L.C. 10/15/65

C

D1301343

▪the
political
world of
american
zionism

the political world of american zionism

BY SAMUEL HALPERIN

EDWARD MINER GALLAUDET MEMORIAL LIBRARY
GALLAUDET COLLEGE
WASHINGTON, D. C.

accession no. 82726

detroit · wayne state university press · 1961

acknowledgments

Some of the material in this book has been published previously in essay form: "Zionism and Christian America: The Political Use of Reference Groups," *Southwestern Social Science Quarterly,* XL, No. 3 (December, 1959), 225–37; "Ideology or Philanthropy? The Politics of Zionist Fund-Raising," *Western Political Quarterly,* XIII, No. 4 (December, 1960), 950–73; and "Zionist Counterpropaganda: The Case of the American Council for Judaism," *Southwestern Social Science Quarterly,"* XLI, No. 4 (March, 1961), 450–63.

Grateful acknowledgment is made to the Morris and Emma Schaver Fund for Jewish Studies for the financial assistance which makes possible the publication of this book.

Acknowledgment for permission to quote is made to the following: Agudath Israel World Organization, New York, publishers of Jacob Rosenheim's *Agudist World Problems* (1941); International Universities Press, Inc., New York, publishers of Morris D. Waldman's *Nor by Power* (1953); and Zionist Organization of America, New York, publishers of Abba Hillel Silver's *Vision and Victory* (1949), and of *Brandeis on Zionism: A Collection of Addresses and Statements* (1942).

COPYRIGHT © 1961

WAYNE STATE UNIVERSITY PRESS

DETROIT, 2, MICHIGAN

ALL RIGHTS RESERVED

PUBLISHED SIMULTANEOUSLY IN CANADA BY AMBASSADOR BOOKS, LIMITED,

TORONTO, ONTARIO, CANADA

LIBRARY OF CONGRESS CATALOG NUMBER 61-10126

956
H19p

preface

Israel today stands as testimony to the power of a visionary idea and the force of a compelling need. About this idea, Zionism, and the events leading to the fulfillment of its political program, much has already been written; but the role of the United States, and especially of the American Jewish community, in the birth of Israel has been either ignored or grossly underplayed.

In a time when the nation's press customarily refers to American Jewry as "almost solidly pro-Israel if not actually Zionist," it is important to examine the genesis of this development in American Jewish public opinion. For American Jewry was not always pro-Israel. Hardly a generation has passed since major American Jewish organizations and leaders blocked the road to Jewish statehood and waged a militant struggle against fellow Jews in the Zionist movement. This fading of opposition and the consequent growth of Zionist influence are the focus for this study of public opinion formation and political action.

My work could not have been undertaken except for the truly impressive scholarship of a host of historians and social scientists. No less valuable were the bountiful writings of numerous Zionist officers, a publication achievement which must rank high in the annals of American social action movements. To all these men and women my debt is profound. Other than acknowledge it here, I can do no more than append a bibliography demonstrating the wealth and diversity of materials awaiting those who would look to our country's many subgroups for a view in microcosm of the American political process.

Those who have labored with me in this study are many. But for the cogent suggestions of Drs. Salo W. Baron, Harold Basilius, William N. Chambers, Abraham G. Duker, Lloyd P. Gartner, Irving Halperin, Ralph K. Huitt, Merle Kling, Robert H. Salisbury, and Mrs. Barbara C. Woodward, I express my particular gratitude, as I do to the helpful staffs of the Zionist Archives and Library in New York and of the Central Zionist Archives in Jerusalem. Thanks are also due to the Wayne State University Research Committee for financial assistance enabling me to travel to Jerusalem and to examine the scholar's paradise of the Central Zionist Archives there. And to my wife, Marlene, mere words cannot record my appreciation for her numerous efforts to share this constant family reading companion with the general public.

Samuel Halperin

Washington, D.C.
October, 1960

contents

tables

abbreviations

AECZA	American Emergency Committee for Zionist Affairs
AJC	American Jewish Committee
AJCOP	*The American Jewish Conference, Its Organization and Proceedings of the First Session* (New York, 1944)
AJCRIC	*The American Jewish Conference, Report of the Interim Committee and the Commissions on Rescue, Palestine, Post-War* (New York, 1944)
AJYB	*The American Jewish Year Book*
APC	American Palestine Committee
AZEC	American Zionist Emergency Council
CCARY	Central Conference of American Rabbis, *Yearbook*
CJR	*Contemporary Jewish Record*
CW	*Congress Weekly*
CZA	Central Zionist Archives, Jerusalem
IJPS	*International Jewish Press Service*
JDC	American Jewish Joint Distribution Committee
JF	*Jewish Frontier*
JS	*Jewish Spectator*
JSS	*Jewish Social Studies*
JP-PP	*The Jewish People—Past and Present* (New York, 1946–55)
JSSQ	*Jewish Social Service Quarterly*
JTA	*Jewish Telegraphic Agency*
LAJC	Library of American Jewish Committee, New York
NP	*New Palestine*
NYT	*New York Times*
PAJHS	*Publications* of the American Jewish Historical Society
PRAA	*Proceedings,* Rabbinical Assembly of America
PYB	*Palestine Year Book*
REC	*The Reconstructionist*
REP-HEAR	U. S. House of Representatives, Committee on Foreign Affairs, *Hearings on H. Res. 418 and H. Res. 419, Resolutions Relative to the Jewish National Home in Palestine,* Seventy-eighth Congress, Second Session (Washington, 1944)
UAHC	Union of American Hebrew Congregations
UJE	*Universal Jewish Encyclopedia*
ZOA	Zionist Organization of America

introduction

I have undertaken the study of the political world of American Zionism in the belief that an adequate understanding of politics requires analyses of interest groups and their activities and that not enough about these politically relevant phenomena is known. By "interest group" I mean an aggregate of persons who, on the basis of a substantial degree of interaction and shared attitudes, make "claims upon other groups in the society for the establishment, maintenance, or enhancement of forms of behavior that are implied by the shared attitudes." *

Specifically, I am concerned here with interacting individuals sharing an interest in the establishment of a Jewish state in Palestine, and with their claims upon other groups in American society. Attention will not be limited entirely to these individuals (known as "Zionists") organized into specific formal groups or associations (popularly termed Zionist "parties") or even to the collectivity of these groups (known as the "Zionist movement"). Rather, my inquiry will be directed to a much broader "public," in this case, all American Jews—those who in particular might be expected to have an opinion, or be affected by, the claims presented by organized

---

* David Truman, *The Governmental Process* (New York, 1953), p. 33. Sociologically speaking, it is also possible to conceive of an interest group as a "social movement," "a group venture extending beyond a local community or a single event and involving a systematic effort to inaugurate changes in thought, behavior, and social relationships." See C. Wendell King, *Social Movements in the United States* (New York, 1956), p. 27. Cf. also Herbert Blumer, "Collective Behavior" in Alfred McClung Lee (ed.), *New Outline of the Principles of Sociology* (New York, 1951), pp. 199–221; and Eric Hoffer, *The True Believer* (New York, 1958).

1

Zionists.* My object throughout is to trace the growth of pro-Zionist opinion beyond the ranks of the organized Zionist movement and into the larger Jewish public of which Zionists constituted only one segment. Accordingly, Zionist leaders will be observed in their attempt "to secure recognition and acceptance from other group leaders and the general public as to the legitimacy of their programs." ** Stated in a somewhat different manner, the attempt to account for the changing character, numbers, and influence of the American Zionist movement will be made by consideration of developments within the broader political world of the American Jewish community,[1] that aggregate of individuals who constituted the immediate "unorganized" or "potential" interest group from which, primarily, organized Zionist associations could derive support and membership.[2]

After sketching the general characteristics of the Zionist movement and its early history in the United States (Chapter 1), we shall observe the effect of external events and crises in the total social system with a view toward determining their effect upon American Zionism and in order to speculate about the relationships between political and general social phenomena (Chapter 2). In the following chapter, we shall survey the institutional and psychological framework or "arena" [3] within which the Zionist movement functioned, after which we shall consider selected organized groups in the Jewish community—religious, protective, and labor—with a view to tracing the development of increasingly pro-Zionist attitudes within these groups as parts of an expanding Zionist public (Chapters 4–6). In so doing, we shall analyze (1) the role of social, economic and ideological predispositions in affecting the reception of claims advanced by the Zionists; (2) the strategy, tactics, and techniques employed by an interest group in attempting to "propagandize" *** for its position; and (3) the growth of interest

---

* Truman, in *The Governmental Process*, views "public" as ". . . an aggregate of individuals who are aware, or who can be made aware, of various possible consequences of the group's actions, including its propaganda" (p. 218).

** Avery Leiserson terms such efforts at achieving "sanction and acquiescence" the "external problem of group representation" as contrasted with the "internal problem" of maintaining order, initiative and morale within the group itself. ("Problems of Representation in the Government of Private Groups," *The Journal of Politics*, XI, No. 3 [August, 1949], 568.)

*** The term "propaganda" in this work implies no moral valuation of the propagandist for, as Truman has ably stated: ". . . attempts to persuade large num-

group "influence potential" which follows upon successful efforts at mass persuasion, nullification of opposition, recruitment of individual supporters, and formation of alliances with other groups in the larger public.

By "influence potential" I mean a group's capacity to affect or modify, either by inducement or sanction, the behavior of other groups and individuals in the direction of the former's objective.[4] In this case, we shall seek to ascertain the degree of Zionist influence over other Jewish groups and over individuals on the single question of the establishment of a Jewish state or commonwealth in Palestine.

Succeeding chapters will consider the role of the total American public or "Christian America" in furthering or impeding the realization of an interest group's aspirations (Chapter 7), and the specific problems of fund-raising and "democratic mold" as they affect a group's objectives among uncommitted sectors of its special public (Chapters 8, 9). Finally, we shall consider the nature of an interest group's propaganda directed at its uncommitted public and against a hostile or competing group (Chapters 10, 11).

More broadly, our inquiry will be concerned with general statements concerning interest group activity which can be derived from this case study of Zionist group efforts. In a concluding chapter I shall offer a number of general statements or hypotheses which help to account for the growth of interest group influence and which serve to illuminate the nature of interest group life. It is hoped that this inquiry into Zionist groups and the Zionist movement may contribute to further advances in the analysis of the general character of the American political system, with particular reference to the role of interest groups. The inquiry may be of particular interest inasmuch as it deals with a non-economic interest group rather than with the labor, business and agricultural associations most frequently investigated by students of the political process.

My data are derived primarily from the official documents and periodicals of a host of American Jewish organizations, studied mainly in the Zionist Archives and Library of New York and the

---

bers of people constitute a basic process in our kind of society. Where social complexity has fostered a diversity of attitudes and where widespread agreement is frequently necessary for effective action, organized efforts to influence and control attitudes are inevitable. In this sense propaganda is simply a kind of communication and is morally neutral" (*The Governmental Process,* p. 222).

Central Zionist Archives of Jerusalem, as well as from the secondary studies of numerous scholars and observers in the fields of Jewish history, sociology and religion. Because the six-decade history of the American Zionist movement is too long an historical period to discuss within the confines of my study, I have devoted predominant attention to the period 1929 to 1948, believing that such a chronological span would yield sufficient materials for the analysis of the central problem at hand—"how does an interest group grow in influence?" The need for an expanded study of this critical generation in American Zionist history is demonstrated by Frank E. Manuel's *The Realities of American-Palestine Relations* (Washington, 1949). On pages 301–302, Manuel claims that "American Zionism in the twenties and early thirties was not a force to be reckoned with seriously." Yet the same author finds the American Jewish community completely transformed and almost solidly pro-Zionist by the mid-forties—only eight pages later in his work.

Words of caution are in order. This is not a study of political "lobbying" or "pressure politics" as commonly understood in folk terms. I am here concerned only with how Zionists mobilized the influence potential to pursue their objectives, not with how they exerted their power in relation to government.[5] This book is not intended to be fully adequate for a complete understanding of the total Zionist phenomenon, since in the interests of manageability I have consciously striven to exclude significant areas of Zionist operations—the redevelopment of Palestine, the ideological discussions at World Zionist Congresses and elsewhere, relations with the British Mandatory for Palestine, the work of other than *American* Zionist groups, etc.[6] Nor is this book intended to act as a guide to understanding the American Zionist movement or the American Jewish community of the sixties, although undoubtedly much of interest and application for the contemporary scene may be found herein. Finally, nothing here discussed is intended as an "exposé" or "unmasking" of any of the participants in the political struggle to be portrayed. The only moral I would impart to my readers is that the associations observed constitute a legitimate segment of the American political scene and, as such, are to be neither condemned nor praised, but studied and understood.

1
the origins, program and early development of american zionism

THE ORIGINS AND PROGRAM OF WORLD ZIONISM

The student of Zionist affairs in America will find it no simple task to determine the nature of the Zionist movement and its goals or the specific quality which distinguishes the "Zionist" from the "non-Zionist." Study of the vast quantity of discussions and explanations of Zionism produced in the United States in the past six decades reveals a broad range of thinking on the aims of, and rationale for, the Zionist program. Yet, despite the existence of this confusing mass of exposition and argument, some basic conception of the nature of Zionism is clearly required in order that readers and investigators may devote their attention to a common phenomenon.

Concerning the origins of Zionism there is considerable uniformity of thinking. Beginning with the destruction of the First Jewish Commonwealth by Babylonian legions in the year 586 B.C., longing for a restoration to Jerusalem's holy Mount Zion became a cardinal feature of Jewish thought, prayer and ritual. When, in 70 A.D., a similar fate befell the restored Second Commonwealth, this time at the hands of Rome, a renewed emphasis on the importance of Palestine to the Jewish people and the Jewish faith again became central to great portions of the observant Jew's daily life.[1] History is replete with instances of Jewish attempts to regain and resettle the Holy Land; the chain of Jewish settlement in that land was never broken.[2]

The modern social and political movement called Zionism is

5

of considerably more recent vintage and is largely tied up with the spectacular career of the Viennese journalist and playwright, Theodor Herzl, whose celebrated book *The Jewish State,* published in 1896, transfigured the Jewish world. Herzl's thesis revolves about several assumptions: (1) The Jews constitute a people or nation in the psychic and cultural sense, but they lack the attributes of political nationality; (2) anti-Semitism and Jewish suffering ("the eternal Jewish problem") is an inevitable consequence of the Jews' "abnormality," that is, their statelessness; (3) Judaism as a civilization or culture is in danger of extinction unless the Jews are enabled to defend themselves physically and to express their unique nature spiritually; (4) a national state is the only institution or means which can guarantee such self-expression and self-defense; (5) Jewish survival and continued Jewish contribution to the mainstream of world culture can be ensured only if the Jews obtain an independent national state. To these assumptions the modern Zionist movement added the proviso that only Palestine, because of its unique associations with Jewish genesis and historical development, could provide the territory for the future Jewish state.[3]

Under Herzl's dynamic leadership the hitherto ethereal vision of a "Return to Zion" became transformed into a practical political movement for the attainment of an international solution to the "Jewish Question"—a Jewish state in Palestine. At the First World Zionist Congress in Switzerland in August, 1897, the "Basle Platform," keystone of the world Zionist movement, was enunciated:

> Zionism seeks to create for the Jewish people a home in Palestine secured by public law. The Congress contemplates the following means to the attainment of this end:
> 1. The promotion by appropriate means of the settlement in Palestine of Jewish agriculturalists, artisans and manufacturers.
> 2. The organization and binding together of the whole of Jewry by means of appropriate institutions, both local and international, in accordance with the laws of each country.
> 3. The strengthening and fostering of Jewish national sentiment and national consciousness.
> 4. Preparatory steps toward obtaining the consent of governments, where necessary, in order to reach the goal of Zionism.

Note that the four operative statements which follow the opening declaration of purpose are all subsidiary to the main objective, "a home in Palestine secured by law." Relative to the interpretation of these operative statements a complex division of opinion among Zionists grew up. Exactly how the Jewish home should be realized, the priority to be given to various measures, the proper interpretation of "Jewish national sentiment and national consciousness," the place of religion, capitalism and socialism in the homeland-to-be, etc., violently agitated the total Zionist movement and caused the formation of numerous and distinctive Zionist "parties." Inevitably, these diverse interpretations of the justification for, and the proposed form of, the desired state produced a host of conflicting and overlapping ideologies representing a mass of claims and counterclaims.

For the purposes of this study, therefore, "Zionism" signifies primarily the goal expressed in the opening declaration of the Basle Platform, and "Zionist" denotes any individual who subscribed or consciously contributed to the attainment of this goal. That such an arbitrary limitation of meaning is based upon more than the author's whim may be indicated by the authoritative statement of the American Emergency Committee for Zionist Affairs, the coordinating agency for all American Zionist parties, which declared in 1943 that

> Nothing more was ever expected of the Zionist than the promotion of this object [a home for the Jewish people]. All special interpretations of Zionism, all accompanying philosophies, are, as it were, private additions to the official policy. *This should be made clear as an answer to various criticisms of the Zionist movement which are in reality aimed not at the movement itself, but at the views held by one Zionist group or another.*[4]

By way of additional elaboration of the meaning of Zionism, particularly as it bears upon the present study, two oft-quoted statements deserve to be cited. Whether every Zionist would accept Louis Dembitz Brandeis' conception of Zionism as accurate is not at all certain, just as a universally satisfactory description of "Jew" and "Judaism" has yet to be found. In any case, Supreme Court Justice Brandeis, the most eminent person ever to lead the American Zionist movement, gave this definition of Zionism which was circulated widely for over three decades:

> Zionism seeks to establish in Palestine, for such Jews as choose to go and remain there, and for their descendants, a legally secured

home, where they may live together and lead a Jewish life, where they may expect ultimately to constitute a majority of the population, and may look forward to what we should call home rule. The Zionists seek to establish this home in Palestine because they are convinced that the undying longing of Jews for Palestine is a fact of deepest significance; that it is a manifestation in the struggle for existence by an ancient people which had established its right to live—a people whose three thousand years of civilization has produced a faith, culture and individuality which enable them to contribute largely in the future as they had in the past to the advance of civilization and that it is not a right merely but a duty of the Jewish nationality to survive and develop. They believe that there only, can Jewish life be fully protected from the forces of disintegration; that there alone, can the Jewish spirit reach its full and natural development; and that by securing for those Jews who wish to settle in Palestine, the opportunity to do so, not only those Jews, but all other Jews will be benefited and that the long perplexing Jewish Problem will, at last, find solution.[5]

An earlier statement by Solomon Schechter, president of the Jewish Theological Seminary of America, also serves to focus upon the common aim of the Basle Platform even while it delineates the multi-faceted appeal of Zionism to American Jews:

Zionism is an ideal, and as such is indefinable. It is thus subject to various interpretations and susceptive of different aspects. It may appear to one as the rebirth of national Jewish consciousness, to another as a religious revival, whilst to a third it may present itself as a path leading to the goal of Jewish culture; and to a fourth it may take the form of the last and only solution of the Jewish problem. By reason of this variety of aspects, Zionism has been able to unite on its platform the most heterogeneous elements; representing Jews of all countries, and exhibiting almost all the different types of culture and thought as only a really great and universal movement could do. That each of its representatives should emphasize the particular aspect most congenial to his way of thinking, and most suitable for his mode of action, is only natural. On one point, however, they all agree, namely, that it is not only desirable, but absolutely necessary that Palestine, the land of our fathers, should be recovered with the purpose of forming a home for at least a portion of the Jews, who would lead there an independent national life.[6]

Following the promulgation of the Basle Platform, the world Zionist movement embarked upon a number of practical enterprises. Fund-raising organizations were established, mass membership associations were founded, Palestinian agricultural colonies and industries were erected, and a program of political negotiation was undertaken.[7] On November 2, 1917, the Foreign Secretary of Great Britain, Arthur James Balfour, issued the policy statement which had been the object of twenty years of forceful Zionist strivings. This famous, and later controversial, "Balfour Declaration" announced:

> Dear Lord Rothschild,
> I have much pleasure in conveying to you, on behalf of His Majesty's Government, the following declaration of sympathy with Jewish Zionist aspirations, which has been submitted to, and approved by, the Cabinet.
> His Majesty's Government view with favour the establishment in Palestine of a national home for the Jewish people, and will use their best endeavours to facilitate the achievement of this object, it being clearly understood that nothing shall be done which may prejudice the civil and religious rights of existing non-Jewish communities in Palestine, or the rights and political status enjoyed by Jews in any other country.
> I should be grateful if you would bring this declaration to the knowledge of the Zionist Federation.[8]

On the basis of this statement of official British policy, Great Britain was awarded the Mandate for Palestine at the meeting of the Principal Allied Powers in April, 1920, at San Remo, Italy. On July 24, 1922, the Council of the League of Nations approved the Mandate and charged Great Britain with "responsibility for placing the country under such . . . conditions as will secure the establishment of a Jewish national home." On September 21, 1922, President Warren G. Harding signed a Joint Congressional Resolution expressing the approval of the American government for the "establishment in Palestine of a national home for the Jewish people." By 1922 a total of fifty-two governments had endorsed the basic political aims of the Zionist movement, and a Jewish national home seemed, if not exactly possible of attainment, at least assured of widespread international support.

Yet thirty years were to intervene before the actual Jewish state was established. In the interim, Jews had to be resettled in Palestine and funds provided for their absorption in the economy, popular support had to be enlisted in Jewish communities around the world, and objections to the eventual state overcome. It is, therefore, to the influential role of American Jewry in these essential tasks that we now turn.

A SURVEY OF AMERICAN ZIONISM TO 1929

As many students of American Jewish history have observed, the interest of Americans in Palestine dates back to the very founding of the United States. Pre-Zionist schemes for a Jewish Restoration to Palestine were not uncommon in both Jewish and Christian circles. Jewish Hovevei Zion ("Lovers of Zion") societies were established in the United States even before Herzl's dramatic call for a World Zionist Congress in 1897.[9] While the earliest Zionist efforts were centered among the hard-pressed masses of eastern Europe, American Jewry was not neglected by the appeals of the movement. American Zionists were involved in all of the international Zionist Congresses and by 1898 they had begun to erect the instrumentalities which would later play such a major role in the winning of American Jewry for the Zionist program. Already American Jewry was seen as the "wave of the future" and, accordingly, it was no mere rhetorical question that Theodor Herzl addressed to his American compatriots in June of 1901:

> A crucial moment has arrived in the history of the Jews. Shall they miss this unprecedented opportunity of laying the ghost of the Jewish question, of ending the tragedy of the wandering Jew? Will the Jews of America, in particular, forget in their own happiness in the glorious land of freedom, how heavy is the bondage of their brethren? [10]

But what a handful of Zionists might perceive as an "unprecedented opportunity" was greeted by most Jews with widespread apathy and by many influential persons as "Ziomania— the curse of the ages." Zionism arrived in the parlors of the respectable as

> . . . a disturber of their peace of mind . . . an offense to their Americanism . . . an obstacle to Jewish adjustment in a democratic environment; it revived memories they wished to forget. The orthodox at the time were steeped in their traditions and rejected innovations; they believed in the Messiah and the Redemption of

Zion, but God had to utter the word. The Jewish labor movement accepted the materialistic conception of history that came from the mind of Karl Marx; they had already written off Jewish nationality as one of the sacrifices the Jews would have to make for the world-revolution; and they regarded Zionists as benighted reactionaries.[11]

The desperately poor and newly-arrived Jewish masses from eastern Europe, on the other hand, were sympathetic to the movement they had fostered in the spiritual degradation of the Ghetto and the Pale. But America was too bewildering, and the daily struggle for economic survival too arduous, to permit them the luxury of much Zionist activity. The glamor of Palestine was too distant; the squalor of the East Side was too close. The Call of Zion was, therefore, limited by actual performance and dedication to a relatively small handful of zealots acting as the "leaven of the Zionist movement in America, keeping the spark of life aglow." [12] When the Federation of American Zionists met in Rochester, New York, in 1914, after almost a generation of labors, less than 15,000 American *shekel*-payers were represented, and the annual budget for the entire American movement totaled a mere $12,150.[13] The Federation had no regular president; Henry Friedenwald, a Baltimore dentist, was its honorary head. No one of national distinction served on its executive or administrative committees. Though many talented Zionist poets and writers, orators and polemicists had left their mark on the Jewish community, particularly among the Yiddish-speaking masses, Zionism was still an Old-World movement, scorned and vilified by those affluent Jews who considered themselves legitimate Americans. The occasional Americanized rabbi or professional who embraced Zionism was merely a "hopeless romantic."

But American Zionism was not to remain long the "eccentric pastime" of a few Reform rabbis, the scholars of the Jewish Theological Seminary, and a handful of laymen. With the advent of famed jurist Louis D. Brandeis to the presidency of the Provisional Executive Committee for Zionist Affairs, a host of talented leaders —for example, Harvard law professor Felix Frankfurter, educator-philosopher Horace M. Kallen, author-producer Lincoln Kirstein, U. S. Circuit Court Justice Julian Mack, merchandiser Nathan Straus, publisher Eugene Meyer, Jr.—rallied to the Zionist program. From a small, decentralized, peripheral group in Jewish society, the

Zionists now quickly developed into a cohesive political group with the best political connections of any Zionist party in the world. Brandeis, Frankfurter and Rabbi Stephen S. Wise enjoyed easy official access to the leaders of the Wilson Administration, including the President himself.

The proclamation of the Balfour Declaration made Zionism even more "respectable" and galvanized the Jewish community into approving action. By 1918 almost 150,000 paid members were counted in the ranks of the newly-formed Zionist Organization of America (ZOA). Additional thousands of Jews affiliated with the religious Mizrachi Organization of America and with several Labor Zionist parties. Indeed, this sudden deluge of popular support for the Zionist ideal led many naïve followers to assume that Zionism had "conquered public opinion" and, consequently, that the Jewish state could be had for the mere asking.[14] This premature judgment was bolstered by the virtually unanimous enactment by the United States Congress on June 30, 1922, of the Lodge-Fish Joint Congressional Resolution approving the ultimate aim of the Balfour Declaration.[15]

Succeeding years, however, found the Zionist cause in America bedeviled by internal factionalism and public apathy while the needs of Palestine imposed unparalleled financial responsibilities upon the movement. After the 1921 Cleveland convention of the Zionist Organization of America, the influential "Brandeis-Mack faction" withdrew from active leadership in the organization over a difference in proposed policies. The less glamorously led majority faction, loyal to Chaim Weizmann's leadership of the World Zionist Organization, was thus left to bear the unprecedented burden alone.[16] Then, too, after the abatement of enthusiasm generated by the Balfour Declaration, American Zionism settled down to the prosaic task of fund-raising for Palestine. For many of its less ideologically oriented adherents, Zionism became just another philanthropy among numerous philanthropies. Formal membership in the Zionist Organization of America fell to less than a sixth of its 1918 strength. Moreover, while directing the remission of almost fifteen million dollars to Palestine between 1921 and 1930, the ZOA itself incurred a debilitating deficit of approximately $150,-000.[17] Cultural and propaganda efforts were virtually at a standstill as every available arm was bent to the solicitation of funds for Palestinian colonization.

Thus, when World Zionist Organization President Chaim Weizmann concluded an American visit in 1928, he carried away "a sad impression" of the fate of American Zionism. The movement, he wrote, was plagued by internecine strife. It had not yet contributed a single *chalutz* (pioneer) to Palestine. He was forced to conclude:

> I honestly confess to one great sin that I have committed. It is a sin of which all of us placed at the head of Zionist affairs have been guilty. We have abused America as a moneygiving machine. Under the pressure to which America has been subject, it has not developed an adequate, healthy, vigorous Zionism. That should be borne in mind when reviewing the work of the past seven years. The Zionist Organization of America has worked under heavy pressure. It was difficult to do all that was required for Palestine, and also develop the other phases of Zionism.[18]

Under such circumstances, Zionists and non-Zionists alike began to view the political program of Zionism as "moribund" or "passé." The distant goal of an independent and self-governing Jewish national home took on religio-cultural overtones rather than its original connotation of sovereign statehood. As the American Vice-Consul in Palestine, George Gregg Fuller, viewed the Zionism of this era: "Jerusalem may one day become the Paris of the Jewish culture and the Vatican of Jewish religion." [19] But his inference was clear: without large-scale immigration from Europe and without adequate funds from America, the Palestinian settlement would never become a viable and independent political entity. It would be permanently confined to a subordinate and dependent status.

On the other hand, Rabbi Abba Hillel Silver, who later led the militant Zionist political offensive before the United Nations and the American Congress, viewed the political phase of Zionism—the securing of international recognition for the right of the Jews to a homeland—as "ended definitely" in 1929 precisely because it had already been "successful." With international sanction already secured for Zionist aspirations, the building of Palestine would henceforth proceed, barring unforseen hindrances, on the basis of a slow economic reconstruction in which Zionism's earlier nationalistic emphasis would be submerged. Wrote Rabbi Silver:

> It is well that the political phase of Jewish Messianism is coming to a close in the upbuilding of the National Homeland. We

shall not have to lay so much stress in the future on the importance of nationalism. We shall henceforth be confronted not with its lack but with its consequences. Hitherto wanting the full complement of the attributes of nationalism, we were constrained to overemphasize its virtues. Many of the spokesmen of our cause were driven to extol nationalism *per se,* which is after all a quite recent and, demonstrably, a quite inadequate human concept. . . . Nationalism is not enough. It is a minimum requirement, not a maximum program. Our national rebirth was made possible by a war in which nationalism was thoroughly exposed and discredited. Nationalism is a means, not an end . . .

Nationalism will not suffice the eternally questing soul of our people. After its national life is secure Israel must push on to the frontiers of the new world—the world of internationalism, of economic freedom, of brotherhood and of peace.[20]

Thus, by any standard—formal membership, funds raised, unity of organization, popularity of appeal—it is apparent that the American Zionist movement of the late twenties was but a foreshadowing of its later strength and prominence. Though some of its partisans might consider the movement ineffectual, and others feel that Zionism had already fought and won its major political battles, American Zionism, viewed from the vantage point of later years, was merely at the midstream of its struggle for influence in the Jewish community.

2
american zionism in its world setting, 1929-48

Only fifteen years after many of its leaders viewed American Zionism as moribund and ineffectual, a much-publicized "Zionist-steam-roller" was advancing with inexorable momentum toward its goal. In place of the 18,031 paid Zionist Organization of America members in 1929, there were approximately 250,000 in 1948. Instead of $2,000,000 remitted to Palestine in 1929, almost $100,000,000 was volunteered in 1948. Sympathetic expressions and material assistance for the Zionist goal were given in every sector of the community. Virtually every formerly hostile and neutralist national organization was constrained to move into a working alliance with the Zionists on a practical, if not on an ideological, basis.

The chronicling and explanation of these changes is the task of this book. But first we shall attempt an overall, historical view of some of the major events contributing to the eventual emergence of an American Jewish community so favorably disposed toward the Zionist program in Palestine. We shall reconstruct as far as possible the social context, the tone and temper of American Jewry as it was constantly modified by the effects of external events and threats to the Jewish people. In this way, we may be able to glimpse certain tendencies to action which existed in significant sectors of the American Jewish community. The admittedly impressionistic historical survey which follows is not offered as an exact and certain guide to the thinking of American Jewry one to three decades in the past. Rather, it is intended as a supplement to, and partial explanation of, the marked changes in Jewish attitudes toward Zionism to be studied more intensively in forthcoming chapters.

Two prevailing sociological hypotheses may be adduced here as having obvious application to the question at hand: "What factors interacted to alter Jewish opinions about Zionist demands?" First, it is hypothesized that "public opinion remains latent until an issue arises for the group; an issue arises when there is conflict, anxiety, or frustration." [1] The historical events we are about to trace—war, depression, and attacks by opposing interests—are held to be the most important of the issues likely to arouse latent public opinion and, thus, to lead to the organization and expansion of interest groups.[2]

Second, despite the magnitude and efficiency of an interest group's propaganda, it is hypothesized that propaganda can succeed in changing opinions, or in mobilizing opinion for action, only where there is an already existent predisposition in that direction. This is to say, the effective propagandist must play upon the fears, aspirations and ideas already commonly held by his "target group," or public. Propaganda is effective only in certain contexts and "unless it is carefully designed to fit the situation, and related to preexisting inclinations, it will not succeed." [3]

In the pages that follow we shall focus upon those *events which apparently aroused Jewish predispositions which could then be exploited by Zionist activity and propaganda.* In this way, we shall be scanning the "total situation" in which Zionist successes were scored, rather than a Zionist interest group registering victory after victory apparently without assistance from the social context in which it operated.

Ideally, a study which attempts to account for changes in public opinion due to the impact of events on predispositions and to the role of propaganda in shaping those predispositions toward desired actions, should include more than a mere cataloging of techniques and media utilized in the exploitation of prevailing attitudes. Highly desirable would be a detailed content analysis of the various themes or appeals employed in various historical periods, as well as some measurement of the relationship between propaganda output and resultant changes in public opinion. At present, studies of such complex phenomena within the Zionist movement are not available.

In the absence of more reliable data, we have chosen to interpolate in the following text some examples of basic Zionist propaganda themes which were *geared to the changing historical condi-*

tion of world Jewry, and directed toward uncommitted Jews as well as the general American public. The use of such themes will be illustrated here in the form of quotations from speeches and articles by prominent Zionists. This selection of quotations is, of course, an impressionistic one; yet, I believe, such excerpts are generally representative of the total propaganda stemming from the Zionist movement in its struggle for influence among American Jews.

Whatever the methodological shortcomings involved, it is hoped that this chapter will enable the observer to "feel," if not exactly to "know," the general configuration of events, predispositions, and Zionist propaganda themes which produced such an unmistakable effect on the outcome of Zionist demands upon the American Jewish community before 1948.

ARAB RIOTS AND THE GREAT DEPRESSION, 1929–33

The dominant reaction of much of American Jewry to the Palestinian Arab riots of 1929 was one of marked solidarity for their fellow Jews in Palestine. Numerous Jewish organizations seconded Zionist demands for the full implementation and protection of Jewish rights in Palestine. A Palestine Emergency Fund to aid the riot victims was immediately and enthusiastically established. Prominent non-Zionists—Julius Rosenwald, Felix Warburg, Herbert Lehman, Samuel Untermeyer and Adolph Ochs—publicly expressed support for the Palestinian cause by making large personal contributions; and in only a few months the Fund netted over $2,100,000. One year later, in memory of the 125 Jews killed in the 1929 rioting, the Zionist Organization of America staged a successful series of memorial meetings throughout the United States. Tens of thousands of Jews not formally affiliated with the Zionist movement joined in these "services for martyrs" which invariably included a call for implementation of the Balfour Declaration.[4]

Zionist activity noticeably accelerated in the face of this first of a series of major Palestinian crises. Zionist leadership forcefully proclaimed the need for Jewish militancy while the Zionist press carried reports of qualitative increases in Zionist interest, of "enthusiastic, well attended meetings . . . in numerous cities which were previously lax and indifferent," and of a "better, heartier Zionist spirit." With the return of the Mack-Brandeis faction to the ZOA (induced in part by "the emergency"), Zionist cohesion, long impaired by bitter factionalism and personalism, visibly improved. Moreover, on the Jewish scene as a whole, Zionists encountered no evidence of anti-Zionist activities, though, they speculated, there surely was some covert antagonism.[5]

The onset of the Great Depression affected the Zionist movement in diverse ways. On the one hand, the fact that Palestine had managed to avoid the deepening world economic crisis (probably as a result of considerable foreign capital investment), while other Jewish committees lay shrouded in gloom, provided Zionists with an appealing message. "When other hopes have lost their meaning," wrote veteran Zionist leader Louis Lipsky,

> . . . when all else in Jewish life lies in confusion, the flag of ZION shall be held high as the symbol of national life reawakened. . . . All other movements have lost their significance, and its devotees have lost their faith. If you will come now and tell the story of achievement in Palestine, thousands of Jews will espouse the cause. . . . It is a moment of unusual opportunity. What could not be built up so speedily in times of prosperity may be built up now. . . .[6]

Interestingly enough, Lipsky's logical analysis of national Jewish demoralization and Zionist opportunity is corroborated by Harry Simonhoff's memoirs of the Zionist movement in Miami in the early 1930's:

> After the letdown following the boom elation, it was not difficult to assemble four or five hundred people to a Zionist meeting that promised a stimulating program. Perhaps there was a reaction from the crass money grubbing of real estate speculation. In those days few tourists visited the Holy Land. Audiences would listen attentively to every word that even a dull speaker had to say about the Palestine he saw.[7]

In those days of economic hardship, much Zionist activity consisted of urging American Jews to shoulder additional economic burdens so that the Palestine venture would not falter. In the depths of the Great Depression, American Jews were constantly exhorted to remember their Palestinian brethren and to make maximum contributions to the United Palestine Appeal or other Palestine funds. Zionism was portrayed as "The Jewish Badge of Pride"; the honor and reputation of the Jewish people as a whole were said to rest upon the very generosity of American Jewry:

> Whatever transpires in Palestine has its repercussion upon the Jews living in every part of the world. A breakdown of our work in Palestine would not only be a staggering blow to the brave pioneers in Palestine who have wrought so finely and borne their trial with matchless courage and dignity, it would not only be a setback to Jewish hopes everywhere, but it would also seriously affect the prestige of Jewish communities throughout the world, particularly that in America.[8]

It is also appropriate to note here that American Jews, who at all other times gave scant evidence of believing that the Jewish state-to-be was intended for persons other than oppressed European and Asiatic refugees, emigrated to Palestine in significant numbers in the midst of the American economic debacle. In the three years between 1933 and 1935, 3,693 persons from the United States (not necessarily native-born Americans) were reported to have arrived in Palestine. Immigration from the U.S. to Palestine in the period 1919–45 was reported to be 8,057 or 2.3 percent of total Jewish immigration. How many of these persons returned again to the U.S. is not known. (See Jewish Agency for Palestine, *Statistical Handbook of Jewish Palestine, 1947* [Jerusalem, 1947], pp. 97–105, and Appendix VI below.)

At the same time, the economic depression adversely affected the American Zionist movement in quantitative terms. Despite a renewed popular interest in Palestine, the membership of the Zionist Organization of America was at its lowest point in years, partially because most of its supporters were drawn from the social classes hardest hit by the depression. For the small merchants and manual laborers whose economic roots in America were only a generation or less in the making, Zionist dues were a luxury. Consequently, the ZOA found itself with a paying membership of less than nine thousand hard core adherents and was forced to abandon much of its public relations and cultural program for lack of funds.

Zionists subsequently began to speak of the phenomenon of an American Jewish community which allegedly believed in Zionism in sentiment, and, perhaps, to the extent of writing a small check for a charitable donation, but which saw no point in paying annual dues of six dollars to a Zionist movement without tangible enemies, and without battles to fight. The Zionist press complained of the deleterious effects on Zionist morale of the lack of an organized opposition or of a dramatic issue upon which to focus Jewish attention. The upbuilding of Palestine was, apparently, widely accepted as a worthy Jewish cause, deserving of an annual contribution to the Jewish National Fund or the United Palestine Appeal, but dues to the ZOA or another Zionist party were an unnecessary item of expense. Thus, concluded Zionist leaders, the Zionist *idea* was a resounding success in terms of popular acceptance and monetary support; the Zionist *organization,* on the other hand, would have to wait patiently for "more auspicious times to appear." [9]

HITLER, ANTI-SEMITISM AND BRITISH POLICY IN PALESTINE, 1933-39

The "more auspicious times" awaited by the Zionist leadership arrived, in part, with the advent of the Nazi party to the government of Germany in 1933 and with the intensification of world-wide anti-Semitism. To be sure, the Zionist and general Jewish press expressed horror, not jubilation, at the news of Hitler's first persecutions of the 600,000 German Jews. At the same time, the rise of Nazism was recognized as a vitalizing challenge to the Zionist movement, as a crisis situation likely to infuse the dormant Zionist organizations with a new lease on life. As President Morris Rothenberg of the ZOA viewed the situation in June, 1933, "a new day in the history of the movement" had arrived. The times called for "rededication to the cause." [10]

During the next four years of Nazi persecution, 165,000 Jews settled in tiny and desolate Palestine. The United States admitted 17,000. As streams of Jews sought escape from Europe, and only Palestine's gates stood open to receive them in large numbers, Zionists and non-Zionists alike joined in emergency fund-raising campaigns to save Jewish lives. "Whatever his rationale," observes Eli Ginzberg, "it became increasingly difficult for any American Jew to maintain a negative attitude toward Jewish expansion in Palestine." [11] Again, Harry Simonhoff's recollection of Miami Jewry's response to the Nazi regime is helpful in recapturing the spirit of the times:

> The reaction of the American Jew was sorrow, fear, anger, and compassion. Of course, the victims of Nazi savagery must be helped to leave their harsh, stepfather land. . . . What about this thing called Zionism? There might be something to the idea of a Jewish state in Palestine. If it is a matter of money, then here is a check.[12]

Probably at the core of some American Jews' pro-Palestine gestures at this time, though positive documentation is impossible, was the fear that Jewish refugee immigration into America, especially in the midst of an as yet unresolved economic crisis, would only aggravate American anti-Semitism. American Jews were eager to rescue fellow Jews from Hitler's reach, but not at the expense of their own security. Some alternative haven had to be found; and since only Palestine was ready to accept appreciable numbers of Jews, ideological objections to Zionism were submerged and reappraised to permit of Palestine's use as a refugee haven or philanthropic project devoid of "political implications." [13]

This renewed interest in Palestine, because it seemed a refugee haven, a fulfillment of Biblical prophecy, a locale of constructive Jewish activity, or because it symbolized other values, was reflected in rising Zionist affiliations, in funds remitted to Palestine and in a marked revival of Zionist activity from its depression doldrums. After several years of restrained press comments on the state of Zionist affairs, *New Palestine* enthusiastically declared: "Seldom in recent years has there been so much Zionist activity . . . old Zionists seem to have taken on fresh life and vigor and new recruits are appearing everywhere." [14]

Jacob R. Marcus attributed this visible increase in pro-Zionist Jewish opinion and activity to subtle psychological processes operative at this time. Many Jews, he wrote for *The American Scholar* audience, who refused to assimilate and disappear into the non-Jewish majority through intermarriage and who, simultaneously, did not wish to identify themselves with any of the existing religious forms in the Jewish community were now able to find meaningful Jewish activity for the first time. Zionism, particularly in its answer to Hitlerism, enabled one to be a "good Jew" without having to attend synagog; Zionism permitted the "secular Jew" to feel a part of his people, enabled him to identify himself with his suffering brethren overseas.[15]

Moreover, continued Marcus, for the Jew "tired of waiting for his Messiah," Zionism signaled the advent of a Messianic Era. The remarkable work of creation in Palestine, which had so strikingly been demonstrated by the advent of the world-wide depression, provided thrilling channels of personal identification for many Jews in an age of economic stagnation and political pessimism. Because Zionists had

> . . . fashioned beautiful modern towns and villages, settled thousands of colonists, drained swamps, built roads, set up model farms . . . erected a great power plant, introduced modern machinery, established new industries . . . gone far to introduce Western standards and ways of living to a primitive land . . . built hospitals and clinics . . . laid the foundation of a great university . . . assembled the largest library in the Near and Middle East . . . established a modern Westernized school system with Hebrew as the language of instruction . . . stimulated a linguistic renascence . . .

reclaimed the desert, established agricultural cooperatives, and achieved much else of a laudable nature, many a Jew found a vicariously idealistic and creative outlet for his new-found Jewish identification. He had come to believe that the social experimentation of Palestine would signal the evolution of a new social order, ". . . an order that will point the way for other peoples. He is confident that the soil that nourished prophetic thought may again become a spiritual center that will give birth to new ethical and scientific gospels." [16]

Under the influence of Palestine's continuing dynamic growth and the need to find accommodation for fleeing German Jewry, Zionist memberships swelled further and numerous organizations officially declared their devotion to the cause of Palestine's rebirth. Yet, declared many a Zionist leader, these new increments of Jewish support were not an unmixed blessing if all that was involved was a feeling of philanthropy and compassion. True Zionism, they stressed, did not share the negative character of "refugeeism"; true Zionism had to be seen as a "constructive movement to solve the Jewish problem of national homelessness." Palestine had to be considered as more than a practical haven for the oppressed; it was also the Jewish answer to assimilation, the expression of the Jewish collectivity to survive as a people with its own land.

Rabbi Abba Hillel Silver, whose leadership seven years later helped to bring about the radical political transformation of American Zionism, expressed this basic Zionist antipathy to philanthropism as an answer to the refugee problem in these words, even while he restated some of the basic themes used repeatedly in explications of the Zionist program:

I believe that we would be making a grave mistake if we base our Zionism today exclusively and entirely upon the motive of persecution, as some Zionists unfortunately have begun to do. Let us not lose sight in this hour of tribulation of the basic and the classic ideals of our movement.

Zionism was more than an escape from persecution. Zionism was a positive movement towards something. It was a movement towards national auto-emancipation. It was a movement towards the upbuilding of a complete Jewish life. It was a movement towards resuming our rightful place, after two thousand years of exile, as an independent people at home, master of its own destinies, fashioner of its own way of life. It was a movement towards the revitalizing of our Hebrew speech and our Hebrew literature and our Hebrew culture. It was a movement towards rationalizing the economic life of at least that portion of our people which will go to Palestine, so that we shall become not a people of *luftmenschen,* but a people of builders and workers and producers. It was a movement towards an ideal wished for, namely, that in our own land we might try to express in concrete forms, to give a local habitation and a name to some of the great economic ideals of our prophets, ideals of social justice and righteousness.

. . . these reasons are just as valid and potent and real today as they were before the invasion of Hitlerism into Jewish life, which seems to many of us to have given a new approach to the Jewish problem.[17]

Some Zionists were visibly heartened by the fact that anti-Zionist expressions were virtually nonexistent in the Jewish community. They also delighted in the patent ability of Palestine to live up to all the Zionist claims for her economic absorptive capacity of German emigrés. At the same time, avowed Louis Lipsky, Zionists ought to recognize that their ideological program was being watered down by its very success in raising money, in absorbing refugees, and in winning Jewish approval. The Zionist movement, he conceded, was becoming a captive to the constant crises and emergency needs of the Jewish people:

> The Zionist movement is being molded more and more, to an ever larger extent, by accidents and emergencies, and less and less through the free expression of the inner revolt against intolerable spiritual and intellectual servitude [consequent upon Jewish national homelessness] . . . the building of Palestine is constantly being determined not so much by what Jews feel and desire, but by the pressure which is brought to bear upon Jewish life by hostile alien forces. . . . The larger part of our effort is conditioned by, and made contingent upon, the circumstances of immediate catastrophe, the implacable urgings of the emergency of the day.[18]

Despite these misgivings about the growing philanthropization of their movement, American Zionists had no choice but to exploit the issue of Jewish suffering because of the need for saving Jewish lives from European anti-Semitism. If the Palestinian enterprise was not to falter, funds had to be found and, after all, the non-Zionist philanthropist's dollars were as good as any others. As a partial remedy for their dilemma, however, Zionists tried to depict the value of Palestine as a spiritual homeland *for all Jews*. A culturally creative and economically prosperous Palestine, they claimed, would bestow blessings on all Jewry, not just the dispossessed Jews of Europe.

In this effort to show American Jews how they, too, would benefit personally from the Zionist program, Zionist propagandists were aided by a growing American anti-Semitism which, in turn, was fed by the economic insecurity arising out of the Great Depression and by funds and encouragement from Joseph Goebbel's Ministry of Propaganda in Berlin. It was hardly a coincidence that the decade of the 1930's was both the time of Hitler's rise to power and also the spawning season of William Dudley Pelley, Gerald Winrod, George Deatherage, Joe McWilliams, Gerald L. K. Smith, the German-American Bund, the Order of '76, the Knights of the White Camellia, the "Buy Christian!" campaigns and, especially, Father Charles E. Coughlin and his incendiary *Social Justice*. Native anti-Semitism did not overlook "Zionist connections" with Franklin D. Roosevelt's "Jewish-Zionist-Communist Conspiracy," as they called the "New (Jew) Deal" with its Sidney Hillman, Samuel I. Rosenman, Benjamin V. Cohen and Felix Frankfurter Jewish leadership.[19]

Under the circumstances, American Jews experienced increasing insecurity and anxiety about their own destiny, as well as that of their European brethren. Some Jews began to wonder if Hitlerism might not triumph even in the United States and, therefore, they turned to numerous internationalist and liberal movements designed to protect civil liberties and combat fascism.[20] Other Jews urged a policy of Jewish withdrawal from public attention, hoping that in this way the charges of Jewish domination of America might be manifestly proven false. Some of these Jews were also inclined to finance the collection of the "True facts about the Jews" (such as was done by the *Fortune* magazine survey of American Jewry in 1936) for dissemination among the general public in the hopes that thereby it would be seen how very negligible was Jewish economic influence in America.

Still other Jews reacted to attacks on the Jewish grouping by self-affirmation and self-assertion in much the manner experienced by Theodor Herzl four decades earlier. Challenged as it was in ethnic and religious terms, the "will to live" of the Jewish people brought about a massive revival of nationalistic sentiments. To many Jews, Zionism seemed like the natural, long-range solution to perennial anti-Semitism.[21]

With its appeals for Jewish auto-emancipation and self-respect, Zionism was thus able to fill a patent void in American Jewish life; many American Jews came to view Zionism as a movement to normalize their own position in the United States. Zionism, it was believed, would give the Jew equal status with peoples of other national origins who had also settled away from their ancestral homes. In the words of Jacob R. Marcus, identification with Palestine provided the dignity and pride necessary to cope with the discrimination Jews occasionally experienced even in America. While some Jews chose to become assimilated into the non-Jewish majority in the face of danger, far more,

> . . . under the influence of Zionism, with a knowledge of the history of their past, have accepted with patient dignity the added disabilities of a difficult period. Zionism has prevented the *morale* of many from completely collapsing. It has bolstered up a pride that cannot easily be broken down by prejudice; the consciousness of their own worth is, to some, ample compensation for the aloofness and bland disregard of their fellow Americans. Zionism brings

them comfort; it instills new hope in them by emphasizing the fact that they belong spiritually, at least, to a group with whom they share a tradition of a courageous past and the hope for a better future.[22]

Moreover, predicted Rabbi Jacob J. Weinstein in a similar article, the establishment of a Jewish homeland in Palestine would positively affect the Jews of America by removing the stigma of homelessness and minority existence that has played an important role in conditioning non-Jewish attitudes toward the Jews in their midst. Jewish self-esteem would be elevated, and Jews would be saved from "the demoralization and self-hatred that are the inevitable by-products of anti-Semitism." A Jewish Palestine would not only "dissipate the necessity for apologetics in which many Jews feel impelled to indulge," but would "prove an inspiring source of Jewish cultural contributions to their various homelands." In sum, concluded Rabbi Weinstein, the Zionist program was relevant to the American Jew because it would deepen his self-respect and self-confidence as a Jew and guard him against despair in the face of growing American anti-Semitism, because it would normalize the status of the Jewish people and because it would enrich Jewish culture. The evils of anti-Semitism could not but be mitigated by such a dynamic transformation of the Jewish people.[23]

Under the impetus of new Arab riots against the *Yishuv* (the Jewish settlement in Palestine), American Jewry responded in 1936 with larger contributions to Palestine and still larger enrollments in Zionist bodies. All organizations concerned with the protection of Jewish rights in Palestine were mobilized under Zionist guidance for emergency rallies. Representations were also made before the American public and government by a "National Front" of Jewish organizations. (See Chapter 10.) American Jewry was exhorted as never before to stand by its Palestinian brethren.[24]

With the rumor of the pending enactment by the British government of severe restrictions on Jewish immigration into Palestine, restrictions tantamount to abandonment of the Balfour Declaration's promise of a self-governing Jewish national homeland, Jewish political activity rose to heights unparalleled since 1929. Zionists and non-Zionists joined in protests to the British government and appeals for assistance from the American people. At the behest of the National Emergency Committee on Palestine, formed by the Zionists on October 10, 1938, more than one hundred mass public demonstrations were held on October 23 and scores of other protest rallies took place on November 2 (Balfour Day). A national Day of Prayer on February 11, 1939, was reportedly widely observed by hundreds of thousands of Jews as an indication of their opposition to a British plan which would have left the Jews of Palestine as a permanent minority in the midst of an independent Arab state. Fifty-one United States Senators, 194 Representatives and thirty state governors voiced similar sentiments at the time, as did numerous non-Jewish organizations and a large segment of the American press. In the words of a staff member of the American Jewish Committee, the support extended by Americans from all walks of life for the eventual realization of the Balfour Declaration seemed more apparent than ever. Never since 1917 had there been "so much widespread discussion of the Palestine situation and so many expressions of anxiety about the future of a Jewish homeland." [25]

More important for the ultimate goals of the Zionist movement, British policy in Palestine radically altered the conception, shared alike by Zionists and non-Zionists, that Jewish statehood was, at best, a very long-range objective. Maurice Samuel, one of the best known of the Zionist speakers and publicists, explained the changing timetable of Zionist goals in this manner:

> How much of the Zionist program did I hope to see completed within thirty-five or forty years? . . . I did not think I would live to see the proclamation of a Jewish State. Like most other Zionists —the great majority, I believe—I was not much concerned with the thought of a state as such until it became clear that the British Mandate over Palestine was being abused, and that without the freedom and instruments of statehood there was no possibility of continuing to build.[26]

> Despite the renewed interest in Palestine and despite the crystallization of Jewish opinion in the direction of statehood, brought about by British and Arab actions there, official Zionist publications still conceded, as after the Arab riots of 1929, that the Zionist *organization* seemed to lag far behind popular acceptance of the Zionist *idea*. Memberships in the ZOA increased from 8,484 in 1932 to 43,453 in 1939. Hadassah more than tripled its 1932 membership of 20,000 in the same period. Funds remitted to Palestine by the United Palestine Appeal mounted almost sevenfold. No organized anti-Zionist expression existed anywhere in the community. Numerous

non-Jewish groups and individuals cooperated with the Zionists on a regularized basis. Major Jewish groups, like B'nai B'rith and the American Jewish Committee, were working alongside the Zionists in various political demonstrations and representations. Nevertheless, the Zionist groups of America were admittedly very far from their goal: the effective mobilization of as many of America's five million Jews as would enable Zionist spokesmen to speak with authority on behalf of the American Jewish community.

That appeals based upon crisis and catastrophe alone did not constitute the whole of the Zionist propaganda arsenal or provide the only motivations for participation in the Zionist movement should be stressed before we attempt to describe additional historical events and their effects upon the American Zionist movement. Throughout the fifty-year period of American Zionism's strivings for a Jewish state, many persons found numerous "intangible compensations" in Zionist membership and activity. Zionism was not only a crisis-bred and crisis-nourished phenomenon; it was also a social enterprise of the first order, permitting its adherents to partake of fellowship, to wield power, to gain recognition and prestige, and to fulfill all of those interpersonal functions for which human associations are brought into existence. Samuel Koenig's sociological study of a typical American Jewish community in 1938 is only one of a number of sources which might be cited for an apt illustration of this point:

> Most of the gatherings inspired by the [Zionist] movement are largely devoted to fund raising, and consist of tea, bridge, and theater parties, luncheons, dinners, concerts, etc. This is particularly true of the women's organizations which are the strongest numerically and the most active. Reports and informative and inspirational talks by local and out-of-town speakers, whereby the interest in the Zionist cause is sought to be aroused, are, as a rule, part of these gatherings, but their general character is mainly social. Individuals belong to those organizations chiefly because it is the thing to do, because they offer social opportunities, and because they serve a "good cause." [27]

WORLD WAR II AND THE NAZI EXTERMINA-
TIONS OF JEWRY, 1939–45

The outbreak of World War II in September, 1939, came as no surprise to the mass of American Jews. Hitler's policy toward the Jews had occasioned a virtual Jewish counter-declaration of war on Nazi Germany as early as 1933. Mass demonstrations against Nazi policies and economic boycotts against German goods had become a characteristic feature of the American Jewish community fully half a decade before Hitler's invasion of Poland and, as Lawrence Fuchs has recently observed, no other American social grouping was as "internationalist" and "interventionist" as were the Jews in the late 1930's.[28] On this social scene of Jewish readiness to "do something" about Hitler, the Zionist movement represented one of a number of movements contending for Jewish support as an answer to Hitlerism. While the Communists called for a militant "United Front Against Fascism," and a few affluent Jews called for a "hands off Europe" policy of American isolation, the Zionist movement advanced its program for a progressive and vigorous Jewish Palestine as a refutation of Nazi calumnies about Jewish "moral degeneracy" and as a potential base of democracy in the impending struggle against Hitlerism.

In this connection, it should be remembered that world Jewry, taken as a whole in 1939, had no choice of loyalties between the contending powers as it did in World War I when Jews, perforce, fought with the armies of all the major combatants. In 1914, large numbers of Jews lived in central Europe and the Turkish Empire, as well as in Russia, western Europe and the United States. Both Germany and the Allies, accordingly, were sympathetic to specifically "Jewish interests," such as Zionism. In 1939, however, practically all Jews were irrevocably wedded to the anti-Axis coalition because of Hitler's anti-Semitic program. Moreover, Allied promises to the Jews regarding Palestine were not forthcoming since the Jews enjoyed no bargaining power, and since such promises might serve only to irritate the neutralist Arab nations which had to be wooed as potentially hostile powers.[29]

Initially, the war seemed to affect the American Zionist movement negatively by promoting a sense of letdown, rather than of buoyancy. Many convinced Zionists were entirely diverted by the war. Jewish confidence sagged under the weight of the *Wehrmacht's* early victories. World attention now focussed on international spokesmen and marching armies. Palestine, albeit a vital Allied supply base, seemed more peripheral to the maintenance of Jewish life than ever before.[30]

Zionist leadership fought this tendency, calling for increased American Jewish awareness of its responsibilities now that the mass of European Jewry was cut off by war. "In the hands of American Jewry," declared a British Zionist in the American Zionist press, "lies the hope, the power and the inspiration for our people. . . ."[31] The American Emergency Committee for Zionist Affairs utilized similar themes, along with those of "democracy" and "patriotism," in its efforts to mobilize American support for a Jewish Army based on Palestinian recruits:

> As self-respecting Jews, we must insist that the Jewish people, rising to national stature in Palestine, be permitted both to exercise the elementary right of self-defense and to make their full contribution to the defeat of Hitler. As loyal Americans and lovers of freedom, we must insist, with all the emphasis at our command, that the vital front in the Near East be strengthened by every man that can be thrown into the struggle.
>
> We must speak out. He who lets fear stifle his voice or indifference dull his ardor falls short of the performance of his full duty to the cause of freedom and democracy, to America, to the Jewish people and the Jewish Homeland. . . . Fellow-Zionists! Assume the responsibility which world events impose upon you. Take up the challenge. Impress your communities with the urgency of the matter. . . .
>
> If we stand up now as men and women, as Americans and as Jews, we can make certain that the Star of David will be carried to the inevitable victory of the Allied cause, along with the banner of our Republic and the flags of all the free peoples of the world.[32]

After the entry of the United States into the war following Pearl Harbor, perceptive observers of the Jewish community sensed a "sobering change from a mood of uncertainty to that of confidence." Jews now felt that they were not alone in their fight against Hitler. Greater interest in Judaism was manifested everywhere.[33] At the same time, however, widespread dissatisfaction was voiced with the apparent inability of Zionist leadership to mobilize large numbers of American Jews behind the Zionist program despite the patent assistance being rendered to the cause of Jewish unity by Hitler's attacks on the Jews. Moreover, in terms of Zionist ineffectiveness with official policy-makers in Washington, there was a prevalent reference to the "Conspiracy of Silence" in which the Roosevelt Administration sent various greetings to the Zionist movement, but studiously avoided any reference to Palestine indicative of official America's former pro-Zionist inclinations. As a subject of governmental policy statements, Palestine was widely felt to be a subject "embarrassing" to the war effort.[34]

New events manifestly agitated the American Jewish community in the summer and fall of 1942. From that time on, the Jewish press bore witness to a veritable revolution in the status of the Jews. The Jewish people under Nazi rule, declared the first sketchy press reports, were not merely being persecuted and harassed as Jews had been for thousands of years but were being physically annihilated under a massive Nazi "Master Extermination Plan." The "Jewish problem" of Europe was being given a "permanent solution," and a non-Zionist solution at that! Whole Jewish communities were said to be methodically uprooted and transported to "liquidation centers," never to be seen or heard from again. Rumors of seemingly fantastic proportions—two million Jews already killed—were given wide circulation in both the Yiddish and Anglo-Jewish presses.[35]

Official United States government confirmation of many of these veiled reports and rumors came on November 25, 1942, when the State Department presented the prominent Zionist leader Dr. Stephen S. Wise with evidence documenting the existence of a personal order from Adolph Hitler to "special German units" commanding the extermination of no less than 5,000,000 Jews by December 31, 1942.[36] A few months later, further proof, including photographs of massacres, was circulated in tens of thousands of copies when the American Jewish Congress released *Hitler's Black Record* and The American Federation of Polish Jews published *The Black Book of Polish Jewry*. What some newspaper columnists had previously scorned as "too vast for credulity" now was corroborated by incontestable evidence.

The reaction of American Jewry, indeed of much of the American public, was one of deepest chagrin and horror. Numerous protest meetings, some attracting as many as 100,000 persons, were held from coast to coast under the auspices of Jewish and non-Jewish groups. Fraternal organizations, Zionist groups and rabbinical associations dispatched delegations to the White House and the State Department. Orthodox Jewry was summoned to a day of prayer and fasting. Half a million Jewish workers in the New York area staged a ten-minute work stoppage, while Mayor Fiorello La Guardia called for city-wide prayers. Radio stations observed minutes of solemn tribute to the butchered victims. Yiddish newspapers appeared on the newsstands wreathed in black borders. Contributions to overseas philanthropies spontaneously mounted. Preliminary steps for the convening of an American Jewish Conference were taken with widespread popular fanfare. (See Chapter IX.) The United States Senate adopted a resolution condemning the Nazi atrocities. Forty thousand spectators viewed Ben Hecht's Madison Square pageant, "We Will Never Die!" dedicated to the memory of the first two million martyrs.[37] And, amid all these demonstrations of deep concern with the fate of European Jewry, Zionists spared no effort to connect the suffering of the Jewish people with the aims of their movement. Zionism, as this contemporaneous statement of Louis Lipsky aptly illustrates, offered American Jews a program to follow in the light of the European tragedy:

Greater trials the Jewish people have never suffered in the long history of martyrdom. The story of today is incredible; but the incredible has become real. Never before have we faced critical times with more awareness of the threat to our survival, than we do today; and with more determination not to endure the cruel status into which we have been forced. It is now appreciated—as never before—that the homelessness of the Jewish people must come to an end. There must come to an end the consistent necessity of pleading for rights denied and flouted, without our names appearing even as complainants. The basic abnormality of Jewish life is its homelessness and the absence of normal conditions in which Jewish life may reveal its authentic features. We cannot abide longer in honor and self respect as a scattered, defeated people.

There is no choice. We must assemble all our strength and force the Gates of Justice; standing there as a united people until justice is done. Or we shall be doomed for generations to an ignoble existence and ultimate disappearance as a people. We of this generation are charged by history to end the chapter of martyrdom and begin the chapter that shall be called the Fight of an

Ancient People for Freedom. Let us not be unworthy. Let us face our duty with courage, intelligence and sacrifice.[38]

On March 19, 1943, a Joint Emergency Committee for European Jewish Affairs was formed by representatives of the four major Jewish "defense" or "anti-defamation" organizations (B'nai B'rith, American Jewish Congress, American Jewish Committee and Jewish Labor Committee), Synagogue Council of America, Agudas Israel, Union of Orthodox Rabbis of America and the American Emergency Committee for Zionist Affairs, with a view toward preparing recommendations for the Anglo-American Refugee Conference to be held in Bermuda beginning April 19. A memorandum presented to the conference by this most representative body of American Jewry ever assembled called, among other things, for British liberalization of the White Paper immigration quotas: "VII. Overriding pre-war political considerations, England should be persuaded to open the doors of Palestine for Jewish immigration and the offer of hospitality made by the Jewish Community in Palestine should be accepted." [39]

But the Bermuda Conference, like the Evian Conference on Refugees held in 1938, offered no solutions for the millions of Jews and other refugees trapped in Europe. Nothing was said about the restrictive White Paper of 1939 in the innocuous press reports issued by the Bermuda conferees. The Jewish press was shocked and indignant. More protest rallies and more delegations to the State Department were dispatched by Zionist and non-Zionist groups alike. Congressman Emanuel Celler's appraisal of the Bermuda Conference was typical of numerous cynical expressions of Jewish public opinion:

> When the Bermuda Conference on Refugees opened it assumed the usual pattern of diplomatic lack of candor and plentitude of verbiage. . . .
> True, we cannot expect miracles, but we want more than palaver, telling us what cannot be done. The conference was a "nice" gesture. . . . Words were stretched into conferences, conferences into learned reports, and reports into satisfied conscience. What now?
> Victory, the spokesmen say, is the only solution. In the meantime, let the millions guilty of no wrong doing be trampled to death, their lives snuffed out by lethal gases and guns, the women

outraged and the children mangled. After victory, disembodied spirits will not present so difficult a problem; the dead no longer need food, drink, and asylum.

Two million Jews dead already, but we are told to wait, wait until nazi *blutbaden* "liquidate" the refugee problem for us. . . .[40]

Shortly after the close of the Bermuda Conference, an "aroused American Jewry," speaking through the American Jewish Conference, adopted the pro-Zionist Resolution on Palestine calling for a Jewish commonwealth in Palestine. (See Chapter 9). Thereafter, an aggressive Zionist leadership increasingly demanded Jewish auto-emancipation instead of continued begging of help from "the conscience of the Christian world." As news reports from Europe revealed that Hitler was rapidly making good his promise to destroy European Jewry, Zionist spokesmen became more dubious about the possibilities of receiving succor from the leaders of the democracies. A forthright *demand* for a Jewish commonwealth, not the halfway *pleas* for larger immigration quotas, came to constitute American Jewry's minimal expectations of the postwar world. Typical of such Zionist appeals based upon the alleged failure of the world to halt the slaughter of Europe's Jews are these two excerpts from widely quoted addresses by Rabbi Abba Hillel Silver, who after 1945 had no peer for his militant leadership of the American Jewish community:

The world is not moved to greater exertions in our behalf when we speak of saving refugees instead of building a Jewish State. The world was not greatly moved by our desperate pleas in behalf of our millions of doomed fellow-Jews now lying dead in their nameless graves, many of whom might have been saved. The great democracies heard the tortured cry of a dying people. They wagged their heads in sympathy and then proceeded to speak in the barren legalism of constricted hearts, of their inability to intervene in the domestic affairs of other nations and of their own inviolate immigration laws.[41]

Spiritual palsy attacked the world, and our moldering age found all sorts of excuses for doing nothing. There were transportation difficulties. There were immigration laws. There was a war on. Nowhere was there any appreciable exertion to rise above the quiddities of technicalities and the barriers of routine. And so, millions of our precious sons and daughters perished who might otherwise have been alive today.

The United States is not without its full share of blame for this terrible failure. Our country did not open its doors wide to rescue the trapped men, women and children. It did not offer even temporary asylum to them in numbers commensurate with the enormity of the tragedy. Actually, the number of visas which were granted was far below the quota allowed by our immigration laws. . . . America found it possible to transport and to admit to the United States more than a quarter of a million Nazi and Fascist prisoners and to give them domicile for the duration of the war. It did not find it possible to do as much for Jews who were its friendliest Allies.[42]

What the "conscience of Christian civilization" and the leaders of the anti-Axis coalition had not done for the suffering Children of Israel, the Jews would now have to do for themselves. The Jewish people, proclaimed the Zionists, would have a secure homeland of its own. Obviously, ran the appeal, only Palestine, in view of its hallowed historical connections with the Jewish people and because of the remarkable colonization efforts of Jewish pioneers, provided a satisfactory site for such a "solution" to the Jewish problem.

The conclusion of hostilities in Europe brought American Jewry the unexpected news that fully 6,000,000 Jews had been exterminated in Hitler's concentration camps. Instead of earlier reports of one or two million casualties, two-fifths of the entire Jewish people had been destroyed. Only 80,000 of Poland's prewar population of 3,300,000 Jews and 10,000 of Lithuania's estimated 150,000 remained alive. An appreciable number of American Jews, possibly a majority, had lost close relatives in the holocaust. Few American Jewish families had not suffered the loss of a friend or, at least, the personal knowledge of one of the murdered victims. The American Jewish community, with its strong Old World ties, suddenly was wrenched loose of its loved ones.

Moreover, the European survivors of Hitler's blood-bath, approximately 463,000 persons, were in many cases still living behind barbed wire in the "liberated" concentration camps; only their guards had changed.[43] There was no place to go. The gates of Palestine were locked by the White Paper of 1939. The gates of America were bolted by immigration laws. Few of the survivors desired to stay in the Europe of their unhappy memories.

It was at this point that the Zionist propaganda machine rolled into high gear. In the name of the martyrs and survivors of Europe, American Zionists and, indeed, virtually all Jews demanded "historic justice" for the Jewish people and a guarantee

EDWARD MINER GALLAUDET MEMORIAL LIBRARY
GALLAUDET COLLEGE
WASHINGTON, D. C.

that Jewish national homelessness would be ended in the postwar world by the establishment, not of new refugee camps, but of an independent Jewish commonwealth. The query which Zionists addressed to the statesmen of the United Nations was in no way different from that which they had posed to their own people a few years earlier:

> How long is the crucifixion of Israel to last? Time and again we have been stretched upon the rack for other peoples' sins. Time and again we have been made the whipping boy for blundering governments, the scapegoat for defeat in war, for misery and depression, for conflict among classes.
> How long is it to last? Are we forever to live a homeless people on the world's crumbs of sympathy, forever in need of defenders, forever doomed to thoughts of refugees and relief? . . . ought not, the incalculable and unspeakable suffering of our people and the oceans of blood which we have shed in this war and in all the wars of the centuries; should not the myriad martyrs of our people . . . be compensated for finally and at long last with the reestablishment of a free Jewish Commonwealth?
> Is not this historic justice and is this world today not reaching out so desperately and so pathetically for a new world order of justice? Should we not be included in that world order of justice? Are we not deserving of it? [44]

JEWISH PUBLIC OPINION IN 1945–46

World War II and Hitler's mass liquidation of European Jews apparently exercised decisive influence on the organizational fortunes of the American Zionist movement. While all previous attacks on the Jewish grouping—the Arab riots of 1929 and 1936–39 and the repressive British Palestine policies of 1938–39—tended to increase Zionist membership and funds remitted to Palestine, nothing like the postwar surge in Zionist popularity was ever before recorded. Direct Zionist memberships exceeded half a million by 1948, with the ZOA alone increasing its dues-paying adherents by 2,900 percent since 1932 and almost 600 percent since 1939. Mizrachi Women's Organization and Hadassah (Women's Zionist Organization of America) also increased their membership more than tenfold since the depths of the depression. *Shekel* sales mounted 2,100 percent between 1932 and 1948 to reach the figure of over 950,000 paid supporters of the World Zionist Congress. Additional millions of Jews were also associated with the Zionist movement in peripheral capacities by virtue of their contributions to one of the numerous Zionist funds, by representation in the American Jewish Conference, or by membership in any of over fifty national organizations engaging in practical work in Palestine or in upholding Zionist political demands.[45]

Further evidence of the opinions on Zionism held by American Jews may be gathered from the comprehensive poll conducted by the Elmo Roper organization, first released by Senators Robert Taft and Robert Wagner on November 16, 1945, and later by the *New York Herald Tribune* on November 22, 1945. Based upon a national cross-section of American Jews, the survey revealed the distribution of opinions on the two conflicting statements.

(1) A Jewish state in Palestine is a good thing for the Jews, and every possible effort should be made to establish Palestine as a Jewish state, or commonwealth, for those who want to settle there;

(2) Jews are a religious group only and not a nation, and it would be bad for the Jews to try to set up a Jewish state in Palestine or anywhere else.[46]

It should be noted that although American Jewry had known for several years of the Nazi decimation of *some* Jews, at the time of the poll American Jews were just beginning to learn of the full extent of the slaughter and of *their own personal losses* in the European holcaust. Under the circumstances, Zionist propagandists hardly had time to exploit these traumatic revelations to the maximum. Moreover, the critical situation of the 500,000 Jewish Displaced Persons in Europe, which so agitated the Jewish community during 1946–48, had not yet fully developed. In all likelihood, therefore, Jewish opinion probably moved even further in the direction of support for a Jewish state than the Roper survey indicates. This, in fact, was the case with certain organized groups in the Jewish community, such as the American Jewish Committee and the Jewish Labor Committee, which cooperated with the Zionists to a far greater extent in 1947–48 than they did immediately after the cessation of hostilities in 1945. (See Chapter 5.)

Furthermore, attention should be directed to the fact that the Roper poll purposely cast the questions employed in their most maximal form. Thus, the word "state" was used rather than "homeland," the latter enjoying far wider acceptance. The purpose of such phrasing was deliberately "to require respondents to vote on the most stringent form of the issue and thus . . . give the results a higher indicative value."

Also to be considered in any assessment of the poll's gauging of Jewish opinion are two of Roper's comments on the overall

TABLE 1.   The Roper Poll of 1945

	PERCENT PRO-JEWISH STATE	PERCENT ANTI-JEWISH STATE	PERCENT UNDECIDED
NATIONAL TOTAL	*80.1*	*10.5*	*9.4*
BY AGE			
21–34 years	77.9	13.6	8.5
35–49 years	79.1	12.4	8.5
50 years and over	82.9	6.0	11.1
BY ECONOMIC STATUS			
Prosperous	73.9	17.5	8.6
Upper middle	75.4	14.6	10.0
Lower middle	84.1	8.0	7.9
Poor	79.3	8.8	11.9
Professional	76.1	14.2	9.7
Proprietors and executives	79.8	12.3	7.9
White collar workers	83.1	9.1	7.8
Labor	81.7	5.8	12.5
BY RELIGIOUS PREFERENCE			
Attend religious services	86.6	9.4	4.0
Do not attend services	70.1	15.4	14.5
Orthodox	86.6	5.9	7.5
Conservative	82.9	9.6	7.5
Reform	71.5	19.8	8.7
BY GEOGRAPHICAL SECTION			
Northeast	81.0	9.9	9.1
Middle West	80.1	11.4	8.5
South	67.0	18.5	14.5
Far West	83.2	5.8	11.0
BY LANGUAGE ABILITY			
Speaks English well	78.9	12.1	9.0
Speaks English brokenly	84.3	4.6	11.1
Does not read English	80.0	7.6	12.4

results: (1) the percentage of "undecided" respondents was unusually low in view of the complexity and the controversial nature
of the issue; and (2) the interviewers, who had been instructed to
report whether they had the impression that their respondent
answered hesitantly or in a manner indicating that his mind was
already made up reported that 77 percent of all those who favored
either the pro- or anti-state positions answered readily and with a
high degree of firmness.[47]

In short, if the Roper poll is assumed to be an accurate
measurement of the opinions on Zionism held by the American
Jewish community in 1945, then the independent observer must
also acknowledge the general truth of the claims advanced by
Zionist propagandists to the effect that the goal of their movement
was "overwhelmingly" endorsed by American Jewry. Indeed, such
a notably non-Zionist observer as the historian Oscar Handlin
concludes a study of the Zionist question in precisely this manner:
"After 1945 American Jews stood almost solidly behind the
Zionists. Only a relatively small group in the American Council
for Judaism thereafter remained apart." [48]

Parenthetically, there is also some evidence to support the
Zionist claim that the American public in general was largely
sympathetic to the aspirations of their movement. Another poll,
this one representative of the total American population, was published by the American Institute of Public Opinion in December,
1945. It indicates that 55 percent of the total sample had "followed the discussion about permitting the Jews to settle in Palestine," and, of these persons, 76 percent favored and 7 percent opposed such settlement, while 8 percent were undecided and 5
percent held miscellaneous opinions. Among informed non-Jews,
therefore, pro-Zionist opinions were virtually as prevalent as
among Jews in general. While the crucial words "Jewish state" or
"Jewish commonwealth" were absent from the formulation of the
question, this poll seems to indicate a fairly clear-cut non-Jewish
tendency to agree with the Zionist program in Palestine.[49]

By way of summarizing the state of American Jewish opinion
toward Palestine and Zionism shortly after the close of World War
II, the observations of Eliezer Kaplan, Treasurer of the Jewish
Agency and noted Palestinian Zionist leader, may be noted briefly.
While Kaplan may not qualify as an objective observer, his de-
tachment from American Zionism, together with the fact that his

views of February, 1946, contrast so sharply with his characterizations of American Jewry only six years earlier,[50] and that his remarks were addressed to top Palestinian leaders for internal consumption, rather than to "domestic Zionist consumers," lends credibility and utility to his view of the spirit of American Jewry in early 1946.

A "profound change" had recently occurred in the American Jewish community, contended Kaplan; the change was not limited to the official Zionist organizations, but extended to "the simple Jew" and to public leaders in most American cities. American Jews were now ready to shoulder huge financial burdens for Palestine; the one-hundred-million-dollar United Jewish Appeal quota for 1946 was three times that of 1945 and, moreover, "not the Zionists, but American Jews in general," were the chief supporters of Palestine in the fund-raising drive.

Apart from the financial effort of American Jewry, continued Kaplan,

> I should also tell you of the growing sense of Jewish solidarity and of the widespread readiness to take part in the struggle for our national future. This is in fact the message I was asked to convey to you at all kinds of gatherings, of labour and middle class circles, of Zionists and non-Zionists, of young and old alike.

With specific reference to American Jewish testimony before the Anglo-American Commission of Inquiry on Palestine in January, 1946, Kaplan averred:

> . . . I must confess . . . that I found it difficult at times to determine whose bearing was more Zionist and whose appearances made a deeper impression—that of Zionists or non-Zionists . . . those who hoped to find evidence of a split between Jews and Zionists have erred greatly. It is a fact that practically all testimonies given and memoranda submitted were conceived in the same spirit . . . the attempt [by the American Council for Judaism] to drive a wedge between Zionists and non-Zionists and to represent the Zionist movement as a group of extremists or a small minority has ended in complete failure. . . . American Jewry is more interested today in Zionism and Palestine than ever it was before.[51]

SUMMARY AND CONCLUSIONS

Viewing the efforts of organized Zionists as part of a total situation of interacting events, it seems that "history was on the side of the Zionist program." Most of the external historical events affecting the Jewish grouping in this period—the Arab riots of 1929 and 1936–39, American anti-Semitism, the rise of Hitler, the German refugee problem, the British White Paper policy of 1939–48, and the annihilation of the European Jewish community—seem to have had a positive relationship to Zionist power and influence in the American Jewish community. All of these events were apparently interpreted as threats to the shared interests of the Jewish group. Indeed, it might be said that the status of the Jewish people as a whole had undergone a revolution in the social upheavals of the mid-twentieth century. Changes in the life of the Jews, in turn, led to a search for new "answers," new programs permitting adjustments to a radically transformed environment.

Zionist leaders, as foregoing quotations have illustrated, were acutely aware of the relevance of this changed social context for their movement. They seemed to understand that, under such conditions of social unrest, large numbers of American Jews "were seeking for answers they did not have, reassurance that the answers they did have were right, and ways of implementing the answers of whose rightness they were convinced." [52]

Zionist propaganda, accordingly, labored to represent Zionism as the most logical answer to the problems confronting the Jewish people. The measure of their success in this undertaking is indicated, in part at least, by the Roper poll of 1945 and by the meteoric rise of Zionist and pro-Zionist organizational fund-raising and affiliations from 1929 to 1948.

Once again, the hypothesis posed at the outset of this chapter to the effect that public opinion is highly sensitive to critical events and that it passes from a latent to an active state when an issue of consequence arises for the group concerned seems supported and validated by the experience of the American Zionist movement.

Moreover, it may readily be seen that some events have greater effect on public opinion than others. Both the economic depression of the early 1930's and World War II before the involvement of the United States, for example, negatively affected Zionist organizational fortunes by making the Zionist program seem superfluous or peripheral to the main interests of American Jews. Other factors, such as the rise of Hitlerism and American anti-Semitism * in the thirties and the Arab riots of 1936–39, appear to be related to moderate increases in funds for Palestine and in formal Zionist membership figures. To still other factors—the British White Paper policy of 1939–47 and, especially, the massacres of European Jewry at the hands of the Nazis—must be attributed vastly more intense reactions with, consequently, much more marked increases in Zionist power and influence.

For purposes of analysis, it is possible to separate the various historical events confronting the Jewish people and then to describe the manner in which Zionist propaganda sought to relate its program to the event. Actual Jewish acceptance of the Zionist goal, however, should not be viewed as a response to a single stimulus. Rather, it seems more likely that Jewish support for the Zionist position can only be adequately interpreted as a complex phenomenon composed of interrelated factors such as socio-economic status, religious outlook, and social motivations, *plus* the effects of a number of events. Two quotations may serve to demonstrate this essential conclusion.

First, Brooklyn Congressman Emanuel Celler (whom *Time* magazine once called "Zionist Celler"), relates the manner in which he became "emotionally dominated" by the Zionist program "into which, for a decade I was to pour my energies, my restlessness and my drives":

> The Nazi terrors had brought many Johnny-come-latelies into the Zionist fold. I suppose I could be counted among those. The reasons were of compelling force. No country would take the Jews. There was the historic association of the Jews with Palestine for two thousand years. There were the Jews already in Palestine who, since before the turn of the century, were draining the marshes, re-

---

* Always intensely aware of what anti-Semites are saying of them, American Jews gave considerable attention to the 1948 election platform of Gerald L. K. Smith's Christian Nationalist Party calling for "the immediate deportation of all supporters of the political Zionist movement" and the outlawing of the Zionist "international machine and all its activity." See Lawrence H. Fuchs, "Sources of Jewish Internationalism and Liberalism," in Marshall Sklare, (ed.), *The Jews: Social Patterns of an American Group* (Glencoe, Ill., 1958), p. 667 note.

viving the tired, wasted soil, building for the day of statehood. There was the virus of anti-Semitism which no country in the world had yet succeeded in eradicating. The insistent extolling of tolerance as a virtue reveals the pose of condescension.[53]

An opponent of organized Zionism, Morris Waldman, Executive Secretary of the American Jewish Committee, also analyzed the temper of American Jewry in much the same way, attributing the predominantly pro-Zionist orientation of the Jewish community to not one, but a series of factors, including historical events and Zionist activities:

> We are dealing with a social complex. Many years of propaganda, virtually uncontested, reinforced by ten years of most tragic events in Jewish history, have generated a widespread pessimism among the Jews of this country . . . with respect to the permanence of Jewish emancipation which, up to these events, had a progressive history of about one century. Our people are depressed and greatly worried even over their future here. This pessimism combined with the fact that Palestine has proven to be the greatest refuge for the fleeing Jews of Europe, has made possible the acceptance on the part of a vast majority of Jews in this country of the idea that Palestine offers the most promising solution and has promoted a friendly and sympathetic attitude toward Zionism which is credited with the great achievement reflected in the Jewish settlement. By contrast, the destruction of Jewish life in the greater part of continental Europe, emphasizes in their minds that world Jewry's, and particularly American Jewry's, efforts to help European Jewries, and expenditures during the past thirty years, aggregating hundreds of millions of dollars (philanthropic and private) though of temporary help have been utterly without permanent profit. . . .
>
> Zionism has been very skillfully propagated as the only solution by appealing to sympathy for the terrible plight of the Jews in Europe. The Jewish public, horrified by the unspeakable savagery of the attacks upon these Jews, with their hearts bleeding for their sufferings and profoundly disturbed over the seeming indifference of Christendom and the effect of all of this upon Jews everywhere, are in the emotional state where they can be, and have been, readily persuaded to regard Palestine as the main, if not the only solution. . . .[54]

Finally, by way of tactical considerations, the Zionist reaction to the historical events of 1929–45 amply illustrates the applicability of political scientist Avery Leiserson's generalization that where an interest group's primary concern is with influencing other groups, "morale tends to be artificial, a product of emergency, crisis, propaganda and force, something to be whipped up to dramatic displays of solidarity and self-sacrifice lest it give way to weariness, boredom and apathy." [55]

However much Zionist leaders might rue their growing loss of organizational independence in the face of various crises and catastrophes, the desperate needs of European Jewry and of the Palestine upbuilding would not permit American Zionists to forego the temptation of an easy appeal based upon the alleged dangers to Jewish interests arising out of this or that emergency. Zionist propaganda, which assiduously attempted to distinguish between "philanthropy and refugeeism," on the one hand, and "Zionism and national constructiveness," on the other, increasingly became imprisoned by the patent desirability of exploiting world events. In the process of mobilizing popular support, Zionists gradually came to be concerned not so much with whether or not individuals and groups upheld Zionist objectives for the right reasons, as with the question of whether or not support could be obtained on *any* convenient terms. Obviously, the omnipresence of a crisis situation provide Zionist propagandists with extremely suggestive appeals for the building of their political interest group.

3

the american
jewish community:
arena for conflict

The struggle of the Zionist movement for power and influence in the United States cannot be described without a substantial understanding of the American Jewish community—the specific political arena in which Zionism contended with various opponents for the advancement of its objectives. Only against a backdrop of conflicting Jewish claims—deriving from differences in national origin, religious outlook, socio-economic status, ideological persuasion, and organizational attachment—can the shifting fortunes of the Zionist movement be adequately portrayed and analyzed.

Unfortunately, however, the raw materials for a political understanding of American Jewry are not readily available. No truly comprehensive study of the Jewish community has yet been undertaken [1] and, therefore, a representative picture must be pieced together from numerous, but incomplete, investigations.

THE NATURE OF AMERICAN JEWRY

A conception of American Jewry which would be acceptable to every interested party has never been evolved and, given the heterogeneous nature of the group concerned, probably cannot be attained in the foreseeable future. One may safely contend that the Jews constitute the largest non-Christian group in the United States, but any attempt to categorize Jews solely as one of the three major American religions will ignore the large number of secu-

larists, agnostics and atheists who identify themselves or are perceived by others as part of the Jewish community. Similarly,
references to the Jews as an ethnic or national grouping will overlook the extremely varied national origins of American Jews, the
absence among them of commonly-accepted criteria of nationality,
and the preference of American Jews themselves for a predominantly religious definition.[2]

Accordingly, in the interests of workability, American Jews
will be defined as a "religious-ethnic-cultural subcommunity" [3]
existing within the larger American "nation of nations" or "nation
of minorities." Jews can thus be considered as members of a major
religious faith, as a component of America's ethnic population,
and as those who share a specific cultural pattern on the American
scene. This broad conception will also account for the widespread
Jewish interest in and aid for overseas Jewries, as it implicitly includes the shared history, common traditions, and sense of kinship
which are central to the continuance of international Jewish
group life.[4]

Major characteristics of American Jewry which appear relevant to the development of American Zionism in the two decades
prior to the establishment of Israel include the following:

THE "NEWNESS" OF AMERICAN JEWRY

The year 1954 marked the tercentenary of the arrival in
America of the first twenty-three Jews at the Dutch port of New
Amsterdam. Earlier, Jews were known to have participated in
Columbus' first voyage. Nevertheless, a glance at the following
table will demonstrate the relatively recent arrival of the majority
of American Jews.

While the greater part of American Jewry is thus only one
or two generations removed from Europe, the curtailment of immigration after 1924 nevertheless produced a situation in which,
by 1940, over 70 percent of American Jewry was native-born, and
90 percent had lived in the United States fifteen years or more.[5]

The character of Jewish immigration to America suggests
several political relevancies. In the first place, one might reason-
ably expect considerable variance in the social outlook of the

TABLE 2.   Estimated Jewish Population Growth in the
United States [6]

YEAR	POPULATION
1790	3,000
1840	15,000
1850	50,000
1880	250,000
1900	1,000,000
1914	3,000,000
1928	4,228,000
1943	5,199,200

early as contrasted with the later immigrants, variance which might tend to make cooperation among Jews difficult. Secondly, as a result of the variable degree of Americanization in the Jewish grouping, one might conjecture: (1) the first settlers to arrive had greater social status, more knowledge of the American political system, greater economic means and more abundant leisure than the newcomers, thus permitting them to exert influence in public affairs out of proportion to their numbers; (2) conversely, the bulk of the Jewish community, having only recently arrived here, was too preoccupied with economic and social adjustment, and too inexperienced in American political life to exercise political influence commensurate with their numerical strength; and (3) the majority of the Jewish grouping, having only recently experienced suffering in Europe, or still having friends and family abroad, might be receptive to stimuli from sources beyond their immediate American social environment; that is, many American Jews might be expected to show keen interest in events affecting European Jewry.

GEOGRAPHICAL DISTRIBUTION OF THE JEWISH POPULATION

The Jews of Europe, traditionally excluded by law from agricultural pursuits, constituted a predominantly small town and urban population. This pattern was faithfully reproduced upon migration to the United States. According to a Bureau of the Census survey of religious bodies conducted in 1936, 4,770,000 Jews resided in the United States. Of these, 4,640,000 were listed by the Census as living in 967 "principal communities" and only 13,000 dwelt in 9,579 smaller communities. New York City was estimated to be the home of over 2,000,000 Jews. Jews were distributed in other predominantly urban locations as shown in Table 3.[7] It may also be noted that in the fourteen largest American cities with a total population of 500,000 or more each, 78 percent of the entire American Jewish population was concentrated.

TABLE 3.   Distribution of Jewish Population in
United States Cities, 1936

POPULATION OF JEWISH COMMUNITY	NUMBER OF CITIES OR TOWNS
Over 100,000	3
75,000–100,000	3
50,000– 75,000	4
30,000– 50,000	1
20,000– 30,000	12
15,000– 20,000	2
10,000– 15,000	21
8,000– 10,000	12
5,000– 8,000	15
2,000– 5,000	61
1,000– 2,000	84
101– 999	478
Less than 100	260

While Jews were thus to be found in almost a thousand predominantly urban areas from coast to coast, their residences classified by states reveal a far more restricted choice of location. In the six populous states of New York, Pennsylvania, Illinois, Massachusetts, New Jersey and Ohio were found in 1936 over 68 percent of the total Jewish population in the United States. These, together with seven other populous states (California, Connecticut, Michigan, Maryland, Minnesota, Missouri and Texas), included over 90 percent of American Jewry.[8] In more recent years, Jews have tended to move, with the general population, to southern California and Florida, but there has been no marked tendency to migrate to other hitherto sparsely populated areas.

Another indication of the nature of Jewish population concentration in 1936 can be readily gained from Harry S. Linfield's observation that the Jews, approximately 3 percent of the total American population, constituted the following proportions of total settlement: a maximum of 16.70 percent in New York and a minimum of 0.21 percent in North Carolina, 11.0 percent in cities with a total population of 100,000 or more, 2.77 percent in cities of 25,000–100,000, 1.22–0.63 percent in other urban areas, 0.38 percent in rural incorporated places, and a mere 0.10 percent in rural unincorporated areas.[9]

The geographical concentration of American Jewry raises the question of the political importance of their places of residence. One might speculate, for example, that such dense settlement lent the Jews greater strength in certain areas than they would have exerted had they been spread around the nation in exact proportion to their total numbers, that is, a mere 3 percent of the population. Conversely, centered only in several states and cities, the Jewish grouping might be expected to wield little influence in broad areas of the United States. As for the relevance of such geographical concentration to Zionist efforts to organize American Jews for their program, the suggestion is obvious that such organization was facilitated by the closeness of Jewish settlement and the consequent need to expend funds and effort in only a few areas rather than over the entire continental expanse of the United States. Then, too, since the Jews constituted a predominantly urban population, Zionist organizational efforts would be abetted by the relatively greater availability of such media of communication as local Jewish newspapers, and the existence of numerous neighborhood Jewish institutions (the synagog, religious school, community center, and so forth), all of which might not have been available had the Jews been dispersed across the rural expanses of the nation.

SOCIO-ECONOMIC STATUS OF AMERICAN JEWS

Data on the socio-economic composition of the American Jewish community, while incomplete, discloses one salient fact. Considering the relatively recent arrival of American Jews and the dire economic circumstances in which most of them debarked here, the Jews enjoy a remarkably high economic status. Survey categories based on income, occupation and educational attainment all reveal a considerable disparity between the levels of the Jews and those of other immigrant groups arriving in America at almost the same time. Indeed, the Jews seem to approximate the economic, if not the social, status of such well-established groups as the Episcopalians, Congregationalists and Presbyterians.[10]

Occupationally, influenced in large part by their urban predilections, the Jews present a vastly different structure from the general population: [11]

TABLE 4.   Jewish Occupational Structure

	JEWS %	TOTAL LABOR FORCE %
Trade and Commerce	40	13.8
Manufacturing	20	26.3
Professions	11	6.5
Farming	0.5	17.5
Others	27	36.6

Within these categories it is estimated that 60 percent of the Jews were wage and salary earners, 29 percent proprietors, and 11 percent professionals.

Availing themselves of superior urban facilities and their more abundant economic means, American Jews have also managed to obtain a significant degree of higher education and to support an extremely prolific variety of their own schools, periodicals, and other cultural institutions.[12]

The relevance for our purposes of the foregoing features of Jewish socio-economic status is limited to internal conditions in the Jewish group itself; the attempt will not be made to gauge the influence of the Jews vis-à-vis non-Jewish groups in the society. But from the available data the supposition arises that much of the Jewish grouping was possessed of both the wealth and probably the leisure either to embrace and support, or else to reject and oppose the Zionist program. In either case, the resources which could be committed to the choice would be considerable.

DIVERSITY AND CONFLICT IN THE JEWISH COMMUNITY

A profound diversity and conflict was present in the American Jewish community only a generation ago and has today not entirely vanished. The greatest single factor making for community discord was the divergent ethnic origin, and attendant social stratification, of the succeeding immigrations from the Old World to the New. Historians and sociologists have referred to a three-phase series of Jewish migrations to America and have traced the divisive factors following therefrom. The migrations included: (1) the "Sephardic"—the descendants, few in number, of the venerable Jewish culture of pre-1492 Spain, who arrived before or about the time of the American Revolution (bearing such names as Cardoza, Carvalho, Seixas, and Pereira); (2) the "German"—immigrants primarily from central Europe who reached America between 1840 and 1880 (with such family names as Schiff, Warburg, Oppenheimer, Guggenheim, Lehman); and (3) the East European—the most numerous group composed of Russians, Poles, Lithuanians, Rumanians, and others, whose main contingents arrived in the United States between 1880 and 1924.[13]

Each of these "waves" of immigrants brought unique traditions and values from their old habitats and proceeded to create institutions in their own image. As each wave became acculturated to the new-found conditions it rose with comparative rapidity in the American economy. And, in turn, each resented the poor immigrant "greenhorns" who arrived daily to build their homes in America.

To aid in understanding the reception of the Zionist ideal by this heterogeneous community another schematic generalization used by students of the Jewish community may be useful—the three major "blocs" which were so noticeable a feature of American Jewish life in the recent past.[14] It will be seen that the members of these blocs, albeit united by the common characteristic of "Jewishness," evidenced vastly different perspectives or patterns of "identifications, demands and expectations." [15]

The "Right Bloc"—This was principally the older German or Austro-Hungarian stratum composed of affluent bankers, merchants, brokers, and professionals. Its predominant religious expression was Reform Judaism, a product of the era of Jewish Emancipation in post-Napoleonic Europe. Organizationally, this bloc expressed itself through charitable associations, the fraternal order of B'nai B'rith, and the select group of influential persons constituted to represent and protect Jewish rights, the American Jewish Committee. This was the bloc most integrated into American life, considered "modern and enlightened" by itself and "un-Jewish and assimilated" to many in the "Left" and "Center" Blocs. For the "Right Bloc," Judaism was defined strictly as a religious grouping; they resented the ethnic and national channels of Jewish expression followed by their co-religionists to the left.

The "Center Bloc"—Thousands of religionists and secularists, constituting an amorphous mass of sweatshop and factory workers, peddlers, "low prestige" businessmen, and a limited number of professionals were included in this bloc. Mostly of East European origin and, therefore, largely Yiddish-speaking, this lower middle or laboring class either adhered to the traditional religious forms of Orthodoxy, developed the new Conservative movement in Judaism, or stood aloof from religious affiliations altogether. For most, Judaism was defined in national and cultural, as well as religious, terms. The struggle for integration into American society absorbed their major efforts well into the decade of the 1940's; but this bloc, nevertheless, provided the reservoir of Zionist strength in such groups as the American Jewish Congress and the Zionist Organization of America and increasingly came to dominate other mass membership organizations such as B'nai B'rith and Jewish War Veterans.

The "Left Bloc"—A complex grouping of predominantly East European labor unionists and labor ideologists; this bloc dwindled as the Jews found more attractive economic positions. Here militantly internationalist and anti-Zionist fraternal societies, such as the Workmen's Circle (Arbeiter Ring), shared socialist ideology with Zionist fraternalists in the Jewish National Workers' Alliance (Farband). Farther to the left, Stalinists in the Jewish People's Fraternal Order opposed their laboring brothers on issues of socialism and Zionism but were, nevertheless, able to make common cause in the propagation of Yiddish culture and in the fight against "capitalist exploitation."

The political relevance of these antagonistic blocs for Zionist destinies in America will be more readily apparent after the extended discussion of the following three chapters.

OLD WORLD TIES

Driven from their former homes by persecuting mobs or gnawing hunger, American Jews cherished little attachment to the governments or national states from which they had emigrated. While many other nationality groups sent their male members to America in order to seek wealth and then return with it to waiting families and friends, the Jewish pattern of immigration generally involved entire families on a permanent basis. Indeed, while other groups returned to Europe at a rate never less than 25 percent of their total numbers, Jews emigrating from the United States constituted only 4.58 percent of their total numbers during the period of 1908–42.[16]

In the absence of a national homeland of their own and of solid attachments to their countries of recent origin, the Jews directed their sentimental attachments to the "Old Country" to home towns, or at most, to regions. Thousands of fraternal associations (*landsmanschaften*), uniting comrades from the Old World, sprang up around America. Distinctions of *Litvak* (Lithuanian) or *Galicianer* (Galician) became potent aids for the maintenance of group loyalties. These, together with the fact that almost every American Jew was only a generation or two removed from a European origin, and that virtually all still had relatives in Europe, gave American Jewry the character of a community rooted here yet intensely concerned with brethren abroad. Like the American Italians, Poles, Czechs, Lithuanians, Syrians and Irish who aided the movements of national liberation of their people, and who sent considerable monetary assistance to friends and relatives overseas, American Jews experienced similar loyalties and sentiments.

As American Jewry increased in numbers, it naturally grew in relative importance to the totality of world Jewry. With the destruction of almost two-fifths of the Jewish people at the hands of Nazi Germany, American Jewry, by virtue of its numbers and wealth, suddenly found itself heir to the leadership of the survivors.

TABLE 5. Relative Percentage of American Jewry to World Jewry [17]

YEAR	JEWS IN U.S.	PERCENT OF WORLD JEWRY
1900	1,000,000	9.1
1939	4,900,000	29.3
1945	5,200,000	47.3

The attitudes and responses of American Jewry to this new-found responsibility, particularly toward the Zionist political program, comprise the central concern of this study. It need only be pointed out here that the Jewish group's shared sentiments of mutual help for other Jews were not without decisive importance for the making of the American Jewish community itself; for in the process of aiding their overseas brethren, American Jewry became transformed in both organizational life and social perspective.[18]

THE EFFECTS OF AMERICANIZATION ON THE JEWISH COMMUNITY

Much of the heterogeneous character of American Jewry can be explained by the absence of the compulsory religious community which characterized the Jewish people in the two thousand years following the destruction of the Jewish state in 70 A.D. In all lands away from Palestine, often termed collectively "Diaspora" —"Dispersion" or "Galut"—"Exile," wherever Jews were to be found, the obligatory demands of the Jewish religion were the chief integrating force in Jewish life. This religion, encompassing ideas of God, Law (*Torah*) and Palestine, provided a type of spiritual fatherland which enabled the landless and stateless Jew to withstand the enmities of a frequently hostile environment. In the externally-imposed physical ghettos of central Europe, or in the self-imposed, self-governing *kahal* (community council) of Poland, Jewish social, cultural and religious life became an inseparable whole, diverging considerably from the Gentile world around it and providing the individual with a "primary group" which absorbed all of his interests and loyalties.

With the "Era of Emancipation and Enlightenment" following the Napoleonic Wars, world Jewry emerged gradually into Western civilization. As Jews became accepted as legitimate citizens of their respective countries, instead of pariahs condemned to civil exclusion, they developed interests apart from their hitherto exclusively Jewish environment. Now, rightfully part of a larger Gentile community that very often possessed greater attractions and prestige, the Jew's time, energy and money were increasingly expended on pursuits outside the primary Jewish group.

Under the circumstances, Jewish group loyalties, religious and otherwise, were weakened. A wide variety of institutions and outlooks—all involving Jewish attempts at adjusting to the majority environment—appeared. The former monolithic nature of the Jewish group was replaced by separate philanthropic, cultural, religious and political approaches to Jewish survival. Indeed, concern for the continued existence of the group waned as adjustment to the larger society proceeded, as internal group sanctions withered, and as the general secularizing and nationalizing influences of western Europe reached the Jew. Jewish life became increasingly characterized by a growing indifference to the perpetuation of a distinctive group; assimilation into the majority culture became a purposeful goal of many Jews.

In the United States, this process of deteriorating Jewish group cohesiveness was accelerated by entrance into the vast "Melting Pot." Scholars have speculated that because the Jews were confronted with the freest political and economic atmosphere they had ever experienced away from Palestine, the tendency to vanish into the American scene was, initially at least, marked in the extreme. That is, the economic and cultural opportunities of America caused Jews, like other immigrant groups, to drift farther from their historic past until it seemed to many observers that a distinctly Jewish existence in America was impossible.[19] One index of this rapid decline in Jewish identification is provided by statistics on a distinctively Jewish cultural pattern—the use of the Yiddish language. According to the 1930 federal census, 1,750,000 persons declared Yiddish as their mother tongue. But only a decade later the number had fallen to 1,222,000 persons in a considerably enlarged Jewish population.[20] Similarly, while the circulation of Yiddish newspapers amounted to 750,000 in 1917, it fell to 535,000 in 1927 and 425,000 in 1944.[21]

Time was to show that the American Jewish community, while discarding many of its historic forms, was abandoning neither the faith nor the fold. Newer communal manifestations more suitable to the American scene—fraternal lodges, community and synagog centers, Young Men's Hebrew Associations, federations and welfare funds, "defense organizations," Sunday schools and, not least significantly, Zionist groups—became the accepted channels for manifesting Jewish identification and interest. In fact, the disintegrating effects of Americanization were gradually offset by other American norms, such as respect for religious affiliation. The militant atheism so prevalent in some Jewish quarters prior to World War I became a faint shadow of its former self as American Jewry accommodated itself to the high prestige accorded by American middle-class culture to religious observances (like church-going) and pluralistic affiliations (that is, joining many organizations).[22]

Thus, as the forces of Americanization affected ever greater numbers of world Jewry, former expressions of Jewish identification were remolded and exchanged for new ones. But, no matter how radically transformed, the Jews in America were still sufficiently differentiated from their environment to provide a distinct object of study and analysis.

The foregoing remarks about the assimilationist character of much of American Jewry suggest a host of relevant hypotheses for our study. In the first place, to the extent that Jews were oriented outward toward the majority culture, claims presented by members of their own, the minority, culture would be received inversely. That is, for those Jews who cared little about their membership in the Jewish group, the Zionist program would offer scant interest since, almost by definition, the Zionist program is a uniquely Jewish approach.

Again, to the extent that Jews were active in organizations and activities of the majority culture, they would have much less of a contribution to make to Jewish groups, Zionist or otherwise. Also, in the degree that Jews looked to Gentile reference groups for their attitudes, the opinion of such non-Jews concerning Zionism would be proportionately important for the success of Zionist claims.

Moreover, with American Jews tending to lose distinctively Jewish cultural traits, Zionist appeals would have to be framed in a manner intelligible and palatable even to assimilated Jews. For example, increasingly unable to communicate with the Jewish public via the Yiddish press, Zionists would have to resort to all of the conventional American media for disseminating information. Unable to contact their target group in the synagog alone, Zionists would have to work within the fraternal lodge, veterans' post, labor union, and community center.

THE ORGANIZATIONAL LIFE OF AMERICAN JEWRY

Enough has already been said concerning the divergent values and perspectives within American Jewry to indicate that the social group with which we are concerned is hardly an uncomplicated and homogeneous whole. Nowhere is this salient fact more clearly expressed than in the maze of Jewish voluntary associations which produce the spectacle of "organized chaos" so familiar to students of Jewish communal life.

Unlike centuries of Jewish life in the Diaspora based upon community solidarity and a sense of collective responsibility to the organized religious community or congregation, American Jewish communal life is arranged at random without the benefit of any all-inclusive base. As Arnold Gurin has concisely remarked of the

Jewish community, "within the voluntary framework of American organizational life we have a wide variety of patterns, a high degree of *laissez-faire,* a considerable amount of anarchy, disorganization, and irresponsibility; as well as some highly organized and integrated structures." [23] While the majority of the local Jewish communities have slowly managed to establish overall "welfare funds" (sometimes called "Jewish federations" or "united appeals") to mediate conflicts in the allocation of charitable contributions, there exist no institutions broad enough to encompass the entire Jewish community on a national basis. Each local social organization, each congregation, is virtually a law unto itself.

Attempting to account for this variance from the congregational unit as the basis of traditional Jewish life, Rabbi Jacob B. Agus attributes the root cause to America's liberal tradition with its emphasis upon individual freedom:

> If there be a pyramid of values in American culture, the sovereignty of the individual constitutes its apex. It is not at all taken for granted that the individual is to be regarded as part of any community axiomatically and automatically. As the focus of all values, he is at liberty to choose out of the organic cluster of values and institutions that is Judaism whatsoever may appeal to him and reject whatever does not suit his fancy. In consequence, the American Jewish community is actually a loose association of organizations, ministering to one or another Jewish or general ideal.[24]

Unchecked by the formal sanctions at the disposal of Jewish communal organizations in the Old World, the American Jewish community evolved into a highly competitive, loosely integrated arena of diverse interests and perspectives. Approximately three hundred national associations and tens of thousands of local organizations vie for members and contributions in furtherance of worthy causes—social, fraternal, cultural, philanthropic, religious, protective, and labor. Virtually the only objective they hold in common is allegedly that of bettering Jewish life.[25]

The multiplicity and diversity of organized Jewish life immediately suggests that the task of any group attempting to effect claims from the totality of the community would be difficult indeed, and that efforts to do so would probably have to proceed in a piecemeal fashion, organization by organization. Also, because national organizations could not frequently control their local chap-

ters or branches, the claims of a group seeking to organize and influence the entire Jewish population would have to be advanced
community by community, and not merely on the national level.

With no overall association to control the multitudinous constituents of the Jewish community, even if agreement could once
be attained, cohesion would be difficult to maintain. Furthermore,
the program presented by a new group would have to be radically
different in some significant respect if it were to be received as
anything more than "just another activity" which would compete
with a host of existing organizations and programs.

In fact, attempts to organize all of American Jewry have invariably foundered on the rocks of the vested interests of professional and lay leaders or died because of public apathy. Sincerely
held ideological differences, or what many Jews believe is chronic
inability to agree on anything, have also been stumbling blocks to
Jewish unity. (The ironic equation, "Two Jews Equal Three Opinions!" is a standard cliché of Jewish conversation.) These factors
will become increasingly evident as we trace the development of
American Zionism, the most ambitious and most successful effort
to mobilize the entire American Jewish community for a single objective.

4

zionism and religious organizations

PROPAGANDA AND ALLIANCES: THE TACTICS OF BUILDING INTEREST GROUP STRENGTH

Surveying the growth of pro-Zionist opinion in diverse sectors of the American Jewish community as well as in certain areas of the overall American society, we shall be particularly concerned with Zionists' efforts to bolster their power potential by attracting existing national Jewish organizations and their constituents to the Zionist political program.

At the outset, it must be recognized that a group's establishment of alliances with other groups is a characteristic feature of the political process in the United States. On this point, one would do well to ponder the observation of political scientist David Truman. Considering the fact that any interest group constitutes only a tiny minority of those active in political competition, alliances with other organized interests are eminently practical, if not inevitable. In a democratic society cherishing the notion of majority agreement as the desired prerequisite for decision-making,

> . . . groups often find it essential to make alliances in order to assert their claims effectively. Alliances are a means of enlarging a public, and the facilities of allied organizations are channels through which a friendly group's propaganda may flow . . . such channels have for the membership of the allied group a prestige and influence greater than that of any "outside" group. Access to these channels, therefore, reduces the hazards facing an outside group.[1]

That Zionist leadership conceived of its goal in essentially identical terms is indicated by the frequency with which Zionists

61

were exhorted to remember Herzl's sagacious command to proceed with "Kibbush Ha'Kehilloth—The Conquest of the Communities." In a similar vein, ZOA President Louis Lipsky's early prescription for a conversion of American Jewry declared: "We must attach ourselves to every form of Jewish regenerative activity in which the quality of our national vision may be applied, and color it with that quality." [2]

The manner in which the Zionist movement proceeded to "attach itself" to an ever larger public of organized Jewish interests will not, however, exhaust our attention in the following chapters. We shall also want to ascertain the contributions to Zionist strength, other than mere moral support, which were obtained by the successful conclusion of alliances with, or an infiltration of, existing Jewish organizations. Finally, we shall be interested in tracing the techniques used by the Zionists in their campaign, and the factors external to the movement itself which abetted or delayed their eventual victory.

MAJOR CHARACTERISTICS OF AMERICAN JEWISH RELIGIOUS GROUPS

Religious activities do not occupy everyone in the American Jewish community in terms of the commonly-accepted religious classification of Americans as Protestants, Catholics, or Jews. Nevertheless, the numerical strength, leadership and useful organizational forms nominally associated with America's three major Jewish religious denominations—Orthodox, Conservative, and Reform— made the conquest of organized religion a logical first objective for the Zionists. If the authoritative approval and encouragement of rabbinical and lay leaders could be secured, the effort to convince American Jewry of the validity and urgency of the Zionist message would be immeasurably enhanced. If not, Zionism could never claim to represent American Jewry.

Attempting to achieve its objectives in the collective name of American Jewry—indeed, of world Jewry—Zionist leaders scrupulously avoided becoming identified with any single branch of Judaism. Instead, they maintained an air of benevolent neutrality on the respective merits of Reform, Orthodoxy and Conservatism and sought to influence all three alike, manipulating their support as a lever to gain entrance to and acceptance in other sectors of the Jewish fold.[3]

But, as we shall see, because of differences in ethnic origin, economic status, social outlook, theological credo and, undoubtedly, differences in the effectiveness of the Zionist maneuvers, the Zionist program was not universally or simultaneously accepted by American religious groups. Some religious leaders became Zionism's most steadfast proponents and others its greatest antagonists. Some religious groups rallied to the Zionist banner immediately while others remained aloof or hostile for fully half a century.

Although we shall not attempt to delineate the total structure of doctrine and outlook which unite and differentiate America's three major Jewish denominations, or "movements" as they are more popularly called, it is necessary to point out some of the major characteristics of the groups concerned, since these characteristics were significant factors in conditioning religious group attitudes toward the Zionist program.[4]

Orthodox Judaism attempts to preserve the traditions and practices of the Jewish faith as they are believed to have been ordained by God and transmitted and interpreted by Moses and other great teachers of the Jewish people. Orthodox Jews are the traditionalists of Judaism, observing dietary laws, using the Hebrew language in prayer, and holding to a considerable body of tradition-derived customs and ceremonies. While there has been considerable development, enrichment, and even innovation in Orthodoxy, fundamental tradition, not change, characterizes Orthodoxy's world outlook.

Reform Judaism, or Liberal Judaism, advocates the observance of only those laws and ceremonies which are considered to have application, purpose and beauty in the present day. While the Orthodox accept the entire body of oral and written law as hallowed by tradition, Reform constantly adapts and simplifies according to an interpretation of modern needs. The ethical teachings of the Prophets are generally exalted over the legalities of the Five Books of Moses.

Conservative Judaism is an attempt to find a middle ground between Orthodoxy and Reform. Recognizing a need to reconcile ancient law and practices with the modern era, it has made some concessions, primarily in ritual. At the same time, Conservatism seeks to preserve Hebrew, the dietary laws and the bulk of traditional observances as vital forces in Jewish life.

A new, and yet small, movement—Reconstructionism—has originated within the Conservative group and seeks to reorganize the totality of Jewish life, reinterpreting Judaism in the light of modern thought, but without advancing to the extremes once practiced by Reform. Reconstructionism views Judaism as "a religious civilization," not merely a religious creed. Hence a place in Jewish life is assured for everything "positively Jewish," including secular Zionism.

These major branches of American Judaism are organized into national lay and rabbinical associations for purposes of consultation; but each local congregational group is largely independent and self-sufficient, except for the central publication of textbooks and the training of rabbis. While the attempt has been made to tie these movements or denominations together along ideological lines, and provide a common creed and ritual for each synagog or temple, differences between congregations are so marked that no single, authoritative policy is likely to be followed by every local unit. Reform practice in one city may resemble Conservatism in another; congregations of a single movement in the same city will often diverge widely in ritual, in attitudes toward Judaism and Zionism, and in other ways.

While each Reform and Conservative rabbi and congregation is represented in the national organizations, the vast majority of the Orthodox synagogs, estimated to total about 3,000 of America's 3,728 congregations (in 1937),[5] completely lack national organizational affiliations. The organization of America's Jewish religious groups as of the year 1945, according to their own unverified claims, appears in Table 6.[6]

Thus, Orthodox-claimed "affiliations" (the term never being clearly defined) outnumbered those of Reform and Conservative Judaism combined. Yet, due to their greater degree of cohesion, superior organization, higher economic and social status, and wider concern with secular activities, the Reform groups constituted the most influential religious force in Jewish communal affairs. Orthodoxy, for much the opposite reasons, and because of its gradual loss of members to Reform and Conservatism, was considered the least potent force in the same area.[7]

TABLE 6.   Lay and Rabbinical Religious Associations

LAY ASSOCIATIONS

DENOMINATION	NAME	FOUNDED	NUMBER OF CONGREGATIONS	MEMBERSHIP
Orthodox	1. Union of Orthodox Jewish Congregations	1898	450	400,000 "direct"; 1,500,000 "indirect"
	2. Union of Sephardic Congregations	1929		numerically insignificant
Reform	Union of American Hebrew Congregations	1873	320	60,000 families; 250,000 persons
Conservative	United Synagogue of America	1913	350	400,000

RABBINICAL ASSOCIATIONS

(There are at least ten others, mostly Orthodox in outlook)

DENOMINATION	NAME	FOUNDED	MEMBERSHIP
Orthodox	1. Union of Orthodox Rabbis	1902	500 rabbis (mostly foreign-born and trained)
	2. Rabbinical Council of America	1922	300 rabbis (mostly American-born and trained)
	3. Assembly of Hebrew Orthodox Rabbis	1920	125 rabbis
	4. Federation of Orthodox Rabbis of America	1926	(not known)
Reform	Central Conference of American Rabbis	1889	475 rabbis
Conservative	Rabbinical Assembly of America	1900	354 rabbis

ZIONISM AND ORTHODOXY

The Rise of Religious Zionism   Most of the West European Orthodox rabbis of Herzl's day considered his political approach to the "Jewish Problem" a blasphemous act of rebellion against the will of God. Secular attempts to normalize the position of the Jews by providing a sovereign state were regarded as defections from "Jewish

Fate" and as cynical machinations likely to lead to complete assimilation, since such attempts emanated from secularists and other
"destroyers of the traditional faith."

But in eastern Europe, where Jewish suffering was greater
and where the de-Judaizing influences of the Emancipation era had
not yet penetrated, lay and rabbinical traditionalists alike generally
responded to the call of Zion. Mizrachi, a religious Zionist movement, founded in Vilna, Lithuania, in 1902, was firmly entrenched
in the United States by 1913 when Rabbi Meyer Berlin arrived
in New York to guide its program. Aided by such friendly rabbis
as Levinthal in Philadelphia, Schaffer in Baltimore, Ashinsky in
Pittsburgh, Ginsberg in Rochester, Schoenfeld in Milwaukee and
Estersohn and Pereira Mendes in New York, Orthodox Zionist
sentiment mushroomed among the ever increasing settlement of
East European immigrants.[8]

These predominantly poor newcomers, steeped in Jewish traditions and loyalties—if not entirely "observant" in their daily lives
—with experiences of persecution fresh in their memories, were
soon to embrace enthusiastically the practical chores of the Zionist
program. But, as late as 1922, the leading American Zionist of his
day recognized the priority of his movement's uncompleted work
in this segment of the community:

> Zionism makes its appeal to the Jewish masses—that large element
> which lives closely associated in industrial, social, intellectual and
> religious Jewish life; still animated, more or less, by sturdy Jewish
> ideals; speaking, more or less, the Yiddish language; becoming
> American without cutting themselves off from the springs of Jew-
> ish life; which is not too wealthy and therefore snobbish; which is
> poor, but becoming more well-to-do. . . . It is this mass, which has
> its own habits and customs and expresses them in its own institu-
> tions . . . which we aim to convert into supporters of Zionism.[9]

It was equally clear to many Zionists that the synagog was the
most likely institution in which potential converts to the cause could
be found, for there lay latent powerful emotional influences, formal allegiances to tradition, faithful adherences to ancient Jewish
ideals, upon which the Zionist movement could build.[10] Already,
virtually every Orthodox *shul* (synagog) had become a veritable
den of Zionist activity: the locale of appeals for funds, the launching ground of mail and telegram campaigns, the base for Hebrew-

Zionist education, and the meeting hall of Zionist Organization of America branches, Hadassah chapters and Young Judaea clubs.[11]

Despite the fact that the leaders of American Zionism and the mass of their followers were not particularly Orthodox in their observances, Orthodoxy found itself able to join a growing Zionist alliance with other Jews. In his brief American visits, Abraham Isaac Kuk, the revered Chief Rabbi of Palestine added spiritual weight to the traditionalists' practical program for "redeeming the Holy Land of Zion." The force of Kuk's personality and writings provided the inspiration and rationalization for Orthodox co-operation with Zionist secularists, and his teachings became the cornerstone upon which the majority of American Orthodoxy based its ardent support of the Zionist movement.[12]

Orthodox Zionists did not confine their efforts to the relatively limited circles of the Mizrachi Zionist organization; members of the multi-party Zionist Organization of America affiliated with Ortho-dox congregations far outnumbered their Mizrachi and Hapoel Mizrachi (religious labor) counterparts.[13]

In short, with one notable exception, most Orthodox Jews—like their Conservative brethren—whether formally committed to the Zionist program or lending support in the roles of sympathizers or "functional members," constituted American Zionism's most dependable, if not most powerful, allies.[14]

Agudas Israel   While a firm alliance with Zionism characterized most of Orthodox Jewry, a small and extremely vocal group of Orthodox anti-Zionists provided the notable exception. Their ac-tivities on the American scene during the crucial decade when Zionist political fortunes were being resolved in the United States and in the United Nations were not without importance.

Despite the growth of religious Zionist sentiment in eastern Europe after 1897 a number of pious Jews rejected all efforts of mortal man to "force the hand of God" in so vital a matter as the redemption of the Holy Land. At the Silesian Kattowitz Confer-ence in 1912 a vehemently anti-Zionist organization, Agudas Israel (League of Israel),[15] was formed, dedicated to the promotion of Jewish interests solely on a religious basis.

Unlike most anti-Zionists, the founders of Agudas Israel did not oppose Zionism as being too nationalistic; in their view, the

Jews had been divinely ordained forever as "a kingdom of priests
and a holy nation." But Agudah emphasis was placed upon a national religion and not upon those attributes of nationhood stressed
by Zionist secularists: territory, language, culture, and sovereignty.
Moreover, because Zionism as a secular movement refused to recognize the primacy of Jewish law, as interpreted by the Orthodox
rabbinate, it was held to be the dread enemy of all faithful Jews.
Beloved Palestine was regarded as a place for Jews to realize the
joys of a full religious life, never as the Zionist's political "solution
to the Jewish problem."

To this end, some Agudah leaders, notably Isaac Breuer, im-
migrated into Palestine, opened a central Palestine office, and created a Zion-centered ideology which preached the preparation of
the Jewish people for its reunion with Palestine under the sovereignty of God. But since our historical era was considered to be only
the pre-Messianic age and not the God-willed time of actual Redemption, Agudah authorities scrupulously avoided all traffic with
"short-cuts" like Zionism, "defections" like Reform Judaism, and
other enemies of Divine Law who refused to await the pleasure
of the Almighty.

Though claiming rigorous avoidance of political concerns,
Agudas Israel often opposed Zionists in testimony before the League
of Nations, aligning itself on the side of the Arab and Jewish anti-
Zionist spokesmen. Thus, after the Arab riots of 1929, Agudas
Israel presented a nine-page document to the British Colonial Office supporting the anti-Zionist Passfield White Paper, denying the
validity of the Balfour Declaration, urging the British not to recognize the legitimacy of the Jewish Agency for Palestine, requesting
the entrusting of the Agudah with full responsibility for further immigration into Palestine, and asking that Zionist pioneering immigration be curtailed.[16]

In the United States, the influence of the Agudah was insignificant until the rise of Hitler and the outbreak of World War II
forced a considerable number of its European leaders to seek
asylum in the New World. The new arrivals, mostly members of
the Hasidic movement, sought to establish replicas of their East
European communities on American soil. They immediately clashed
with the more Americanized Orthodox who hoped for a synthesis
of Western thought and the Jewish heritage.[17] Agudas Israel's second American national convention in 1940, for example, issued a

ringing denunciation of secularist Judaism and called upon the Mizrachi to abandon Zionism and return to the "true faith" of the past.[18]

But by 1941 the outbreak of war and its attendant intensification of Jewish plight in eastern Europe, where the Agudah's primary strength was concentrated, induced the next convention to adopt a more guarded program on *Eretz Israel* (Palestine). World Agudah President Jacob Rosenheim (himself a refugee in London from his native Germany) told the assembled delegates they could gladly join with other Jews in redeeming the Holy Land and in enabling pious Jews to fulfill the *mitzvah* (religious duty) of settling in Palestine, but for the truly religious Jew, life in *Eretz Israel* would be "a happiness in itself" even if no Jewish state or national home were ever to be established.

The Baltimore convention thereupon reaffirmed the official policy of the 1937 Great Rabbinical Council of the Agudas Israel World Organization (see Appendix III), declared its readiness to negotiate with other Jewish organizations on the fate of Palestine, and reiterated earlier demands that the rebuilding of *Eretz Israel* should proceed solely on the basis of Torah law.[19]

With an allied victory in sight by 1944 and the fate of Palestine certain to be decided soon after the conclusion of hostilities, Agudas Israel felt compelled to take measures assuring it of a place in all such negotiations on Palestine. Joining the Zionist-led attack on the restrictive White Paper of 1939, the Agudas Israel convention demanded that its representatives be included whenever the fate of Palestine was under discussion. While not yet prepared to endorse Zionist demands for a Jewish commonwealth or state, the organization served notice that it would insist upon massive Jewish immigration into the Holy Land and upon the maintenance of Jewish rights already secured by the Mandate, a political document formerly unacceptable to the group.[20] Rabbi Eliezer Silver, President of the American branch of the Agudah, also utilized the occasion to castigate arch-enemies by declaring that American Jewish unity would be impossible "as long as the reformed rabbis, who represent an infinite minority in Jewish life, will continue to impose their leadership on Jewish organizations." [21]

A final indication of the gradual but virtually complete abandonment of the Agudah's original position on Zionism may be obtained from the official statement of London Agudas Israel representative Harry Goodman, who told the press in March, 1945, that Zionists and Agudists then differed only on the question of religion in the proposed Jewish commonwealth. Most Zionists maintained that religion was a private matter of conscience, while the Agudah favored the adoption of official state policies administered by rabbinical authorities. Warning against the dangers of "forty various Jewish bodies acting separately" in postwar conferences, Goodman conceded that the erstwhile foe of Zionism legitimately represented one of the two major trends in world Jewry. Orthodoxy, of course, was the other. Consequently, the two movements should be able to cooperate.[22]

Agudas Israel's about-face on the Zionist question can be traced most directly to the precarious position into which its sister Agudah organizations had been led by underestimating both the speed of the Zionist reclamation of Palestine and the intensity of Jewish need in eastern Europe. Prominent Palestinian Agudah leaders consistently warned the World Agudah Organization in London and New York that its policies were "barren" and "isolationist," since they failed to take a clear stand either for or against the practical work then rapidly proceeding in Palestine.

Isaac Breuer, for example, the same Agudah leader who in Frankfurt, Germany, had, in 1919, declared Zionism to be "the most formidable enemy that has ever arisen against the Jewish people," [23] now condemned the Agudah's world leadership for its failure to seize the opportunity provided by the Mandate "for the building of a *Torah* home in *Eretz Israel.*" Those same leaders were now being forced to scurry to the Palestinian homeland in order to save their lives. Chided Breuer in 1943, seven years after he had fled Germany for Palestine: "The leaders of the Agudah did not understand the times. They saw the trees, not the forest; they lacked historical perspective." [24]

At the same time, the mass of Agudah laborers in Palestine (the Poale Agudas Israel party), unwilling to be bypassed by the constructive processes going on around them, established agricultural colonies and cooperatives and began to negotiate with the Zionist leaders of Palestine for various forms of assistance, including land and loans. With Zionists pressing claims for a Jewish commonwealth, the Palestinian Poale Agudah, too, resolved to work for what they conceived to be the only effective guarantee that its remnants from

Europe would be absorbed and rehabilitated—"a Jewish political regime—Commonwealth—in an undivided Palestine." [25]

Thus, with the European Agudah organization destroyed, and the bulk of its Palestinian movement allying with the Zionists, American Agudas Israel, too, moved ever closer to a *rapprochement* with the Zionist movement of the United States.

ZIONISM AND REFORM JUDAISM

Early Pronouncements on Zionism   The most politically influential of American Jewry's three religious denominations, Reform Judaism, constituted for over half a century "the greatest organized obstacle in the path of Zionism." [26] Composed originally of what we termed the "Right Bloc" in the American Jewish community, Reform adherents included many of the oldest, wealthiest and most socially prominent families in American Jewish life.

Even before the birth of political Zionism had set into motion the contending forces within American Reform Judaism which were later to crystallize into Zionist and anti-Zionist opinion, the founders and shapers of Reform had expressed their unequivocal opposition to any program or doctrine envisioning Jewish "national rebirth" in Palestine. At the founding, in 1841, of America's first Reform temple, Gustav Poznanski uttered the momentous slogan which was to become the rallying point of powerful forces opposed to Zionism: "This country is our Palestine, this city our Jerusalem, this house of God, our Temple." [27]

By the late 1860's, Isaac Mayer Wise, a revered builder of American Reform, had assumed a position theologically antithetical to the Palestine ideal. And, in 1890, under his guidance, the Central Conference of American Rabbis adopted the first of a series of resolutions placing American Reform Judaism unquestionably in doctrinal opposition to the "Return to Zion." With impetus supplied by Herzl's call for the First Zionist Congress, the Central Conference affirmed earlier anti-nationalist pronouncements in 1897 and

Resolved, that we totally disapprove of any attempt for the establishment of a Jewish state. Such attempts show a misunderstanding of Israel's mission which from the narrow political and national field has been expanded to the promotion among the whole human race of the broad and universalistic religion first proclaimed by the Jewish prophets . . .

We affirm that the object of Judaism is not political nor national, but spiritual, and addresses itself to the continuous growth of peace, justice, and love in the human race, to a messianic time when all men will recognize that they form "one great brotherhood" for the establishment of God's kingdom on earth.[28]

Other eminent Reform rabbis similarly castigated the rising "Ziomania." Chicago's fighting liberal, Emil G. Hirsch, made invidious comparisons between the ancient Palestinian Temple sacrifices and the Chicago slaughterhouses. Kaufmann Kohler equated Zionism with "degeneracy" and "demoralization."[29] All available evidence seems to indicate that the overwhelming majority of the Reform rabbinate concurred in Isaac Mayer Wise's oft-quoted characterization of Zionism as "a momentary inebriation of morbid minds and a prostitution of Israel's holy cause to a madman's dance of unsound politicians."[30]

These learned rabbis were reacting to Zionism as products of the entire intellectual and theological orientation of their age. Flowering in the nineteenth century of decaying autocracy, expanding democracy, and irresistible optimism over "Universal Progress," Reform Judaism regarded much of its Palestinian heritage as irrelevant and troublesome "excess baggage." Since society was believed to be moving inexorably in the direction of progress for all, the Jew included, Reform saw no point in bewailing the loss of the ancestral homeland, a mere "Middle Eastern Ghetto."

Formally considered an *am,* or people, with distinct cultural-national traits, the Jewish group was now re-defined to conform to the prevailing religious categories of Europe. Use of the Hebrew language dwindled. References to Zion in the prayer books were expunged or denatured. Increasingly radical approaches toward the elements of Jewish distinctiveness were adopted. Reform temples came to be considered by traditionalist Jews as little more than Christian churches devoid of crosses.

The Dispersion was welcomed as a blessing and regarded as a "mission" to bear witness to God's goodness and the truth of ethical monotheism. "If Judaism is a religion, and the Jew a missionary of faith," reasoned the early Reformers, "a return to an ancestral land is more than unnecessary; it is undesirable. It check-mates the very purpose of Jewish existence." [31] To the first Reform Jews in America and western Europe, who knew but little of the suffering of their co-religionists in Czarist Russia, Zionism seemed an Oriental "philosophy of despair based on a lack of trust in de-mocracy and the moral evolution of man." [32] Pogroms in the East were interpreted by Reform as "occasional lapses in the march of Universal Progress"; small price, indeed, for the privilege of being "servants of the Lord."

Moreover, nineteenth-century Reform—so well described by Nathan Glazer as "the religion of economically comfortable Jews who wanted to be accepted by the non-Jewish world"—resented Zionism on non-theological grounds as well.[33] For Zionism seemed to them to repudiate the widening political emancipation of the Jews, threatened friendly relations with non-Jews, and impugned the national loyalty of the Jew wherever he lived. How could the Jew claim improved civil status and come to be accepted as a full-fledged participant in the life of his national state as long as he re-mained interested in the welfare of a foreign country? Far from providing a solution to the Jewish problem, Zionists were endanger-ing the painfully won position of the Jews by presenting tangible evidence of dual loyalty to the waiting anti-Semites who main-tained that the Jews were eternal strangers in every land. To Re-form, therefore, Zionism was not only mistakenly reactionary, it was actually a menace to Jewish security! [34] Theological argumenta-tion and biblical exegesis were thus wedded to socio-economic in-security and "advanced ideas" of Universalism in order to form an obdurate and tenacious opposition to the Zionist program.

Not every Reform rabbi in nineteenth-century America em-braced the fight against "Ziomania," however. Maximilian Heller in New Orleans, Gustav Gottheil (of Reform's premier Temple Emanu-el) in New York, Jacob Raisin in Charleston, Max Raisin in Paterson, New Jersey, were all numbered among early propo-nents of "The Return." [35] Famed Civil War abolitionist Bernhard Felsenthal in Chicago even rejected the basic Reformist credo of an "Israelite mission": ". . . individual Jews have no special mes-sage to deliver to mankind. From Palestine, from a Jewish *Muster-staat* (model state), our so-called mission can best be fulfilled." [36] And Reform rabbinical professors Caspar Levias and Max Schloes-singer, writing in 1899 and 1907, respectively, gave additional evidence that the ideological case against Zionism was far from complete. Both admonished Reform to come to an understanding with Zionism instead of brandishing the threat of excommunication. "Reform Judaism will be *Zionistic* or it will *not be at all*," prophesied Schloessinger.[37]

This older generation of "renegade rabbis" was followed in turn by the younger—Stephen S. Wise, Judah L. Magnes and Abba H. Silver. Dynamic orators, they made a tremendous contribution to the struggling American Zionist movement, for they "had poise and social prestige, these 'westerners,' their English was impeccable, and they were invaluable for refuting the charge that Zionism was a foreign product, capable of appealing only to the un-Americanized." [38] Nevertheless, reminisced veteran Zionist leader Louis Lipsky, the conversion of a Reform rabbi to Zionism was an "occasion for great rejoicing: it meant that a breach had been made in the enemy's citadel." [39]

But the handful of dissenters only served to intensify the anti-Zionist ire of the Reform majority. Pro-Zionist professors were purged in 1907 from the Hebrew Union College, Reform's rabbinical seminary,[40] and the Central Conference of American Rabbis, by its continuous barrage of anti-Zionist resolutions and proclamations (adopted in 1898, 1899, 1906, 1911, 1917, 1918, and 1920), earned the reputation of Zionism's "Enemy Number One." In the aftermath of Zionism's first great victory, the Balfour Declaration, Reform rabbinical delegations even carried their opposition to the League of Nations in testimony against "Jewish nationalism." [41]

The "Non-Zionist" Phase of Reform   By the time Great Britain was granted the Mandate for Palestine in 1922, the emphasis within Reform had shifted from vehement hostility to a position of "non-Zionism." Henceforth, Reform leaders would cooperate in the spiritual, cultural, economic and social upbuilding of the internationally sanctioned Jewish homeland in Palestine. On the other hand, they would presumably continue to oppose all Zionist "political machinations" calculated to achieve independent statehood. By this policy, Reform could accommodate itself, without great inconsistency, to the post-World I Zionist victories, at the same time minimizing the political implications of the renascent Jewish national homeland and transforming the return to Zion into a long-term, religio-cultural project.

Thus, failing to defeat Zionism, Reform joined it in the philanthropic endeavor of aiding a Jewish community which, Reform leaders confidently believed, would not mature into statehood for many years to come, if ever.[42] To this end, the Central Conference of American Rabbis voted in 1924 to participate in the Non-Partisan Conference for Palestine and, four years later, to endorse the proposed economic upbuilding of Palestine by a union of non-Zionist forces led by the eminent Reform layman Louis Marshall [43] and the Zionist cohorts of Chaim Weizmann.

Some Reform Zionists, notably Rabbi Stephen S. Wise, were wary of this new-found friendship of their erstwhile foes, fearing that the sudden influx of philanthropic interest would dilute the virility and purity of Zionist ideology. Others were confident that the change in Reform, albeit sudden and not fully observed by certain rabbis' pulpit discourses,[44] was nevertheless genuine. For example, Rabbi Barnett R. Brickner, President of the Ohio State Zionist Region, returning from the 1930 annual meeting of the Central Conference of American Rabbis, told a convention of the Zionist Organization of America that the just concluded restoration of the traditional *Kol Nidre* chant and *Hatikvah* (the "Zionist national anthem," now Israel's national anthem) to the Reform *Union Hymnal* was an event of significant proportions, since it occurred at a

. . . conference of Reform rabbis, where the word Zion has been *tref* [unclean] for many, many years, which uses a prayer book from which has been deleted every reference to and every hope for a reconstituted Jewish life in Palestine. Coming from a group of men who were nurtured on a theology that we are Jews by religion alone, and denying every vestige of national consciousness for the Jewish people, it was apparent that not the shades of the old founders abided but that a turn in events had taken place.[45]

With Hitler's accession to power and the consequent forced exodus of Jews from Germany, the Reform rabbinical conference reinforced its earlier pledge to aid the Jewish Agency's appeal for funds needed in the resettlement of the emigrés. Palestine, it was recognized, offered unusually good opportunities for the rehabilitation of a comparatively large number of Hitler's victims. Irrespective of their views on Zionism, therefore, all Reform rabbis were exhorted by the Conference to support the fund drives in their communities.[46] Again, the following year, the CCAR expressed "its profound joy and satisfaction at the economic, cultural, social and spiritual progress of the new Palestine" and rejoiced at the ability of the tiny land to provide a haven for so many fleeing Jews.[47] However, Zionist partisans, urging that "the aspiration of the Jewish people for the restoration of Zion be made an important part of our [liturgical] service," were narrowly defeated by a Conference vote of 45-43.[48]

At the same time, in accordance with its central maxim of periodic self-evaluation in order to compensate for "ideological and material changes in Jewish and general life," the CCAR decided [49] to devote its next meeting to a reassessment of the fifty-year old "Pittsburgh Platform," long considered the authoritative formulation of basic Reform principles and ideals.[50] Undoubtedly behind this decision to re-evaluate the validity of this pillar of American Reform thinking was a growing Zionist opinion among the rabbinate. Reform Zionists, despite their large increase in numbers, were still laboring under the stigma of promoting a movement inimicable to the spirit of their religious creed. For, in the 1885 Platform, the founders of Reform had peremptorily asserted the absolute incompatibility of Reform Judaism and political Zionism:

> We recognize, in the era of universal culture of heart and intellect, the approaching of the realization of Israel's great Messianic hope for the establishment of the kingdom of truth, justice, and peace among all men. We consider ourselves no longer a nation, but a religious community, and therefore expect neither a return to Palestine, nor a sacrificial worship under the sons of Aaron, nor the restoration of any of the laws concerning the Jewish state.[51]

That a majority of Reform rabbis no longer subscribed to these sentiments, however, may be readily inferred from the 1935 "Statement of 241 Reform Rabbis" which lauded the principles and ideals of the Palestinian labor movement, declared the prophetic ideals and the "Social Justice Program of the CCAR" to be "especially compatible" with those of Labor Palestine, and commended all Jews to give their hearty support to the Histadrut (General Federation of Labor in Palestine) and to the American League for Labor Palestine.[52]

Additional evidence of the far-reaching change of attitudes extant in the Conference may be implied from the defensive tone of its non-Zionist Presidential message: Rabbi Samuel H. Goldenson found it necessary to assure his assembled colleagues that those who were not associated with the Zionist movement were certainly not lacking in Judaism or Jewish values; they, too, held the best interests of Judaism dear to their hearts. He also voiced the traditional Reform fear that a new emphasis more favorable to Zionism would render a lesser place of importance in Jewish life to religious and spiritual values which would then be replaced by more secular and political influences. Drawing upon the authority of the Prophets, Rabbi Goldenson stressed the importance of ensuring a high moral and idealistic level in the projected Palestine endeavor, for only in this way would non-Zionists find the rationale for participating in the rebuilding of *Eretz Israel*.[53]

Two papers on Reform and Zionism were then read by leading non-Zionist and Zionist rabbis, Samuel Schulman and Abba Hillel Silver, respectively. Discussion of these papers revealed a broad distribution of opinion in the Conference. James G. Heller urged those rabbis who feared secular nationalism to form a "Reform Judaism party" in Zionism with a program designed to increase religious emphasis without divorcing religion from Jewish nationhood and peoplehood concepts. Rabbi Samuel S. Cohon, on the other hand, summed up traditional non-Zionist, religiously-oriented Reform feelings with the thesis that the Pittsburgh Platform view of nationalism was still valid, (1) because the majority of Jews in the world would continue to live outside of Palestine, (2) because Jews were no longer a nation and had to integrate into their lands of residence and, (3) because such integration was possible only as a religious community, without national allegiances other than to their adopted lands. A synthesis between these two opposing points of view was attempted by Rabbi Barnett Brickner in the form of a "spiritual Zionism," an "inspiriting force that will come when Jews are living what they believe to be a fully creative life." Recognizing that "no Zionist wants all the Jews in Palestine," this speaker sought to reconcile the two views by appealing to a commonly accepted value—the prospect of a viable and spiritually creative Jewish people everywhere in the world.[54]

On the basis of the foregoing papers and discussion, the Conference proceeded to revise the Pittsburgh Platform's stand toward Zionism. A resolution introduced by three Zionist rabbis sought to initiate a policy of "neutrality" and of "mutual respect and tolerance" in place of the traditional deep dissent from the Zionist program. Their original resolution, which would have resolved that the CCAR "harbors at present no opposition to Zionism," was not accepted. Instead, a revised and weakened resolution was adopted by the Conference:

> Whereas, at certain foregoing conventions of the Central Conference of American Rabbis, resolutions have been adopted in opposition to Zionism, and
>
> Whereas, We are persuaded that acceptance or rejection of the Zionist program should be left to the determination of the individual members of the Conference themselves, therefore
>
> Be it resolved, That the Central Conference of American Rabbis takes no official stand on the subject of Zionism; and be it further
>
> Resolved, That in keeping with its oft-announced intentions, the Central Conference of American Rabbis will continue to cooperate in the upbuilding of Palestine, and in the economic, cultural, and particular spiritual tasks confronting the growing and evolving Jewish community there.[55]

Thus, fifty years after the enactment of the militantly anti-Zionist plank of the Pittsburgh Platform, American Reform rabbinical opinion had evolved to the point where a collectively negative stand on Zionism was abandoned in favor of an individual approach signifying a wide difference of opinion in the Conference.

Only two years later, proceedings in the CCAR reflected a further abandonment of the traditional Reform attitude of antipathy toward Zionism. Meeting in Columbus, Ohio, in 1937, under the shadow of both native and German anti-Semitic outbursts, the Conference adopted a new set of "Guiding Principles of Reform Judaism," the "Columbus Platform," as it was popularly termed.

In the lengthy discussions attending the adoption of these "Principles," the Conference rejected a draft by Rabbi Samuel Schulman which would have de-emphasized nationhood in favor of the non-Zionist religious-centered approach.[56] But far more indicative of Reform's growing Zionist temper was the adopted Principle V proclaiming: "Judaism is the soul of which Israel is the body." This statement also more fully recognized the peoplehood of Israel, the hallowed memories and hopes of Palestine, and "the obligation of all Jewry to aid in its [Palestine's] upbuilding as a Jewish homeland by endeavoring to make it not only a haven of refuge for the oppressed but also a center of Jewish cultural and spiritual life." [57]

Pro-Palestine forces were simultaneously at work among Reform laymen as well. Consequently, the Union of American Hebrew Congregations resolved in 1937:

> We see the hand of Providence in the opening of the Gates of Palestine for the Jewish people at a time when a large portion of Jewry is so desperately in need of a friendly shelter and a home where a spiritual, cultural center may be developed in accordance with Jewish ideals. The time has now come for all Jews, irrespective of ideological differences, to unite in the activities leading to the establishment of a Jewish homeland in Palestine, and we urge our constituency to give their financial and moral support to the work of rebuilding Palestine.[58]

Thus, both Reform Judaism's rabbinical leadership and laymen went on record as favoring previously opposed conceptions of a "Jewish people" and as looking to Palestine as a spiritual *center* rather than as merely another land of Jewish residence. Pro-Palestine sentiment was rising in Reform, eclipsing the anti-Zionism of Isaac Mayer Wise and Kaufmann Kohler. But the day had not yet arrived when Zionist adherents could persuade Reform to endorse officially the movement it had formerly defamed.

The Resurgence of Anti-Zionism   Careful to preserve its 1935 neutrality formula, the Central Conference of American Rabbis from 1937 to 1942 did little more than implement previous resolutions designed to promote the Palestinian renascence and to aid Jewish refugees.[59] However, Zionist rabbis within the Conference were not idle. Rabbi Edward L. Israel, a member of the Executive Committee of the Zionist Organization of America, was elected Executive Secretary of the Union of American Hebrew Congregations, a position of considerable importance in molding lay thinking throughout American Reform.[60] Another member of the ZOA's Executive Committee, James G. Heller, was elected President of the CCAR, itself. Zionist sentiment also prevailed among the leadership of Reform youth groups; Richard Bluestein, President of the National Federation of Temple Youth, declared at the second biennial convention of that organization:

> . . . liberal Judaism must embrace *Eretz Israel* completely and wholeheartedly. We should have as one of our primary tenets the spreading of complete understanding of the significance of Zionism. . . . Let us, therefore, petition our parent body, the Union of American Hebrew Congregations, for a more positive stand on Zionism than that adopted by that body some years ago.[61]

Following Rabbi Heller's inaugural suggestion, the Central Conference agreed to appoint a Committee on Palestine

> . . . to cooperate with all the agencies striving to make it a Jewish homeland, to put the force of the liberal rabbinate behind the beneficent and creative work of Zionism. This can be done without committing those who still adhere to a theoretical opposition to the movement. All can unite in aiding the actual work . . .[62]

With the ideological opposition of the Conference officially withdrawn and Zionist figures occupying key positions in the Reform movement, the time was at hand for Reform Zionists to capitalize on their hard-won gains. A suitable occasion presented itself when, following the Allied defeats in Libya and in the South Pacific, the American Emergency Committee for Zionist Affairs proclaimed American Zionism's immediate task to be the mobilization of American public opinion in favor of a distinctive Palestinian fighting force, Jews fighting Nazism under the Jewish flag. In addition to its utility in the defense of Palestine, such a force would ostensibly provide a bargaining pawn in postwar negotiations on the fate of Palestine.[63]

At its 1942 meeting in Cincinnati, the CCAR was confronted with a proposed resolution of thirty-three rabbis who demanded that the Conference add its voice to other expressions of Jewish public opinion promoting the cause of a Jewish military force.[64] This resolution immediately occasioned controversy, with most of the rabbis lined up according to their sympathies on the broader question of Zionism; for, claimed non-Zionists, the "nationalist implication" of such a resolution represented a clear emasculation of the CCAR's neutrality formula of 1935.

The debate on the Zionist-sponsored motion revealed the general tenor of non-Zionist thinking: Rabbis Samuel Goldenson and Edward Calisch argued that since no motion to *oppose* a Jewish army had been proposed, though some rabbis felt so inclined, the motion *for* a Jewish force should similarly be withdrawn for the sake of harmony. Rabbi Henry Barnston reminded the Conference that there was sufficient room for the Jews of Palestine to enlist in other armies rather than to demand a separate Jewish unit. Rabbi Louis Wolsey expressed the fear that "the formation of a Jewish Army is going to confuse the attitude of America towards the Jew" and that the CCAR, a purely religious body, would become engrossed with questions of "militarism." Finally, Rabbi Irving Reichert objected to the resolution as a certain indication that "the nationalistic aspirations of the Jews in Palestine took precedence over the welfare of American Israel." [65]

With irreconcilable differences of opinion clearly expressed, the Conference proceeded to measure the question of support for a Jewish Army by a roll-call vote, the first in many years. The Zionist-sponsored resolution was adopted 64-38, with twenty-seven rabbis requesting their negative votes to be specifically recorded.[66]

Reform's twenty-year truce on the Zionist question was ended. Zionist protagonists had won an important but, in effect, a pyrrhic victory. Though the official voice of the Reform rabbinate was added to a growing list of Jewish Army supporters, an influential minority of non-Zionist leaders, sensing that their posture of silence was being mistaken for assent, reacted to its defeat by waging open and protracted warfare with the advancing Zionist movement. Within a year their zeal was to culminate in the formation of the American Jewish community's first, and only, organization avowedly dedicated to the fight against Zionism.

With the CCAR no longer to be relied upon as a bulwark to save Reform Judaism from the incursions of "Jewish national chauvinism," a group of six Reform rabbis, under the leadership of Philadelphia's Louis Wolsey, met to discuss ways and means of returning Reform to its "prophetic and universal" ideas.[67] Their discussions led to larger meetings, on March 30 and April 6, 1942, wherein twenty-four rabbis rallied to the call to "do something" about the mounting Zionist victories. All present agreed that their beloved CCAR would lie increasingly at the mercies of the Zionists, unless men of their persuasion could be organized to resist the "nationalists." Widespread agreement was also expressed that anti-

Zionist feeling was latent among many Jews, that "nationalistic Judaism" was not worth living, and that Reform's failure to grow in recent years had been due largely to its timidity vis-à-vis Zionism. A concerted attack on Zionism could, they felt, be profitably exploited in order to fashion a positive religious program in much the same way that the dynamics of the old quarrel over ritual had contributed to the growth of Reform and the decline of Orthodoxy.

But on the question of tactics the rabbis expressed divided opinions. Rabbi William Fineshriber, for example, allegedly favored the organization of a pressure group within the CCAR in order to combat the Zionists. Such rabbinical effort would clearly require lay financing in order to offset the spending of the Zionists in their efforts to win over Reform. In any case, the CCAR must be regained; secession, in order to wage war on the Zionist-dominated Conference, was considered out of the question. Other rabbis proposed the publication of an anti-Zionist organ of opinion and the use of radio and public forums. Still others suggested a larger conference of "like-minded men" who would deliberate further and concretize effective procedures. Despite fears that such a meeting outside the CCAR would produce a schism in Reform and that the anti-Zionist minority would, accordingly, lose face, the decision was made to call a national rabbinical conclave of non-Zionist rabbis at Atlantic City on June 9–10, 1942.

The group of twenty-four then sent a letter to CCAR President Heller informing him of their intentions and elucidating their reasons for the proposed meeting. Accusing him of violating the 1935 neutrality resolution by not declaring the Jewish Army motion out of order and by lending his signature, along with other Zionists, to an advertisement in the *New York Times* which aligned the Conference with the Zionist demand for a Jewish military force, the non-Zionists condemned the controversial resolution as an expression of a mere one-fourth of the Conference, since it was voted at a poorly-attended meeting. Finally, as their price for an end to the proposed non-Zionist rabbinical conference, the group suggested the appointment of a "non-political and non-Zionist," but "pro-Palestine," committee to work out a platform acceptable to all.

On May 11th, non-Zionist Rabbis Samuel Goldenson and Louis Wolsey met with James Heller and Solomon B. Freehof, the latter men representing the Conference. Heller censured the non-Zionist group as a secessionist movement, likely to disrupt the unity of Reform. Instead of the Atlantic City meeting he urged a special session of the entire CCAR. According to later non-Zionist reports, Heller allegedly promised that such a meeting would (1) revive and strengthen the 1935 neutrality plank; (2) adopt a by-law making neutrality on the Zionist issue a permanent rule; (3) acknowledge as a mistake the passage of the Jewish Army motion; and (4) agree to discuss fundamental issues such as the relationship of Zionism to Reform, a *rapprochement* between Reform Judaism and Zionism, and the essential ideas of Reform. At this meeting, in short, the Zionist gains would be erased and the Conference could adhere once again "to an economic and cultural reconstruction of Palestine, but not to any political or nationalistic activity, purpose, or interpretation." [68]

At the behest of Goldenson and Wolsey, the Atlantic City conclave was postponed temporarily but, a few days later, after a straw vote revealed that many of the non-Zionists could not attend the proposed special session of the CCAR, the question of a separate non-Zionist convocation arose again. With a Zionist victory certain should the entire Conference be assembled, the group of twenty-four non-Zionists attempted to win concessions by negotiation on a more limited scale. Warning Heller that they would proceed with their own plans unless he unilaterally met three conditions, the group again stressed its devotion to the maintenance of reform unity. The conditions demanded of Heller were: (1) a "vigorous letter" to the entire membership of the CCAR apologizing for his condemnation of the dissenters as "schismatics"; (2) a resolution to the Executive Board of the CCAR promising that the Conference would "under all conditions and at all times" maintain a state of neutrality on Zionism; and (3) an assurance that the Jewish Army resolution would be expunged from the Conference record. Perhaps recognizing this ultimatum as a valuable precedent which could block all future Zionist inroads into Reform, Rabbi Heller refused.

The Atlantic City Conference The die cast, the non-Zionists issued a statement categorizing Heller's proposals for a special CCAR meeting as "provocative of a situation whose only issue would be disruption and schism." They then proceeded to call their own rabbinical conference for June 1–2 at Atlantic City. A manifesto, marked "not for release to the press or to any news-gathering agency," suggests that non-Zionists still hoped the Zionists would yield in the face of concerted non-Zionist action:

> We like-minded men have appeased the Zionists with consent, assent and co-operation from Convention to Convention, until their victories through the years have been so cumulative that they now know no bounds. The day had to come when we must cry "halt." The conditioning of American Jewry by a Jewish flag and a Jewish Army and a state in Palestine and a dual citizenship in America, is more than we can accept. The secularist creed has overreached itself. We have been watching with anxiety the secularistic tendencies in American-Jewish life, the absorption of large numbers in Jewish nationalistic endeavors, the intrusion of the Palestine issue as an irritating factor in intracommunity relations, the persistent public expression of extremists who presume to speak for all American Jewry, the efforts to cultivate and promote the sense of psychological difference between American Jews and their fellow Americans which plays into the hands of our enemies, the unremitting efforts of certain groups to put American Jews behind programs of international political pressure, the reduction to secondary importance of the traditional religious basis of Jewish life. . . . We refuse any longer to be religious acrobats. We cannot pact with the untenable position in society which nationalism as a creed imposes upon us.

Invitations sent to 160 Reform rabbis known to be unaffiliated with the Zionist movement yielded eighty-two responses, of which forty-five said they would attend, nine would attempt to attend, twenty-one expressed sympathy with the group but were unable to attend, and three took the trouble to proclaim their Zionist bent and complete opposition to the group's aims.

As the conference assembled, press releases stressed the Reform rather than the anti-Zionist nature of the proceedings. Papers prepared for the gathering included: "The Message of Reform Judaism to American Israel and World Jewry," "Lay-Rabbinical Cooperation," "The Hebrew Union College," "A Program for Enlightenment," [69] and "Post-War Problems of the Jews." But the opening speeches swiftly removed any doubt as to the aims of the conference. Morris S. Lazaron delivered an unreserved attack on the motives and patriotism of American Zionists,[70] and Louis Wolsey predicted that the conference would contradict the Zionists' claim that their movement represented four million Jews and "the totality of Jewish life." [71]

Following the reading of the rabbinical papers and the appointment of a committee to interest laymen in financing a non-Zionist program on a national scale,[72] the conference issued a press release entitled "A Statement of Principles by Non-Zionist Rabbis," [73] adhered to eventually by ninety-two Reform leaders—the "Goy [Gentile] Nineties," as their Zionist colleagues quickly dubbed them. An introduction to these "Principles" stated:

> The special reason for our gathering is in the growing secularism in American Jewish life, the absorption of large numbers in Jewish nationalistic endeavors and the tendency to reduce the religious basis of Jewish life to a place of secondary importance. A further reason for taking counsel together is in our realization that at this time more than ever all men for their own good . . . should give every emphasis to those moral and religious values and principles that transcend boundary lines and hold all men in a common bond of human fellowship.

Principle I further developed this theme of the interdependence of peoples and implied that Jewish destiny could not be divorced from general "evil forces" at work in the world. The "Statement" did take cognizance of the fact, however, that "unhappily we Jews are often the first victims of the distemper of peoples and suffer most from the maladjustments of society."

Principle II dealt with a declaration of faith in the democratic way of life and the prophetic ideals, as embodied in the American Bill of Rights, with the hope that the forthcoming peace settlement should be in consonance with these principles.

The non-Zionists' serious dissent from the Zionist endeavors of the day was expressed in Principle III:

> Realizing how dear Palestine is to the Jewish soul, and how important Palestinian rehabilitation is towards relieving the pressing problems of our distressed people, we stand ready to render unstinted aid to our brethren in their economic, cultural and spiritual endeavors in that country. But in the light of our universalistic interpretation of Jewish history and destiny, and also because of our concern for the welfare and status of the Jewish people, living in other parts of the world, we are unable to subscribe to or support the political emphasis now paramount in the Zionistic program. We cannot but believe that Jewish nationalism tends to confuse our fellow-men about our place and function in society and also diverts our attention from our historic role to live as a religious community wherever we may dwell. Such spiritual role is especially voiced by (Reform) Judaism in its emphasis upon the eternal prophetic principles of life and thought, principles

through which alone Judaism and the Jew can hope to endure and bear witness to the universal God.

This handiwork of the Atlantic City rabbinical conclave, and the subsequent formation of the lay-dominated American Council for Judaism, were met by the Zionists with unprecedented hostility. Zionist ranks were closed to meet the common foe. Every rabbi was forcefully invited to "stand up and be counted" in one camp or the other. At least 214 Reform rabbis declared for the Zionist position.

The Formation of the American Council for Judaism   Undeterred by the scope of the Zionist attack, the non- or anti-Zionists (meaningful distinctions between the two soon vanished in the fury of contending contumely) proceeded to organize support for a "righteous onslaught on Jewish nationalism." On November 2, thirteen of the non-Zionist rabbis met in the Philadelphia study of Louis Wolsey. There, Sidney Wallach, until then associated with the American Jewish Committee, outlined his approach to an effective program of anti-Zionist public relations. Thereupon, the group agreed to retain Mr. Wallach's services, raise an initial sum of $25,000, and carry the news of the contemplated organization to their respective cities. The question of the incipient organization's goals—"pro-Reform or anti-nationalist"—was left in abeyance pending an investigation of potential financial and rabbinical support. Several of the rabbis favored the group's identifying itself with the largest possible number of American Jews; Wallach proposed that a place be found in the new organization even for irreligious anti-Zionists. Other rabbis warned they could have no traffic with a non-religious crusade, even one aimed at Zionism.[74]

A second meeting, on November 23, heard evidence that the anti-Zionist position would be supported in influential lay circles. Rabbi Jonah B. Wise of New York, a national chairman of the United Jewish Appeal and Executive Director of the Joint Distribution Committee, reported by letter on a November 16 meeting of prominent New Yorkers sympathetically inclined toward the group's program.* Henry Wolf, a leading member of the American

---

* The meeting on November 16 was attended by Alan M. Stroock (son of the late president of the American Jewish Committee), William Rosenwald (president,

Jewish Committee, was quoted concerning the current struggle of an anti-Zionist bloc for control of the Committee. Wolf assured Rabbis Wise and Wolsey that sums far exceeding the hoped-for $25,000 would be made available in the near future, either through the election of an anti-Zionist president of the American Jewish Committee or, failing that, through the secession of anti-Zionist forces from the Committee and their entrance into the germinating lay-rabbinical anti-Zionist alliance.

On the suggestion of Wallach that it would "look better" for a rabbi than for a lay person to direct the activities of the group, Rabbi Elmer Berger was chosen Executive Director. A name for the new organization, "American Council for Judaism," was then unanimously chosen. Suggested by Rabbi Lazaron, this name met the desires of the group's potential financial backers and coincided with the views of Adolph Rosenberg, President of the Union of American Hebrew Congregations (who earlier suggested that the anti-Zionist group would succeed only if it adopted a "positive view," with Americanism as its central theme).

The assembled rabbis also pooled information on current Zionist maneuvers. They criticized Rabbi Israel Goldstein for reportedly using his position as President of the Synagogue Council of America for Zionist purposes; Rabbi Julius Gordon, allegedly acting without authority in his role of Chairman of the CCAR's Palestine Committee; and Rabbis James G. Heller and Barnett R. Brickner for appointing almost exclusively Zionists to vacancies on CCAR commissions. In a more positive vein, Rabbi Fineshriber reported that the group had highly-placed friends in the State Department who were "considerably annoyed" at the Zionist pressures then being exerted on Congress.[76]

With financial assistance from important lay figures assured, the group obtained articles of incorporation from the New York

National Refugee Service and a chairman of the United Jewish Appeal), Paul Baerwald (honorary chairman, Joint Distribution Committee), Arthur Hays Sulzberger (publisher, *New York Times*), Maurice Hexter (executive vice-president, New York Jewish Federation), George Backer (president, Jewish Telegraphic Agency), Samuel Leidesdorf (treasurer, New York United Jewish Appeal), Edgar Nathan (president of Manhattan Borough), and Henry Ittelson (head of Commercial Investment Trust). Others whose views were heard, although they did not attend, were Judge Samuel Rosenman (a confidant of President Roosevelt), Lewis Rosenstiel (head of Schenley Distillers), Nathan Ohrbach (a prominent New York merchant), Alexander Kahn (managing editor, *Jewish Daily Forward*), and Judge Joseph M. Proskauer (a leading member and later president of the American Jewish Committee).[75]

Legislature and tax deduction status from the federal government. In April, 1943, Lessing J. Rosenwald of Philadelphia placed his financial resources and abilities at the disposal of the American Council for Judaism and was elected its President. A lengthy "Statement of Views" was issued by the Council on August 31, 1943, and offices and executives were established to promote the anti-Zionist cause within Reform and in the American Jewish community at large.[77]

Meanwhile, as it became increasingly clear to the Zionists that their victory on the Jewish Army resolution was producing the first organized anti-Zionist group in American Jewish history, desperate attempts were made to confine the dissenters to activities within the Central Conference of American Rabbis itself. On January 5, 1943, a meeting of seven Zionists, six members of the Council for Judaism and three neutrals, all rabbis, took place in Baltimore. Conference President Heller, appealing to commonly held goals of "unity in Reform" and the "welfare of Palestine," suggested the liquidation of the American Council for Judaism, in return for which he would obtain a by-law guaranteeing the CCAR's future neutrality on the Zionist question. Heller argued that the net effect of the Council's activities could only be to create schisms in Reform and injure the Jewish settlement of Palestine, even though the anti-Zionists' fire was directed only at Zionist ideology. After all, reasoned the Zionist representatives, the average person, Jew or Gentile, could not distinguish between opposition to Zionism and opposition to Palestine; if hostile officialdom detected that the Jews were divided, the gates of Palestine would surely be shut to further Jewish immigration.[78] Undaunted by these appeals, Rabbi Wolsey notified Heller on February 4 that a mail vote of the Council's rabbinical members found them "solidly against liquidation." [79]

Thus, when the Central Conference again convened in 1943, it was confronted with the spectacle of a house divided against itself. Many of the anti-Zionists were boycotting the Conference session and rabbinical spokesmen for the American Council for Judaism were actively circularizing Reform congregations. Faced with this situation, the Executive Board of the CCAR commended President Heller for his efforts to avert a permanent division of the Conference and urged "all shades of opinion . . . to refrain from organizing fractional groups or in issuing public statements representing the opinion of such fractional groups." [80] Rabbi Heller then reported on the events leading up to the "break of Jewish unity," casting no aspersions on the sincerity of his colleagues in the Council as was done by later Zionist propagandists. On the contrary, he conceded that the founders of American Zionism's first organized opposition

> . . . are men who have the same love of God and Israel as we have. Without question, in all that they have done, they have been activated by a deep conviction . . . that thereby they were defending ideals and ways sacred to them, and, as they thought, in dire jeopardy.[81]

Heller admonished, however, that good intentions are never sufficient, for actions have a logic of their own and dire consequences must result from faulty actions.

Continuing, in his Presidential message to the Conference, to analyze the events which had followed in the wake of the Jewish Army resolution of 1942, Rabbi Heller charged that the formation of the American Council for Judaism could not be justified by this act alone. The Jewish Army resolution was not a repudiation of the 1935 "neutrality formula," though he could understand how it furnished a convenient excuse for bringing diversity on the Zionist question before the public. He also noted that, in addition to serious clashes in the press on such issues as "nationalism *vs.* religion" or "universalism *vs.* particularism" which did the Jewish cause no service, the Council for Judaism, by attempting to organize local chapters, had precipitated bitter inter-congregational and inter-rabbinical feuds in the Reform family.

Urging that this unfortunate state of affairs be remedied by returning this "difference of opinion" to the Conference proper, President Heller recognized the essentially rabbinical character of the Zionists' foes. After all, he argued, the American Council for Judaism, even though it did contain some laymen, was organized and controlled by rabbis, its statements were signed only by CCAR members, and rabbinical leadership and initiative were paramount throughout the organization. Furthermore, since the whole question of the Council's existence represented a theological reversion to Reform Judaism as it stood at the turn of the century, the Conference had a right and a duty to deal with the question.[82]

Rabbi Heller went on to direct considerable criticism toward methods of the Council for Judaism, its "misunderstanding" of Zionist ideology, and its "irresponsible" attacks on existing Reform bodies, such as the Union of American Hebrew Congregations and the CCAR itself. In particular, he attacked the Council's preoccupation with charges of dual loyalty, "arbitrary communal organization," and so on. In conclusion, he recommended that, in the best interests of Jewish unity and Reform, the American Council for Judaism should promptly disband.[83]

The Conference then engaged in a round table discussion on the "Compatibility of Zionism and Reform Judaism," an academic question in view of the actual events of 1942–43. At the conclusion of debate, the Conference, removing the last tenuous hint of doctrinal reservations vis-à-vis Zionism, resolved:

> The attempt has been made to set in irreconcilable opposition "universalism" and "particularism." To the members of the Conference, this appears unreal and misleading. Without impinging the right of the members of the Conference to be opposed to Zionism, for whatever reason they may choose, the Conference declares that it discerns no essential incompatibility between Reform Judaism and Zionism, no reason why those of its members who give allegiance to Zionism should not have the right to regard themselves as fully within the spirit and purpose of Reform Judaism.[84]

Following upon this measure, the Zionist bloc, patently dominant in the Conference, moved the adoption of a particularly forceful resolution:

> The American Council for Judaism was founded by members of the C.C.A.R. for the purpose of combatting Zionism. The Zionist Movement and masses of Jews everywhere, shocked by the rise of this organization at a time when Zionists and others are laboring hard to have the gates of Palestine reopened . . . could not avoid . . . seeing in it an example of what they had come to consider the constant opposition of Reform Judaism to Zionist aspirations. This impression does grave injustice to the many devoted Zionists in the C.C.A.R. and to the Conference, itself.
> Therefore, without impinging the right of Zionists or non-Zionists to express and to disseminate their convictions within and without the Conference, we, in the spirit of amity, urge our colleagues of the American Council for Judaism to terminate this organization.[85]

As was to be expected, discussion preparatory to the adoption of this motion occasioned caustic debate. Rabbis Samuel H. Goldenson and Joseph Rauch introduced a minority report on the proposed resolution encompassing the view that it was beyond the authority of the Conference to adopt a position which would deny freedom to certain of its members. In so doing, they submitted that:

> . . . the group of Rabbis who organized the American Council for Judaism have no other object than to serve Jews and Judaism. . . . That the American Council was organized by Rabbis was due to the fact that it was within the Central Conference of American Rabbis that a sharp distinction was felt between those who took the Nationalist approach to Jewish life and destiny and the others who took the non-Nationalistic view.[86]

These rabbis and others, including several Zionists, implored the Conference to recognize that the anti-Zionist Council for Judaism had been organized because no other medium existed for the propagation of the non-nationalist viewpoint. Insisting upon the inherent right to organize and express one's views, the minority vigorously condemned vilification, vituperation and intolerance on the part of Zionists and refused to surrender their ideals for the "sake of unity." The view was clearly implied that what was demanded of them was not unity but rather *conformity* to world Zionism.[87]

With considerable ill-feeling, the Conference recorded its collective will on the majority resolution and, in a roll-call vote, registered 137 votes for the measure, forty-five opposed and ninety-six abstentions.[88] The result makes it evident that Zionist opinion, though powerful, was not so unmistakably dominant as to constitute a clear rebuke of the Council's position. Perhaps for this reason, as well as that of hesitancy to impugn the motives of their rabbinical colleagues in the American Council for Judaism, few rabbis considered the resolution in its literal sense. No serious proposal for CCAR sanctions against the dissenters was consequently considered.

From 1944 on, non-Zionist sentiment within the Central Conference of American Rabbis could take only minor protest action as the increasingly pro-Zionist character of Conference actions became manifest. At the Cincinnati Conference of 1944 three incidents traceable to the activities and ideology of the anti-Zionist Council for Judaism occupied the attention of the CCAR. First,

President Heller's protest about letters being circulated to various congregations by the Council was referred to the Arbitration Committee for investigation. That committee, citing the Code of Ethics adopted by the Conference in 1940, found these letters, written to congregations in support of an anti-Zionist interpretation of Judaism, were contrary to the spirit of the code and "not conducive to the promotion of relationships of dignity and esteem amongst rabbinical colleagues" because they drew "invidious distinctions between the teachings of the incumbent and those of a predecessor."

Second, when the Executive Board sought Conference approval of a resolution commending Rabbis Solomon B. Freehof and James G. Heller for their efforts at the American Jewish Conference,[89] efforts directed at strenuously promoting a resolution for a Jewish commonwealth in Palestine, objections were raised which questioned whether such a move would be in harmony with the spirit of neutrality supposed to prevail on the question of Zionism. President Freehof answered that such objections were groundless since the CCAR delegates to the American Jewish Conference were free to vote as they wished; the CCAR's organizational neutrality would remain unimpaired. This interpretation was shared unanimously by the Committee on the President's Message and the congratulatory resolution was subsequently enacted.[90]

The Congregation Beth Israel Controversy   At this same session of the Central Conference, however, American Reform was faced with a third and far more serious issue reflecting loss of cohesion, this time in the form of a challenge from a militant congregation dominated by leading members of the American Council for Judaism. Recalling earlier anti-Zionist pronouncements of the CCAR, these irate laymen protested against the "departure" of the Conference "from the historic patterns and essential principles of American Reform Judaism as enunciated at Philadelphia in 1869, and as stated and restated at Pittsburgh in 1885, at Rochester in 1920, and at Columbus in 1937." [91] Congregation Beth Israel of Houston, Texas, one of the wealthiest, largest and oldest Reform temples in the South, enacted caustic resolutions of protest against the CCAR, Union of American Hebrew Congregations and Hebrew Union College, charged "betrayal of classic Reform," and declared itself to be the champion of "authentic" Reform Judaism.[92] Moreover, a pamphlet campaign to attract other congregations to this "classic," anti-Zionist Reform program was undertaken and justified as

> . . . a mission with which no force or factor could be permitted to interfere, namely, to serve individually and collectively as missionaries among its own people and to safeguard at least a segment of the Jewish people of this nation against indictment before the Lord for worshipping a false god, ZIONISM.[93]

Summoning the recorded testimonies of recognized Reform founders and leaders—Abraham Geiger, Samuel Holdheim, David Einhorn, Samuel Hirsch, Isaac M. Wise, Kaufmann Kohler and David Philipson—Congregation Beth Israel adopted a set of "Basic Principles" on November 23, 1943, which simultaneously repudiated the actions of the CCAR since 1942 and heralded a return to "legitimate" Reform.[94] These "Principles" quickly became the subject of nationwide discussion and precipitated violent controversy in Jewish circles for over a year. With regard to Palestine and Zionism, the Congregation articulately declared:

> We are Jews by virtue of our acceptance of Judaism. We consider ourselves no longer a nation. We are a religious community, and neither pray for nor anticipate a return to Palestine nor a restoration of any of the laws concerning the Jewish state. We stand unequivocally for the separation of the Church and State. Our religion is Judaism. Our nation is The United States of America. Our nationality is American. Our flag is the "Stars and Stripes." Our race is Caucasian. With regard to the Jewish settlement in Palestine we consider it our sacred privilege to promote the spiritual, cultural, and social welfare of our co-religionists there.[95]

This renewal of Pittsburgh Platform principles, coupled with ample expressions of American patriotism, came before the Conference when the Executive Board moved that CCAR President Freehof's answer to these accusations of Beth Israel, should, in view of the "able and comprehensive" nature of the reply, be made "the official response of our Conference to Congregation Beth Israel." This action was taken only after several non-Zionist rabbis forcefully expressed convictions that such action would drive the Houston congregation out of Reform, that the Beth Israel charges and platform were "one of the finest things that has happened in recent years in American Jewish life," that the Conference talked about freedom of speech but denounced those who practiced it, and that, "in making drastic pronouncements often carried by a small majority," the CCAR was virtually excluding some dissenters.[96]

To the accusations of this "Texas Classical Reform Temple," CCAR President Solomon B. Freehof retorted on March 21, 1944. Conceding that today's Reform Judaism as expressed in utterances of most members of the Central Conference did indeed represent a departure from some of the ideas laid down by Reform Jewish leaders in past generations, Freehof charged that the Texas "classicists" were behaving in the manner of Orthodoxy:

> It is only Orthodoxy which dares not depart from "classic" patterns laid down by past generations. It is the principle of Orthodoxy that all laws authentically deduced from past laws are sacred and represent the will of God, and that customs which have been widely accepted in the past have the force of law and may not be abolished even when circumstances change. But Reform Judaism is a liberal Judaism. It proclaims the right of each generation to change customs and rituals and even to restate doctrines, provided the essential principles of Judaism are preserved and strengthened by such changes.

Freehof further condemned Beth Israel's by-laws conferring non-voting or "second-class membership" on congregants who espoused Zionism, *Kashrut* (dietary laws), or an extensive use of the Hebrew language. "Your object is definite," wrote Rabbi Freehof; "you wish to exclude those who disagree with you on any one of the above points." As for Beth Israel's charge that the CCAR had become "Zionistic," Freehof countered that, on the contrary, it had merely ceased to be anti-Zionist:

> The manifest fact now is that there are many, perhaps even a majority, of our members who are both convinced Zionists and convinced Reform Jews. These rabbis do not find their Reform Judaism and their Zionism to be mutually incompatible. It is obvious, then, that there has been a definite change of mood in our Conference. Therefore, in harmony with liberal principles, this new mood was acknowledged in our 1943 Resolution. We recognized the fact, plainly observable in the life of hundreds of our Reform Rabbis, that Reform and Zionism are quite compatible.[97]

Dissatisfied with this official reply, Congregation Beth Israel prepared a new anti-Zionist broadside, quoting revered names in

Reform and pronouncements by such stellar figures as the historian of Reform, David Philipson, all of which were intended to prove that Reform and Zionism were manifestly "irreconcilable." Specific acts of the Conference—the Jewish Army resolution of 1942, the endorsement of CCAR delegates to the American Jewish Conference, the "Zionist record of the CCAR," the 1943 resolution finding no incompatibility of Reform with Zionism, the suggestion that CCAR members in the American Council for Judaism should resign without a similar invitation to Conference members in the Zionist Organization of America—were singled out by Congregation Beth Israel as proof that the Conference was no longer neutral. Furthermore, Beth Israel queried:

From whence comes the authority to the Central Conference to abandon underlying, fundamental principles? It should not be necessary to remind you [President Freehof] that laymen were responsible for the beginning and the development of the Reform movement, and that it was in the nature of a definite breaking away from *Rabbinical* Judaism. Do not laymen still have an important stake in its perpetuation? Have they given the Central Conference a mandate to abandon the fundamental and underlying principles which characterize the chief difference between it and Orthodoxy? [98]

As for the "esteem" in which members of Congregation Beth Israel held the CCAR's "Zionist" resolutions, they later declared:

An informal resolution passed by a majority cannot at one fell swoop wipe out the facts of history, commonly accepted, over a period of more than one hundred years. The passage of a resolution by a group, no matter how learned nor by how large a majority, for instance that "we have changed our minds and the world is flat and not round" would not change the fact. . . . A study of the history of Reform Judaism rejects absolutely the compatibility of Reform Judaism and Zionism. Facts are facts and resolutions do not alter them. [99]

After dealing with Houston's war of polemics against organized Reform, the CCAR turned to other matters and tacitly ignored the organizing activities of the American Council for Judaism. Most Reform rabbis declared that the strife-ridden Central Conference, laden with a host of religious concerns, should be guarded from further divisions on the Zionist question. Renewed debate in the Conference was considered unlikely to change additional minds, especially since the realities of world politics and the state of American Jewish opinion had not yet produced unanimity on the Palestine problem.[100]

Having attained their major objectives, the Zionists were content to allow the Conference a respite from the vexatious debates. Besides, many of the tactical goals pursued by the Zionist movement after 1945 could be supported by the vast majority of the American Jewish community, Zionist and anti-Zionist alike. For example, active Zionist allegiance was not required to join in denouncing the White Paper of 1939. In fact, Zionist and anti-Zionist rabbis found a growing field of agreement as they appeared before Congressional committees and executive officers to protest against the "discriminatory treatment" of Jews practiced by the British Mandatory government. Of course, in every case, the anti-Zionists were careful to cloak their political representations in the garb of "humanitarianism" and "democracy" rather than as part of a Zionist design to achieve a Jewish state.[101]

Similarly, with no dissent expressed, the CCAR, in 1946, joined with general Jewish and Zionist opinion in protesting the British arrest of the Palestinian leaders of the Jewish Agency, condemned "other acts of violence and terror tantamount to the inauguration of war by the British authorities on the Jews of Palestine," castigated the White Paper of 1939 and other "infamous," "oppressive," "tyrannical" and "provocative" acts, and dispatched a committee of rabbis to petition President Truman to use his good offices for the attainment of various Jewish objectives in Palestine.[102]

The greatest organized obstacle in the path of Zionism was thus manifestly vanquished after half a century of arduous struggle waged by a bloc of Reform rabbis who were simultaneously devoted to the Zionist program. Having succeeded in discrediting Classical Reform's anti-Zionist ideology, in removing outspoken anti-Zionists from positions of prominence in the movement, and in elevating their own members to the leadership of the CCAR,* Reform-Zionists had achieved a notable victory. Obviously, the Conference was not a solidly Zionist body; the price which would have to be paid in order to achieve such homogeneity was readily apparent. Further inroads

* Rabbi Abba Hillel Silver was simultaneously President of the CCAR, Chairman of the American Zionist Emergency Council, and President of the Zionist Organization of America (1946). Zionists also dominated the more important CCAR commissions and were delegated by the CCAR to sit on the executive board and joint commissions of the Union of American Hebrew Congregations.[103]

into the CCAR could only be purchased at the expense of further disruption in Reform cohesion and in the consequent strengthening of the anti-Zionist American Council for Judaism. The Zionists chose not to pay this price for a gain of so limited utility.

Reform's Changing Conception of Zionism   The foregoing account would be incomplete and misleading if it attributed official Reform's marked change of attitude toward Zionism solely to the efforts of Zionist partisans who were simultaneously associated with Reform Judaism. Hand in hand with the activities of organized Zionist blocs, external historical events and social conditions within Reform itself were combining to force an abandonment of the "classical," anti-Zionist position.

First, and foremost of these was the changing composition of Reform's laity and rabbinate. Originally German-Jewish in character, and therefore "out of bounds" to the "socially inferior" East Europeans, Reform temple memberships became increasingly accessible to Russian and Polish Jews as they climbed the economic ladder. After the leveling effect of the Great Depression and particularly after the vast social changes of the forties, many *nouveau riche* East European Jews entered into the hitherto exclusive circles of Reform, B'nai B'rith, and other associations. Former Orthodox Jews, eager to achieve the higher social status associated with the affluence of Reform, were drawn into the temples. Widespread assimilation, particularly among the wealthy German Jews, had removed the "Old Guard" leadership of temple after temple, providing the newcomers with the opportunity to reshape Reform in their own image.[104] By 1930, according to a survey of forty-three Reform congregations in eleven major cities, temple memberships were composed of equal proportions of Jews from German and East European homes. Among the foreign-born respondents alone, 57 percent hailed from eastern Europe, only 33 percent from Germany.[105] In the Reform rabbinate, too, German predominance vanished with the passage of time. With very few exceptions, Reform pulpits came to be staffed almost exclusively by products of East European households.[106]

This striking transformation of Reform membership and leadership was, of course, more than nominal. In the train of the traditionally-educated new members there came an increased attention to ritual and ceremony, a greater use of Hebrew prayer and

melody, and, most significant, the changes in attitudes toward
Palestine and Zionism which we have already chronicled. Generations nourished on the two-thousand-year-old dream of Zion restored could find little sympathy with early Reform's antipathy
to the Zionist movement.

A graphic representation of this changed outlook toward Zionism carried into Reform by the younger generations of rabbis is
contained in the following tables [107] dealing with the ninety rabbinical signers of the anti-Zionist "Statement of Principles" (June
2, 1942) and the 214 Reform Zionist endorsers of a counter-state-
ment. Note that the Zionist position increases almost directly with
the recency of the college class:

TABLE 7.   Alumni of Hebrew Union College in the CCAR

CLASSES OF	BELONG TO CCAR	SIGNED ZIONIST STATEMENT	PER-CENT	SIGNED ANTI-ZIONIST STATEMENT	PER-CENT	NON-COMMITTAL	PER-CENT
1883–93	10	1	10	7	70	2	20
1894–03	38	5	13.2	19	50	14	36.8
1904–14	36	9	25	10	27.7	17	47.2
1915–24	65	23	35.3	15	23	27	41.5
1925–34	115	52	45.2	21	18.2	42	36.5
1935–42	77	33	42.8	13	16.8	31	40.2

Comparing graduates of Stephen Wise's Zionist-oriented Jewish
Institute of Religion with graduates from the Hebrew Union College during the same period reveals a striking picture of the differences in attitudes engendered by the two Reform seminaries:

TABLE 8.   Alumni of Jewish Institute of Religion in the CCAR

	BELONG TO CCAR	SIGNED ZIONIST STATEMENT	PER-CENT	SIGNED ANTI-ZIONIST STATEMENT	PER-CENT	NON-COMMITTAL	PER-CENT
J.I.R. Graduates 1926–42	86	65	75.5	1	1.1	20	23.2
H.U.C. Graduates 1926–42	188	84	44.5	33	17.5	71	37.7

Adding the graduates of the two schools since 1926, the results reveal a marked Zionist disposition among the younger generation of Reform leaders:

TABLE 9.   The CCAR and Zionism, Younger Rabbis

ALL CLASSES	BELONG TO CCAR	SIGNED ZIONIST STATEMENT	PER-CENT	SIGNED ANTI-ZIONIST STATEMENT	PER-CENT	NON-COMMITTAL	PER-CENT
1926–42	274	149	54.3	34	12.4	91	33.3

Finally, considering the entire Central Conference of American Rabbis (which in 1942 included forty-nine rabbis graduated from neither the Jewish Institute of Religion nor the Hebrew Union College—of whom twenty-six signed the Zionist statement and six the anti-Zionist document), the alignments were:

TABLE 10.   The CCAR and Zionism, Entire Membership

BELONG TO CCAR	SIGNED ZIONIST STATEMENT	PER-CENT	SIGNED ANTI-ZIONIST STATEMENT	PER-CENT	NON-COMMITTAL	PER-CENT
476	214	44.9	90	18.9	172	36.2

Closely related to this changing social composition of Reform was the fact that the movement as a whole, while managing to replace the families of German origin with newcomers from eastern Europe, seemed on the verge of stagnation. In fact, during 1930–40, when marked changes of attitude toward Zionism were recorded, Reform actually lost members. And, as the table indicates, Reform's ability to create new congregations was but a shadow of earlier decades:

TABLE 11.   Reform Congregational and Family Affiliations [108]

	1873	1900	1910	1920	1930	1940
Congregations	56	88	198	222	282	302
Families	2,700	9,000	17,000	31,000	60,000	59,000

Reform temples, by and large, simply were unable to keep abreast of the dynamic growth recorded by Conservatism.[109] With the vast reservoir of American Jewry moving in the direction of Neo-Orthodox or Conservative affiliations, Reform leaders sought an explanation of their failure to attract new members.

Anti-Zionists were certain that the failure could be traced to Reform's timidity and ambivalence on the Zionist question. But a larger number of Reform Jews believed that the mass of American Jewry, reared in East European homes, was repelled by Classical Reform's innate hostility to Zionism. The ethical monotheism preached by Reform, they argued, lacked the warmth of the pioneering achievement, vibrant Hebrew culture, and idealistic self-sacrifice, all associated with the Zionist ideal. Perhaps Zionism contained vital motive forces which could be harnessed to give new life to Reform Judaism. It was all too apparent, observed one rabbi, that:

> Reform congregations, largely Zionist in membership or led by outright Zionist rabbis, display a high degree of vitality and are prominent in the Reform Movement. The congregations which insist on the original anti-national principle have tended to split up and have made room for newer congregations which are loyally affiliated with Reform Judaism but in which Zionism is quite at home.[110]

Thus, on a purely pragmatic basis, many Reform leaders were persuaded that the very survival of their movement depended on an accommodation with Zionism and its myriad appeals to traditionalist Jews, the reservoir from which the Reform membership of the future must inevitably draw.

Finally, the Reform generation which saw the rise of a well-nigh universal anti-Semitism, even in this freedom-loving land, began to question the validity of its ideology of "Universal Progress." "The First World War and its aftermath of pogrom and fascism had tempered the naive optimism of an earlier day," observed Rabbi Bernard Bamberger.[111] While the age of the Pittsburgh Platform encouraged the belief that the realization of Israel's Messianic era was approaching, the age of Hitler and Father Coughlin made it clear that radical means of saving the Jewish people were needed. With the physical destruction of European Jews proceeding at an unprecedented rate, only the most fanatic of anti-Zionists could afford the luxury of besmirching the Zionist endeavor specifically designed to rescue the threatened communities. Reform Jews might still have reservations about the validity or wisdom of Zionist ideology, but few would risk being labeled an "enemy of Israel" by an open hostility to Zionism.[112]

ZIONISM AND CONSERVATIVE JUDAISM

The Rise of Conservatism   The American Zionist movement derived its most unanimously enthusiastic and dedicated supporters from the ranks of Conservative Judaism, the newest religious alignment in the American Jewish community. Drawn from the great "Center Bloc" of American Jewry, these Jews—products of recent immigration from eastern Europe—were tied by bonds of tradition, kinship, and social outlook to the effort of Jewish national restoration in Palestine. Seeking to achieve a synthesis of Jewish tradition and modern culture, they retained and cherished the age-old hope of rebuilding Zion. Frequently corresponding with family and friends still in Europe, they shared a growing sense of frustration with each report of outrages committed against their brethren overseas. Although engrossed in the economic and social struggle to sink roots into American soil, they never abdicated the self-imposed responsibility of aiding fellow Jews to reach Palestine.

The Jewish Theological Seminary in New York City, forerunner of the Conservative movement, was founded as late as 1887, largely as a protest against what was felt were the de-Judaizing excesses of Reform's Pittsburgh Platform. But upon the death of Sabato Morais, its founder and its first president, the Seminary virtually ceased to function. Only with the great new influx of Orthodox Jews from eastern Europe around the turn of the century were new life and meaning infused into it.

This huge entry of poor and seemingly "benighted" Jews from the "Barbaric East" was deplored by the Americanized, successful Reform Jews of central European background who had already achieved great eminence in business and in the professions. At first an impregnable wall of social isolation separated the "aristocracy" with their "church-like" temples from the predominantly traditionalist "huddled masses" of New York's East Side. Few, if any,

Reform congregations opened their doors to greet the newcomers. Moreover, the Central Conference of American Rabbis gave little encouragement to the formation of Reform temples composed of the few East European congregants willing to accept beliefs and practices contrasting so sharply with their former Orthodoxy.[113]

Yet a *modus vivendi* between the two social groups was unavoidable. For their part, the Russian Jews were eager to enjoy the high social status achieved by the *Yahudim* or German Jews. The *Yahudim,* on the other hand, ardently wished to "Americanize" and "enlighten" the Russian newcomers lest the latter's "bad manners" reflect unfavorably on the position of the Jews in America. To this end, charity was condescendingly administered by the "Uptown" set to the lower East Side crowd, in the fervent hope that the Easterners would thereby become more "civilized."

In the realm of religion, Reform Jews searched about for some medium capable of breaking Orthodoxy's Old World influence upon the new immigrants without, at the same time, driving them into the camp of the radical Jewish socialists, then organizing to overthrow "The System." Unable or unwilling to absorb the newcomers themselves, Reform needed a "more American," a "more modern" version of Orthodoxy with which to assimilate the millions of daily-arriving Easterners. Accordingly, influential Reform laymen revived the dormant Jewish Theological Seminary, imported the outstanding scholar Solomon Schechter to be its head, and provided funds to enable the Jewish Theological Seminary to reach and attract the great masses from eastern Europe.[114]

The Reform laity which constituted the majority of the Seminary's Board of Directors built better than they hoped. In the relatively short span of four decades, the new "Conservative" brand of Judaism promulgated by the Seminary was sweeping the membership of formerly Orthodox homes and challenging the century-old Reformists in numbers, wealth and the eminence of its rabbis and laymen.

It was Schechter, perhaps more than any other individual, who won for the tiny Zionist following in America its first great accretion of strength—the Conservative movement in Judaism.[115] Despite the threats and imprecations of the Seminary's Reform-dominated Board of Directors, he warmly and decisively espoused the doctrine of Jewish national restoration in Palestine [116] and served on the Federation of American Zionists' Administrative

Committee, thus scandalizing the anti-Zionist Reformists in the Hebrew Union College even while he heartened and emboldened the Zionist camp. Moreover, great scholars at the Seminary, all appointed by Schechter—Louis Ginzberg, Israel Friedlaender, Mordecai M. Kaplan, Judah L. Magnes and Israel Davidson—persisted in granting succor to the growing Zionist "heresy" by virtue of their numerous writings, speeches and other Zionist leadership activities.[117]

Schechter and his faculty viewed the re-establishment of a Jewish homeland in Palestine as much more than a mere political program; for them it was a religious imperative. For them, the Jewish *Torah,* the God-idea of Israel, the Jewish people and the land of Palestine constituted an indissoluble partnership, the well-being of all being necessary to the health of any single element. The Hebrew language, Jewish folkways, the Zionist colonization of the Holy Land—these became the very essence of "Jewish civilization"; for, held Schechter and his disciples, Judaism was too catholic, too broad, to be viewed merely as a religious faith in the manner advocated by Reform rabbis in the Central Conference of American Rabbis.

Naturally enough, under the influence of such forceful teachers and unequivocal teachings, the graduates of the Jewish Theological Seminary ("Schechter's Zionists," as some dubbed them) carried the Zionist message to all parts of the United States, until one could safely say that where stood a Conservative synagog there stood a Zionist base.[118]

Conservative Pronouncements on Zionism   Meetings of the Conservative Rabbinical Assembly of America (RAA) were consistently characterized by their continuing expressions of sympathy for the growing Zionist movement. In 1927, a leading Zionist and Conservative rabbi, Israel Goldstein, could declare without fear of contradiction that the RAA was "the rabbinical bulwark of American Zionism," and that Conservative Jews viewed Palestine with "an intuitional, unreasoning and mystic love . . . ," and like *Torah,* "as an ultimate, a thing that is good in itself, whose welfare we seek for its own sake." [119] A few years later, RAA President Mordecai M. Kaplan praised the achievements of Jewish Palestine in the days of the early Nazi terror, and urged the integration of the Zionist ideal with the totality of American Jewish life. To this end, he suggested that the Zionist Organization of America be broadened to consist, not of individual members alone, but "in the main of representatives of all religious, cultural and educational institutions whose membership look to the restoration of Palestine as the symbol of Jewish reawakening throughout the world." Such a recommendation coming from the RAA would not be amiss, he thought, because "every one of us, to a man, has in conviction, teaching and action given proof of his loyalty and devotion to the Zionist cause." [120]

Another Rabbinical Assembly President, Eugene Kohn, speaking in 1937, recalled that Conservative endorsement of Zionism was nothing new and that, indeed, whatever strength Zionism possessed in America was largely due to Conservative efforts. However, he noted, the RAA, in addition to an absolute dedication to the "preservation and enrichment of the religious tradition of our people" in Palestine, advocates a specific point of view on the Zionist settlement of Palestine, namely, the promotion of a laboring, cooperative society without "capitalistic exploitation and speculative investment." Feeling that the time was ripe for a "collective expression of our interest in Zionism" in terms of concrete Zionist policies, the RAA then approved a comprehensive "Pronouncement on Zionism." [121]

Occasioned by Great Britain's announced intention to partition the Holy Land further (1937), the "Pronouncement" denied that the proposed restriction of Jewish territory represented "a reflection upon the moral quality, or the practical validity of our ideal." Rather, declared the Assembly, Britain's policy represented

> . . . the violation not alone of sacred traditions and long established historic association, but of pledges solemnly made, and covenants solemnly entered upon. It is but another "devil's triumph" achieved by the forces of lawlessness and terrorism at present raging throughout the world.[122]

Reaffirming the allegiance of the RAA to the World Zionist Organization and the Jewish Agency for Palestine "as the only legitimate representatives before the nations of the world of the Zionist Movement and of the Jewish people as a whole on questions touching the political aspects of our activity in Palestine," the "Pronouncement" went on to affirm:

> It was an act of brute violence which drove the Jew out of Zion. Only through an act of justice will they be restored. Firm in

their faith that justice will ultimately and inevitably triumph in the world, the members of the Rabbinical Assembly re-assert their faith in the ultimate triumph of Zionism.[123]

In recognition of the community of interests between the two groups, the Zionist Organization of America, in 1938, granted the RAA the right to elect three delegates to its national convention. The Assembly, honored at being the first national group so treated, drafted plans to effect a still more "organic relationship" between the two movements and pledged its "continuing, untiring support" to the Zionist cause.[124]

Joseph Zeitlin's 1937 study of the American rabbinate adds an empirical note reflecting the exceptional degree to which Conservative rabbis embraced the Zionist program. Based upon the survey replies of 118 rabbis, approximately 31 percent of the membership of the Central Conference of American Rabbis (Reform), the Conservative Rabbinical Assembly of America and the Orthodox Rabbinical Council of America, Zeitlin found rabbinical favor for the following suggested solutions to the "Jewish Problem" (1.00 denotes a "major solution"; .50, "minor solution"; .00 no solution):

TABLE 12.   1937 Rabbinical Thought on the "Jewish Problem" [125]

SUGGESTED SOLUTIONS	REFORM	CONSERVATIVE	ORTHODOX	ENTIRE GROUP
1. Self-removal of Jews from prominent places in business, politics, intellectual endeavor	.04	.03	.13	.05
2. Good-will conferences between Jewish and Gentile leaders	.55	.51	.53	.53
3. Militant fight against anti-Semitism	.59	.60	.48	.58
4. General education to raise level of the population	.88	.81	.69	.83
5. Improved religious training	.80	.82	.79	.81
6. A Socialist economy	.59	.80	.38	.63
7. Emergence of an international spirit	.86	.92	.61	.84
8. Zionism	.54	.91	.82	.71

The year 1939 found an eminent Conservative rabbi, Solomon Goldman, at the helm of both the Zionist Organization of America and the American Emergency Committee for Zionist Affairs at a time when American Zionists fought to weather the crisis occasioned by the MacDonald White Paper with its limitations on Jewish immigration and settlement in Palestine. Hailing Rabbi Goldman's new leadership and the ensuing strengthened emphasis on "the spiritual and cultural values inherent in the Zionist program," Conservative rabbis also blasted the White Paper, pledged Palestine the full "mobilization of the material and moral support of American Jewry," and beseeched their congregations to double their efforts for the reclamation of the Jewish national home. The assembled rabbis also established a permanent Palestine Committee to: (1) "explore and create avenues through which the Synagogue can make its unique and characteristic contributions to the Zionist movement in Palestine more felt and more stimulating," and (2) "render more effective the services of the members of the Rabbinical Assembly as a body in the advancement of the aims and purposes of the Zionist movement." [126]

Additional resolutions of the RAA indicate the Conservative rabbinate's virtually unanimous and continuous support of Zionist objectives.[127] In the realm of concrete achievements directly attributable to the Zionist affiliations of the Assembly, "Palestine Sabbaths" were observed in congregations throughout the nation. To the anti-Zionist charge that Zionism was a "secular" movement, thousands of Conservative synagogs held special prayer services, invoking God to lend His aid to the fortunes of the Zionist movement. Permanent Palestine Committees were organized in many synagogs to supervise the collection of funds for Palestine and the dispatch of telegrams and resolutions at propitious moments in Zionist political campaigns. Some congregations even voted to join the Zionist Organization of America *en masse*, billing ZOA dues and synagogal memberships simultaneously and incorporating local Zionist activities into the congregational program.[128]

Finally, as with Orthodoxy, Palestine and Zionism were subjects which permeated the Conservative religious school, influencing a rising generation of young American Jews. One poll of Conservative educators in the mid-forties illustrates the extent to which sympathetic dispositions toward Zionism were fostered by Conservative rabbis and teachers alike:

TABLE 13. The Teaching of Palestine and Zionism in Conservative Religious Schools [129]

ASPECT OF TEACHING	RABBIS		PRINCIPALS, WEEKDAY TEACHERS		SUNDAY SCHOOL TEACHERS	
	CSP * %	MDC ** %	CSP %	MDC %	CSP %	MDC %
1. Importance of Palestine in shaping Jewish history, past and present	71	96	81	92	90	94
2. Importance of Palestine as a solution to the problem of Jewish homelessness	86	94	86	94	91	93
3. The need for a Jewish Commonwealth	77	87	87	96	82	90
4. The need for a cultural center for world Jewry	77	93	81	94	83	83
5. Realization of prophetic ideals of the Bible, as exemplified in the Palestinian collectives	26	41	41	58	33	62

* Current School Practice
** Most Desirable Condition

ZIONISM AND RECONSTRUCTIONISM

A fourth religious "movement" on the Jewish scene, and one which contributed substantially to the shaping of influential rabbinical and lay opinion, was the small intellectual association known as the Jewish Reconstructionist Foundation. An outgrowth of the thinking of Mordecai M. Kaplan and other prominent members of the Conservative rabbinate, Reconstructionism never became a distinct sectarian trend enlisting mass support. Rather it acted largely as an omnipresent elite, lending intellectual authority, and gentle criticism, to various objectives and stages of Zionist growth.

The "Reconstructionist Program," promulgated in the first issue of the Foundation's official organ (1935), gave succinct expression to the group's New Deal-ized conception of the role of Palestine in Jewish life:

> We consider the establishment of Palestine indispensable to the life of Judaism in the diaspora. We seek to enable Jewish civilization so to root itself in the soil of Palestine as to make of that land the cultural center for Israel's intellectual and spiritual rebirth. We oppose any attempt to render Palestine the object of imperialist aims or the victim of private profit-seeking. We endorse every effort toward the establishment of a cooperative commonwealth in Palestine based upon social justice and social cooperation.[130]

A more graphic illustration of the importance ascribed to the Zionist restoration of Palestine was contained in the Foundation's official seal, with its accompanying explanation:

> The form is that of a wheel. The hub of the wheel is Palestine, the center of Jewish civilization from which all the dynamic forces of Judaism radiate. Religion, culture and ethics are the spokes by which the vital influence of Palestine affects and stimulates Jewish life everywhere and enables it to make its contribution to the civilization of mankind. . . .[131]

At the same time that Reconstructionists embraced the goal of restoring Zion, they declared that Zionism, however essential, was only an instrument in the greater task of producing a renascence in Jewish life. Accordingly, they would work within the Zionist movement for a complete reorganization of American Judaism as well as for the rebuilding of Palestine. To these two-fold ends, leading rabbis from all three branches of Judaism united in the Reconstructionist movement to make a continuing contribution in the years following 1935.

Utilizing their energetic magazine, *The Reconstructionist* and a prolific stream of books, Reconstructionist-oriented rabbis issued frequent commentaries on desired changes in Zionist ideology and tactics.[132] Working within their respective rabbinical associations and congregations, they exerted important influence in behalf of the Zionist cause. For example, one Reform rabbi, Roland B. Gittelsohn, avers that Mordecai Kaplan's Reconstructionist school was largely responsible for the adoption of the pro-Palestine plank in Reform's 1937 "Guiding Principles." In place of Reform's former narrow conception of "Americans of Mosaic persuasion," Kaplan's thought helped to promote the "Jewish peoplehood" perspective, thus enlarging Reform Jews' ideological view and "bringing them back to the love of Zion." [133]

Finally, rabbis identified with the Reconstructionist program constituted some of Zionism's most facile publicists, effective speakers and competent leaders.[134] Accordingly, though it numbered less than three hundred formal members in 1945, the Reconstructionist Foundation must be recognized as a strategic ally in the Zionist movement's rise to a position of political influence in the American Jewish community.

SUMMARY AND CONCLUSIONS

Religious denominations in the Jewish community had achieved an almost complete consensus on the Zionist question by the mid-forties. Orthodox and Conservative Judaism, always implicitly attached to the Palestine ideal, were by then clearly on record as favoring the establishment of a Jewish state, or commonwealth, in Palestine. Beginning with a basic hostility to Zionism, Reform had also evolved into a movement predominantly disposed in favor of the Zionist program, although in the process of evolution an active opposition group had emerged to counter the main current of development.

We have seen that the role played by established ideologies can be initially decisive in predisposing a group one way or the other in respect to claims of another group. Undoubtedly, the ideological objectors to Zionism in Classical Reform and in the Agudas Israel were as sincere in their opposition based on religious convictions as were the doctrinally favorable adherents to Zionism in Conservatism, Reconstructionism, and the bulk of Reform and Orthodoxy. Ideological attachments, however, are clearly tempered by economic status, ethnic origin, and personal experience, as the case studies of these denominations show. Moreover, ideological barriers seem to be insubstantial when contradicted by the press of events in the life of groups, whether external (the rise of Hitlerism, native anti-Semitism, the appeal of Labor Palestine) or internal (shifting character of group membership, need for an organization to keep abreast of the times in order to acquire members). Ideological predispositions, it can therefore be said, are important but not conclusive; attitudes do change in reference to new events and conditions, and under the influence of dedicated partisans of a countervailing idea.

Our study has also indicated something about the role of the total society in shaping the perspectives of a public within it. For example, the fact that basic Zionist demands had been recognized by the League of Nations and the American government by 1922 seems initially to have influenced Reform to switch to a position of "non-Zionism" rather than remain in opposition to world opinion and official Washington policy. Again, the fact that pro-Zionist sympathies in America were so widespread apparently influenced immigrating Agudah leaders from Europe to seek a *modus vivendi* with the developing American acceptance of Zionism. On a narrower scale, too, the fact that pro-Zionist attitudes were so prevalent among American Jewry seems to have had a "bandwagon" effect, inducing onlooking American Jews to participate in the "popular thing to do."

The following chapters will illustrate some of these conclusions anew and present additional clues as to the manner in which an interest group succeeds in increasing its influence by acting upon additional groups in its public. For the present we shall conclude by summarizing the probable accretions to Zionist strength which followed upon the conclusion of the pro-Zionist alliances we have traced above.

In the first place, Zionist demands received authoritative approval from over one thousand American rabbis speaking individually or through their rabbinical conferences. Thus, the prestige and sanction of religion were imparted to the Zionist ideal and transmitted to over half a million families formally affiliated with thousands of congregations in all three major branches of American Judaism. Dynamic rabbinical spokesmen, particularly those drawn from the ranks of Reform, actually rose to the head of the Zionist movement, lending it something of the air of a massive religious crusade directed by talented orators and well-trained organizers.

On the basis of the enthusiasm generated by influential laymen and their rabbinical leadership, thousands of congregations participated in the concrete tasks of Zionist work by providing membership for the actual Zionist "parties," by donating considerable sums to various Zionist funds, and by collectively signing letters and telegrams to officials of the American government. Religious organizational channels—the synagogal press, the classroom, the summer camp, the pulpit—were opened to the Zionist cause, thus helping to shape the thinking of much of the adult Jewish community as well as the generations of the future.

In short, no observer of the Jewish religious scene in 1946–48 could fail to conclude that the Zionist movement was deriving much of its moral, political and financial support from the rabbis, national religious associations and local congregations of all three American Jewish denominations. By contrast, only a few rabbis and a smaller number of temples could be found to oppose the Zionist program. Looked at somewhat differently, the student of Zionist power would have found a vastly altered political scene if the authoritative voices of religious Jewry had not so unmistakably given their assent to the practical demands of the Zionist movement.

5
zionism and jewish defense organizations

American Jewish life has been dominated for many years not by the synagog and the temple but rather by the diverse policies and actions of numerous secular Jewish organizations; consequently, Jewish affiliations in the United States cannot be measured entirely in terms of religious group membership and synagog participation. For many Jews, membership in one of these secular organizations was a substitute for religion and virtually their only contact with American Jewish life; for others, it was an important supplement to their religious affiliation.

Among the most influential secular Jewish groups are the national "defense organizations." The term refers to those associations dedicated primarily to the fight against anti-Semitism, infractions of Jewish rights, and discriminatory treatment of Jews, both in the United States and abroad. Though for the most part these organizations also had positive programs based on fraternalism or the promotion of Jewish integration into the American scene, the concern with Jewish "defense," "protection," or "anti-defamation" may be singled out as their dominant and common feature.

The internecine struggles and institutional rivalries of these groups, on the one hand, and their heterogeneous composition and leadership, on the other, gave tone and temper to both the American Jewish community and the American Zionist movement in the two decades prior to the establishment of the State of Israel. In this chapter and in the one to follow we shall trace the influence of Zionism on several major national Jewish defense organizations.

AMERICAN JEWISH COMMITTEE

Founded in 1906 for the purpose of preventing any "infraction of the civil and religious rights of Jews, in any part of the world," the American Jewish Committee was second only to the Reform Judaism movement in its long-standing rejection of the Zionist program. Although from its inception East European and Orthodox elements were represented on the Committee, effective control of policy was always in the hands of a predominantly wealthy group of Jews with German and Reform backgrounds. Numbering only a few dozen men in its early days and, at most, a few hundred such leaders until the mid-forties, the Committee was generally recognized as the most influential lay body in the community. It could be counted upon to speak out in the name of American Jewry on every question affecting the status of Jews.

Before World War I the influence of the Committee in American Jewish affairs was never successfully challenged. As the authoritative voice of outraged American Jewry, the Committee in 1911 obtained the abrogation of a commercial treaty with Czarist Russia as retaliation for the discriminatory treatment accorded American Jews traveling in that country. Philanthropic aid to alleviate the plight of distressed overseas Jewry was another major undertaking of the Committee; in 1914 it took the initiative in organizing an American Jewish Relief Committee, which later became the powerful relief and resettlement vehicle, the Joint Distribution Committee. But the major activities of the AJC were centered about the domestic struggle against anti-Semitism, discriminatory legislation, and other impedimenta to Jewish adjustment in the United States. To this end, the Committee took a leading role in the fight against restrictive immigration quotas, the Ku Klux Klan, and Henry Ford's anti-Semitic *Dearborn Independent*.[1]

The American Jewish Committee's characteristic approach to the solution of Jewish problems was a general aversion to publicity, mass demonstrations, and "noisy" techniques likely to call attention to the Jewish grouping. Preferring to make its influence felt at a high governmental level, and in a quiet, unassuming manner, the Committee's leadership often took exception to the "extremist" methods employed by the more vocal and belligerent

American Jewish Congress, the Zionists, and later, the anti-Zionist American Council for Judaism.

To the Jewish masses largely derived from East European and essentially traditionalist backgrounds, the American Jewish Committee was synonymous with German, Reform, non-Zionist, "upper crust," "assimilationist," and "escapist" Jewry. The Committee's early leadership, a veritable "Whos Who in American Jewry" consisting of prominent jurists, lawyers, bankers, brokers, merchants, and publishers—Cyrus Adler, Irving Lehman, Louis Marshall, Adolph Ochs, Julius Rosenwald, Jacob Schiff, Oscar Straus, Lewis Strauss, Cyrus Sulzberger, Felix Warburg—was frequently attacked by the Jewish press and the more popularly based organizations as a "self-anointed, self-appointed and self-perpetuated" minority. The Committee's "Jewish values" and desires for Jewish survival were also considered entirely too questionable for the important position in Jewish life occupied by such an eminent and selective organization. Moreover, the abundant funds and exceptionally competent professional staff which distinguished the Committee from many other Jewish associations were said to be responsible for an "undue" and "excessive" influence exerted by these "marginal Jews" over the totality of American Jewish communal life.[2]

The nature of political control in the Committee, before its "democratization" in the forties, can be seen in its by-laws of 1936. Provision was made for three classes of members: Class A members, numbering approximately three hundred, were named for three-year terms from the 198 communities having a Jewish population of one thousand persons or more. These prominent local personalities were chosen either directly by a "sustaining membership," that is, by wealthy contributors to the Committee, or by the boards of directors of local Jewish philanthropic federations or welfare funds. Class B members consisted of thirty-two delegates from nineteen national Jewish organizations, including fraternal lodges, Orthodox and Conservative lay and rabbinical bodies, and Hadassah, the Women's Zionist Organization of America. Finally, Class C members-at-large, numbering some thirty persons, were elected for one-year terms by the annual meetings of the full Committee. These members were usually outstanding leaders and/or wealthy philanthropists in the American Jewish community, co-opted in every case by a governing council within the AJC, called the "Executive Committee."[3]

Nominally, therefore, the vast majority of the American Jewish Committee was composed of community representatives chosen by the local philanthropic federations. Actually, effective power rested with the nationally-chosen members-at-large and the self-perpetuating Executive Committee. According to an analysis made in 1943, only one of the AJC's fourteen officers was a delegate of a local federation, and none were appointed by the eighteen national organizations affiliated with the Committee. Furthermore, of the seventy Executive Committee members, only ten represented welfare funds and national organizations. Apparently, therefore, it was the Class C members-at-large who controlled the AJC and directed its policies, including those relative to Zionism.[4]

At the same time, although the local personalities (Class A members) were not decisive in controlling national Committee policy, these three hundred "community representatives" did often dominate their respective Jewish communities and were able to channel Committee policy downward. The American Jewish Committee, many an observer of Jewish affairs consequently claimed, exerted "an extraordinary influence, in some cases amounting to control, of the public acts of the American Jewish community, both nationally and locally." [5]

As might be deduced from the foregoing treatment of the AJC's socio-economic structure and from previous discussions of Reform and German-American Jewry's attitude toward Zionism, the Committee, from its very inception, refused to assist the struggling Zionist movement. On the contrary, behind Reform's early doctrinal antipathy to Zionism were outstanding leaders of the Committee.

For their part, the Zionists regarded the Committee as an arch-rival, hardly less formidable than the theology-wielding Reform rabbis of the Central Conference of American Rabbis. Louis Lipsky, for many years America's "Zionist Number One," relates how the AJC was early made a prime target of the Zionist political offensive:

> We just could not abide its undemocratic constitution. It was a self-appointed body. It was contemptuous of public opinion, and invariably took the unpopular side. We, organizers of a free Jewish opinion, upon which Zionist success depended, felt that we had to fight the American Jewish Committee or be faithless as Zionists and Americans.[6]

"Non-Zionism," 1918–38 Zionism's victory in the attainment of the Balfour Declaration temporarily stilled the air of contention

between the warring camps. Like the Reform movement, the American Jewish Committee accepted the vague conception of a Jewish national homeland for its religio-humanitarian significance and tacitly ignored the nationalistic, ideological, and political implications of the event. In a public statement of April 28, 1918, the Committee declared its readiness to

> . . . cooperate with those who, attracted by religious or historic association, shall seek to establish in Palestine a center for Judaism, for the stimulation of our faith, for the pursuit of development of literature, science, and art in the Jewish environment and for the rehabilitation of the land.[7]

Thereafter, the Committee joined with other Jewish organizations in a memorial to President Wilson asking that the forthcoming peace conference recognize Jewish claims to Palestine and confer the Palestine Mandate on Great Britain. President Louis Marshall and other officers of the Committee were also instrumental in convening "Non-Partisan Conferences for Palestine" in 1924 and 1925. These meetings culminated in the "Pact of Glory" of 1929—the Zionist-non-Zionist cooperative venture of a Jewish Agency for Palestine intended to provide the material and moral support for the realization of the opportunities presented to world Jewry by the Mandate. Individual members of the Committee also played a prominent role in the formation in 1925 and 1926 of important pro-Palestine organizations, such as the American Friends of the Hebrew University ("To receive and maintain funds to aid in the support and development of Hebrew University and to disseminate information concerning the Hebrew University and its activities"), and of the Palestine Economic Corporation ("To afford an instrument through which American Jews and others may give material aid on a strictly business basis to productive Palestinian enterprises and thereby further the economic development of Palestine and the resettlement there of an increasing number of Jews").[8]

Following the Arab riots of 1929 and the issuance of the restrictive Passfield White Paper of 1930, the leadership of the Committee joined with the Jewish Agency for Palestine

> . . . in expressing its profound disappointment with the policy of the British Government as enunciated in the White Paper of October 20, 1930; a policy which the Committee deems to have no

basis in either the Balfour Declaration or the Mandate and to be a fallacious interpretation of these two charters underlying the trusteeship of Great Britain on behalf of the League of Nations. . . .

Shoulder to shoulder with leaders of the Zionist movement, the Committee offered "its wholehearted cooperation" to the Jewish Agency in its efforts to reverse Britain's assault on the development of the Jewish national home.[9]

The Committee maintained its sympathetic association with the Zionist reclamation of the Holy Land during most of the 1930's but, with the establishment of the enlarged Jewish Agency in 1929, ceased issuing policy statements on Palestine, relegating such concerns to its representatives on the Agency.[10] For example, when in August, 1936, Judge William M. Lewis, acting President of the Zionist Organization of America, telegraphed Committee President Cyrus Adler requesting that he protest to the State Department against Great Britain's rumored suspension of Palestinian immigration, Adler replied that the Committee's policy of leaving all pertinent matters on Palestine in the hands of the Jewish Agency was adequate even to the present situation. Unlike other American Jewish organizations, which made angry, well-publicized representations before the State Department over the threatened immigration restrictions and the renewal of Arab rioting, the Committee's Executive decided that it would not dispatch its own protest delegation to Washington. Rather than cause its members "to act in relation to Palestine in a dual capacity," the Committee held that Palestine's interests "will best be served through the medium of the Jewish Agency speaking in the name of its diversified membership." [11] In this declaration, the Committee was reacting as it had in similar situations involving attacks upon Jewish interests. Thus, while the American Jewish Congress and other mass membership bodies were advocating a militant public campaign of economic boycott and mass protest meetings against Hitlerian anti-Semitism, the American Jewish Committee preferred the quieter policy of private negotiations in official circles.[12]

The Partition Controversy, 1938–39   The swift-moving course of events centering on Palestine soon caused the Committee to abandon its position of beneficent aloofness in favor of a more partisan policy. With prolonged Arab-Jewish enmity at new heights in

1937, Britain's Peel Royal Commission threw a bombshell into the Jewish world by proposing the partition of Palestine and the establishment of a tiny, independent Jewish state and a larger Arab state. While Zionists split sharply on the alleged merits of the diminutive Jewish homeland-to-be, non-Zionist opinion was jarred by the distinct possibility of a sovereign Jewish state being proclaimed in their day. Contrary to their earlier expectations that it would be hundreds of years, if ever, before Jewish immigration into Palestine would provide a numerical majority over the prolifically multiplying Arabs, a Jewish State, albeit a small one, was now actually proposed by the British. In the words of one contemporary wag, non-Zionists were alarmed that Jews had prayed 2000 years for a Palestinian Restoration and now *it had to happen to them!*

Opposition to such a possibility was soon mirrored in the activities of Maurice J. Karpf, President of the Faculty of the New York Graduate School for Jewish Social Work, a spokesman for the influential Committeeman, Felix Warburg, and, as such, a prominent non-Zionist member of the Jewish Agency. Karpf told numerous audiences that non-Zionists opposed partition and the consequent Jewish state for a host of "emotional, economic, social, cultural and political reasons," as well as "on principle," since they considered a Jewish state "dangerous" to the Jewish people. Anticipating the queries of his Zionist critics, Karpf conceded that the non-Zionists had stumbled into an unanticipated pitfall:

> If you ask why they entered the Jewish Agency, they answer that when they entered the Agency they did not expect that within their lifetime the Jewish State would be a problem for consideration. . . . Now that a Jewish State is actually proposed, and may almost be had for the taking, they suddenly find themselves forced to face a problem they did not envisage; and they are frank to say they will not accept a Jewish State.[13]

Like Felix Warburg, who earlier had threatened that the non-Zionists would leave the Jewish Agency if Zionists persisted in pursuing statehood,[14] Karpf declared that many non-Zionists were pressing for a "declaration of non-cooperation with the Zionists in the Agency" and for an end to the collection of those funds for Palestine that were to be used "for the creation of the very thing . . . they opposed by profound conviction." [15]

Faced with a revolutionary change in the prospects for the

Jewish national homeland and unable to rely upon their small representation in the Agency, the American Jewish Committee, speaking for its predominantly non-Zionist constituency, once again embraced a policy of independent political action. A resolution of January 16, 1938, announced the Committee's unalterable opposition to partition, a policy which "ignores all of the guarantees embodied in the Balfour Declaration," and authorized Committee officers to seek "a just, equitable and workable solution of the present Palestine problem." Meanwhile, in the absence of a "better" formula, the Committee would continue to support the Mandate [16] and the joint Zionist and non-Zionist fund drive of the Keren Hayesod (Palestine Foundation Fund).[17]

Consequent upon the enduring unrest in Palestine and numerous rumors of a reported change in British policy, the AJC's Executive Committee chairman cabled Chaim Weizmann, President of the World Zionist Organization, of the American Jewish Committee's hope for a continuing British exercise of the Mandate "in accordance with the principles of the Balfour Declaration." Morris D. Waldman, AJC Executive Director, was also dispatched to London to represent non-Zionist views in the impending British-Zionist negotiations on Palestine.[18] A letter to all corporate members, dated October 19, 1938, declared that the Committee's officers were endeavoring, "by all legitimate means, to keep the doors of Palestine open for immigration of our afflicted brethren and to protect them within the framework of the Balfour Declaration." At the same time, the leadership spurned the activist course of the Zionists who, with their allies, were embarked upon a vigorous campaign to mobilize public opinion against the British restrictions in Palestine; it affirmed its categorical opposition to "emotional appeals at mass meetings or otherwise." [19]

As long as an actual Jewish state was not at issue, the Committee gave evidence of its willingness to assist all "proper" and "legitimate" actions on behalf of Palestine. However, these demonstrations were consistently garbed in the role of "philanthropy" lest the Committee become identified with the "political" motivations of "less-integrated" American Jews. Thus, when the Jewish world was alarmed at British moves in Palestine, the Committee found itself able to participate in the Zionist-initiated high level representations to the American government, but it assiduously avoided the mass protest rallies called by the American Jewish

Congress and other Zionist bodies. On October 10, 1938, the American Jewish Committee joined the American Jewish Congress, B'nai B'rith, Jewish Labor Committee, Jewish War Veterans, Zionist Organization of America, Hadassah, Union of Orthodox Rabbis of the United States, Mizrachi, Council of Jewish Agency for Palestine, Palestine Foundation Fund, Jewish National Fund, Poale Zion, "Illinois Emergency Committee" and the "Washington, D.C., Emergency Committee," in presenting a statement to Secretary of State Cordell Hull asking that the government of the United States ". . . take suitable action to urge upon the British Government a reaffirmation and a fulfillment of its pledge to facilitate the establishment of the Jewish National Homeland and to assist and encourage immigration of European Jews into Palestine." [20] Nine days later, the AJC was again represented in a delegation to British Ambassador Sir Roland Lindsay and, in March and July, 1939, it submitted new protests to Prime Minister Chamberlain and the State Department over Britain's discriminatory treatment of Jews and her violations of the Mandate for Palestine.[21]

Zionist-Non-Zionist Negotiations, 1940–42   With the outbreak of World War II and the attendant exacerbation of Jewish suffering in Europe, the American Jewish community manifested increased concern for its overseas brethren. The significance of Palestine as a haven for the persecuted refugees accordingly became more pronounced. The growing need and a sense of common frustration led Jewish leadership to seek new avenues of cooperative effort. Accordingly, beginning with the spring of 1941, a series of negotiations between Sol M. Stroock, President of the American Jewish Committee, and Chaim Weizmann, representing world Zionism, took place in New York with the object of reaching an accord on the question of Palestine and Zionism.[22] The exploratory conversations were gradually broadened to include representatives of the American Emergency Committee for Zionist Affairs, the American Jewish Congress, B'nai B'rith, and the Jewish Labor Committee. On March 19, 1942, all of these groups, except the Labor Committee, gave evidence of an evolving consensus for common action by dispatching a delegation to the State Department in protest over Great Britain's precipitation of the *Struma* incident.[23] High hopes were entertained by the Jewish press that this new-found concord could be carried over to the reconstitution of the inactive American wing of the Jewish Agency and other Palestinian projects.

At these joint meetings, the AJC, represented at first by Louis E. Kirstein and later by President Maurice Wertheim, pledged its continued loyalty to the "non-ideological" upbuilding of Palestine, but attacked the "nationalist program" which some Zionists and the American Jewish Congress were allegedly attempting to impose upon American life. In the view of AJC President Maurice Wertheim, Jewish nationalism constituted a grave threat to American Jewry and, therefore, the Committee would never consider "abandoning our fundamental point of view—that we are Americans of the Jewish faith, of American nationality, and that we can never permit anything that threatens to affect this status." [24]

The bone of contention in the Zionist-non-Zionist conversations was the question of whether or not Zionism must necessarily be equated with nationalism. Some members of the Committee, like Executive Secretary (later vice-chairman of the Executive Committee) Morris D. Waldman, viewed the two as distinctive ideologies in an internal exchange of organizational correspondence:

> Not all Nationalists are Zionists, nor are all Zionists Nationalists . . . there are among our own inner group men like Dr. Adler and myself, who entertain no objection to the establishment of a State in Palestine, who see in the creation of such a State little danger of impairing or embarrassing the status of Jews in any country outside of Palestine. We do reject Jewish Nationalism, which means the organization of the scattered Jewry of the world into an international political unit or entity, and we object to the existence of the World Jewish Congress as the Parliament of such an international political Jewry. This does not mean that Jews may not, as Jews, be politically active.[25]

At the same time, wrote Waldman, the Committee's past record of cooperation with the Zionists made it logically impossible for it now to combat Zionism publicly, even though the majority of the Executive Committee opposed a Jewish state; once having made it clear that they would not endorse the idea of a Jewish state, the Committee's leaders had, in effect, promised that they would not combat Zionism either.

Waldman then proceeded to decry the activities of Rabbi

Morris S. Lazaron and other anti-Zionists who seemed to be motivated primarily by self-interest, "by fear of the effect of these things on their own position." Expressing the feeling that this "fear motive is getting to be the *leitmotif* in all the Committee's decisions," he controverted the anti-Zionist charges of dual loyalty which some AJC members were hurling at the Zionists: "I have found few, if any, Christian fellow-citizens who question our loyalty to America because of our interest in, and support of, a Jewish Palestine." [26]

But other members of the Committee, led by Justice Joseph M. Proskauer of the New York Supreme Court, indicated their utter disbelief in the possibility of arriving at any agreement with the Zionists. Viewing a Jewish commonwealth, even in the indeterminate future, as a "Jewish catastrophe," they called for the creation of an organization to promote the view that Jewry was a political unit neither here nor in Palestine. Representing this "rising tide, not of non-Zionism, but of anti-Zionism," Judge Proskauer explicitly threatened vacillating Committee leadership with a loss of support and organizational competition from new quarters unless the AJC publicly countered Zionist aspirations:

> I am satisfied that from every point of view of safety for Jews in America there has got to be an open, vocal Jewish dissent from nationalism and political Zionism; and if the American Jewish Committee doesn't make itself the mouthpiece of this public position, some other organization will have to.[27]

President Maurice Wertheim represented a middle position in the American Jewish Committee. While sanguine about the possibilities of reaching a compromise with the Zionists on Palestine questions, he did not doubt that nationalism and Zionism were rightfully equated with one another. Questioning whether the nationalistic emphasis of some Zionists "is not, in this country at any rate, more of a liability than an asset in the attainment of their goal," he indicated that cooperation was possible only on the basis of an explicit rejection by American Jews of the "improper nationalism" promoted in America by the American Jewish Congress and the World Jewish Congress. Wertheim held that leading Zionists, like Rabbi Stephen S. Wise, Nahum Goldmann, and Louis Lipsky, all spearheads of the World Congress movement, were confusing the status of American Jews with the "proper nationalism" of the Jewish state-to-be in Palestine. Unless Zionists renounced their nationalistic program for America, Wertheim warned, there would be only one alternative open: "our Committee would have to make its position crystal-clear, forthrightly, and forcibly, and then . . . 'go to the country.' " [28]

With Zionist-non-Zionist cooperation clearly threatened by the lack of an acceptable definition of the relative scope of nationalism and Zionism, Zionist leaders moved quickly to allay the non-Zionists' fears. Nahum Goldmann, President of the World Jewish Congress, condemned all descriptions of the World Jewish Congress being a "World Jewish Parliament and a World Jewish Government" as either "a silly misunderstanding or a malicious calumny." Citing earlier statements of his own and of Stephen S. Wise, Goldmann stressed the voluntary and consultative nature of the World Jewish Congress and denied that it had ever interfered with the internal autonomy of any Jewish community. Finally, he provided an authoritative statement of the Zionist position which subsequently served as a basis for a tentative Zionist-non-Zionist entente. Avowing that a large measure of the present controversy was due to the impossibility of translating Hebrew words adequately into English, Goldmann stressed that none of the terms for nationalism employed in the present debate implied any kind of political allegiance:

> Neither Zionism nor the World Jewish Congress movement has ever considered the idea of a Jewish nation in the Diaspora, with political allegiance to any international Jewish authority. Cooperation of Jews in the Diaspora is possible only on a purely voluntary basis for the defense of human rights and the realization of common aspirations. Only in Palestine—and that is the meaning of Zionism—can the Jewish people achieve full nationhood by establishing its own state to which its Jewish citizens, those living there, will owe political allegiance. Jews in the Diaspora countries are citizens of their respective countries; to these countries and to them alone do they owe political allegiance. But can this elementary truth mean that Jews are not allowed to cooperate with other Jews, that they cannot be united with other Jews all over the world by a common past, by a common present, by a common future, or, in a word, by a common destiny? To conceive of allegiance and loyalty to this country or any other democratic country in this exclusive way is unjust not only to the Jewish people but also to the conception of American Democracy.[29]

Chairman of the Palestine Executive of the Jewish Agency, David Ben-Gurion, then visiting in New York, also hastened to assure President Wertheim that Zionism would not impair the civil status of American Jewry:

> No Zionist questions that American Jews owe their allegiance to America on exactly the same basis as all other Americans. Whatever view they hold on the nature of the ties which bind together Jews of different countries, it in no way impairs the allegiance of American Jews to America. If necessary a competent Zionist authority will declare that there is nothing in the programme or the practice of Zionism which conflicts with the above.[30]

Substantially on the basis of this explicit Zionist "renunciation of Diaspora Nationalism," AJC leaders agreed to continued talks with the Zionist; and at Wertheim's Connecticut home in June, the "Cos Cob Formula" was successfully drafted. Non-Zionists would henceforth work with Zionists toward the following goals:

a) For the maintenance of Jewish rights under the Mandate in Palestine for the immediate future;

b) For the fulfillment of the original purposes of the Balfour Declaration, whereby through unrestricted Jewish immigration and large-scale colonization under a regime designed for this purpose, Jews may constitute a majority in Palestine and establish an autonomous commonwealth, it being clearly understood that

   (1) In such a commonwealth, all the inhabitants, without regard to race or religion, shall enjoy complete equality of rights;

   (2) The establishment of this commonwealth will in no way affect the political or civil status and allegiance of Jews who are citizens of any other country.[31]

But agreement had come too late. By this time the Zionist question had sundered the Central Conference of American Rabbis and anti-Zionist rabbis were carrying their drive against "Jewish Nationalism" into the American Jewish Committee in an effort to commit its vast financial and moral influence to their cause.[32] Such leading members of the AJC as attorney Morris Wolf and Judge Joseph Proskauer, dissatisfied with the failure of the Committee to denounce the Zionist "corruption" of American

Jewish life, were simultaneously encouraging the formation of the anti-Zionist American Council for Judaism and opposing the effectuation of any such compromise agreement as was represented by the Cos Cob Formula. Indeed, Wolf, Proskauer, Lewis L. Strauss and a considerable following were reportedly threatening secession from the Committee and entrance into the American Council for Judaism unless the AJC abandoned its non-Zionist platform and aligned itself openly with the emerging anti-Zionist coalition of Reform rabbis and wealthy laymen.[33]

With a split in the ranks of the Committee brewing, Maurice Wertheim, for reasons of ill health, announced that he would relinquish the presidency. Negotiations with the Zionists were "temporarily" broken off, the Committee announcing that it would soon formulate a unilateral statement on Palestine. Moreover, in what constituted a direct affront to the Zionists, frankly anti-Zionist Judge Proskauer was named by the Nominating Committee as Wertheim's successor, the choice to be submitted for final ratification to the January, 1943, annual meeting of the AJC.[34]

Meanwhile, the various Zionist organizations of the United States had agreed upon a common political objective at the joint Biltmore Conference in May, 1942: the establishment of Palestine as a Jewish commonwealth. In non-Zionist circles, this demand was widely regarded as a sweeping victory for the "extreme" Zionist position, since it called for an independent Jewish Palestine instead of the mere lifting of barriers to further Jewish immigration.* (See Chapter 9.)

With the Zionist position clearly recorded in the form of the Jewish commonwealth resolution, the thirty-sixth annual meeting of the American Jewish Committee convened on January 31, 1943. Retiring President Maurice Wertheim, reporting on the progress

---

* Proskauer, for example, wrote of the Biltmore Platform:

> The passage of this resolution greatly strengthened the chauvinistic endeavors of extreme Zionists to secure immediately the creation of a Jewish State.
> I could not understand how anyone could expect that a land, whose population in 1942 was two-thirds Arab and one-third Jewish, could then be organized as a purely Jewish state. I believed then, as I believe now, that the Biltmore Resolution showed a lack of a proper sense of timing. My own attitude . . . was that the real objective at that time should not be statehood; that it was the part of wisdom to follow the Balfour Declaration and the provisions of the mandate in their clear enunciation of the right of free Jewish immigration into Palestine; and that the solution of the political problem ought to be postponed until there was a greater parity in population.[35]

of his negotiations with Zionist groups over the past two years, conceded that a common statement of principles to which all factions within the Committee could subscribe was clearly not feasible; an attempt to produce one would only produce greater diversity and, perhaps, even split the Committee. Rather than seek a bilateral agreement, therefore, Wertheim advised the assembled Committee to "determine exactly what it felt on the subject of Palestine, in order that the negotiations might proceed from a sound base." After quoting conciliatory statements by Nahum Goldmann as evidence of "an ever-narrowing gulf which it is my fervent hope may some day be bridged forever," Wertheim relinquished his leadership.[36]

The AJC then proceeded to a consideration of a "Statement of Views with Respect to the Present Situation in Jewish Life," proposed for adoption as the official policy of the Committee by Judges Proskauer, Irving Lehman, Samuel I. Rosenman, and George Z. Medalie. The sections on Palestine,* the heart of the "Statement" which had already been approved by the Executive

---

* The full text of the Palestine sections reads:

We recognize that there are now more than half a million Jews in Palestine who have built up a sound and flourishing economic life and a satisfying spiritual and cultural life, and who now constitute substantially one-third of the population, and that while this Palestinian immigration has been a blessed amelioration of the condition of this large number of Jews, and has helped to bring about a great development of the country itself, settlement in Palestine although an important factor, cannot alone furnish and should not be expected to furnish the solution of the problem of post-war Jewish rehabilitation.

We affirm our deep sympathy with and our desire to cooperate with those Jews who wish to settle in Palestine.

With respect to the government of Palestine, we recognize wide divergence of opinion and that *under existing conditions there should be no preconceived formula at this time as to the permanent political structure which shall obtain there.* Since we hold that in the United States as in all other countries Jews, like all others of their citizens are nationals of those nations and of no other, there can be no political identification of Jews outside of Palestine with whatever government may there be instituted.

We endorse the policy of friendship and cooperation between Jews and Arabs in Palestine and urge that every possible avenue be followed to establish good will and active collaboration between them.

We approve for Palestine an *international trusteeship* responsible to the United Nations for the following purposes:

    (a) to safeguard the Jewish settlement in and Jewish immigration into Palestine and to guarantee adequate scope for future growth and development to the full extent of the economic absorptive capacity of the country.

    (b) to safeguard and protect the fundamental rights of all inhabitants.

    (c) to safeguard and protect the holy places of all faiths.

    (d) to prepare the country to become, *within a reasonable period of years,* a self-governing Commonwealth under a Constitution and a bill of rights that will safeguard and protect these purposes and basic rights for all.

Committee, suggested that there be no preconceived formula for Palestine's ultimate future and that an international trusteeship under the United Nations was the best immediate proposal.[37]

In support of this program, Judge Proskauer took the floor to answer the Zionist members of the AJC who had already announced that they regarded the "Statement" as a marked retrogression from the Committee's previous sympathy for Palestine.[38] Addressing himself to Judge Levinthal, who in his role as President of the Zionist Organization of America stood as the chief opponent of the program, Proskauer averred that all endeavors "to effect a compromise on ideologies or principles" were perfectly futile; such efforts would only "split this American Jewish Committee into bits and destroy its usefulness as a factor for the achievement of the good of Jewry." He argued further that the "Statement" was intended to provide a compromise of action, not of principle. Proskauer also revealed that several leading members had threatened to resign from the AJC because they believed that it did not go far enough in denouncing the whole Zionist program; some of the anti-Zionist suggestions he had heard in the last week, Proskauer confided to Levinthal, "would make your blood freeze in your veins." Then, referring to his nomination to the presidency of the American Jewish Committee, Proskauer declared simply: "I shall accept it on the basis of this paper and on no other basis." [39] Finally, invoking the unity and welfare of the Committee and of world Jewry as values to be protected from any impending schism in the group, and warning of grave consequences certain to follow a rejection of the "Statement," Proskauer challenged the Zionist members present: "I am giving almost of my life's blood to postpone this Zionist controversy, to hold out the hand of friendship and fellowship to the most ardent Zionist . . . the issue of peace or war rests not on us; it rests on you." [40]

At the conclusion of this virtual ultimatum to adopt the "Statement" or to face a breach in the cohesion of the group, the assembled AJC members approved the non-Zionist program and elected Judge Proskauer as their new president.[41] But in order to hold out new hopes for an eventual understanding on the Zionist question, the leadership was authorized to enter into renewed negotiations with Zionist organizations on the basis of the adopted "Statement."

The Committee and the American Jewish Conference, 1943
Anticipating the outcome of the American Jewish Committee's
January 31 meeting, Zionists were already proceeding with their
plan to mobilize American Jewry in behalf of a Jewish commonwealth. Over the signature of Henry Monsky, B'nai B'rith's
Zionist president, an invitation to meet in Pittsburgh for the purpose of considering the postwar status of world Jewry and for the
upbuilding of Palestine had been issued on January 6 to thirty-
four national Jewish membership organizations.

The AJC's interpretation of this latest Zionist move was a
correct one. Zionists, in Waldman's view, had despaired of reaching a *modus vivendi* with the leadership of the Committee and,
therefore, had "decided to corral as many Zionist complexioned
organizations as possible in order to secure mass support for the
maximum Zionist program as reflected in the so-called Biltmore
resolution which contained a demand for a Jewish commonwealth." [42] Waldman claims he immediately telephoned Weizmann
and attempted to convince him that the Committee was being misinterpreted, that Proskauer was "undergoing a change of attitude
vis-à-vis Palestine," and that the non-Zionist-Zionist negotiations
would again be resumed after the January 31 meeting of the AJC.
He also asked Weizmann to see that the forthcoming Pittsburgh
meeting adopt no resolution endorsing the Biltmore Platform, as
such an attempt to "overwhelm" the American Jewish Committee
would only widen the gap between Zionists and non-Zionists. Weizmann apparently relayed Waldman's message to other Zionist leaders, for the Pittsburgh meeting took no specific action on Palestine.
Instead, the conference resolved to convene a broader, elective
"American Jewish Assembly," representative of the entire American
Jewish community, which would formulate Jewish demands for
the postwar world.

Writing in the Zionist Organization of America publication
New Palestine, February 19, 1943, Louis Lipsky announced that
the American Jewish Committee's adoption of the "Statement of
Views" of January 31 marked the "end of a long discussion" with
the non-Zionists. The Committee's previous pro-Palestine policy
seemed threatened by its new "ideology"; Lipsky thought he detected an unmistakable "anti-Zionist attitude in language." The
AJC-Zionist talks, which had proceeded for a full fifteen months,

were now definitely concluded. Henceforth, announced Lipsky, any renewed Zionist negotiations with the Committee would have to take place under the jurisdiction of the proposed American Jewish Assembly.[43]

Numerous Jewish organizations hailed the forthcoming Assembly as a long-overdue step toward Jewish unity. Groups like the American Jewish Committee and the Jewish Labor Committee, which alone had refused invitations to the preliminary Pittsburgh conclave, were immediately attacked as "saboteurs" and "wreckers" of Jewish welfare. Virtually the entire Anglo-Jewish and Yiddish press combined to demand that the recalcitrant groups join in the common endeavor.[44] Accordingly, the AJC, which at first labeled the impending Assembly "untimely," delegated Proskauer, Lehman, Medalie, Alan M. Stroock and Joseph Willen to meet with a committee composed of Henry Monsky, Stephen S. Wise, James G. Heller and Robert Goldman, representing the Assembly.

A conference between the two delegations took place on February 20, ending with an oral agreement to be ratified by the respective organizations involved. The exact terms of this agreement were later bitterly disputed by both sides. However, a letter from Proskauer to Monsky, dated February 23, gave his account of the agreement: (1) The proposed "Assembly" would be re-titled a "Conference"; (2) The objective of this conference would be to secure a large measure of unanimity on a postwar program for world Jewry for presentation to the Peace Conference; (3) "Such agreement is to be purely voluntary, each participating organization and individual retaining, irrespective of the vote of the conference, complete freedom of action." [45]

Another letter from Proskauer to Monsky, sent on March 26, shows that the American Jewish Committee was continuing to have qualms about the projected meeting, no matter what its final form. Stigmatizing the project as "a quasi-political 'Assembly' that would consider itself empowered to speak for and act in this country for Jews no matter to what extent they might hold varying beliefs," Proskauer revealed his fear that Jews might be accused of "dual loyalties":

> On principle, the American Jewish Committee is unalterably opposed to any plan that would seem to set up the Jews as a separate political enclave, and your project, with its local and regional delegates, its elaborate electoral machinery, and its very title

"American Jewish Assembly" will certainly have this implication.

Surely we must studiously avoid not only the reality, but the appearance of creating parallel or subsidiary political machineries through which sections of America's population would rule themselves, deal with the national government, or negotiate with other governments in the interest of their group.

To avoid these pitfalls, he proposed a different type of meeting—a "Conference" of various groups of differing opinions with the object of reaching areas of common ground. "Such a Conference," Proskauer suggested,

> . . . would not make any claim to speak on behalf of the totality of American Jewry; it would not attempt to bind or coerce its own minorities or in any way challenge their right to express their point of view or to take any action they deem fit or proper.
>
> It would not claim to be the elected and authoritative instrument of the four million Jews of the United States.[46]

Proskauer's concern for the rights of minorities was, of course, partly dictated by the vulnerable position of the AJC. As he later conceded in his memoirs, the Committee "was not a mass organization. We relied for leadership on ideas rather than on numbers." [47] In any popularly-based forum of American Jewry, then, the Committee was likely to be outvoted.

Nor was the distinction between an "Assembly" and a "Conference" a mere quibbling of a legalistic mind. The distinction represented a subtle safeguard intended to protect the American Jewish Committee against any Zionist claims emanating from the projected meeting; unlike "Assemblies," held Proskauer, "Conferences" could not take binding votes.[48] To promote the interests of the Committee further, he also insisted that Conference delegates be chosen in part from among local community leaders, where there was a reservoir of Committee sentiment, rather than entirely from the mass national Jewish organizations where Zionists presumably constituted a majority.

After prolonged correspondence and negotiations, Zionist leaders, eager to construct a forum representing all American Jewry, accepted Proskauer's major demands. With these concessions from the Zionists in the form of a change of name and a more widespread election of local personages, the Committee had "saved face" after its earlier hostility to the Conference. With every day bringing strengthened demands for "Jewish unity," Proskauer now abruptly agreed to enter the Conference. Apparently, this action came as a surprise to even so well-informed a figure as AJC Executive Secretary Morris Waldman, whose memoirs provide this account of Proskauer's unilateral action:

> . . . either because he genuinely desired "unity" in American Jewish life or feared to carry the responsibility for organizational isolation in the face of the hue and cry throughout the country for unity—or perhaps for both reasons—Proskauer, who had always been impatient with committees, acted on his own and capitulated to the pressure of Wise and Monsky, both very persuasive gentlemen. When he reported this at a meeting of the Administrative Committee we were all deeply disturbed.[49]

Confronted with severe criticism of his action, Proskauer threatened to resign the presidency of the American Jewish Committee. But since the position of the organization had already been compromised, Committee leadership, for all its apprehension, agreed to enter the Zionist-engineered American Jewish Conference.

The Zionist press rejoiced at the news that "a mere change of name" from "Assembly" to "Conference" had induced the American Jewish Committee to abandon its boycott of the proposed meeting. An editorial in the American Jewish Congress' official organ, for instance, held that the AJC's insistence on a "Conference" as "a loose gathering of representatives of various groups who meet to exchange opinions without any *a priori* obligation" was intended to free it from the responsibilities subsumed by an "Assembly" acting in the name of an integrated community. Nevertheless, *Congress Weekly* confidently concluded that the AJC had lost its organizational freedom:

> All precautions that may be taken to maintain the voluntary and non-binding nature of the Conference will . . . be of little consequence. Once the Conference convenes, it will assume responsibility not to one or another of the participating organizations, but to the Jewish people as a whole. It will not be so easy for any group to leave the Conference without facing the condemnation of our people throughout the world. The Conference will be held together, not by constitutional rules or legal formulas, but by the pressure of the unparalleled tragedy which has befallen our people and the inexorable necessity of finding a common program of action.[50]

This prediction, illustrative of the hopes of the rapidly growing Zionist groups, proved to be only half correct. The American Jewish Conference, the most elaborate and representative gathering of American Jewry ever assembled, did go on to enact a Palestine Resolution echoing the Biltmore Platform's demand for a Jewish commonwealth. Of the 501 delegates to the Conference, approximately 480 backed the Zionist-sponsored position; only four opposed it. Alone among the sixty-five national organizations represented in the Waldorf-Astoria ballroom, the three AJC representatives chose to vote against the widely-hailed proposal. Indicating that the Committee did not oppose a commonwealth "on principle" but did regard this demand as "untimely," Judge Proskauer promised that his organization would cooperate with the Conference in "other areas" for common Jewish action.

On October 24, however, the Executive Committee of the AJC abruptly announced its secession from the Conference without submitting the question to a referendum of the total AJC membership or awaiting the next annual meeting, less than three months away. This unexpected withdrawal shocked Jewish opinion; the American Jewish Committee was instantly condemned in unprecedented fashion in virtually every corner of the community. Few observers would grant that the Zionist question alone was the decisive factor in the Committee's actions; rather the AJC was vilified and denounced—simultaneously with the so-called "lunatic fringe" in the anti-Zionist American Council for Judaism—for its "obvious unwillingness" to accept majority rule and to limit its organizational independence, as witness these typical comments from the Yiddish press:

THE MORNING JOURNAL: The decision of the American Jewish Committee to withdraw from the Conference cannot be regarded otherwise than as an act of national sabotage in the most critical moment of Jewish history. . . . THE DAY: With its position taken against the Jewish Commonwealth and Jewish unity, the American Jewish Committee has isolated itself to a large extent from Jewish life in America. . . . THE ALLIANCE VOICE: The action of the American Jewish Committee has clearly proved that it is an anti-democratic body which does not believe in majority decisions but which wants to dictate to the Jewish masses and to blot out the national hopes and aspirations of the Jewish people.[51]

Similarly, the autobiography of Morris Waldman again provides a valuable source of information on American Jewry's state
of mind at this time:

> The withdrawal of the American Jewish Committee from the
> Conference created greater excitement in the Jewish community
> of America than any domestic event in my recollection. Our ac-
> tion was hailed with a storm of criticism and invective on the part
> of virtually the entire Jewish press . . .[52]

Only a handful of anti-Zionists and "assimilationists," on the other
hand, lauded the Committee's "independence of action"; Proskauer
and others on the Executive Committee reportedly were dismayed
at the widespread and nearly unanimous condemnation of the
AJC by the leaders of American Jewry.

In the three months following the AJC's unpopular action,
four members of the Executive Committee and forty-five members
of the General Council resigned in a much-heralded public protest movement. Furthermore, ten of the eighteen national organizations affiliated with the AJC—the fraternal orders of Brith
Sholom, Brith Abraham, Free Sons of Israel and Progressive Order
of the West, the Zionist women's organization, Hadassah, and the
religious lay and rabbinical bodies, Rabbinical Assembly of America, Union of Orthodox Jewish Congregations, United Synagogue
of America, Women's Branch of the Union of Orthodox Jewish
Congregations and Women's League of the United Synagogue of
America—severed relations with the "isolationist," "negatively-
Jewish" American Jewish Committee. Resolutions of protest also
showered upon the New York office from resentful affiliates in the
interior; the Camden, New Jersey, and Minneapolis Federations
of Jewish Charities resigned, and the Jewish Community Councils
of Los Angeles, Tulsa, Detroit, Memphis, Passaic, Bridgeport,
Schenectady, Kansas City and the New England Council of Jewish
Federations and Welfare Funds forcefully demanded that the AJC
repair its "error" and return to the Conference.[53]

Though the AJC's withdrawal from the American Jewish Conference produced a reaction leading to the resignation of only forty-
nine of the 420 corporate members, the more widespread loss of
organizational support must be considered a severe blow to the
Committee's communal foundations. Henceforth, bereft of its
Orthodox, Conservative and fraternalist affiliates, the Committee

assumed the air of a Classical Reform lay group which, in fact, its leadership had predominantly resembled.

After a tour of fifteen large cities in which he attempted to explain and justify the AJC's secession from the American Jewish Conference, Waldman reported to the 1944 annual meeting. He noted a widespread pessimism over the future of world Jewry and universal demand for Jewish unity in order to meet threats to Jewish existence. He also pointed to abundant evidence of the average American Jew's resentment at the AJC's separatist policy. Only a vast "program of education" would be able to convince the masses of the Jewish community, said Waldman, that Zionism was a false and dangerous doctrine.

With regard to the organizing drive then being waged by the American Council for Judaism, Waldman informed the AJC of suggestions that had been frequently broached to him on his tour: the AJC and the Council for Judaism, "having the same anti-Zionist object," should be merged. To this idea he had replied that only opposition to Jewish nationalism united the two groups, the former being engaged in the task of protecting Jewish rights, the latter aiming, "at least nominally and ostensibly," at a revitalization of Reform Judaism. Waldman advised that the AJC refrain from seeking the dissolution of the Council for Judaism, even though he only partially shared the anti-Zionist group's philosophy of Jewish life and could not commend the "ambiguity of its purpose." While the Committee had forthrightly dared to pursue a course of action independent of most of American Jewry, it clearly would not be advisable, cautioned Waldman, for the unpopular AJC to join with the even more despised anti-Zionist Council for Judaism.[54]

Despite its severe loss of organizational support, the Proskauer-led Executive Committee formally refused a return to the American Jewish Conference. A motion that the AJC re-enter the Conference with a declaration supporting all of the Conference program except the Jewish commonwealth goal was decisively defeated (77 to 14), the pro-Zionist contingent of fifty members having previously resigned from the AJC.

Thus, Zionist leadership had failed, regardless of the magnitude of its victory in the American Jewish Conference, to corral the influential American Jewish Committee for its stable of allies. In time, however, other events were to constrain the Committee to support Zionist objectives. One of these decisive factors was undoubtedly the Zionist-led hail of vituperation which descended upon it, preventing it from pursuing its primary objectives in the Jewish community. Although the AJC was never accused of placing too much reliance upon public opinion, it found a *modus vivendi* with Zionism essential when public hostility impeded its Jewish-defense program. By 1947, this same group, which in 1943 was unwilling to support a plea for a somewhat ambiguous Jewish commonwealth, was to be found in the vanguard of the struggle for a Jewish state. But in late 1943 that time seemed remote indeed.

"Independence of Action," 1943–47   In the next few years, AJC leadership dedicated itself to getting off the fire kindled by Zionist partisans following the evaporation of hopes for a Zionist-non-Zionist alliance. While seeking to restore its badly damaged communal prestige, the Committee assiduously attempted to avoid Zionist wrath. Instead of waging the militant non-Zionist crusade once threatened by Wertheim and Proskauer, the AJC repeatedly offered Zionists its hand in friendship. At the same time, care was taken to assure its constituency that the AJC had always followed a "consistent policy" toward Palestine and Zionism. Above all, the Committee sought to maintain its organizational independence and not become, in the words of one staff member, "a tail to the Zionist kite."

Ruling out the possibility of a reconciliation with the Zionist-dominated American Jewish Conference, the AJC proceeded with measures to repair its organizational foundations by converting itself into a national, non-Zionist membership organization. First, the select group of influential laymen, sensing their numerical weakness vis-à-vis the Zionists, amended their laws to permit a popularly based membership program. Chairman of the Executive Committee Jacob Blaustein told the 1944 annual meeting that henceforth participation in the AJC would be open to all like-minded Jews around the country who would, in turn, organize themselves into local chapters in order to propagate the group's aims. He felt confident that many Jews then identified with the Zionist cause would, if properly "enlightened" about both the "full implications of the extreme maximum political Zionist program" and the true position of the American Jewish Committee, reject Zionism in favor of the Committee's positive approach to Jewish life. Moreover, continued Blaustein, to broaden the Committee's organizational base from its original half-dozen members into the thousands did not represent "any fundamental departure from the long and honorable tradition of modesty regarding the efforts and achievements of the American Jewish Committee, which has consistently refrained from doing anything merely for the publicity it would derive." It was, however, essential to develop a proper, wider public appreciation of the Committee's program so that Committee effectiveness might be enhanced.[55]

After launching its campaign for mass support, the AJC next sought to remove the stigma of anti-Zionism attached to it by the Zionists and other Jews while, at the same time, it attempted to do something for the surviving Jews of Europe. Acting independently, it attacked the White Paper of 1939 in a memorandum sent to British Ambassador Halifax on January 17, 1944. The Committee urged the Mandatory government to re-examine its policy toward Palestine "in the light of the present needs of European Jewry." Making it clear that the AJC "does not at this time urge determination of the final constitutional status of Palestine," the memorandum reaffirmed its traditional support for the Balfour Declaration and for Palestine as "a center for the development of Jewish life and for the continuation of cultural creativity." Recommendations for a Holy Land international trusteeship and a guarantee of "adequate scope for the future expansion of the Jewish community in Palestine" were also reasserted. The Committee then concluded with a vigorous denunciation of the MacDonald White Paper "which discriminates against Jews as such." [56]

Judge Proskauer's official statements in succeeding months also gave patent testimony to the American Jewish Committee's ardent desire to avoid conflict with the Zionists without, however, being forced to adopt the Jewish commonwealth formula. In written testimony before the House Committee on Foreign Affairs in February, 1944, the AJC lauded the constructive work being done in Palestine, recognized its cultural significance, recommended further economic development, stressed the great role which Palestine could play in Jewish rescue, but objected to the Zionists' demand for a commonwealth. Again, the AJC proposed an international trusteeship until the "final status" of Palestine could be determined by "as yet unpredictable circumstances." [57] The AJC's official position, as expressed before Congress, thus contradicts Proskauer's oft-repeated declarations to the effect that it did not oppose a Jewish state or commonwealth "on principle," but only objected to the Zionists' "timing." For the fact is that the Zionist-backed Wright-Compton resolutions made no immediate demand for statehood but merely expressed Congressional approval for appropriate measures to the end that . . . the Jewish people may *ultimately* reconstitute Palestine as a free and democratic Jewish commonwealth." [58]

Following the initial failure of this Zionist campaign to commit the Congress of the United States to the commonwealth goal, the American Jewish Committee again stressed its devotion to Palestine and Judaism while it firmly criticized the Zionist political offensive for "confusing" the American people about what the Jews wanted:

Certainly the international controversy publicly raised by the [Wright-Compton] resolution served no useful purpose. The hearings before the House clarified nothing. On the contrary they caused increased confusion. They created the sad and humiliating spectacle of the United States Congress being used as a forum for conflicting Jewish ideologies. The debates between the Zionists and anti-Zionists on the very essence of Jewish group life and on the role Palestine occupies in Jewish religious thoughts could only have confused American public opinion—and did. . . .

Zeal and wisdom are not always synonymous. Nor is a counsel of moderation necessarily an expression of hostility to the main objective, which is the fullest possible development of the Jewish settlement in Palestine.[59]

But soon new reports of Nazi atrocities in Europe and British brutality in Palestine in late 1944 visibly jarred the American Jewish community, Zionists and non-Zionists alike. Exploiting powerful and deep-seated Jewish predispositions to help their European brethren, Zionist leaders stepped up the tempo of their campaign for maximum immigration into Palestine. In this they were joined by previously hostile elements. Under these tragic circumstances, Proskauer's attitude toward Zionism was undergoing a decided change. The Committee's president, Waldman reported, had many opportunities to meet Zionist leaders and had been obliged to study Jewish affairs more closely.[60]

In addition, President Roosevelt's and Governor Dewey's pro-

Zionist pledges to the Zionist Organization of America on the eve of the 1944 presidential election [61] had placed the American Jewish Committee in an awkward, "out-of-step" dilemma. The leaders of the AJC, always anxious to be portrayed in the role of "good and loyal Americans," were embarrassed by the sudden turn of events which found them arrayed against seemingly official American policy toward Palestine.

After Roosevelt's re-election, Waldman recommended, on November 6, 1944, that the AJC change its policy and lead a "united front" of Zionists and non-Zionists in a revived Jewish Agency. By doing this, he advised, the Committee could

> . . . gracefully withdraw from its controversial position vis-à-vis the Zionists, and so liberate itself from the unpopular position in which it allowed itself to be falsely maneuvered. As members of the Agency, a number of us will have the opportunity to press for our non-nationalist views—and with greater effect.[62]

Early in November, Proskauer and twenty-eight leading AJC members consequently wrote to World Zionist Organization President Chaim Weizmann indicating their willingness to aid in the reconstitution of the moribund Jewish Agency for Palestine.[63] Nothing materialized from the offer, however, probably because the Zionist-dominated American Jewish Conference had already met the Zionists' need for a forum representing the "collective will" of American Jewry.

On February 16, 1945, Judge Proskauer proposed to strengthen the non-Zionist hand by yet another maneuver: he invited the American Jewish Conference, American Jewish Congress, Jewish Labor Committee, and Agudas Israel to an "informal conference" to consider postwar peace problems. The Zionist reply came from Louis Lipsky, Chairman of the American Jewish Conference Executive Committee. Lipsky criticized Proskauer's proposal as a duplication of the more representative work of the Conference. Instead of creating new agencies which would "lead to confusion and tend to prejudice the attainment of our objectives," Lipsky proposed that the AJC rejoin the Conference. The pro-Zionist American Jewish Congress, also led by Lipsky and Rabbi Stephen S. Wise, simultaneously rejected Proskauer's invitation on similar grounds. But the Jewish Labor Committee and Agudas Israel, neither one a member of the American Jewish Conference, accepted; thus was formed what the Zionists later called an "unholy, anti-Zionist united front" to speak for their respective sectors of American Jewry at the forthcoming San Francisco Conference on International Organization (UNCIO).[64]

Terming "most unfortunate" both the failure of his efforts at "Jewish unity" and the position of the American Jewish Conference that it be the sole representative of all shades of Jewish opinion, Proskauer went on to pursue some type of "face-saving" *rapprochement* with the Zionists. An official statement of March, 1945, lamenting that Jewish factionalism played into the hands of anti-Semites, appealed for "Zionist understanding" of the AJC's position even while it indicated disbelief in the practicality of Zionist political aims:

> We say to our Zionist friends: we may not join in your present political demands, but we love Eretz Yisroel, the land of Israel, no less than you do; we are prepared to work with you in getting the answer to all these difficult questions. Why, then, must you have conflict with us because we say it is inexpedient, unwise and dangerous to the safety of Palestine itself presently to go to the extreme of your demands? Why must you submerge all these practical questions, and, in the middle of a great world war, cast everything upon the hazard of the urging of your ultimate political position, which from any point of view is at the present time academic?
>
> American Jewry has a right to look to its leadership and say: What have you done? Where are you going? . . . You have built up for us a picture of combativeness and dissension in which fighting groups act in open and bitter hostility. And the anti-Semite rejoices and echoes the Hitlerism: Divide and Conquer. . . .
>
> Let us have peace. *Let us cease to wrangle over what may happen in Palestine years from now.* Let us face the issues of today and tomorrow, face them together. . . .[65]

Clearly, the Committee was in a difficult position. Unwilling to embrace the political approach of the Zionists, it was subjected to caustic criticism for its self-styled independence, which was interpreted by the now Zionist-disposed Jewish community as "wrecking activity" little short of "direct sabotage" of the aims and aspirations of the Jewish people.[66] Moreover, this campaign of pro-Zionist invective was proving effective in limiting the influence of the Committee's other, and infinitely more central, domestic programs in the fight against anti-Semitism. One anonymous staff document, circulated to Committee leaders in 1945, warned that they must adopt a "positive" and "creative" philosophy if local AJC chapters were to be kept together. These only recently founded chapters, cautioned the writer, could not

> . . . be held together by antipathy to or disinterest in "political" Zionism. If the Committee is to remain in direct and overt opposition to political Zionism, it will become but another American Council for Judaism. It will inherit the prejudice that is widespread against this organization. It will attract "cranks." It will never broaden its base and will have to dispense with the help of the majority of the American rabbinate. Without the support of the rabbinate, particularly the Reform rabbinate, the American Jewish Committee can hardly hope to carry through a systematic educational program.

As a way out of its unhappy circumstances, the AJC was urged to adopt a new and "dynamic, America-oriented" philosophy, with an outright declaration that the "ultimate hope of a political state for Jews in Palestine" is not incompatible with the Committee's basic concerns. Only in that way would the stumbling blocks to local organization be removed and the "danger of schism" removed, as it had been in the Union of American Hebrew Congregations, the National Council of Jewish Women and other non-Zionist groups.[67]

This "positive" and "creative" declaration recommended by the staff paper was never promulgated. In practice, however, the American Jewish Committee moved ever closer to parallel, if not identical, action alongside the Zionists. During 1945 and 1946, Proskauer and Blaustein, in close collaboration with Nahum Goldmann of the Jewish Agency Executive, made repeated representations to President Truman and the State Department for the admission of 100,000 immigrants into Palestine, an objective basic to any Zionist effectuation of statehood. Testifying before the Anglo-American Committee of Inquiry in January, 1946, Proskauer still maintained a preference for an international trusteeship while diplomats continued the search for alternatives to independent Jewish statehood.[68]

But, with the fate of Palestine coming unmistakably to a turning point, the American Jewish Committee's leadership granted Proskauer broad, discretionary powers, including the right to support the partition of Palestine and a Jewish state "in the absence of any preferable practical alternative." Proskauer, accordingly, told the United Nations Special Committee on Palestine (UNSCOP) in May, 1947, that if partition were voted by the General Assembly, the AJC would support the decision to the limit. All during the crucial summer of 1947, Proskauer and Goldmann were in constant communication, pressing for United States acceptance of the UNSCOP proposals for the partition of Palestine. Finally, on October 11, 1947, the American Jewish Committee officially endorsed the majority UNSCOP plan for separate Arab and Jewish states. In the troubled days that followed, the AJC publicly opposed several plans which would have meant the permanent freezing of the Jewish settlement in Palestine as a dependent minority. Indeed, once having concluded that there was no "preferable practical alternative" to statehood, the AJC became a steadfast and influential ally of the Zionists in their many appearances before the United Nations and the executive branch of the United States government.[69]

On January 18, 1948, in an address before the forty-first annual meeting of the American Jewish Committee, entitled "Our Duty as Americans—Our Responsibility as Jews," Judge Proskauer gave further indications of the Committee's complete acceptance of the necessity for a Jewish state. Four days later, leaders of the American Zionist movement accepted Proskauer's "conversion" as a sign that he might now be included formally in future Zionist work.[70] And, in fact, after the establishment of the State of Israel, Judge Proskauer proudly reminisced over his actions in behalf of a Jewish Palestine:

> For my own part, I think I have shown that I followed a consistent and considered course. After the criticism to which I was subjected in earlier stages by some extremists in the Zionist ranks, I take satisfaction in quoting the statement of the Prime Minister of Israel that the people of Israel will never forget my "noble efforts." [71]

Summary and Conclusions   Thus was consummated a forty-year record of American Jewish Committee ambivalence toward the Zionist goal of a Jewish state. It is clear that no seasoned ideology of non-Zionism guided the Committee in the various stages we have traced. Unlike Agudas Israel's doctrinal rejection of a non-Messianic restoration of Palestine or Classical Reform's theological adherence to a Divinely-ordained mission of Jewish dispersion, fear of dual loyalty and the alleged effects of the existence of a Jewish state upon the security of American Jews vis-à-vis their Christian neighbors seem to have strongly motivated the American Jewish Committee's leaders. The philanthropic upbuilding of Palestine and the humanitarian rescue of European Jews for settlement in a Jewish national homeland could be consistently pursued by the Committee only so long as an actual Jewish state, whose actions might reflect discredit on United States Jewry, was not a practical possibility.

With a program implicitly dedicated to making the position of its constituency more secure against anti-Semitism, it is not surprising that the Committee reacted strongly to the growing violence and bitterness of the Palestine conflict. Because the Jewish position in Palestine and in the Displaced Persons camps in Europe was becoming more desperate by the day, the Committee feared new outbreaks of "irresponsible" Jewish actions. As one staff member put it, AJC leadership concluded that the possible political evils resulting from the creation of a Jewish state were of lesser consequence than an anticipated uprising of Jewish D.P.'s in Europe, or similarly desperate action resulting from a growing sense of frustration in the face of the continuing Palestine impasse. Under the circumstances, they began to wonder whether a Jewish state was worse than prolonged Jewish unrest. At least, they reasoned, after the state was established "the daily papers in New York would no longer carry headlines screaming of King David hotel explosions and hangings of British sergeants" by Jewish terrorists.[72]

While it is true that the dominant socio-economic elements in the Committee tended to incline toward the anti-Zionist ideological position of early Reform Judaism or of the later American Council for Judaism, it is more accurate to view the Committee's shifts in tactics as "a disguised struggle for organizational power and prestige," [73] rather than as a deep-seated attitudinal antagonism to Zionism. Zionism, after all, was not the chief concern of the Committee; the domestic struggle against anti-Semitism was. When the Committee found itself "out of step" with other sectors of the Jewish community, particularly with B'nai B'rith and the Reform rabbinate, which were necessary to carry on its program of anti-defamation, a change of tactics was clearly required. Accordingly, the Committee urged a revived Jewish Agency for Palestine and a "common Jewish front" at the United Nations Conference. The need for further conciliation was demonstrated by the political events of 1945–47, which made it clear that some sort of Jewish state would be established regardless of the Committee's stand on Zionism. Continued antipathy to statehood now served no useful purpose; it would only serve to alienate the Committee from its financial and moral supporters in the Jewish community, most of whom were loudly clamoring for support of the UNSCOP partition proposal. In the words of one AJC staff advisor, opposition to Zionist goals now would be suicidal, especially in the face of the twin facts that "almost no popular non-Jewish voice has been heard in this country against the idea of the Jewish State" and that the Jewish masses had been whipped up to a fiery pitch by "the self-centered and demagogical wing of the Zionist leadership." Moreover, some prominent Committee members, notably Judge Edward Lazansky, were demanding that the AJC recognize the positive desirability of a Jewish state.[74]

In the final analysis, then, the Committee's belated support for an independent Jewish state must be attributed primarily to political necessity rather than to any change of heart about Zionism or solely to the successful maneuvers of Zionist leadership. The Committee was never "converted" to Zionism nor even deprived of its organizational independence, as were virtually all other national Jewish organizations. When AJC members finally added their political influence to that of the organized Zionists in support of Jewish statehood, it was on a basis of equality and not of servility. The American Jewish Committee, in short, preferred an "evil end to an endless evil"—the uncertain prospects of a Jewish state to prolonged international and domestic unrest over the "Jewish Question."

B'NAI B'RITH

Founded by German-American Jews in 1843, the international order of B'nai B'rith (Sons of the Covenant) is the oldest, largest and most influential of the mass Jewish organizations based upon a fraternal program. Organized into lodges from coast to coast, no Jewish institution except the synagog is a more universal feature of American Jewish life. With a program combining the defense of Jewish rights, philanthropy, mutual aid services and social conviviality, B'nai B'rith, perhaps more than any other organization, succeeded in bridging the social, economic, religious and ideological chasms which divided the American Jewish community before the 1930's. With its youth organizations and college campus affiliates (Hillel Foundations) B'nai B'rith numbered approximately 200,000 members in 1944. Of these, 112,000 men were organized into 660 lodges, 50,000 women into 460 auxiliaries, and 18,000–20,000 dues-paying students into 141 campus units.[75]

With the consolidation of the Jewish community after the halting of immigration in 1924, B'nai B'rith rapidly lost its original German and Reform character. Every shade of opinion and background was to be found in its ranks, although, of course, as the Jewish grouping became more rooted in America, the composition of the lodges tended to give middle-class, East European Jews a numerical predominance. It is interesting to note that all B'nai B'rith presidents after 1925 were descended from East European immigrants, while the same phenomenon did not occur in the more "Germanic" American Jewish Committee until 1948. It was largely due to these new leaders, widely-respected for their Jewish learning and devotion, that the B'nai B'rith passed from the confines of a parochial fraternal order to the more demanding role of a principal motive force in Jewish life. As Judah Pilch observed of the Order in the early forties:

> While the rank and file of the B'nai B'rith is still keeping itself aloof from real Jewish organizational work, holding on to the form of fraternalism that does not demand maximum participation in Jewish life, the tendency of its leaders is to bring the organization in closer contact with all types of work which are essential for Jewish survival.[76]

We must turn to the role of this leadership, as it speaks in the name of a large constituency, in order to gain an understanding of one of American Zionism's principal allies in the struggle to win the support of American Jewry for a Jewish state.

Early Assistance to Palestine B'nai B'rith's philanthropic concern for Palestine antedates the birth of the modern Zionist movement; financial aid was extended by lodges to Palestinian settlers
as early as 1865. The B'nai B'rith lodge founded in Palestine
in 1888 came to number some of Palestine's most distinguished
Jews (Bialik, Dizengoff, Sokolow, Ussishkin, and others). Gifts were
extended by the Order before World War I to the Hebrew National Library and the Haifa Technion. In 1925, scholarships at
the Hebrew University and housing for new immigrants were
provided, and donations totalling $200,000 were presented to the
Jewish National Fund in 1936 and 1941 for the establishment of
agricultural colonies. Finally, numerous forests, welfare agencies,
kindergartens, a teachers' college, youth hostels, the Palestine Hebrew Cultural Fund, the Haifa Nautical School and the Daniel
Sieff Research Institute were endowed by the generosity of the
Order.[77]

During the dark days of the world-wide depression in the
thirties, B'nai B'rith exhibited much interest in the prosperity
of Palestine and the rapid growth of the Jewish settlement there.[78]
With Hitler's rise to power and the intensification of American
anti-Semitism, B'nai B'rith reported a sharp rise in popular interest
for its anti-defamation program and a marked movement to help
fleeing German Jewry.[79] And, when the Zionist Organization of
America summoned a "non-partisan, non-political" National Conference for Palestine in Washington (January 20–21, 1935), B'nai
B'rith responded enthusiastically to the call. Assured by ZOA President Stephen S. Wise (also a prominent *Ben B'rith*) "that there
was no intention to commit any Jew or any organization . . . to a
policy other than the support of Palestine upbuilding," B'nai B'rith
President Alfred M. Cohen became a leading sponsor of the mass
meeting in which fifty national organizations and one thousand
community representatives participated. Honored by election to
the chairmanship of the Committee on Palestine Reconstruction
and chosen to speak to the entire nation on a coast-to-coast radio
network, Cohen lent enormous prestige to the Zionist-sponsored
conference. Later, too, he told his fellow fraternalists that "every
Jew worthy of his heritage is interested in the upbuilding of Palestine so that it may become the home of all Jews who choose to
live there, and . . . a refuge for the oppressed and persecuted." [80]

In succeeding months, apparently without internal opposition,

Cohen proceeded to press for a non-ideological program for the rebuilding of Palestine. The fact that Palestine's doors were open to save persecuted Jews, in the view of President Cohen, militated against overt anti-Zionist sentiment:

> Of course, there are still those to whom the idea of a national Jewish homeland is repugnant; but the acceptance of Palestine as a place in which to help Jews make a good life is universal.
>
> So the old-fashioned anti-Zionist has become merely a non-Zionist. He looks with no hostility at the Palestinian enterprise; he wishes it well if it will make a good home for the homeless; he gives his money to it even. But he still frowns on political Zionism which, however, seems to be no burning cause.
>
> The hot fires of controversy between Zionists and their opponents have cooled off. The controversies of Zionism are now within the family and have to do with social and economic policies in Palestine.[81]

The "hot fires of controversy" were again stirred up, however, on the "partition question" of 1937–38. But, unlike the American Jewish Committee, which dropped its non-Zionist role long enough to oppose actively the "political implications" of a Jewish state, B'nai B'rith took no official stand on the question. That its leadership was troubled, however, by this most "momentous problem in two thousand years . . . whether they [the Jews] shall be suddenly transformed into nationhood with all the implications and responsibilities which inevitably attach to a Sovereign State," is clearly apparent from President Cohen's admonitions to the Zionists to be calm in the face of this "tremendous responsibility." Speaking in behalf of his heterogeneous constituency, he cautioned the Zionist leaders to consider: "Will the creation of a Sovereign Jewish State serve the highest interests of the Jew?" and "In the present unsettled world conditions is the time propitious for the creation of such a Sovereign State?" [82]

The Monsky Era With Britain's withdrawal of the statehood offer, B'nai B'rith's anxieties were quelled and its leadership rallied alongside the Zionists and other Jewish groups in combatting Great Britain's White Paper policy which threatened to annul the promise of a Jewish national homeland, B'nai B'rith's new president, Henry Monsky, participated in the formation of Zionism's political arm, the "Emergency Committee for Zionist

Affairs," made representations before the British and French ambassadors, joined in delegations to the United States Secretary of State, cabled protests to Prime Minister Chamberlain, and arranged conferences with non-Jewish national organizations (for example, the Federal Council of Churches of Christ). Zionists gratefully acknowledged the use of B'nai B'rith's influential contacts: "The many channels of action which you opened directly and indirectly have led to an intensification of public interest in Jewish aims in Palestine." [83] In addition, the national B'nai B'rith contributed a "substantial sum" of money to the Zionist Emergency Committee and urged its numerous lodges to join with the Zionists in mass protest meetings and other forms of political action.

Avoiding outright commitments to Zionist ideology which might occasion schismatic tendencies in some lodges, Monsky increasingly led the B'nai B'rith into a working alliance with the Zionists and their fund-raising institutions. In addresses before the 1940 and 1941 National Conferences for Palestine, Monsky pledged the "unqualified support" of 150,000 B'nai B'rith members to a "sacrificial support" of the United Palestine Appeal and exhorted the assembled delegates:

> Whether you are a Zionist or not, whether you look upon Palestine as a national Jewish homeland, a cultural center, or a haven of refuge does not matter one whit. You have the responsibility and the duty to support to the point of sacrifice the magnificent instrumentalities of the U.P.A. for the rebuilding of Palestine in the light of present history.[84]

Again, at the 1941 convention of his organization, Monsky reviewed Jewish achievements in Palestine—"a thrilling chapter in Jewish history"—and lamented "that the Jews of America were lacking in the vision and the statesmanship twenty years ago or more to actively embrace the Palestinian program." In view of the catastrophic position of the Jewish people, he concluded, B'nai B'rith must redouble its past efforts and recognize the "sacred responsibility" of giving unreserved support to the redemption of Palestine.[85]

The close association of B'nai B'rith with the practical objectives pursued by the Zionist movement paid additional dividends to the Zionist cause early in 1943 when Monsky's sympathies were utilized as a springboard for the organization of the American Jewish Conference. Whereas an invitation by Zionist groups would certainly have been rejected by several influential national organizations, Monsky's call for a meeting to discuss the postwar status of Palestine and world Jewry was eventually accepted by almost every important group in American Jewry.[86]

At the American Jewish Conference, Monsky and B'nai B'rith Secretary, Maurice Bisgyer, played leading roles, Monsky being elected to the governing Praesidium of three. Almost two hundred of the delegates and alternates were reportedly members of the fraternal order, sixty-five of whom organized themselves into a "B'nai B'rith bloc," one of nine at the Conference. In fact, according to one press report, there were so many district past presidents and B'nai B'rith women leaders present that at times the Waldorf-Astoria ballroom looked like a B'nai B'rith Supreme Lodge Convention.[87] Though previously informed by Monsky that membership in the B'nai B'rith bloc committed no one to support the Palestine Resolution of the Conference (that is, the Zionist "Biltmore Platform"), every bloc delegate voted with the Zionists. Monsky himself was accorded the privilege of seconding the resolution moved by Rabbi Abba Hillel Silver. With excitement at fever pitch in the crowded hall, Monsky prophetically declared: "This resolution when adopted will become a historical document, vital to the future fate and destiny of the people of Israel . . . I claim the privilege, one that I shall cherish for the rest of my life, of seconding the motion." [88]

Following the withdrawal of the American Jewish Committee from the Zionist-dominated Conference, the question of B'nai B'rith's official stand on a Jewish commonwealth came before the Supreme Lodge on May 6, 1944. Some Zionist partisans urged the organization officially to endorse the Palestine Resolution. On the other hand, a few non-Zionists reportedly demanded that B'nai B'rith emulate the secessionist example of the American Jewish Committee. With the basic Zionist objective of gauging Jewish sentiment already attained, other Zionists saw no advantage in precipitating a conflict in the already favorably-disposed fraternal order. Under the circumstances, with neither partisan side really able to force the issue to a head, B'nai B'rith resolved to continue its full participation in the pro-Zionist work of the Conference (Monsky continuing on the Praesidium) but to take no official action for or against a Jewish commonwealth.

At the same time, President Monsky made it clear that the

spectacle of Jewish disunity, precipitated by the American Jewish Committee's separatist policy, would solve none of the pressing Jewish problems. As justification for his policy of cooperating with other groups in the Zionist-controlled Conference, Zionist and non-Zionist alike, Monsky reminded his brothers:

> Our enemies make no distinction between Jews. The Jewish slave-labor battalions of the Nazis are made up, I am sure, of Zionists and non-Zionists, of bankers, doctors, lawyers, businessmen, laborers, assimilationists, and non-assimilationists, devoutly religious Jews, and those of our people who are indifferent to their religion—the simple, basic, and unchangeable fact is they are made up of Jews.[89]

In the following half-decade of arduous striving for a Jewish state, numerous B'nai B'rith members and leaders were to be found alongside the organized Zionist groups and working within the Zionist-oriented American Jewish Conference. In both financial drives and political campaigns many B'nai B'rith lodges proved a most reliable asset. Though never officially endorsing the Zionist ideology or calling for a Jewish state, the organization's effective deeds compensated for any hesitancy of language. In any evaluation of American Zionism's increasing power and influence potential in the mid-forties, therefore, the respected leadership, numbers, and financial assistance of B'nai B'rith must certainly be taken into account.

AMERICAN JEWISH CONGRESS

A third "defense organization," and one which played a central role in Zionism's struggle to mobilize American Jewish support, was the American Jewish Congress. Originally established during World War I to secure Jewish civil rights and prevent discriminatory legislation following the conclusion of hostilities, the American Jewish Congress was a conscious and deliberate product of Zionist leadership and thought. With the American Jewish community firmly dominated by "self-appointed" anti-Zionist and assimilationist leaders, Zionist groups felt the need to organize a mass following. The supreme political importance of such a countervailing organization was later described by Louis Lipsky in his memoirs of early American Zionism:

> Suppose we were unable to rally, in due time, a majority of American Jews under the banner of Zionism; and the bulk of American Jewry remained unorganized, or, if organized, were marshalled against our interests? In a way, the American Jewish Committee claimed the hegemony in American Jewish life. That leadership might be challenged by, say, the Independent Order B'nai B'rith or the Union of American Hebrew Congregations. All three bodies could be relied upon not to be friendly to the Zionist programme.

> We therefore thought it of utmost importance to bring into existence a new American representative body, all-inclusive if possible, democratically elected, in order to ensure, first—the creation of an authentic personality to speak for American Jewry; second— to mould that body into a likeness satisfactory to Zionist hopes; and third—to have a forum towards which our propaganda might be directed.[90]

Fostered by such outstanding Zionist personalities as Rabbi Stephen S. Wise, Louis D. Brandeis, Louis Lipsky, Felix Frankfurter, Bernard G. Richards, Julian Mack, Nathan Straus and Pinchas Rutenberg, massive popular elections, unparalleled in Jewish history, occurred in June, 1917. Thereafter, 300 delegates, elected by some 335,000 ballots, assembled to approve the Balfour Declaration and to press for a minority rights program at the Versailles Peace Conference of 1919.

Although the Congress was originally intended as an *ad hoc* body to deal only with issues raised by the war, its Zionist leadership saw an opportunity to develop an effective rival to the non-Zionist American Jewish Committee and therefore decided to make permanent use of the physical instrumentality and the emotional appeal provided by such a popularly-based organization. To that end, the American Jewish Congress was reorganized in May, 1922, with a program designed "to further and promote Jewish rights; to safeguard and protect such rights wherever and whenever they are either threatened or violated; generally to deal with all matters relating to and affecting specific Jewish interests." [91] And, according to its Constitution, the Congress gave unmistakable testimony to its pro-Zionist character by specifically pledging to further the development of the Jewish national home.

Its membership drawn largely from the broad "Center Bloc"

of American Jewry, the American Jewish Congress was virtually indistinguishable from the Zionist Organization of America. Rabbi Wise, President of the ZOA from 1936 to 1938 and a leading Zionist spokesman for fifty years, headed the Congress for virtually the entire period of 1925–49. Louis Lipsky, President of the ZOA throughout the twenties, was also "Number Two Man" in the Congress for more than two decades.[92] During this time no significant Zionist move failed to evoke the enthusiastic support of the Congress and most of its one hundred affiliated national organizations.[93]

The "Congress movement," as it was often called, exerted influence far beyond its immediate organized membership. At the American Jewish Conference sessions of 1943 and 1944, for instance, the "Congress bloc" was second in size only to the General Zionists. (Congress strength in 1943 numbered 111 of 501 delegates; 92 of 487 in 1944.) Moreover, when the Congress bloc cast its vote in favor of "the establishment of Palestine as a Jewish Commonwealth through free immigration under Jewish administration and control," it simultaneously represented the official views of the more than 300,000 Jews represented in its major affiliates: American Federation of Polish Jews, Council of Jewish Fraternal Federations, Free Sons of Israel, Independent Order Brith Abraham, Independent Order Brith Sholom, Progressive Order of the West, United Galician Jews of America, and United Roumanian Jews of America.[94]

In contrast to the "quietist" techniques employed by the more cautious American Jewish Committee, the Zionist-complexioned American Jewish Congress staged economic boycotts of German products, organized massive public protest meetings, promulgated fiery, denunciatory proclamations, and openly castigated British policy, non-Zionist "timidity," or official Washington resistance to the Zionist demands. *Congress Weekly,* the organization's widely-circulated magazine, invariably was to be found in the forefront of Zionist-sponsored campaigns, whether for funds, an abrogation of the White Paper, a call for a Jewish Army, a mobilization of Jewish opinion in the American Jewish Conference, or a drive to establish a Jewish state.[95]

In conclusion, it is presently impossible to measure the exact contribution the Zionist activities of the American Jewish Congress made in influencing the broad masses of the Jewish community and in impelling other national groups to support Zionist objectives more actively. At the same time, the consistently outspoken Zionist record of the Congress, its numerical strength, and its contacts with other Jewish organizations permit of no other conclusion than that the Zionist movement here created a useful instrument in the long march toward a Jewish state. In this respect, the secularist Congress joined with the Conservative religious movement in providing the hard core of American Zionism.

NATIONAL COUNCIL OF JEWISH WOMEN

A fourth and final association to be considered here was not, strictly speaking, a "defense organization," but rather a Jewish women's organization dedicated to a broad program of social services and international and Jewish affairs, including the defense of Jewish rights. Founded in 1893, the National Council of Jewish Women sought to unite American Jewish women regardless of differences in ideology, social class, or religious affiliation. Numbering approximately 65,000 members in 1944, located in 215 American communities, the Council was composed primarily of women from upper- and middle-class families, generally of Reform religious background.

Until 1943 the "non-ideological" Council avoided taking a stand on the question of a Jewish Palestine. In that year, however, preparatory to the convening of the momentous American Jewish Conference, the Council's National Convention recorded itself in favor of the "immediate abrogation of the White Paper of 1939," "unrestricted immigration of Jews into Palestine," and the "uninterrupted and continued upbuilding of Palestine in the spirit of the Balfour Declaration." In line with the foregoing non-Zionist program, its delegates to the American Jewish Conference specifically recorded an abstention on the Zionist-backed demand for a Jewish commonwealth.[96] Ultimately, however, the Council of Jewish Women was forced to choose between the widely different non-Zionist courses of action of the American Jewish Committee and the B'nai B'rith, between independence of action and Jewish unity for Palestine.

The Council's refusal to go along with the overwhelming majority of the Jewish community in support of a Jewish commonwealth, reported Sidney Hook (who had been retained to evaluate the Council's programs and policies), immediately generated extensive "bitterness and resentment and, in some places, active opposition." [97] Excerpts from Hook's "limited circulation" survey serve to indicate the nature of the opinions among American Jewry which gradually forced various non-Zionist groups either to align themselves with positive support for Zionist objectives or else to risk organizational isolation. In the face of the fiercely pro-Palestine sympathies harbored in virtually every corner of the community, organizations were invariably induced to give more than mere "lip service" to the cause of a Jewish Palestine.

Characterizing the Council's position on Palestine as inadequate because it was "too neutral," Hook urged the Council to remedy its past lack of warmth and appreciation for Palestine and to give substance to its verbal professions of sympathy for "the uninterrupted and continuing upbuilding of Palestine." In the past, the Council's actions seemed to suggest "a desire to stand in the calm of a storm center, to avoid offense by saying the least that can be said, to divert the ire of extremists. . . ." If the Council desired to avoid being maneuvered by political Zionists or anti-Zionists into positions where it appeared to be taking the side of one or the other, then its statements, advised Hook, must no longer be "formulated primarily with an eye on how they will be received by other Jewish groups rather than with a courageous faith in the validity of Council's positive position." Finally, reviewing the many admirable features of Jewish Palestine which were "independent of political questions" and which could serve to enhance and strengthen American Jewish life, Hook recommended that the Council "meet the Palestine question squarely" and adopt specific projects of a cultural nature to aid the upbuilding of the Holy Land.

Recognizing the probable consequences of further indecisiveness toward Palestine, the Council moved in 1946 to adopt concrete measures—the training in America of Palestinian social workers and financial grants to the Hebrew University—designed to aid the Jewish community in Palestine.[98] On the one hand, the Council remained uncommitted to the commonwealth program and to specific aspects of "Zionist ideology"; on the other, it forfeited the type of organizational independence vis-à-vis Zionism which had painfully been achieved by the American Jewish Committee. Without winning a complete victory or obtaining an enthusiastic convert, Zionist leadership was at least assured that the organizational influence of the Council would not henceforth be marshalled against the Zionist cause.

SUMMARY AND CONCLUSIONS

The record of defense organization responses to the Zionist program reveals once again that the Zionist movement rose to the pinnacle of its influence in the American Jewish community both directly and indirectly. In some organizations, notably the American Jewish Congress and to a lesser extent B'nai B'rith, Zionists constituted the membership and leadership so completely that there was virtually no meaningful distinction between such groups and the Zionist political parties (ZOA and Hadassah, for example). In these cases, the needs of Zionism and Palestine provided appealing activities and interests which could be carried on as part of the groups' regular programs. Conversely, the aspirations of organized Zionist parties constantly derived strength from the concurrence and direct support of such allied and cooperating groups.

In other groups, such as the American Jewish Committee and the National Council of Jewish Women, the strategy of Zionist parties and their allies was directed primarily at influencing more affirmative responses to Zionist demands. Failing to enlist such groups behind an explicit avowal of all Zionist objectives (as contained in the Basle and later Biltmore Programs), they attempted to win approval for a few, such as free Jewish immigration and colonization in Palestine. At the very least, Zionists labored to "neutralize" these influential groups as serious rivals to Zionist demands and to prevent the appearance of articulate anti-Zionist expressions. When this was finally accomplished, such groups traveling part of the way with the Zionists lent the movement as a whole much of its *indirect* support and helped to legitimize the claims of Zionist leaders to hegemony in the Jewish community.

If we bear in mind the relative nature of what constitutes "Zionist victory," we may fairly state that the American Zionist movement achieved considerable success by the mid-forties in

lining up defense organizations as allies for its program, in preventing outspoken anti-Zionist opposition, and in countering such
a group as the American Jewish Committee, which insisted upon
"independent action." What proportion of the credit for this
emerging Zionist victory can be attributed to the skillful campaigns of the Zionists themselves (for example, propaganda against
the American Jewish Committee's "escapism" and the utilization
of Henry Monsky and B'nai B'rith in the American Jewish Conference), how much to the peculiar psychological bent of the
Zionists' opponents (the AJC's fear of "bad publicity" for the
Jews), and how much to responses to historic events (Arab riots,
the plight of the D. P.s, White Papers, Hitlerism), is a matter of
conjecture. Certainly all of these factors played some role as co-
determinants of the gradually emerging character of an American
Jewish community overwhelmingly inclined, regardless of the
motives involved, to support the Zionist program in Palestine.

6

zionism and jewish labor

COMPETING IDEOLOGIES OF THE
JEWISH LABOR MOVEMENT

The development of American Zionism clearly shows that various sectors of American Jewry, though ostensibly united by devotion to a common objective, whether religious expression or defense of Jewish rights, were poles apart in their receptivity to the Zionist program. Similarly, among the broad masses categorized loosely as "Jewish Labor," the appeal for a Jewish state met with varied responses ranging from enthusiastic assent to passionate rejection. With regard to ethnic origins and economic status, this grouping enjoyed comparative uniformity, but on ideological questions like Zionism, Jewish labor was as sharply divided as other religious and secular organizations.

The roots of this conflict lie deep in the Old World heritage of the Jewish community. Russian Jews, oppressed by the anti-Semitic policies of Czarist regimes, increasingly turned to various revolutionary programs for the solution of the "Jewish problem." Many of them, forerunners of members of the Communist party, assiduously denied concern with Jewish survival and resented any energies expended on activities other than the "class interests of the proletarian revolution." Some even looked forward to the day when the Jews would vanish as a distinct group in the aftermath of universal socialism. Other Marxists, organized into the General Alliance of Jewish Workers (Bund), proclaimed the existence of a specific "Jewish proletariat" and heralded the use of Yiddish and secular Jewish culture as important weapons for spreading Socialist doctrine among the working class Jewish community.[1]

Both Bundists and the undifferentiated Jewish Marxists rejected all movements not based upon the class struggle theories of their Socialist apostles. Zionism, obviously, was such a movement. With its primary tenet of Jews everywhere constituting "One People," Zionism could only be regarded, by Bundists and Bolsheviks alike, as a "sinister deviation from the true path . . . a mirage, compounded of religious romanticism and chauvinism." "Reactionary," "bourgeois," and "obscurantist," the Return to Zion was widely scorned as a diversionary threat to the best interests of the working class, interests which must be international, not national, in character.[2]

These same anti-Zionist and anti-nationalistic ideologies were carried into the sweatshops of American industry by the East European immigrants who arrived before the turn of the century. Traveling by a different road and impelled by a totally different motivation, the early leaders of American Jewish labor, notes C. Bezalel Sherman, arrived at the same conclusions as the Reform Jewish rabbinical authors of the Pittsburgh Platform of 1885, namely, that the Jews did not constitute a distinct people, and that mankind was standing on the threshold of a Utopia in which all men would be rid of human injustice. Accordingly, declared the first American conference of Jewish workers' organizations in 1890, seven years before the first World Zionist Congress: "We have no Jewish question in America. The only question we recognize is the question of how to prevent the emergence of 'Jewish questions' here. . . . The world is our fatherland, socialism our religion." [3] Joseph Schlossberg, one of the first major union leaders to embrace the Palestine dream, similarly recalls the wall of antagonism that greeted early Zionist efforts:

> Like the pioneers in the Palestine desert and swamps, the Jewish workers did pioneering work in the American industrial jungle, but they knew nothing of what their own kith and kin were doing in the Middle East. To the Jewish workers of America, Zionism was a hobby of the bourgeoisie. The abolition of capitalism was the great objective, and that meant the abolition of the sweatshop.[4]

Thus reasoned the class-conscious and often Jewishly-alienated leadership which early came to dominate the great clothing industry trade unions (for example, International Ladies' Garment Workers Union and Amalgamated Clothing Workers) and the socialist fraternal order Workmen's Circle (Arbeiter Ring). Drawn largely from origins in northern Russia, Poland and Lithuania, this leadership ardently espoused anti-Zionist, anti-capitalist and anti-religious philosophies with almost equal facility. Strong proponents of labor solidarity, they established close ties with the general American labor movement and therein came to be considered the legitimate representatives of approximately half a million Jewish workers.

As economic opportunities narrowed and physical assaults on Jewish life and property mounted, broad masses of East European Jews, particularly from the pogrom-ridden Ukraine, flowed into the United States at the rate of 100,000 persons per year. Zionism, having swept eastern Europe after the first Zionist Congress, was a movement of great attraction among these newer arrivals; the appeal to unite with fellow Jews in the cause of Jewish national rebirth vastly outweighed the exhortations of their Bundist union leaders to "crush the exploiting Jewish bourgeoisie."

Jewish labor leadership's divergence from the ideals and aspirations of the rank and file produced a striking feature of Jewish trade unions before 1910: the seeming inability of the workers to remain organized in times of industrial peace. This recurring event, noted by many historians of the American labor movement, has been interpreted as a spontaneous reaction on the part of the Jewish masses to the irreligious and assimilationist policies of their leadership. The rank and file, "too raw, too inexperienced, too bewildered and too immature politically" to oppose their leaders openly, resisted in the only way they knew how —by dropping out of the unions as soon as strikes were terminated. By contrast, the *landsmanschaften* and fraternal orders, composed of Jews from essentially the same social stratum, thrived with orientations that were pro-Zionist and sympathetic to religion.[5]

To be sure, pro-Zionist expressions among the rank and file were not limited to passive non-cooperation in the Bundist-led unions. Unable to express their Palestinian interests in existing labor groups, New York workers founded the first Labor Zionist group, the National Radical Verein Poale Zion, following the Kishinev pogroms of 1903. Six years later, the Jewish Socialist Labor Party (Poale Zion) was formed in Chicago and, in 1912, a

Zionist fraternal order—Jewish National Workers' Alliance (Farband)—was established to rival the Bundist-dominated Workmen's Circle. (Arbeiter Ring).[6]

Despite dissatisfaction with existing labor leadership on the part of Socialist-Zionist workers, the anti-Zionist union chieftains reigned largely unchallenged until the dramatic issuance of the Balfour Declaration kindled Jewish hopes for a Palestine reborn.[7] But even then organized and widespread labor support for the Zionist cause was not at hand. The international sanction given to the Zionist goal might have led the average Jewish worker in 1918 to realize that Zionism was not the "reactionary dream" he had been told it was,[8] but the channelling of pro-Zionist sympathies into usable political power had not yet been accomplished. Genuine Jewish labor unity on the Palestine question may truly be said to date only from the eve of the State of Israel's birth in 1948.

Much of Jewish labor continued to stand aloof from the Zionist effort during the twenties.[9] Absorbed in the struggle to win economic security in their new homes, they had little effort to spare for the work then in progress in Palestine. But while the unionist masses remained detached, their leadership never ceased to belabor the "Zionist reactionary menace." The *Jewish Daily Forward,* spokesman for the Bundist-led proletariat, consistently sided with "bourgeois" non-Zionist financiers and philanthropists like Felix Warburg and Louis Marshall in their efforts to colonize Jews in the Soviet Union's Biro-Bidjan project in preference to supporting Zionist settlement schemes in Palestine. Thus, Left and Right joined to combat the Zionist program; "rarely did politics make stranger bedfellows." [10]

THE "GEWERKSCHAFTEN" CAMPAIGN FOR PALESTINE

Not every Jewish labor leader closed his eyes to the Palestine experiment, however. As early as 1923, American Jewish trade unionists were enlisted in aid of the Histadrut, the General Federation of Jewish Labor in Palestine, the first trade union in the Middle East. On purely "humanitarian grounds," Max Pine, Secretary of the United Hebrew Trades, agreed to head a labor fund for the promotion of trade unionism in Palestine. Dubbed the "Gewerkschaften" campaign (from the Yiddish for United Hebrew Trades), this philanthropic venture gradually enlisted the support and interest of union after union, leader after leader, Jew and non-Jew alike.

Non-Zionist efforts to limit labor's aid for Palestine to purely financial channels soon proved futile. Zionist propaganda exalting the key role of the Histadrut gradually led up to an analysis of the "Jewish problem in its entirety"; Jews became familiar not only with the Histadrut but also with the entire range of Zionist activities in Palestine. Access to Jewish labor was thus partially gained through a fund-raising mechanism; Zionist positions on immigration, land acquisition and cooperative life soon became common currency in trade union parlance.[11] Years of ideological opposition to Zionism were in this manner gradually worn away by the practical task of providing funds and moral support for a dynamic Palestinian trade union movement which was to grow from a mere 23,000 workers in 1923 to 175,000 by the mid-forties —three-fourths of all the Jewish workers in Palestine.

Spurred on by the plight of European Jewry at the hands of Hitler and various fascist regimes, on the one hand, and by glowing tributes to Labor Palestine from visiting American delegations, on the other, *Gewerkschaften* (renamed National Committee for Labor Palestine in 1936) markedly increased its penetration of labor groups year by year. In its first campaign of 1923–24, solicitations were conducted in 63 communities and $51,000 was raised. Gradually, however, over 500 localities were involved in the drive until $3,365,000 was collected in 1948. Contrasted with the 360 delegates from 158 organizations who came to the 1926 *Gewerkschaften* convention, 3,012 delegates representing 1,012 organizations attended a similar assembly in 1944. In addition, another 2,000 organizations had become affiliated with the annual campaigns to which over 150,000 individuals and numerous organizations, both Jewish and non-Jewish, contributed. Special divisions of the campaign operated in the United Hebrew Trades, Ladies Garment, Amalgamated Clothing, United Hat, Furriers, Typesetters, Printers, Pocketbook Workers and Bakers unions, Pioneer Women's Organization, Poale Zion Party, Jewish National Workers' Alliance, Left Poale Zion Party, League for Labor Palestine, the youth movements of Hechalutz, Habonim, Hashomer Hatzair, more than four hundred branches of Workmen's Circle, and over two thousand *landsmanschaften* and local societies. No other organization faintly approached the campaign's comprehensive coverage of the American Jewish labor community.[12]

Meanwhile, distinctive Labor Zionist organizations, bolstered by the writings of Palestinian theoreticians (Berl Katznelson, Ber Borochov, A. D. Gordon, and others), were advancing a synthesis of Zionism and Socialism among the Jewish masses. Though never very prominent numerically,[13] Labor Zionist groups provided American Zionism with steadfast political support, generous financial contributions, and a unique perspective of looking at Palestine as a dynamic, progressive and idealistic entity. In fact, it may be the achievements of Labor Palestine—agricultural collectives and cooperatives, reclamation of the desert, draining of malarial swamps, educational and medical services of Histadrut, and so forth—which provided the greatest attractions for American sympathizers, regardless of their Zionist party or independent affiliation. Indeed, Labor Zionism virtually permeated the entire Yiddish press, commanded the admiration of the American rabbinate, and called forth wide support in the multi-party Zionist Organization of America.[14]

THE JEWISH LABOR COMMITTEE

Zionist efforts to attract organized Jewish labor to its cause did not stop at the promotion of *Gewerkschaften* campaigns or at the erection of separate Labor Zionist organizations. Hand in hand with these efforts to influence Jewish labor opinion others aimed at acquiring the overt support of "the official voice of Jewish workmen"—the Jewish Labor Committee. Formed in 1934 as an outgrowth of the AFL Labor Chest to aid labor victims of Fascism, the JLC, by 1942, represented three international unions (International Ladies' Garment Workers, Amalgamated Clothing Workers, and United Hat, Cap and Millinery Workers), 116 locals, the fraternal order of Workmen's Circle, and 765 other labor groups, a total Jewish membership of almost 500,000.[15] Advocating a program of "international labor unity" and representing units of both the AFL and CIO, the Jewish Labor Committee claimed, and by and large was accorded, the unique distinction of speaking for the totality of Jewish workmen.

The legitimacy of a distinct Jewish-American labor movement had long been recognized in the larger councils of American labor. In view of the marked predominance of Jews in unions of the clothing industry, a specific "Jewish labor bloc" with interests in the problems of anti-Semitism, refugees and Palestine was considered appropriate by non-Jewish labor leaders. Other cultural or national groups—Italians, Negroes, Irish—had also long been accorded this status.

To this scene of pluralistic tolerance of "Jewish unionism," the Jewish Labor Committee came not as a successor and substitute, but as a coordinator of opinion. If Jewish interests were not adequately served by the demands of the Labor Committee, important "Jewish unions"—the ILGWU, Amalgamated and Hatters —and prominent Jewish labor leaders—David Dubinsky, Sidney Hillman, Max Zaritsky, Jacob Potofsky and Joseph Schlossberg— were available. Their views on Jewish problems were certain to command an audience and respect in the general labor movement independent of the JLC. Thus, from its inception, the loosely federated JLC moved slowly on controversial matters, aware of its dependence on a heterogeneous constituency, watchful of potential internal conflicts.

Moreover, the Jewish Labor Committee's claim to represent "Jewish labor" was increasingly undermined by three sociological facts (not to mention the continuous attacks of its arch-rivals, the Jewish Communists): (1) Jews rapidly vacated their places in industry to more recent non-Jewish immigrants in order to take up white-collar, commercial and professional occupations—"Jewish unions" were not really Jewish any more. (2) Like the Labor Zionists, the composition of such "proletarian" groups as the Workmen's Circle increasingly shifted from laborers to small shopkeepers and proprietors. (3) A large proportion of the Jews who remained in industry became labor leaders and management operators rather than manual workers. Thus, both the terms "Jewish" and "labor" were subject to important qualifications. Evidence is supplied by the following data taken from the American Jewish Committee's study, *Jewish Labor in the United States:* [16]

TABLE 14. Jews in the American Labor Force

YEAR	PERCENT OF RUSSIAN JEWS IN MANUFACTURING	PERCENT WHO WERE EMPLOYEES	PERCENT OF MEN'S CLOTHING WORKERS WHO WERE JEWISH
1900	60	96	—
1913	—	—	80
1934	14	63	—
1950	—	—	25–30

Despite this multi-faceted change in the Jewish occupational structure, the Labor Committee assumed a prominent position in the Jewish community. Dedicated to the belief that "Jewish problems cannot be isolated and can be solved only upon recognition everywhere of the rights of Jews to unqualified citizenship," the JLC became a fourth Jewish "defense organization" (the others: B'nai B'rith, American Jewish Committee and American Jewish Congress). In cooperation with them, the Labor Committee participated in numerous anti-Nazi demonstrations, supported the economic boycott of German goods, rescued labor leaders from the holocaust of Europe, and generally participated in a broad range of overlapping and supplementary activities designed to combat anti-Semitism and discrimination and to promote the best interests of the Jewish people.[17]

Concerning Zionism, the JLC traditionally remained aloof from all "political representations" in behalf of a Jewish Palestine. Even though many of its local constituents actively supported the *Gewerkschaften* campaign and adopted pro-Zionist resolutions, the JLC was widely regarded as a Bundist-dominated national organization. Official expressions of Committee opinion and editorials in the Committee-dominated *Jewish Daily Forward* were notably cool toward Zionist activities in America, although they not infrequently lauded the constructive tasks of Jewish labor in Palestine.[18] In practice, however, the JLC joined with virtually the whole of American Jewry in lending valuable assistance to Zionist objectives by protesting the anti-Jewish discriminations of the White Paper of 1939.[19]

As the plight of European Jewry worsened, the JLC came under increasing popular pressure to participate in a common program of Jewish action. Although invited by B'nai B'rith's Henry Monsky to participate in a conference of thirty-four national organizations on postwar Jewish problems, including Palestine, it declined to send representatives. There followed several months of stormy internal discussions in which the Committee's leadership sought a position on Palestine acceptable to both the Bundists and Zionists represented in its National Executive. Finally, the Committee adhered to the anxiously awaited convocation of American Jewry in the American Jewish Conference.[20]

At the Conference, JLC spokesman Israel H. Goldberg revealed the group's program relating to Palestine, emphasizing that the national leadership made no attempt to commit its constituents to a final position on Palestine. JLC policy was to "find only points of agreement and avoid those of disagreement among our own constituents." [21] Accordingly, the Committee felt able to proclaim to the assembled representatives of American Jewry:

> We declare our solidarity with organized Jewish labor in Palestine and its demands regarding Jewish immigration into and colonization in Palestine.

> We demand the immediate annulment of the White Paper and the guarantee of free Jewish immigration, land purchase and colonization in Palestine.[22]

The JLC would not go farther than this. On the controversial Palestine resolution calling for the creation of a Jewish commonwealth, it registered an official abstention, "because there is no unanimity among its membership on this question." [23]

Succeeding weeks found the Jewish press alarmed over rumored conflicts on the Zionist issue within the Labor Committee. Strengthened by the American Jewish Committee's secession from the American Jewish Conference, "die-hard" Bundists in the group were allegedly urging the JLC to follow suit. Pro-Zionists in the Jewish Labor Committee were equally insistent on a policy of greater cooperation with the mass of American Jewry through the instrumentality of the Conference. Eventually, a compromise was reached which reflected this lack of organizational solidarity: the JLC agreed to remain within the American Jewish Conference and to participate in the Commissions on Rescue and Post-War Reconstruction, but it simultaneously boycotted the Interim Committee, the Conference executive organ, and the Commission on Palestine charged with implementation of the Jewish commonwealth resolution.[24] Continuing to walk a tightrope between Bundists and Zionists, the Committee thereafter extended something less than full support to the Zionist-oriented Conference.

On the basis of the nearly unanimous pro-Zionist declaration of the American Jewish Conference, the Zionist political offensive aimed at non-Jewish Americans now went into full operation. Because the JLC was still unavailable as a forum for presenting Zionist demands to the general labor movement, Zionist members of Committee constituents organized a new vehicle. Under the chairmanship of President Max Zaritsky of the United Hatters, and with CIO and AFL Presidents Philip Murray and William Green as honorary chairmen, the American Jewish Trade Union Committee for Palestine was formed in the spring of 1944. Almost immediately the new group, claiming to represent "hundreds of thousands of organized Jewish workers in the United States" in both major labor federations, endorsed the full gamut of Zionist demands for the "ultimate reconstitution of Palestine as a free and democratic Jewish Commonwealth," for the abrogation of the White Paper of 1939, and for the passage of the pro-Zionist Wright-Compton Congressional resolutions.[25]

Unable to elicit pro-Zionist sanction from the Jewish Labor Committee, American Zionist leadership had at least prevented the influential group from following the independent, non-Zionist course pursued by the American Jewish Committee. With the Laborites neutralized inside the Conference, along with other non-Zionist groups, The American Jewish Trade Union Committee for Palestine began to line up Jewish and non-Jewish labor support for a Jewish commonwealth. The Jewish Labor Committee was thus bypassed; Zionists went on to obtain substantial political support.

After the Second Session of the American Jewish Conference in December, 1944, however, the Jewish Labor Committee once again emerged to assume a position of crucial importance for Zionist objectives. The admission of the Jewish People's Fraternal Order, the Communist-dominated Jewish section of the International Workers' Order, at this meeting profoundly shocked the staunchly anti-Stalinist Labor Committee. Notified that the Conference Interim Committee had voted 20-5 on August 1, 1944, to recommend membership for the JPFO, the National Executive of the Labor Committee declared that it would not participate in the forthcoming Conference session since the Conference seemed to be entering into a partnership with the Communists. Prevailed upon to state its objections against the JPFO to the General Committee of the Conference, the Laborites dispatched four vice-chairmen to protest the admission of the "Communist-front" group.[26]

The initial spokesmen for the Committee, P. L. Goldman, avowed that the admission of the Order was not, as some had charged, a convenient excuse for the JLC to leave the Conference, although, he admitted, "I will not say that there are not in the Jewish Labor Committee elements that would like to get out of the Conference for other reasons."

Isidore Nagler, a second spokesman and a prominent Zionist, declared that the admission of the Communist JPFO would produce a "profound reaction" on the part of the AFL and that the Committee could not, therefore, work with a group whose openly stated intention was the "penetration and destruction of the trade unions." Recalling the Palestinian Communist party's record of abetting Arab "revolutionists" in their rioting against the Jewish colonists, and reminding the General Committee of his own role in the formation of the American Jewish Trade Union Committee for Palestine, which in turn had done so much to induce state labor federations and the central labor bodies to adopt resolutions favoring a Jewish commonwealth, Nagler pleaded with the Zionist majority on the Conference General Committee not to harm the JLC, which was "composed of trade unionists who are heart and soul with our [Zionist] movement." [27]

Notwithstanding these arguments of the Committee's delegation, an "overwhelming majority" of the American Jewish Conference, motivated, no doubt, by eloquent testimony to the effect that the Conference should provide a forum for all Jews without respect to ideology, voted to confer membership upon the leftist Jewish People's Fraternal Order. Despite numerous appeals to JLC leadership to "be democratic" and to accept the majority decision of the Jewish community, the Labor Committee thereupon seceded from the Conference. Once again, the JLC followed the precedent set by the leading non-Zionist organization, the American Jewish Committee.[28]

As in the American Jewish Committee's alleged "breach of

Jewish unity" and "betrayal of Jewish welfare" in 1943, the Labor Committee's secession precipitated a vehement Zionist propaganda offensive and a campaign of vilification from the pro-Zionist Yiddish press. This widespread condemnation intensified when it was learned that the "proletarian" Laborites would join with the "bourgeois" American Jewish Committee and the "clerical" Agudas Israel in a non-Zionist united front as consultants to the State Department at the forthcoming United Nations Conference on International Organization in San Francisco.[29]

With the Zionist-led United Hatters Union already committed to a pro-Zionist platform, Sidney Hillman's Amalgamated Clothing Workers, the second of the JLC's "Big Three" international unions, breached the Labor Committee's non-Zionist position by adopting a forthright demand for the establishment of a Jewish commonwealth.[30] Rumors also abounded that Hillman intended removing the Amalgamated from the JLC, partially over dissatisfaction with the latter's failure to adopt a more pro-Palestine policy.[31]

Rank and file repudiation of the JLC "neutralism" also came from another source, the pro-Soviet Trade Union Committee for Jewish Unity, formed on March 3, 1945 by 85 delegates from 51 trade union organizations representing "tens of thousands of Jewish members." This body immediately announced its intention of countering "the destructive anti-unity role of the Jewish Labor Committee, the self-anointed spokesman for Jewish workers," and promptly applied for admission to the American Jewish Conference, charging that "had the Jewish Labor Committee given those workers they so badly misrepresent an opportunity to vote on the question, the overwhelming majority would have voted to remain within the Conference." [32] At the same time, the Committee for Jewish Unity petitioned the American and British governments for the abrogation of the White Paper of 1939 and demanded that an end "be put to Jewish wandering and . . . every Jew that so desires be entitled to enter Palestine as of right and to settle among his own people there." [33]

Events on the international scene moved swiftly. By 1947 some plan for the partition of Palestine was widely expected in diplomatic circles. Faced with a need to make some definite choice, and with virtually every sector of the Jewish community rallying to support proposals for a Jewish state, the JLC suddenly shifted its tactics from a position of "neutralism" to one of vigorous support for the demands of the Zionist-dominated Jewish Agency for Palestine and aggressively rallied opinion behind proposals for the Jewish state-to-be, largely by utilizing its extensive contacts with labor groups both here and abroad. Thereafter, when the partition of Palestine had been approved by the United Nations General Assembly, JLC President Adolph Held publicly proclaimed: "I am proud that throughout the deliberations on the Palestine problem in the United Nations, the J.L.C. cooperated fully with the Jewish Agency." [34]

THE AMERICAN LABOR MOVEMENT

We may also conveniently examine at this point the special role played by the general American labor movement. No attempt will be made to catalog the numerous pro-Zionist resolutions adopted by the two great labor federations, the national unions and many state and local labor councils and federations. But from a cursory view of labor documents, to say that Zionist sympathies enjoyed extensive support from American labor is obviously a gross understatement. The American Federation of Labor, for example, frequently boasted of being among the earliest endorsers of the Balfour Declaration and, thereafter, of giving vigilant and forceful aid to the cause of a Jewish national home.[35] The Congress of Industrial Organizations, too, especially after 1944, became a steadfast friend of the Zionist movement.[36] In fact, while the presidents of the two organizations, William Green and Philip Murray, were not on speaking terms, they frequently appeared together on the same platform in support of the Histadrut and the Zionist program in Palestine.[37]

Other prominent labor leaders as well gave their personal approval to petitions, declarations, and programs upholding the Zionist platform. By way of illustration, the initial proclamation of The American Jewish Trade Union Committee for Palestine, calling upon American labor to rally for a Jewish commonwealth, bore the names not only of Green and Murray as Honorary Chairmen, but also of Honorary Vice-Chairmen James B. Carey, Secretary-Treasurer, CIO; William Collins, New York State Representative, AFL; Edward Flore, Vice-President, AFL; George M. Harrison, Grand President, Brotherhood of Railway and Steamship Clerks; James McDevitt, President, Pennsylvania State Federation of Labor; George Meany, Secretary-Treasurer, AFL; Thomas Murray, President, New York State Federation of Labor; Thomas Murtha, President, New York City Central Trades and Labor Council; Rolland J. Thomas, International President, United Automobile Workers, CIO; and Matthew Woll, Vice-President, AFL.[38] The impact of such universal endorsement on Zionist aspirations is difficult to gauge, but that organized American labor provided the Zionist movement with a useful political alliance cannot be questioned.

THE JEWISH BURO OF THE COMMUNIST PARTY, U.S.A.

Data is lacking on the occupational composition of the Jewish Buro of the Communist Party, U.S.A. Communist reactions to the Zionist program may conveniently be treated here, however, since their tactics were so largely directed at infiltrating the ranks of Jewish labor.

Direct Jewish membership in the American Communist party never exceeded several thousand persons [39] and, therefore, it may be assumed that the erratic course of Communist reactions to the Zionist program exerted relatively little influence on the American Jewish community as a whole. Certainly the bitterly anti-Stalinist Bundists, who in such great measure led the Jewish Labor Committee and Workmen's Circle, were not swayed one way or the other by official pronunciamentos emanating from the Jewish Buro of the Central Committee of the CPUSA.

The record of American Communists on Palestine and Zionism is a complicated tale of radical shifts in direction, obviously occasioned by the transitory goals of current Soviet foreign policy. While it would not be profitable to trace the entire span of Communist thinking on the Zionist question, which in any case cannot be fully understood without a lengthy treatment of Soviet foreign policy and the actions of the Palestinian Communist party, certain

Communist declarations will serve to illustrate the kaleidoscopic nature of the Communist "Party line" on Palestine.

At the outset it should be noted that Zionism's fundamental thesis—"The Jews Are One People"—clashes sharply with Marxist assumptions of ineradicable class antagonisms. Furthermore, according to Stalin's development of a Marxist theory of nationality, the scattered and heterogeneous Jews fall far short of many of the attributes necessary for the constitution of a national state. Given these definite ideological tenets, it is not surprising that the dominant flavor of Communist thinking vis-à-vis Zionism was one of scorn and contempt. Thus the *New Masses* of February 19, 1935, declared that Jewish revolutionists had never ceased to regard Zionism as "detrimental to the interests of the Jewish masses" because:

> Zionism is a tool of British imperialism which needs Palestine for its own purposes;
>
> Zionism is dispossessing the Arab peasants and is conducting a colonization by conquest with the aid of British bayonets;
>
> No nation can solve its problems by emigrating to another country, even if Palestine were not so small and so thickly populated;
>
> Zionism draws away the attention of the Jewish masses from the problems of the countries where they live;
>
> Zionism separates them from the masses of other nationalities; As a chauvinist movement it is a breeding ground for fascism.[40]

Communists and Zionists were at constant odds during the thirties, the former accusing the "bourgeois reactionaries" of diverting attention from the "revolutionary struggle," while the latter charged the Moscow-dominated Jewish Buro of the CPUSA with diverting attention from Zionism to "grandiose" colonization schemes in Soviet Biro-Bidjan. Moreover, the ire of world Jewry was widely kindled by the disclosure that Arab rioting in 1936–39 had been incited by Communists, who characterized the bloody disturbances as "revolutions against reactionary imperialism." [41]

This general tenor of Communist denunciations of Zionism continued until the Soviet Union became locked in deathly encounter with Nazi Germany. Then, impelled by the urgency to unite every Jewish force "on a common people's platform of Jewish unity, as part of American national unity, against the main enemy," [42] Jewish Communists moderated their attack on Zionist "national chauvinism." A leading Communist, Alex Bittelman, announced that Communists now held Palestine in high regard since Palestinian Jewry constituted "an important part of our people— a community which is building an organized, national life in that part of the world." American Communists also believed that Jews should support the Zionist demands for a Jewish Palestinian army in order that they might participate in the war "as a free and organized national community." On the other hand, Zionist ideology was still rejected since it was "only one tendency among many in Jewish social life—a tendency which has its own philosophy on the nature of Jewishness and which conducts its own policy as a party on the question of Palestine." Finally, stressing that Communists believed they could work jointly with the Zionists in those trying days, Bittelman praised the efforts of American Zionists and the nationalistic American Jewish Congress to achieve "people's unity" in the Jewish community.[43]

An even closer *rapprochement* with international Zionism was attempted by Bittelman the following year (1944) when he pledged complete Communist support for efforts to abrogate the restrictive 1939 White Paper. At the same time, he warned against "giving this struggle a strict Zionist form," since such partisan efforts would only militate against the essential task of constructing a "united front" to oppose fascism. Pledging that the party would urge "the Jewish workers of America to render all possible support to the Yishuv [Jewish community in Palestine] and to the Histadruth," he castigated his Socialist opponents ("emigré Bundists") in the Jewish Labor Committee and *Jewish Daily Forward,* for attempting to "engineer a new anti-Zionist crusade" in the United States. These "quisling maneuvers must be defeated for the good of the Yishuv and for the good of Jewish unity in America," urged Bittelman. He concluded with a forceful plea for Jewish unity: "Let us go forward with all consistent anti-fascists, Communists and non-Communists, Zionists and non-Zionists, Socialists and non-party workers—to victory." [44]

Thus, the "line" of American Jewish Communists had veered a considerable distance from its original unconditional rejection of the Zionist goal. With Nazi Germany vanquished and a mighty Soviet Union eager to intrude itself into the troubled waters of the Middle East, few observers were surprised to learn that American

Communists, while not approving Zionism, were thenceforth to join the Soviet-approved bandwagon for the establishment of the Jewish national home. Read the resolution of the July, 1945, CPUSA convention:

> Support the just demands of the Jewish people for the immediate abrogation by the British Government of the imperialist White Paper and for the rebuilding of a Jewish National Homeland in a free and democratic Palestine in collaboration with the Arab people, on the basis of the unanimous agreement of the "Big Three" in the Near East.[45]

SUMMARY AND CONCLUSIONS

Zionists presented their demands to a Jewish labor community predominantly disposed to the Marxist, and hence anti-Zionist, philosophy of East European Bundism. Failing initially to evoke the desired support of their goals, Zionists resorted to a variety of techniques designed to secure eventual labor adherence to the Zionist program. The most prominent of these was counter-organization was resorted to once again in the creation of The Bundist-dominated associations (Jewish National Workers' Alliance *vs.* Workmen's Circle). Zionists also erected "umbrella organizations" broad enough to include both Zionists and anti-Zionists, notably the *Gewerkschaften* campaign for the Histadrut, which gave Zionists a popular platform from which to sing the praises of a Jewish Palestine based on labor ideology. Zionists, furthermore, worked within existing labor groups, such as unions and the Jewish Labor Committee, and gradually assumed a prominent, if not entirely dominant, position in them. Counter-organization was resorted to once again in the creation of the American Jewish Trade Union Committee for Palestine, which realized many of the Zionist aims otherwise unobtainable through the Jewish Labor Committee.

The influence of external factors upon the changing fortunes of Zionist aspirations in the United States may be inferred from labor's keen awareness of the fate of its brethren in Nazi-occupied Europe, a fate likely to produce greater tolerance for the work of rescue being performed in Palestine. More directly, the example

of a dynamic Labor Palestine, inspired by the social service activities of the Histadrut labor movement, clearly had an effect on the
thinking of Jewish laborites.

The fact that the Jewish labor movement provided no effective organized opposition to the Zionist program in the mid-
forties, despite its earlier active hostility, cannot, however, be attributed entirely to Zionist operations and the positive external
influences deriving from Europe and Palestine. Also to be considered was the fact that the labor movement, particularly as
"coordinated" by the Jewish Labor Committee, was internally
divided in leadership and outlook. Cherishing its standing with
the general labor movement above all else, the JLC's leadership
studiously avoided taking any stand on Zionism which might
result in rival labor factions presenting opposing views on Palestine to the great AFL and CIO labor federations. At all costs the
"united interest of Jewish labor" must be maintained.

Under the circumstances, a policy of benevolent neutrality
toward Zionism was the most that Zionist laborites could achieve
without splitting the labor movement asunder. Here, as in the
struggle within Reform Judaism, Zionists apparently took what
they could get without risking the possibility that a too-militant
stand would precipitate the organization of an aggressively anti-
Zionist labor organization. Thus, laborites so disposed could participate in the *Gewerkschaften* campaign and in The American
Jewish Trade Union Committee for Palestine without incurring
the official wrath of Bundists in positions of JLC leadership. Both
Reform's Pittsburgh Platform anti-Zionism and Jewish labor's
early Bundist credos were effectively bypassed or neutralized. It
is interesting to note, however, that where the apparently secondary or peripheral issue of Zionism, as represented by continued
adherence of the Jewish Labor Committee to the American Jewish
Conference, collided with a more central issue on which all
factions of the JLC were agreed—anti-Communism—Zionist sympathies were subordinated. The JLC, accordingly, risked Jewish
popular disapproval occasioned by its secession from the American
Jewish Conference in order to maintain its organizational stature
with the anti-Communist general labor movement.

Thus, by 1947, American Jewish labor presented the spectacle
of a virtually united front regarding Zionist aspirations in Palestine. Labor Zionists expressed their sentiments through their own

Zionist parties, fraternal orders, fund-raising campaigns, and through The American Jewish Trade Union Committee for Palestine. Many formerly antagonistic Bundist groups, notably Workmen's Circle chapters, also enthusiastically supported the Trade Union Committee for Palestine and the *Gewerkschaften* campaign. Jewish labor's annual fund-raising drive for Palestine, consequently, was able to increase its collections thirteen fold within a decade. That there were still Bundist ideological objectors to Zionism cannot be denied. Yet the fact remains that no articulate labor indictment of the Zionist program reached the general American public after 1946. Like other sectors of the American Jewish community, Jewish labor and its allies in the general labor movement were mobilized for political activity as the question of Palestine's fate approached a fateful decision in the arena of international politics. If not thoroughly "Zionized" in membership and conviction, the American Jewish labor movement nevertheless rendered important material support for Zionist objectives.[46]

7

zionism
and christian america

THE POLITICAL USE OF
REFERENCE GROUPS

Any effort to document the building of Zionist strength from among the reservoir of potential American supporters must do more than trace the emergence of increasingly pro-Zionist postures on the part of virtually every major Jewish organization in the years preceding the birth of Israel. Attention must also be directed at non-Jewish (or what Zionists preferred to call "Christian") reactions to Zionist aspirations. This is so not only because the mobilization of non-Jewish notables in behalf of their program was a conscious objective of Zionist leaders but also because Zionist strivings with non- and anti-Zionist Jews cannot be abstracted from the total environment of the majority, non-Jewish culture. Indeed, aside from the direct value of non-Jewish contributions to the achievement of Zionist political goals, a challenging question may be raised: Could Zionism have mobilized American Jewry without the active support and encouragement of prominent non-Jews?

Sociological theory and common observation both aver that large sections of every minority group are oriented in their daily lives and values toward the dominant, majority culture rather than toward their own groups. Thus, the "anti-Semitic Jew," or what Kurt Lewin more adequately termed the "self-hating Jew," [1] is familiar to any student of Jewish affairs. With so many Jews haunted by minority-group feelings of inferiority vis-à-vis the possibly more attractive and rewarding reference groups of their Christian neighbors, the reactions of non-Jews to the Zionist program were matters of no small concern in determining the ultimate stand of American Jewry on the Zionist question. In fact, prominent non-Jewish supporters of a Jewish state may be said to have mattered considerably more than similarly situated Jews. Not only could a Christian Zionist make his own financial, moral, or political contribution to the Zionist cause, but his example would serve as a potent influence on that considerable body of American Jews who feared any Jewish move likely to prove distasteful or ill-advised to the non-Jewish majority. To put it another way, since many Jews were eager to identify themselves with the values of the Christian community, Zionism would find Jewish support in the measure that it first won non-Jewish converts to its program.

No matter how effectively Zionist leadership proclaimed its superior morale based upon a "positive philosophy" of Jewish survival and cultural creativity, and no matter how insistently it chided "fear-obsessed" and "timid" non-Zionists (especially those in the American Council for Judaism and, before 1946, in the leadership of the American Jewish Committee) for a too-frequent attention to what non-Jews thought of Zionism, the leaders of American Zionism never completely ignored the need for mobilizing "Christian America" in behalf of a Jewish Palestine. This is not to imply that Zionists operated consciously from a base of social psychological evidence. But, just as Theodor Herzl was keenly aware of the necessity of winning pro-Zionist testimonials from Christian princes and kings as a forerunner to effective work among skeptical Jews, Zionist leaders regularly called for a "systematic program of enlightenment among non-Jews." [2]

NON-JEWISH ORGANIZATIONS AND EFFORTS FOR PALESTINE

Scholars have often observed that widespread American Christian interest in the Jewish Restoration to Palestine preceded the development of the modern Zionist movement by many decades. Recent studies have dealt with one or another aspect of this Christian interest in the early twentieth-century period, culminating with the Congressional Resolution on Palestine of 1922.[3]

Following the Arab riots of 1929, Zionists made several abortive attempts to channel long-standing Christian sympathy for Jewish aspiration in Palestine into political support for the movement. At the behest of the noted Chicago Zionist leader Judge Julian Mack, Rev. Charles Edward Russell formed a Pro-Palestine Federation of America in Chicago in January, 1930. Combining a Pro-Palestine declaration with a platform of Christian-Jewish good will and anti-prejudice education, the Federation succeeded in enrolling many notable Christian clergymen.[4] Another Christian organization, the American Palestine Committee, formed in May, 1932, listed an even more illustrious membership on its letterhead. Headed by Senator William King of Utah, the Committee had as its honorary chairmen Vice-President Charles Curtis, Senator William E. Borah (Chairman, Senate Foreign Relations Committee), and Senator Claude E. Swanson (the ranking minority member of the same committee). Other public luminaries initially included were the Senate minority leader, Secretary of Agriculture, Assistant Secretary of State, Assistant Attorney-General, Solicitor-General of the State Department, Assistant Commissioner of Education, Assistant Commissioner of Reclamation, ten senators, and eighteen representatives.[5]

Despite this impressive roster of supporters and sponsors, Christian Zionist activities were less than wholeheartedly supported by official Zionist leadership. While Zionist periodicals of 1933 carried news of the merger of all existing Christian Zionist groups into a new Pro-Palestine Federation and, consequently, predicted great increases in non-Jewish support for Zionism, Zionist leaders were inwardly less sanguine. Writing to the World Zionist Organization's London Office early in 1934, Morris Rothenberg, president of the Zionist Organization of America, noted that the ZOA had "from time to time, utilized non-Jewish agencies in connection with our political work," but conceded that the new Pro-Palestine Federation was "largely a paper organization concentrated in the person of Mr. [A. Ben] Elias." Aside from a few creditable, albeit sporadic, issues of the *Pro-Palestine Herald,* Rothenberg considered the work of the Federation "negligible." Under the circumstances, he informed London, the ZOA could not support "either Mr. Elias or his methods of procedure." [6]

But even without official American Zionist support, the Pro-Palestine Federation proceeded independently to take such actions as would strengthen the hand of world Zionism. Following the advent of Hitler to power, the Federation addressed Prime Minister Baldwin in the name of "the consensus of enlightened Christian American opinion" and asked that the gates of Palestine be thrown open to receive "the victimized and persecuted Jews escaping from the European holocaust." Declaring that the "restoration of the Land of Israel to the Children of Israel is the guiding star in this great struggle for a better world and a better humanity," the signatories expressed their steadfast devotion to the creation of the Jewish national homeland.[7] Moreover, when in the wake of the Arab riots of 1936, British authorities threatened to curtail Jewish immigration, Christian Zionists promptly convened an "American Christian Conference on Palestine," which voiced its indignant disapproval of any departure from the League of Nations Mandate for Palestine guaranteeing Jewish immigration.[8] Subsequent meetings endorsed the full demands of the Zionist movement in urging Great Britain to cease obstructing Jewish settlement, to restore Transjordania to the areas intended for Jewish colonization, and so forth. In these demands, the Pro-Palestine Federation, headed by Russell, claimed to speak in the name of hundreds of Catholic and Protestant clergymen, cabinet officials, labor leaders, governors, college presidents, professors, and mayors.[9]

Again, when rumors of a proposal to stop Jewish immigration into Palestine spread throughout America in 1938, Christian supporters rallied to the defense of the Zionist cause. Several days after the formation of the Zionist National Emergency Committee on Palestine, a "Provisional Committee on Palestine Policy," organized by 36 lay and clerical leaders, seconded Christian Zionist protestations to Prime Minister Chamberlain. In addition, the Pro-Palestine Federation even went so far as to urge the United States government to intercede directly in Palestinian affairs,[10] thus ignoring the long-standing Zionist procedure of appealing directly to British governments without involving American officialdom. Other organizations, among them the National Council of Catholic Men and the Federal Council of Churches of Christ in America, subsequently endorsed this appeal. Similarly, a petition inaugurated by the *ad hoc* Zionist National Emergency Committee on Palestine and signed by 51 senators, 154 representatives, and 30 governors urged President Roosevelt to take action to eliminate British obstructions to the realization of the Jewish national home.[11] Other examples of Christian contributions to the Zionist offensive against the restrictive clauses of the British White Paper of 1939 include a formal protest to the British government lodged by 28 senators, a denunciatory resolution of 15 of the 25 members of the House Committee on Foreign Affairs, protests of the American Legion, Disabled War Veterans and Veterans of Foreign Wars (all solicited by the pro-Zionist leadership of the Jewish War Veterans), and additional declarations of the Pro-Palestine Federation.[12]

But again, despite such numerous manifestations of genuine non-Jewish support for the execution of the Zionist program as outlined in the Balfour Declaration and the Mandate for Palestine, Christian Zionism had not yet achieved a reliable organizational channel and possessed no voice except the sporadic petitions and manifestos devised by non-Jewish Zionists or solicited hurriedly by Jewish leaders to counter emergencies as they arose. The mobilization, encouragement, and support of a Christian Zionist vehicle for tapping the vast reservoir of latent pro-Zionist and pro-Palestine sympathy was not accorded a place of significance in Zionist leadership priorities.

However, as the progressive ravages of World War II immeasurably exacerbated Jewish suffering in Europe, American Zionists moved their political offensive into "high gear." The shaping and mobilization of favorable non-Jewish opinion was elevated to a conscious, purposeful goal of Zionist leadership. Emanuel Neumann, the Zionist leader directly responsible for this task, thus declared to the assembled Zionist delegates at the May, 1942, "Extraordinary Zionist Conference" (Biltmore Conference) that Zionism's previous efforts with "Christian America" were grossly inadequate to the task at hand. In the past generation, he said, "we Zionists have isolated ourselves from the vital currents of American life and American thought. We have withdrawn into our shell." Henceforth, American Zionism must approach the problem of winning over public opinion on a number of levels. First, on the political level, "It is obvious that we have to convince all those who are in public life of our own united desire and determination to see the Zionist program through and ensure their support." Second, on the moral level, Zionists must impress the "church unions, organizations of clergy and laity, great publicists, teachers and preachers who speak for the Conscience of America. We have to present this to them as a great moral problem, involving great moral issues." Finally, affirmed Neumann, Zionists must use an intellectual

approach and thereby influence "thoughtful America." Having
failed in the past twenty years to deal with State Department research workers, private international organizations, universities,
and research institutions, a concerted effort should now be launched
to influence those experts and scholars concerned with postwar planning in such trouble spots as Palestine.[13]

This formal and more deliberate approach to the exploitation
of Christian sympathy for Zionist aspirations was well on the road
to implementation by the time Neumann's plans were unveiled at
the Biltmore Conference. Under Neumann's direction, and with
the active participation of retired Supreme Court Associate Justice
Louis D. Brandeis, the defunct American Palestine Committee
was being reactivated. Moved by the twin tragedies of oppressive
Hitlerian policies in Europe and oppressive British policies in
Palestine, numerous and influential non-Jews responded to the
invitation of Democratic Senator Robert M. Wagner and Republican Senator Charles F. McNary to form a "vehicle for the expression of the sympathy and good will of Christian America for the
movement to re-establish the Jewish National Home in Palestine."
Thus was reconstituted, on April 30, 1941, the American Palestine Committee, an association that numbered more than 15,000
influential Americans in its ranks by 1946 and that greatly surpassed the limited numbers and influence of the Pro-Palestine
Federation of a decade earlier.

At its very inception, the APC proudly announced a member-
ship including three Cabinet members, former Presidential nomi-
nees, and 68 United States senators and 200 representatives. An
executive council, consisting of such well-known figures as Dr.
Daniel L. Marsh, Professor William F. Albright, Dr. Henry A.
Atkinson, Dr. Carl J. Friedrich, William Green, Eric A. Johnston,
Philip Murray, Judge Frank A. Picard, Dr. Daniel A. Poling, Msgr.
John A. Ryan, Dr. Carl Hermann Voss, Dr. Mary E. Woolley, and
Senators Claude Pepper, Elbert D. Thomas, and Arthur H. Van-
denberg immediately laid plans for the nationalization of the
APC's pro-Zionist program. Field workers were dispatched across
the nation to build the first of more than seventy-five local APC chap-
ters. In addition to more than $72,000 per year (raised to $150,000
annually by 1947–48) disbursed by the national American Zionist
Emergency Council for work among non-Jews during 1943–45,

local ZOA and AZEC chapters were exhorted to provide their Christian Zionist neighbors with funds, clerical services, and moral support. Only in that way could the APC realize its target: "to crystallize the sympathy of Christian America for our cause, that it may be of service as the opportunity arises. Sympathy is like any other force: it is effective only when properly channeled." [14]

One of the first things the APC did was to circulate an impressive declaration entitled "The Common Purpose of Civilized Mankind," a reaffirmation of the "traditional American policy" in favor of a Jewish national home. Issued on November 2, 1942— the twenty-fifth anniversary of the Balfour Declaration—this document bore the signatures of 68 senators and 194 congressmen, including both the Senate and House majority and minority leaders and 18 of the 23 members of the Senate Foreign Relations Committee. Submitted to President Roosevelt and Secretary of State Hull, this expression of "deep-seated sentiment in favor of the Jewish Homeland in Palestine," was afterwards widely distributed in "tens of thousands" of copies. [15]

An even more striking illustration of the degree to which Congressional opinion supported the Zionist program is contained in the statements compiled by the American Zionist Emergency Council in October, 1944. Of the 535 members of the Seventy-eighth Congress, 411 endorsed the Zionist call for immediate American action to sanction a Jewish commonwealth. Representatives of every state in the Union, totaling 86 percent of the Senate and 75 percent of the House, further affirmed the Jewish right to settle Palestine, unhampered by arbitrary British restrictions, such as those imposed by the White Paper of 1939. [16]

Christian sympathizers were by no means limited to the ranks of the American Congress. Prominent non-Jews, in addition to those previously named, who spoke before Zionist gatherings or sent messages of support to the ZOA (culled at random from the pages of *New Palestine,* official organ of the Zionist Organization of America), included Paul V. McNutt, Robert H. Jackson, Harold L. Ickes, William Randolph Hearst, S. Ralph Harlow, Wendell L. Willkie, Walter Duranty, Sumner Welles, Raymond Gram Swing, Marshall Field, III, Van Wyck Brooks, Dorothy Thompson, Freda Kirchwey, Reinhold Niebuhr, Walter Clay Lowdermilk, Owen Brewster, and Claude R. Wickard. Moreover, the Zionist cause enjoyed a favorable press, a fact which Zionist leaders were quick to publicize by issuing a number of collections of pro-Zionist newspaper editorials and syndicated columns.[17]

Operating independently of the "regular" Zionist organizations, various Zionist "Revisionist-front" activities also met with a sympathetic response among the non-Jewish population. These organizations, not subject to the discipline or direction of the American Emergency Committee for Zionist Affairs, rallied a host of Christian supporters for their goal of transferring the Jews of Europe to the shores of Palestine. Included among the honorary chairmen of the "Emergency Conference to Save the Jewish People of Europe" (July 20–25, 1943) were: Dean Alfange, William Green, Arthur Garfield Hays, William Randolph Hearst, Herbert Hoover, Harold L. Ickes, Senator Edwin C. Johnson, Philip Murray, Harrison H. Spangler, Rex Stout, Senator Elbert D. Thomas, Bishop Henry St. George Tucker, Hendrick Willem Van Loon, and William Allen White. Other participants in the conference included: Archbishop Athenagoras, Bishop James Cannon, Ilka Chase, Jimmy Durante, Clark M. Eichelberger, Mayor Fiorello La Guardia, Judge Dorothy Kenyon, Senator William Langer, Elsa Maxwell, Edgar Ansel Mowrer, Admiral Yates Stirling, Jr., Lyman Beecher Stowe, and Sigrid Undset.[18] Hundreds of other prominent personalities, particularly drawn from the entertainment, literary, and news-reporting fields, were also listed as sponsors and supporters of numerous Revisionist groups whose ultimate aim—a Jewish state in Palestine—was identical to that of other Zionist organizations coordinated by the American Zionist Emergency Council.[19]

Among the Christian clergy, too, the Old Testament's prediction of a Jewish Restoration to Palestine was often an article of fundamental belief. As Americans became increasingly aware of Hitler's extermination of European Jewry, basic Christian sympathies for the Zionist program in Palestine were intensified. To give voice to the demand that "an end be put to Jewish suffering," a Christian Council on Palestine was formed on December 14, 1942. Numbering almost 3,000 prominent clergymen in 1946 (particularly drawn from the liberal Protestant denominations), the Council's prestige and authority were utilized in numerous representations to the American public and government on behalf of Zionist goals in Palestine.[20]

An impressive example of the type of invaluable services rendered to the Zionist cause by these lay and clerical groups was the "National Conference on Palestine," convened at Washington's Hotel Statler on March 9, 1944, at a time when controversial Congressional resolutions subscribing to the Jewish commonwealth were under official consideration. Sponsored by the American Palestine Committee and Christian Council on Palestine in cooperation with the CIO, AFL, Free World Association, Union for Democratic Action, Unitarian Fellowship for Social Justice, and United Christian Council for Democracy, the conference assembled 143 "big-name" delegates from 86 American communities and approximately 700 leading Washingtonians, including numerous high-ranking officials, as dinner guests. The conference then placed itself squarely behind the pending Wagner-Taft and Wright-Compton resolutions.[21]

Other meetings on the local level, attended by tens of thousands of Christians in major American cities, pronounced similar goals for non-Jewish supporters who longed to alleviate Jewish suffering and "right an ancient wrong." In the 1944 Zionist campaign for the abrogation of the White Paper, more than 3,000 non-Jewish organizations—unions, churches, Rotary, Lion, Elk, and Kiwanis clubs, YMCA's, ministers' associations, orders of the Knights of Pythias, and farm Granges—passed pro-Zionist resolutions, circulated petitions, and sent letters and telegrams to the Administration and their Congressional representatives. In Meriden, Connecticut, alone, whose entire Jewish population did not exceed 1,500 persons, more than 12,000 letters on the subject of Palestine were reportedly dispatched to President Roosevelt and the State Department. Similar expressions to Washington emanated from 200 non-Jewish organizations in Colorado, from petitions signed by 60,000 persons in South Bend, Indiana, and from Leominster, Massachusetts, 1,000 telegrams. Congressmen expressed "amazement" at such substantial non-Jewish interest in distant Palestine.[22]

Having succeeded in erecting sizable and influential alliances on the national "political" (Congressional) and "moral" (church) levels, Zionist public-relations officials next turned to the academic and local-government levels, again with considerable success. *A Petition to the United States, Respectfully Submitted by Members of the Faculties of American Schools of Higher Learning,* delivered to President Roosevelt in January, 1945, fully seconded the Zionist demands for the ultimate reconstitution of Palestine "as a free and democratic Jewish Commonwealth" and the immediate opening of that country for unlimited immigration and colonization. Bearing the names of more than 150 college presidents and deans, the *Petition* was also signed by about 1,800 faculty members drawn from 250 colleges and universities in 45 states.[23] In addition, pro-Zionist resolutions were enacted by 41 state legislatures and hundreds of municipalities, representing more than 90 percent of the nation's population. *A Petition to the President of the United States from the Governors of Forty-One States,* submitted July 2, 1945, was yet another of the numerous testimonials obtained by the Zionist movement at the summit of its popularity at the close of World War II.[24]

SUMMARY AND CONCLUSIONS

These abundant manifestations of Christian concurrence with Zionist objectives are all the more impressive in the face of the relative paucity of anti-Zionist expression by non-Jews. Anti-Zionist Christian sentiment, which later found a home in the American Friends of the Middle East, was not widely articulated by notable groups or even individual spokesmen before 1948. Efforts by the American Council for Judaism to draw invidious distinctions between "justifiable humanitarian concern" for Jewish refugees and "rabid Jewish nationalism" yielded little more public testimony than a single thin pamphlet of statements by Christians challenging the Zionist position. Two similar pamphlets published by the Institute of Arab American Affairs contained statements by a mere handful of Americans, few of whom compared in stature with the host of influential Christians who had endorsed the Zionist program.[25] While those Protestant denominations that maintained schools and missions in the Middle East were evidencing increased concern for the Arab cause and while the Roosevelt Administration's Middle Eastern policy was frequently rumored to be dictated by pressures from oil companies "working stealthily behind the scenes," the fact remains that significant organized non-Jewish dissent from Zionist claims was not easily identifiable. To be sure, popular apathy and inertia, as well as unorganized and latent anti-

Zionism, were probably much more prevalent than available published data indicate. This apathy, together with expressions of anti-Zionist hostility which Zionist leaders encountered from State Department officials below the rank of Secretary of State, can alone account for the many difficulties experienced by Zionist leadership in their efforts to influence official policy toward Palestine.[26]

To return to the salient finding of this study—the fact of widespread and influential Christian support for the Zionist cause —a supplementary conclusion can be adduced, namely, that expressions of Christian Zionist sentiment were both genuine and indigenous to the American culture. That is to say, Christian concern for Palestine was not a commodity to be called forth whenever it served the purposes of Zionist leadership. Support for Zionist aspirations was often to be found in communities remote from centers of Jewish population concentration. Congressmen with no Jewish constituency to speak of were to be found in the front ranks of the Zionist struggle, ardently promoting the cause which was still rejected by a number of influential Jews. Moreover, while the attention of Zionist leaders was only intermittently focused on the desirability of mobilizing Christian support, the record indicates that much Christian Zionist activity was self-generating. Christian Zionism was not mere response to Zionist proddings; it was as much, or perhaps more, a deeply-felt response to a number of compelling motivations and circumstances. Among these were a humanitarian good will toward the Jewish people, a belief in the moral rightness of the Zionist goal, a desire to fulfill previous international promises to the Jews, a wish to help realize Scriptural prophecies of the Jewish Restoration to the Holy Land, and a revulsion against the horrors of Hitler's policy of Jewish extermination.[27] Obviously, Christian Zionist activities cannot be attributed to any one such factor, certainly not to the universal acceptance of Zionist ideology by an extremely heterogeneous non-Jewish public. What is certain is that in the absence of a more plausible alternative to Jewish suffering, Jews and non-Jews alike united to pursue the Zionist program for the creation of a sovereign Jewish state.

The existence of this coalition of Jewish and Christian Zionist or Christian pro-Palestine interests decisively facilitated the acceptance of Zionist claims by American Jews. Lacking concrete proof for their allegations that the Zionist program would injure the status of American Jewry in the eyes of the general American public, anti-Zionist Jews most assuredly were weakened in their efforts to produce doubts among Jews about the wisdom of a Jewish state. Similarly, influential Jewish organizations, like the American Jewish Committee, that preferred a line of action independent of the Zionists, were caught up in the almost universal demand for prompt enactment of the Zionist program. Thus, late in 1943, Morris D. Waldman, executive secretary of the committee, conceded that:

> On the matter of Palestine the Zionists have an invulnerable position, viz., the Balfour Declaration as originally officially interpreted; the sanction of the League of Nations (Mandate); the endorsement of Woodrow Wilson and both Houses of U. S. Congress; the united self-sacrificing efforts of all elements of world Jewry to build the Yishuv; the remarkable achievements of the Jewish settlers; the sympathy of most Jews for a Jewish Palestine; the weakness of opposition to the theory of a commonwealth or state on the ground that it would prove an embarrassment and danger to Jews outside of Palestine.[28]

Later, after the Committee had tasted several years of massive Zionist attacks for its allegedly "traitorous" and "un-Jewish conduct," another leading staff member urged a *rapprochement* with American Zionists, "especially in the face of the fact that almost no popular non-Jewish voice has been heard in this country against the idea of the Jewish State." [29]

Measured both by direct support for the Zionist cause and by its indirect effects on American Jews, then, Christian Zionist activities made crucial, albeit unquantifiable, contributions to the growth of Zionist influence in the years immediately preceding the establishment of Israel.

8
ideology or philanthropy? the politics of zionist fund-raising

In 1930, organized American Zionism stood on the brink of complete collapse. Leaders and followers alike had generally ceased talking of the near-term prospects for a sovereign Jewish state. As a worldwide political movement, Zionism no longer quested immediately for statehood; Palestine was instead to be developed gradually. Far from being the "potent political lobby" described by many journalists a decade later, Zionism was largely a fund-raising movement dedicated to the economic reclamation and colonization of Palestine. In the words of one contemporary wag, a Zionist was a person who *schnorred* (begged) money from a second person in order to send a third person to Palestine. But even in this regard, Zionist success was feeble at best. Hampered by a crippling organizational deficit, the Great Depression, and a membership that had fallen to less than one-fourth of the 1918 high of 200,000, Zionist remissions to Palestine averaged only $1,000,000 annually.

Little over a decade later, however, memberships in the American Zionist movement rose to almost 600,000 while funds raised for Palestine exceeded $100,000,000 per year. Drawing upon a public of only 5,000,000 persons, organized Zionist fund-raising in America far surpassed the drives of such well-established national philanthropies as the American Red Cross and the American Cancer Society. Indeed, it may not be an exaggeration to suggest that, measured by fund-raising, American Zionism was the most successful political interest group in our nation's history.

This chapter concentrates on a vital yet scarcely-studied dimension of interest group politics: the techniques of financing political action. Specifically, it "tests" an hypothesis implicit in many studies of interest groups and social reform movements, namely, that the concreteness and specificity of an interest group's ideology and program vary inversely with the success of the group's leadership in attracting membership and financial support. In this case, we shall inquire whether American Zionism's marked success in enrolling a large number of members and in collecting unprecedented funds was accompanied by a dilution of the political program adopted by the first World Zionist Congress in 1897: "to create for the Jewish people a home in Palestine secured by public law." Substantively, we shall be concerned with the manner in which Zionists, after repeated failures, came to erect unparalleled fund-raising institutions for Palestine and how these "non-political, philanthropic" mechanisms were subsequently utilized for the attainment of Zionist political goals. But, to students of the political process, this case study should also furnish additional observations of the dynamic quality of group politics—the constantly shifting employment of diverse political techniques, the interminable process of making new alliances, and the ceaseless forging of more attractive propaganda appeals, all of which mark the efforts of interest groups seeking to realize their claims upon other members of society.

"THE MILLIONAIRE APPROACH"

The rebuilding of a desolate Palestine preparatory to establishing the State of Israel in 1948 was a costly venture requiring tremendous efforts and expenditures of both human and financial resources. Many hundreds of millions of dollars were required to reclaim the eroded biblical land and to resettle destitute Jewish colonists and, later, refugees. Coming decades before the enactment of a Marshall Plan or a Point IV Program, Zionist reconstruction in Palestine was a purely voluntary project, its success depending on the devotion and generosity of a widely scattered world Jewry. Therefore, it was immediately apparent to Zionist leadership that the burden of fund-raising for Palestine must be borne by the entire Jewish people if a Jewish state was to be achieved.

After the proclamation of the pro-Zionist Balfour Declaration in 1917 and the granting of the League of Nations Mandate for Palestine to Great Britain in 1920, American Zionism ceased temporarily to act as a "political" interest group. Primary Zionist demands were henceforth directed not at achieving favorable governmental recognition or action, but rather at realizing claims upon other members of the Jewish community; efforts were focussed primarily upon mobilizing the monetary means necessary to build the now internationally-sanctioned Jewish national homeland.

The impoverishment of European Jewry in World War I naturally turned Zionist attentions to American Jewry. But here, too, there were obstacles to successful fund-raising. The newly-arrived East European Jewish masses who constituted over two-thirds of American Jewry, albeit generally sympathetic to Zionism, were absorbed in the mighty struggle to sink economic roots into American soil and, hence, could spare few precious dollars for Palestine. The more established and affluent Jewish notables, on the other hand, were thoroughly suspicious of this new political movement, which they felt might somehow endanger their status in America. Men of great wealth and prominence—like Jacob H. Schiff, Felix M. Warburg, Adolph S. Ochs, and Julius Rosenwald —although known throughout the Jewish world for their generous support of "worthy causes," exhibited scant interest in rebuilding the Jewish national home, a movement they almost universally characterized as an "impractical dream" and/or as a harmful political scheme likely to support anti-Semitic charges of Jewish dual loyalty and lack of patriotism.

Accordingly, the first major Zionist effort to achieve financial viability involved trying to convince the philanthropic "big givers" that Palestine was a "practical, business-like, and realistic" solution to the problem of Jewish suffering in Europe and elsewhere. Or, if Palestine could not be made to seem "a good business proposition," it had at least to be portrayed as a project whose support would imply *only philanthropic generosity,* not as a political and "nationalistic" program likely to be misunderstood by non-Jewish fellow Americans. Beginning with the early 1920's, therefore, Zionist resources were thrown into the struggle to win the financial support of America's wealthier Jewish families. Every prominent leader, from World Zionist Organization President Chaim Weizmann down, was increasingly involved in the interminable fund-raising campaigns which so largely came to characterize post-World War I American Zionism. In the words of a leading Zionist lecturer, fund-raiser and publicist, typical Zionist fund drives could best be described as: "mixtures of public spirit, imaginative kindness, publicity-hunting, social pressure, cajolery, professional slickness, sentimentality, Jewish loyalty, high pressure salesmanship, advertising stunts, and nostalgic echoes of forgotten pieties. . . . a perpetual tug of war between educational effort and surrender to techniques." [1]

But for all their efforts in this period, Zionists were unable to attract more than token support from the great Jewish philanthropists. Sears, Roebuck magnate Julius Rosenwald, for example, could never be convinced that Palestine was a "practical" endeavor; his fabled munificence did not extend beyond the limited endowment of educational and scientific institutions in the Holy Land. Even Felix M. Warburg of Kuhn, Loeb, and Company, the most pro-Palestine of those whom Zionists derogatorily called Jewish "social service barons," never responded to the Palestine cause with anything like the humanitarian largesse which Zionists claimed he "short-sightedly" bestowed on the "bottomless pit" of Jewish charitable activities in Europe. Moreover, Warburg's characteristically non-Zionist perspective on Palestine, relates the president of the World Zionist Organization, was always very different from that which Zionists desired to develop in all Jews:

> . . . for us Zionists it was a movement of national regeneration; for him it was, at any rate in the early stages of his interest, one among the fifty-seven varieties of his philanthropic endeavors— perhaps bigger and more interesting than some others, but not different in essence. His whole upbringing militated against his taking the same view as we did. . . .[2]

THE ENLARGED JEWISH AGENCY FOR PALESTINE

By 1929, two factors, the threatened atrophy of the Jewish settlement in Palestine without extensive outside support and a major Arab attack on Palestinian Jewry exerted sufficient influence on all wings of American Jewry to move them to cooperate in the fashioning of an enlarged Jewish Agency for Palestine. Led by Louis Marshall, president of the influential American Jewish Committee, leading non-Zionists, after protracted negotiations, put aside their reservations about the "political and nationalistic implications" of Zionism and accepted forty-four seats on the governing council of the enlarged Jewish Agency. Along with such eminent European Jews as Sir Herbert Samuel, Albert Einstein, Lord Melchett, Oscar Wasserman and Leon Blum, wealthy Americans would henceforth share equally with Zionists the responsibility for reconstructing Palestine. Since five times as many Arabs as Jews lived in Palestine in 1929, Marshall and other philanthropists who opposed a sovereign Jewish state were satisfied there was "no likelihood that for many years to come, if ever, the Jews will be other than a minority."[3] At the same time, the achievements of Jewish Palestine were sufficiently attractive to warrant men of diverse outlooks combining in a program of common action "on strictly non-political lines." As Marshall proclaimed in 1929 at the signing of "The Pact of Glory" for the establishment of the Jewish Agency, the example of a renascent Jewish Palestine was meaningful to all Jews, Zionists and non-Zionists, because Jewish Palestine

> . . . has accomplished marvels in the last twenty-five years in stimulating Jewish thought among our youth throughout the world. It has brought about a renaissance of Jewish learning and scholarship which has once more made Hebrew a living language. It has given thousands of us, who at one time were indifferent to our history, something to live for and aspire for. Why should not such an ideal be regarded as belonging to all Jews?[4]

To be sure, not all Zionists welcomed this partnership with their erstwhile foes, the philanthropic non-Zionists. Some opposed the union because it would allegedly sidetrack genuine economic development and only grudgingly provide Palestine with "at most five per cent of all monies raised for Jewish purposes in the United States."[5] Others, led by former Zionist Organization of America President Rabbi Stephen S. Wise, were unwilling to join with men who viewed the idea of Palestine as just another Jewish refugee haven like those being promoted by non-Zionist philanthropists in Argentina or Soviet Crimea: "While their help was certainly both desirable and welcome, I felt that admitting them to a position of political leadership and responsibility meant a serious compromise with the basic principle of Zionism. . . . A philanthropic, economic, cultural, or spiritual interest in Palestine was laudable and helpful. But it was not Zionism."[6]

Despite such fears of philanthropy diluting Zionism's ideological content, the majority of American Zionists, laboring under a crippling ZOA deficit of $150,000, quickly succumbed to the temptation and promise of a speedy remedy for their long-standing financial weakness. "For the sake of Palestine," they would compromise the "purity of the Zionist political ideal" and permit non-Zionist late-comers to contribute "their rightful share" to the reclamation of Palestine. Not only would fund-raising problems be immediately solved, they thought, but the entire Zionist movement would gain an aura of respectability from its close association with "big names" like Herbert and Irving Lehman, Henry Morgenthau, Jr., Felix Warburg, Cyrus Adler, Lewis W. Strauss and Sol Stroock. With the philanthropic "large givers" safely in tow, Zionism should then be able to rally added support from the hesitant Jewish masses and from prominent non-Jews who always wanted to see first what the "large givers" were doing. As the Zionist *Congress Weekly* viewed the pact in retrospect:

> At a certain stage of Zionist development in this country, the readiness on the part of Jewish philanthropy to sail with it under one fund-raising banner was certainly an achievement. Zionism, abhorred by some and scarcely tolerated by others, gained entrance—at least for public purposes—into the drawing rooms of the mighty. There were even converts to the cause.[7]

With the proclamation of "The Pact of Glory," Zionist spokesmen triumphantly heralded the "opening of the most fruitful period in the history of modern Jewish times" and "the threshold of a new epoch." Henceforth, they predicted, it would be possible to make of Zionism the most important factor in the Jewish community, since the union of all Jewish forces for Palestine had placed Zionism in an "impregnable" position and given it "a commanding power which should enable it to reach out into all phases of American-Jewish life." From now on the ZOA would cease to be merely a money-raising organism and would return to the earlier, "more political" and "more ideological" side of Zionism.[8]

Measured by fund-raising, however, the effective life of the Jewish Agency was shorter than even its most outspoken critics could predict. In place of the early hopes of raising lavish sums from non-Zionist millionaires, the Zionist press soon featured bitter recriminations against non-Zionists for "failing to fulfill their pledge" to Palestine. Among themselves, Zionist leaders conceded that the Agency was "still-born." [9] The causes of the Agency's demise are numerous and complex and cannot be treated here,[10] but the importance of this experience for the Zionist goal of mobilizing funds was obvious: Jewish financial resources could not be tapped merely by involving several score of wealthy non-Zionist notables in the supervision of rebuilding Palestine. Funds gathered by the Jewish National Fund (Keren Kayemeth) and Palestine Foundation Fund (Keren Hayesod)—the two principal Zionist financial institutions—during the nine years following the creation of the enlarged Agency (1930–38) were only $12,137,000, less than the sums collected by these funds in the nine years preceding the establishment of the Agency.[11] Granted that Jewish fortunes, like those of all Americans, were greatly reduced by the Great Depression, Zionists nevertheless concluded that another way would have to be found to tap American Jewry's financial power.

GENESIS OF THE UNITED JEWISH APPEAL

Beginning in 1929, when Zionist and non-Zionist collaboration had progressed to the point where joint direction of the Jewish Agency for Palestine was considered possible, fund-raising for Palestine was attempted under the "umbrella" of a consolidated annual, nation-wide drive for various Jewish causes. In 1930, for example, an Allied Jewish Campaign with a goal of $6,000,000 was launched, receipts to be divided in the ratio of seven-twelfths for the avowedly non-Zionist relief and rescue organization, the American Jewish Joint Distribution Committee (JDC), and five-twelfths for the Palestine funds. Hampered by the deepening economic crisis, however, fund-raising fell far short of the quota and Palestine received less than a million dollars from the drive. Accordingly, the JDC and Palestine funds parted company in order to seek larger incomes by independent action.

Subsequent fund-raising efforts for Palestine all failed to reach rather conservative goals. Instead of a target of 250,000 persons, the Zionist Organization of America's 1935 "National Zionist Roll Call" enlisted less than 20,000 "registered sympathizers," who paid $1 each. Similarly, a campaign for a $100,000 ZOA "Extension

Fund" netted only $13,500. "At every turn," complained Zionist leadership, "the Organization is hampered by lack of funds in important tasks it must fulfill." [12]

Far more serious for Zionist prospects than this financial weakness, however, was the recrudesence of non-Zionist hostility to Zionist fund-raising, only nine months after a successful and harmonious All-Jewish American Conference for Palestine in January, 1935.[13] In October, 1935, the Executive Committee of the United Jewish Appeal, which for the past two years had conducted a joint drive for the American Palestine Campaign and the Joint Distribution Committee, abruptly announced that the cooperative venture would be cancelled for 1936. Officially, the explanation given was that "the sums raised have not shown an increase commensurate with the great need, nor did they measure up to what was expected of American Jewry." Because of this, independent campaigns were to be undertaken enabling the two beneficiaries "to intensify their special appeals . . . in quarters in which [they] might meet with a more sympathetic response." At the same time, cooperation between the leaders of both campaigns was pledged to continue unabated.[14]

Unofficially, however, the Zionist sector of the Jewish community was alarmed by rumors that the "anti-Zionist rich boys in the J.D.C." were attempting to "starve out" the precariously-financed Zionist movement. The Yiddish press, in particular, carried numerous stories attributing the break to the unilateral action of the Joint Distribution Committee, some of whose philanthropically oriented members allegedly "could not get accustomed to the thought that Palestine should play such a prominent role." [15]

Responding to the philanthropists' challenge that Zionists bear the major brunt of fund-raising efforts for Palestine, the Administrative Committee of the ZOA immediately issued a call for a "United Palestine Front" and a "militant campaign for the acceptance of Zionist ideals on the part of American Jewry." The unilateral decision of the JDC to wage a separate campaign was hailed as a golden opportunity to restore Zionist political propaganda to the "rightful place" from which it had been ousted by the necessity to placate wealthy non-Zionist contributors. Now, for the first time in several years, American Jews would be able to contribute to a United Palestine Appeal, "not as a merger of various relief funds, not disguised as a partnership of competing funds, but as

the symbol of the *national* funds of the Zionist movement." [16] Other
bases of Zionist support, long dissatisfied with the Zionist-philan-
thropist partnership in which Zionist political ideology was diluted
or submerged, also heralded the American Palestine Campaign—
JDC break. *The Reconstructionist,* influential in rabbinical and
intellectual circles, editorially chided the ZOA for having allowed
itself to become subservient to the "large givers" and the "best
techniques" for fund-raising:

> As the material and the moral support of non-Zionists became
> the objective of expert campaigners, the Palestine project was
> transformed more and more into just another philanthropy, an-
> other relief measure to which contributions from the compas-
> sionate were invited. The violent negation of Zionist ideology
> which this implied was recognized, but always condoned because
> of "emergencies." [17]

Subsequently, at a second "National Conference on Palestine," held
on February 8–9, 1936, enthusiastic pro-Zionist delegates, many
from nominally non-Zionist groups, accepted an ambitious quota of
$3,500,000. *New Palestine,* consequently, expressed satisfaction at
this evidence of "the virtual unanimity with which the task of constructive work in Palestine is regarded by all sections of American
Jewry." [18]

But despite this ideological preference of some Zionists to "go
it alone" in Palestinian fund-raising and regardless of how Zionists viewed the state of Jewish support for Palestine, the financial
record told a far different story. Even with the intensification of
Zionist activity and determination to help Palestine, occasioned in
large part by Hitlerian oppression and the renewal of Arab rioting in Palestine, funds raised for Palestine in 1936 totalled only
$1,677,000, less than half of the goal.[19]

Zionist failure to meet the quota for Palestine cannot be explained by the facile conclusion that Zionists did not work hard
enough at the task. On the contrary, Zionist partisans were generally
considered to be among American Jewry's most aggressive and dili-
gent workers in communal affairs. Zionist financial weakness must
rather be attributed primarily to the fact that, while their base
of popular support was large, they had not yet succeeded in capturing major positions of leadership and decision-making in the
Jewish community.

THE POWER STRUCTURE OF
JEWISH PHILANTHROPY

Zionist strength, in practically all countries, was based primarily upon the allegiance of the lower and middle classes. On the
other hand, from the time of the founding of the movement, Zionists were in almost continuous conflict with the economically privileged sectors of the Jewish group.[20] In the United States, the opposition of the rich acted to the detriment of Zionist aspirations
not only by depriving the Palestinian cause of the needed funds,
but also by arraying many of the local Jewish federations and welfare funds against Zionist demands. Increasingly, these community
coordinating bodies, operative in 266 cities and covering 97 percent of American Jewry by 1941, were recognized as the channel
both for unified fund-raising and, more important, for fund allocation.[21] Causes deemed "unworthy" by these dominant local
leaders were usually consigned to oblivion or minor status as the
notion of a unified, once-a-year "umbrella" campaign won widespread community acceptance.

Scientific analyses of the power structure of the American
Jewish community in this period only confirmed the common-sense
observation familiar to many students of Jewish affairs: almost
invariably, leaders of the local welfare funds were men of considerable financial means whose successes in the business world were considered sufficient recommendation for leadership in Jewish affairs.
Unlike some European Jewries, in which spiritual leadership was accorded mostly to scholars in Jewish lore, American communal dominance—especially the power to dispense philanthropy—gravitated
into the hands of those willing and able to "set an example" by
making a large contribution to the local philanthropic fund. As often
as not, moreover, this oligarchy of wealth and power was without Jewish education or even Jewish sympathies. A movement
like Zionism, viewed by many prominent Jews as likely to lower
their status in non-Jewish eyes, was not widely endorsed by local
leaders. Imitating the charitable patterns of the great Jewish philanthropists on the national levels, these local leaders generally
accorded Palestine only token support. Instead, they favored the

so-called "non-ideological and non-political" relief programs of the Joint Distribution Committee, an organization committed to the principle that Jews should be helped to remain in the countries of their birth rather than to emigrate to Palestine. Thus, American Jewish capitalists preferred aid to Jewish colonization in Soviet Crimea and Biro-Bidjan over a "Return to Zion." *

Nor was this type of leadership necessarily confined to the local organizational level of Jewish communal life. In their struggle to gain a position of dominance in the American Jewish Community, Zionists repeatedly charged that an "inter-locking directorate of anti-Zionist plutocrats" controlled the purse-strings of such influential national organizations as the American Jewish Committee, the National Refugee Service, and the Joint Distribution Committee (Joint or JDC). As evidence for their accusations, a study of Jewish leadership by Rabbi Joshua Trachtenberg was widely cited. Trachtenberg had found that, of the forty-two directors of the JDC, twenty-seven were seated on the AJC Executive Committee (total membership: fifty). Of the seventeen JDC Executive Committee members, twelve occupied similar positions in the American Jewish Committee. Clearly, the inter-relationship between the non-Zionist AJC and the "non-ideological," philanthropic JDC was a crucial factor in determining Zionist demands in negotiations with the JDC for joint fund-raising under the United Jewish Appeal.[23]

Because of this demonstrated relationship between non-Zionist leadership and the control of the Joint Distribution Committee, the rupture of cooperative relations between the United Palestine Appeal and the JDC was viewed by Zionists as far more significant than a mere maneuver of competing fund-raising organizations. Among Zionists, the collapse of the United Jewish Appeal could only be interpreted as an attack upon Palestine itself and upon the entire Zionist program, as a clash between the "phi-

---

* Historically speaking, it may be that European Jewry *had* to be rehabilitated in Europe after World War I. Although the availability of more money would have enabled the World Zionist Organization to absorb more immigrants in Palestine, the vast bulk of European Jewry was not willing or able to emigrate. The Zionists, therefore, concentrated upon supporting a selective migration of *halutzim* (trained agricultural pioneers), rather than mass immigration to Palestine. Moreover, since the Soviets did not permit emigration, the failure of Russian Jews to integrate into the new Soviet society by learning new economic skills would have meant their remaining "declassed," and unemployable and, perhaps, ultimately they would have been destroyed along with "the reactionary kulaks." [22]

lanthropy and assimilation of social service barons" and the forces of "positive Jewish survival and reconstruction in Palestine." Accordingly, Zionist leaders once again exhorted their followers to organize on the "grass-roots level," to "Conquer the local Jewish Federations!" and to "Infiltrate the Welfare Funds!" These were the power centers which would ultimately determine the extent of American Jewry's financial support for Palestine.[24]

During the next few years, Zionists did manage to secure greater representation on the governing boards of local federations and welfare funds. At the national level, too, new vitality characterized Zionist fund-raising as the vigorous Zionist Rabbi Abba Hillel Silver assumed the chairmanship of the United Palestine Appeal, a direct instrument of the Zionist movement dedicated to the reclamation of Palestine. Sparked by reports of anti-Semitic outbreaks in Rumania, the spread of Nazi rule to Austria, the rumored plan for a restrictive British White Paper for Palestine, and the successful absorption of large numbers of Jewish refugees in Palestine, United Palestine Appeal income in 1938 exceeded that of 1936 by almost 70 percent—to be sure, still far short of Zionist needs or expectations.[25]

More significant than increases in funds collected, however, was *New Palestine's* reassessment of the "menace" posed to Palestinian interests by non-Zionist control of the welfare funds. Noting that Zionists in several cities had already induced their funds to support Palestine generously, the ZOA organ declared: "There is no reason why propaganda for Palestine cannot be conducted in the midst of a Welfare Fund campaign. . . . It is the duty of Zionists . . . to find a constructive way to place Palestine and concrete Zionist interests in the center of community life. The Welfare Chests may be that way." [26]

Shortly thereafter, Zionist leaders announced that they had accepted overtures from JDC to reconstitute the United Jewish Appeal for 1939. A growing local clamor for "national Jewish unity" in the face of threats to Jewish interests was generally considered to be responsible for the agreement. Though dissatisfied with a subordinate share of the funds, Zionists for the time being would take advantage of the joint campaign to emphasize the "proper role of Palestine in Jewish life" and, thus, eventually maximize their income.

After two years of renewed joint fund-raising through the United Jewish Appeal, Zionist funds were receiving contributions from 3,371 communities, as contrasted with only 700 participating communities five years earlier. Seventy percent of all UJA speakers sent to local communities were being supplied by the United Palestine Appeal rather than by the JDC, and key roles in the joint campaign were being played at all levels by Zionist workers and leaders. Clearly, the philanthropic inclinations of American Jewry, as represented by the United Jewish Appeal, could be harnessed to bring Zionist perspectives before an ever-widening sector of the Jewish community.[27]

DIVORCE AND RECONCILIATION IN 1941

The Jewish community's record of fund-raising in 1941 reveals in abundant detail a long dormant and deep-seated conflict of interests between the Zionists and non-Zionist philanthropists and, therefore, admirably illustrates the power struggle in which Zionists contended for the support and loyalties of American Jewry. This record will also serve to describe the manner in which fund-raising agencies, ostensibly nourished by a philanthropic and humanitarian disposition, may be utilized for the promotion of a political program which might otherwise fail for lack of popular support.

It will be remembered that the history of cooperation between Zionists and non-Zionists in fund-raising presents a checkered pattern of joint drives. For example, in 1930 the cause of Palestine (United Palestine Appeal) and the predominantly European needs of the JDC were combined, but thereafter the two interests went their separate ways. In 1934 and 1935 there were again united appeals followed, in 1936 and 1937, by independent drives. The year 1938 saw individual campaigns, except for communities in which a welfare fund existed; there an initial sixty-forty ratio governed the distribution of funds gathered collectively. In 1939 and 1940, the JDC and UPA combined once again into a United Jewish Appeal; but in 1941, the year with which we are particularly concerned here, fund-raising unity was once again disrupted. This erratic course of events suggests a basic conflict of interests which, in fact, available documents decisively portray.

Beginning in October, 1940, United Palestine Appeal officials led by Rabbi Abba Hillel Silver and Joint Distribution Committee executives headed by Rabbi Jonah B. Wise commenced negotiations for the continuation in 1941 of the combined United Jewish Appeal. The UPA immediately protested against the proposed inclusion in the division of UJA funds, of the newly-founded National Refugee Service, contending that this agency's "comparatively temporary" budget for the absorption of refugees in the United States should be met from sources other than those earmarked for the "far-reaching and long-range programs" of UPA–JDC overseas needs. JDC leaders countered that the creation of the NRS was necessary to care for the 40,000 Jewish refugees who had entered the United States in 1939. Zionists detected other motives and retorted that the philanthropists of the JDC had consciously created the non-Zionist National Refugee Service as a JDC satellite with leadership "indistinguishable and identical" with that of the parent body. In such circumstances, Zionists interpreted the presentation of two separate non-Zionist budgets for the JDC and for the NRS as a cynical attempt to out-vote the Zionist UPA leadership two to one.[28]

Pressed by the JDC to accept the inclusion of the new NRS, United Palestine Appeal leaders, themselves under membership pressure to achieve fund-raising unity, finally yielded and recognized the NRS as a separate beneficiary. To safeguard the proportion of funds earmarked for Palestine the UPA insisted on parity with the JDC in the allocation of initial collections (instead of the old sixty-forty initial ratio) and the division by an allotment committee of all funds over the first $7,500,000 collected.[29] These proposals unacceptable to the JDC, the UPA went on to suggest a number of alternatives, including a sixty-five—thirty-five division, but agreement was not forthcoming. Accordingly, on December 17, 1940, the Administrative Committee of the UPA declared that an independent campaign for Palestine was unavoidable. In line with this course of action, the UPA would submit its own independent quotas to the various Jewish communities, asking them to allocate stated sums for Palestine, regardless of the sums requested by the NRS or JDC.[30]

Upon the announcement of this renewed rupture in UPA–JDC relations, the Zionist press charged that the philanthropist-dominated JDC and NRS were not merely disputing the allocation of funds for competing overseas causes, but were openly encouraging a resurgence of anti-Zionism. *New Palestine,* for instance, protesting Palestine's hitherto second-rate financial status in the United Jewish Appeal, justified its refusal to participate in joint fund-raising with the non-Zionists:

> In the holy name of "unity" and for the sake of local "peace," Zionist leaders too long compromised with those who knew only the philanthropic approach to the Jewish problem and lack the perspective of nationalist solution.
> The result was that allocations for Zionist needs fell far behind the requirements of the times, Zionist education and propaganda languished, and the entire Zionist body politic was in danger of being swallowed up by the gargantua of a unified and large-scale philanthropy, of which it would be but a minor overseas agency. . . . It was only when intolerable conditions became more intolerable, and when the foes of Zionism made very clear their intransigence, that those responsible for Zionist leadership found it impossible longer to subject the movement to humiliation and degradation.[31]

Another exposé of the "true facts" concerning the break came from the pen of Louis Lipsky, former President of the ZOA and Chairman of the American Jewish Congress' Governing Council. Unveiling a "struggle which had been going on under cover for many years," Lipsky charged:

> The United Jewish Appeal had only the appearance of union. Beneath the smooth, non-committal, neutralized words of the campaign, a more or less polite struggle was carried on to subordinate the ideals and objectives of the Zionist movement to the aims and desires of a small but influential group of Jews who are anxious to keep American Jewish life loyal to isolationist, assimilationist ideals, who are always limiting the Jewish interest, always avoiding Jewish identification, always seeking to have Jewish life adjust itself to the fears and negations arising out of an everlasting apology for Jewish existence.[32]

Reciting a long series of instances in which Zionists and anti-Zionists had engaged in covert struggle, Lipsky explained that the issues had never been "fought out in a political arena" because of the anti-Zionists' fervent desire to avoid publicity at any cost. Characterizing such misguided thinking as dominated by obsessive fear of what non-Jews might think if controversies in Jewish life reached the ears of the general American public, Lipsky revealed that until then the truly significant issues in Jewish life had been "confined to conversations in committee rooms, conferences in executive sessions, confidential letters circulated to a limited group of friends, couched in language which is the perfection of camouflage." [33]

Referring specifically to the United Jewish Appeal which hitherto had contained the Zionist-non-Zionist struggle by means of "colorless slogans" and "ingenious percentages and ratios," Lipsky alleged that there were "understandings" among non-Zionist leaders in these joint campaigns to avoid all references to the word "national" and all activities of a political, state-building nature. These "understandings," conceded Lipsky, arrived at in "a social, off-the-record way," were markedly effective in reducing the importance of Palestine, both in terms of popular ideological acceptance and in funds actually raised for Zion. The philanthropists' JDC, with its "short-sighted, palliative program" for "patching up" Jewish life in Europe, thus always came out ahead of Zionism's "practical, long-range vision." The cause of Palestine was progressively minimized in the distribution of funds destined for overseas use. In 1938, for example, Palestine received approximately $2,500,000 of $7,000,000 collected. But in 1939, of $16,200,000 raised, Palestine was allocated only $4,000,000. And in 1940, with $14,500,000 gathered, it would be allotted only $2,900,000. [34]

Answering this non-Zionist drive to minimize funds directed to Palestine, the United Palestine Appeal proclaimed an unprecedented goal of $12,000,000 for its independent campaign of 1941. The UPA demanded that, henceforth, all local welfare fund collections for overseas purposes must be distributed on a 50-50 basis between the JDC and UPA. An experienced UPA staff, led by Henry Montor, immediately proceeded to mobilize pro-Palestine support in communities throughout the nation. Zionist preparations for waging this independent fund-raising campaign gave the impression of unparalleled optimism and self-confidence. [35]

To achieve their ambitious target, Zionists also organized

another National Conference for Palestine in Washington, D.C., on January 25–26. With over two thousand delegates in attendance, including representatives of such prominent non-Zionist organizations as B'nai B'rith, the Central Conference of American Rabbis, and the National Council of Jewish Women, the National UPA Chairman, Rabbi Abba Hillel Silver, delivered a scorching indictment of the philanthropic-minded leaders of American Jewry, who had "lacked the vision" to build up Palestine after the proclamation of the Balfour Declaration. Instead of seizing the opportunity to save thousands of refugees from Europe and build up Palestine at the same time, declaimed Silver, the Jews of America

> . . . chose rather to listen to their omniscient and infallible philanthropic mentors who counselled them to give all aid to the Jewries of Eastern and Central Europe, but only a pittance to that visionary project of impractical idealists in Palestine. One must be realistic, they argued—and what greater realist in the world is there than a successful Jewish banker or broker, and who can question his unerring judgment? [36]

Noting that once again these "realistic philanthropist guides of Israel" were urging American Jewry to waste their money on a new JDC refugee colonization scheme for Santo Domingo, as they had formerly sought funds for the now defunct JDC Jewish settlements of Soviet Biro-Bidjan and Crimea, Silver recounted the events leading up to the demise of the UJA. He then proceeded to tell the assembled delegates that the current feud with the JDC was not merely over the relative proportion of dollars to be given to each agency but was, in fact, motivated solely by the desire of philanthropically-minded anti-Zionists to "strangle" the Zionist movement by the "single device of starving it to death." [37]

At the same time, he disclosed a new and even more threatening maneuver of influential non-Zionists to divert support and attention from Palestine. This threat allegedly emanated from a plan being promoted by the non-Zionist leadership of the Council of Jewish Federations and Welfare Funds to establish a "national advisory budgeting service" which would "evaluate" the needs and relative importance of the various beneficiaries of Jewish charitable contributions. How, asked Silver, could such a committee "evaluate" the role of Palestine or other such ideological preferences?

> . . . to one who is opposed to Zionism, every dollar spent in Palestine, except as it might be spent in elementary relief, is wasted, regardless of how efficiently that dollar may otherwise be expended. On the other hand, those who believe in the upbuilding of the Jewish National Homeland feel that the cause is so worthy and historically so necessary that the millions already spent in Palestine are entirely inadequate.

Given the impossibility of such "objective evaluation" and the prevailing "undemocratic" and "irresponsible" communal organization (i.e., non-Zionist control) of American Jewry, Zionists would never consent to have the validity of their claim dependent on a national budgeting committee.[38] Echoing this determination, the UPA Conference resolved "not to recognize any action by the Council of Jewish Federations and Welfare Funds whose effect will be to substitute . . . dictatorship for democratic control and the autonomy of American Jewish communities." [39] This resolution marked the beginning of a Zionist offensive to defeat the proposed budgeting service with its "impartial" committee of evaluation. Utilizing every medium at their command, Zionists strove to awaken the community to the deleterious effects on Palestine were all budgets to be "censored" by such a body. *Congress Weekly,* for example, editorialized that

> The decision of the Board of Directors of the Council of Welfare Funds to establish a National Budgeting Committee is nothing less than a declaration of war against the Zionist movement, and more specifically the United Palestine Appeal. . . . In effect, the decision is an ultimatum to the groups behind the United Palestine Appeal: either you will be satisfied with the share we are ready to give you; or we will thwart your efforts in the local Welfare Funds; so that either way you will not get a cent more than we are ready to give you.[40]

Characterizing the "controlling interests" of Jewish life as one great philanthropic holding company with interlocking directorates reaching into the JDC, the National Refugee Service, the Council of Jewish Federations and Welfare Funds, and the American Jewish Committee's more "assimilated" and "self-hating" Jews,[41] Zionists attempted to halt the budgeting proposal submitted to a referendum of the local welfare funds.[42] Even the very idea of the referendum itself was subjected to the attacks of the Zionists, who had traditionally been found on the side of those preferring community-wide making of decisions to what they described as "arbitrary judgments" of a few "philanthropic oligarchs" and "social service barons." [43]

The cause for Zionist unhappiness over the impending referendum may be surmised from Louis Lipsky's observation that, far from being a popular ballot which would determine how the mass of Jews really felt, the budgeting service ballot would be confined to a mere five thousand directors of the local welfare funds. Instead of representing the "true wishes" of the 450,000 contributors to such charitable pools, Lipsky felt certain that the balloting would yield almost exactly the same decision as that favored by the "big giver," non-Zionist philanthropists. After all, reasoned Lipsky, "To qualify as a member of a local [welfare fund] Board one must be included in the coterie of 'big givers' in any community. This means that the Boards are composed of persons who are invariably found on the side of the philanthropic view of Jewish life." Furthermore, what kind of "democracy" could the Zionists expect when the impending "loaded" referendum provided one vote for each welfare fund, regardless of its size or importance, when, in other words, the city of Detroit would have a vote equal to that of Nashville? [44]

Zionist fears proved warranted. On May 17, 1941, the officers of the Council of Jewish Federations and Welfare Funds announced that the referendum had approved, by a vote of fifty-four to fifty-three cities, the establishment of the controversial budgeting service. Zionists immediately challenged the CJFWF contention that there was a "clear mandate" for the plan. Conflicting figures were introduced to show that less than one-third of the 166 communities belonging to the Council had voted for the measure, that Canadian towns had been illegally counted in the vote, that agencies unrelated to overseas fund-raising had been included, that communities voting against the proposal were deliberately not counted, and so on. In such "scandalous circumstances," Zionists queried, how could the Council proceed to force a budgeting service upon American Jewry? [45]

Although non-Zionist partisans had thus won the first round

for a national budgeting service whose "evaluations" might minimize allocations to Zionist funds, budget plan protagonists were unable to put the scheme into operation. While the referendum was in progress, new and unexpected events occurred in the conflict over funds for overseas Jewry. The Yiddish and Anglo-Jewish press accelerated their almost unanimous denunciation of the JDC for obstinately refusing to make concessions to the UPA. Some of the welfare funds, now apparently controlled by a majority of pro-Palestine backers, publicly clamored for a reconstitution of the disrupted United Jewish Appeal. Zionists, too, were divided on the merits of the renewed break with the JDC. Some welcomed the opportunity to reassert the primacy of Zionist propaganda in an independent campaign solely for Palestine. Others, particularly in the important Chicago area, feared that the cost of operating an independent campaign, coupled with the powerful opposition of many local anti-Zionist philanthropists, would mean that total funds remitted to Palestine would fall off. Was it not true, they asked, that the JDC and its affluent directors in the American Jewish Committee controlled the "big givers" of New York City, the 1-2 percent of all contributors who donated over half of all the funds raised? [46]

Whatever the motivation involved—the "pressure of public opinion" for Jewish unity, Zionist fears over a loss of funds, non-Zionist reluctance to have continued public controversy characterize the Jewish community in the eyes of non-Jews, or a combination of these factors—a joint statement by Rabbis Jonah Wise and Abba Hillel Silver abruptly announced that once again the JDC and UPA would combine in 1941 in a joint appeal for $25,000,000. The new agreement provided for the division of the first $8,800,000 collected on the basis of $2,000,000 for the NRS (22.9 percent), $2,525,000 for the UPA (28.6 percent), and $4,275,-000 for the JDC (48.5 percent). All additional funds would be distributed by an allotment committee between the JDC and UPA only. The cause of Palestine would thus be assured of a larger portion of the initial funds collected than in 1940, when it received only 23.3 percent. Excluding the NRS allocation, Palestine would receive 37 percent of the initial quota (as compared with the JDC's 63 percent) and an even greater share should the drive surpass its goal. [47]

Zionists rejoiced at this new 63-37 arrangement and wondered why the JDC had "backed down" to such a compromise when, only the previous December, the UPA had offered to accept a 65-35 division. Could it be that the non-Zionists were coming to respect the Zionist movement's growing influence in the communities? Certainly the Jewish public was rapidly showing a new interest in Palestine, proclaimed the Zionist press.[48] *New Palestine,* for example, viewed the renewed merger as approximating "what American Jews would want Palestine to receive." Eventually, predicted the ZOA organ,

> . . . when American Jews are made to realize the vital importance of Palestine to the whole problem of Jewish survival, they will, no doubt, make ampler resources available. But at present, in view of the economies effected by the unification of efforts, it should be possible for the U.P.A. to send as much money to Palestine this year as it would if it ran an independent campaign.

Moreover, Zionists need not worry that the joint campaign would deprive them of the propaganda opportunity of presenting an "affirmative program in our own way."

> Although we are cooperating with philanthropic agencies, we need not and must not soft-pedal the political implications of Zionism. . . . The conduct of a joint campaign . . . frees Zionist energies for other tasks. We can now give more attention to the internal strengthening of our organization. . . .
> We Zionists may well breathe a sigh of relief that we need not accept upon our shoulders exclusive responsibility for a colossal fund-raising campaign in competition with another similar endeavor of equal magnitude.[49]

Thus, once again, Zionists were united with philanthropists in advancing the interests of Jewish Palestine. Several years were to pass before the UPA would receive the greatly augmented largesse of an American Jewry fully mobilized for the "responsibilities of Jewish leadership" emerging from World War II, but significant inroads into Jewish philanthropy had been made. Palestine was receiving increased aid from America, anti-Zionists had not succeeded in "starving out" the Zionist cause, and valuable instrumentalities for bringing the message of Palestine to American Jewry remained intact and at the disposal of the Zionists. Furthermore, the degree to which fund-raising mechanisms were utilized in 1941 for the promotion of Zionist political objectives is amply demonstrated by another reference to the National Conference for Palestine in 1941.

"POLITICS" OUT OF "PHILANTHROPY"

A survey of the Zionist press between 1930 and 1941 reveals that the term "Jewish State," as the ultimate goal of the Zionist movement, had almost entirely disappeared from common parlance. Instead, the ambiguous phrase "Jewish National Home" or, weaker yet, "homeland," was substituted in official expositions of Zionist aims. With the prospect of a Jewish majority in Palestine far from immediate attainment and talk of a Jewish state or *national* homeland offensive to many influential non-Zionist financial contributors, the original Herzlian concept of Zionism largely passed into disuse. The political program of Zionism became more nebulous as Zionist leaders sought to enlarge their public. As Emanuel Neumann, President of the Zionist Organization of America from 1947–49, recalled:

> . . . for many years the "Jewish State" became taboo—not merely on grounds of expediency. The very word was banned from official Zionist use and driven underground. The State was not only impossible of achievement, but of questionable morality. The National Home, interpreted as a spiritual and cultural center, was deemed a nobler and loftier conception—and one which offered practical advantages. A "spiritual center" required little space, no Jewish majority and no political sovereignty. . . . The accent [of this "Spiritual Zionism"] was upon patience, caution and restraint, and the avoidance of risk. Zionist statesmanship was made synonymous with moderation—carried at times to an immoderate extreme.[50]

It was from this state of affairs that a return to "Maximal, Herzlian Zionism," that is, to the political conception of a sovereign state, was brought about in 1941. This decisive change was first displayed in public action, surprisingly enough, not by the self-avowedly political Labor Zionists, the Zionist Organization of America or even the American Emergency Committee for Zionist Affairs representing all Zionist parties, but by the fund-raising National Conference for Palestine of January 25–26, 1941. (In fact, sixteen months of bitter internal contention were to elapse before the American Zionist parties and even the Palestinian Zionist movement were to adopt such a political program). Seconding the demand for a Jewish commonwealth pronounced by visiting Palestinian labor leader and Chairman of the Executive of the Jewish Agency David Ben-Gurion at this conference,[51] Rabbi Silver reminded the assembled UPA leaders:

> What are all our efforts for? What are we aiming at? We have no new aims. We accept no substitute aims. Our is the historic and millennially unsurrendered and uncompromised aim of rebuilding Israel's national life in Israel's historic national home. Our aim is a Jewish Commonwealth. Such a Jewish Commonwealth was the clear intent of both the letter and the spirit of the Balfour Declaration. Two decades of legal hairsplitting and sundry White Papers have not succeeded in whittling down the clear, full-orbed intent of that historic document or in giving moral sanction to any deviation from it.[52]

Thereupon, the Conference forthrightly declared its belief that "only by large-scale colonization of Jews in Palestine, with the aim of its re-constitution as a Jewish Commonwealth, can the Jewish problem be permanently solved." [53]

Obviously, Zionist control of such an instrumentality as the National Conference for Palestine, to which numerous non-Zionist groups enthusiastically subscribed, paid substantial dividends in political as well as financial advantage. The contribution of fund-raising to the eventual success of Zionist aims in America thus can never be measured in terms of dollars alone. Utilizing platforms provided by fund-raising occasions and exploiting genuine humanitarian impulses, Zionists were gradually able to persuade American Jews of the desirability and practicability of their program. Eventually, the *demands,* if not the motivations, of "non-political" fund-raising organizations and "political" Zionist groups became virtually indistinguishable.

ZIONISM'S FINANCIAL TRIUMPH

At the close of World War II, the full impact of Hitler's "Jewish policy" was felt by American Jewry, most of whom were themselves only a generation removed from European origins. Jewish solidarity intensified when the world learned of the massacre of six million Jews. The Zionist political solution for the homelessness of the remaining European survivors won widespread acceptance when it was advanced by a rejuvenated movement under the dynamic leadership of Rabbi Abba Hillel Silver. In the period from 1940 to 1948, Zionist Organization of America membership leaped from 43,000 to more than 250,000; Hadassah (Women's Zionist Organization of America) membership rose from 73,000 to 243,000; sales of *shekolim* (voting rights for World Zionist Congress elections) skyrocketed from 171,567 to 954,886.[54]

Similarly, Jewish fund-raising—the most universal expression of Jewish identification and communal participation—greatly exceeded all previous records. Many communities doubled their United Jewish Appeal contributions each year from 1943 to 1948, while the total number of givers doubled from 1945 to 1946 and rose yet another 70 percent by 1948. Thousands of persons who had never before been involved in Jewish community activities pledged their first contributions of the UJA; and the UJA, in turn, tripled its collection goal in a single year. Local welfare funds, long feared by Zionists for their non-Zionist complexion, devoted an increasing share of their income to the United Jewish Appeal— 53.3 percent in 1941–45, 71.6 percent in 1946, 72.2 percent in 1947 and 75.0 percent in 1948.[55] American Jewry, which had given only $14,500,000 to the joint UJA drive of 1940, increased its gifts to $35,000,000 in 1945, and then dramatically to $103,000,000 in 1946, $118,000,000 in 1946, and $150,000,000 in 1948. With a potential public of only 5,000,000 persons, UJA collections in 1948 exceeded the entire national collections of the American Red Cross by as much as 400 percent and those of the American Cancer Society by almost 1200 percent! [56]

The Zionist share of this greatly augmented income rose to $56,000,000 in 1947 and to over $70,000,000 in 1948, as contrasted with less than $3,000,000 raised in 1940. Compared with approximately $14,000,000 remitted to Palestine by Zionist funds between 1901 and 1929 and $8,000,000 sent from 1930 to 1939, American Jewry donated over $200,000,000 between 1939 and 1948. Funds remitted to Palestine in 1948 alone exceeded $90,000,000. Additional untold millions of dollars were also simultaneously flowing to Palestine from individual family and personal donations, private investment, tourism, commercial transactions, commodity transfers, and numerous small-scale fund drives for particular Palestinian projects and institutions.[57]

Of far greater political significance than the actual sums collected was the fact that Zionist funds received an ever-increasing proportion of the total funds collected for overseas purposes until, in 1949, the United Palestine Appeal was allotted almost $8,000,-000 more than the world-wide programs of the JDC. Also notable was the increasing UPA share of the total receipts garnered by the UJA:

TABLE 15.   United Palestine Appeal Allocations as a Percentage
of United Jewish Appeal Collections [58]

1939	26.1	1945	42.8
1940	24.1	1946	41.5
1941	28.5	1947	39.0
1942	29.2	1948	45.5
1943	34.6	1949	47.4
1944	40.1	1950	51.1

Moreover, by this time the "non-Zionist" JDC was itself expending more than $15,000,000 annually on various Palestinian projects. These impressive material contributions describe better than any words the dramatic shift in JDC attitudes toward the Palestinian cause:

TABLE 16.   Expenditures of the Joint Distribution Committee
on Its Palestine (Israel) Program [58]

1914–1917	$1,037,977	1946	$ 2,333,700
1918–1920	3,828,441	1947	6,879,500
1921–1932	4,601,993	1948	15,458,100
1933–1939	1,769,804 a)	1949	24,081,900
1940–1945	6,510,779 b)	1950	19,642,500
		Total	$86,144,694

a) Exclusive of $860,000 expended on cultural activities.
b) Exclusive of investments in the Palestine Economic Corporation in the amount of $646,307.

SUMMARY AND CONCLUSIONS

Fund-raising for Palestine thus serves as a convenient barometer of the strength and influence of the Zionist movement in the American Jewish community. Clearly, Palestinian Zionists were not reaping all of the dollars destined for overseas purposes in 1948; considerable sums were also expended in Europe and elsewhere in the pressing work of aiding the survivors of Hitler's Europe. Equally clear, however, was the fact that the rebuilding of a Jewish Palestine was no longer subordinated to other "worthy Jewish causes." Having increased its collections through the United Palestine and United Jewish Appeals more than thirty fold in less than a decade, Palestine emerged second to none in the philanthropic attentions of American Jewry.

As we have seen, this was not all accomplished at once. Rather it was the product of a number of Zionist attempts, some ill-fated and premature (like the "Millionaire Approach" and the enlarged Jewish Agency for Palestine), to organize the financial potential of American Jewry in behalf of a Jewish Palestine. But despite widespread public apathy, the presence of a heterogeneous Jewish population, and the activities of numerous influential opponents, American Zionists were gradually able to make common ground with the great majority of their potential public—the Jews of America. Since conditions in the Jewish community militated against direct ideological appeals for "radical political solutions" like statehood and national independence, Zionists instead utilized the only effective bridge uniting diverse sectors of their public. This was the bridge of *philanthropy,* the sole ground on which a community beset by institutional rivalries, competing social and religious ideologies, and mutually hostile socio-economic groups could meet for a measure of common action.

To say that Zionism successfully energized its latent public by relating its program to a potent philanthropic impulse is not to conclude that Zionism surrendered or diluted its political objective of a sovereign state. On the contrary, we have seen that precisely at the same time that Zionist memberships and monetary collections were spiralling upwards, the militant, political program of "Maximal, Herzlian Zionism" was reaffirmed as the central goal of the movement. Far from being fluid and imprecise, the Zionist goal after 1941 was clearly one of achieving political hegemony in Palestine, even though such a goal might be rejected by many of the affluent contributors upon whom the Zionist movement largely depended for economic support. In short, the American Zionist experience documented here does not confirm the hypothesis affirmed by many writers to the effect that an ideological loosening invariably accompanies the growth of an interest group's size and wealth.

Broadening their popular base by infiltrating and influencing already existent associations or by erecting new "umbrella organizations" (such as the National Conference for Palestine), Zionists added "educational content" to the ordinary philanthropic appeals of saving Jews and helping the poor unfortunates. In this way, ever larger portions of American Jewry came to view Palestine Zionistically—not in terms of mere temporary disaster and palliative relief, but rather as a "long-range and permanent, political solution to the Jewish problem." In this way, too, the deep conflicts dividing the Jewish community, and which had defied all previous efforts at communal organization, became sufficiently controllable to permit Zionists to mobilize and channel Jewish public opinion into political action.

Through the instrumentality of annual conferences for Palestine, independent or joint fund-raising campaigns, Palestine Days, and local welfare funds, Zionists ceaselessly labored not only for dollars but for acceptance and support of their goals. Intra-Zionist cohesion, always a problem, was also enhanced by fund-raising activity. Coming together on the common platform of a fund-raising affair, Zionists of diverse persuasions—Labor, Religious, Cultural, Political—developed new patterns of cooperation and accord even while they influenced and transformed non-Zionist members of synagogs, fraternal orders, "anti-defamation" organizations and women's clubs.

Within the arena of fund-raising for "worthy causes," Zionists were also able to convert, or at least to overpower, the philanthropically disposed objectors who, had they not been neutralized or corralled in some type of joint endeavor with Zionism, might have organized effective obstruction to the further advance of Zionist influence. Here, too, Zionists found it possible to vie with and largely overcome those groups whose primary objection to Zionism was not ideological but rather was dictated by the fear that their own local interests would suffer from the competition of a dynamic Palestine making continuous claims upon American Jewry, claims which would militate against local cohesion and fund-raising for local purposes.

Finally, the various institutions and the gradually developed annual "habit" of American Jews giving to Palestine eventually produced sufficient unity of thought to permit political action. Resolutions enacted by the Zionist-led National Conferences for Palestine were even more militant than those adopted by American Zionist organizations. Indeed, while Zionists paved the way in constructing effective channels for the direction and utilization of popular opinions, it was the "non-Zionists," speaking with their dollars and political resolutions through fund-raising conferences, local welfare funds and pro-Palestine philanthropic organizations who lent such considerable force to Zionist claims that American Jewry was virtually united behind their program.

The evidence of our study does not support the contentions of some Zionists that the eventual achievement of their objectives is entirely attributable to the political skill of their leaders. For there were also important changes in the perspectives of non-Zionist philanthropists which help account for the marked shift in the allocation of philanthropic funds to Palestine. In this connection, one overly facile conclusion proferred by some anti-Zionists is that the JDC's staff had become infiltrated and gradually dominated by Zionist partisans who then "perverted the true purposes" of the JDC. To be sure, such an influential person as Joseph Schwartz, JDC executive secretary and later head of the Bonds for Israel Government organization, may well have considered himself a Zionist.[59] But, probably, a more adequate explanation is that Jewish philanthropists were forced by the press of historical events to develop a new perception of their self-interest.

When, late in 1945, a study mission headed by U.S. Commissioner of Immigration Earl Harrison (and including Joseph Schwartz) recommended to President Truman that 100,000 Jews be admitted to Palestine immediately, as there was no other way to normalize the uprooted lives of Europe's Jewish Displaced Persons, the die was cast.[60] The leading figures of the Joint Distribution

Committee, much concerned with anti-Semitism and other such threats to their personal security in America, were faced with difficult choices. Either the JDC had (1) to urge that America's gates be opened wide to welcome the homeless Jewish survivors—and some Jews were certain this would mean "importing more anti-Semitism" into the U.S.—or (2) to risk the consequences of "unfavorable publicity" from continued Jewish unrest and violence in Palestine and in the D.P. camps, or else (3) to support Palestinian immigration promptly and in wholesale fashion. Large-scale immigration into Palestine would, of course, strengthen the hand of political Zionists, might even enable the Zionist leadership to establish a sovereign Jewish state after all. But would this not be better from the viewpoint of "good Jewish-Christian relations in America" than the likely prospects of Jewish D.P.'s confined in Dachau and Bergen-Belsen attacking their American G.I. guards, infinitely better than the actual daily newspapers carrying screaming headlines of King David Hotel explosions and hanging of British sergeants by Palestinian Jewish terrorists? [61]

The time had come to order priorities anew. At the sacrifice of their prized record of consistent opposition to Zionism with all of its "political, ideological, and nationalistic content," American philanthropists now shifted from refugee relief in Europe to nation-building in Palestine. "Zionism," correctly concludes one perceptive student of this period, "resolved the dilemma of American Jewry; it provided a home for the remnants of European Jewry without incurring an immigrant exodus to the United States." [62]

In retrospect, then, the prosaic task of raising dollars for Palestine illustrates an obvious political facet: by exploiting deep-seated predispositions toward psychological insecurity as well as philanthropic generosity, and by employing diverse techniques, Zionists achieved a considerable accretion to their power and influence potential. Distinctions between "philanthropic humanitarianism" and "political Zionism," in effect, came to lose their practical if not their ideological significance. Zionists and non-Zionists, regardless of ideological differences, joined hands pragmatically to make possible the same goal—a Jewish state in Palestine.

9
the democratic mold:
the american jewish conference
of 1943

In characterizing the operations of American interest groups, David Truman develops the concept of the "democratic mold." By this term Truman reminds us that every organized interest must conform to the prevailing expectations and normative standards of the total society in which it operates, or else risk the opprobrium and opposition of the very public it seeks to influence. Specifically, organizations in American society are expected to act "democratically." This does not mean that oligarchical tendencies are absent in group life; it does aver that, at the very least, interest groups must pay lip service to "democratic ideals" and seek to accomplish their ends through the forms, language and processes associated with democracy.[1]

In this chapter, we shall carry the record of the decisive consolidation of American Jewish opinion behind the Zionist program one step further by studying a particularly striking example of Zionist utilization of democratic techniques—elections, ballots, majority rule, representation, campaign platforms, resolutions, the appeal for unity, and the like—for the attainment of their goals. The example chosen is the momentous American Jewish Conference of 1943.

It may be noted at the outset that Theodor Herzl, the founder and first leader of the political Zionist movement, was no novice at synthesizing the demands of the democratic mold with the exigencies of practical Zionist politics. As early as 1898, at the Second World Zionist Congress, Herzl made this oft-repeated statement of basic Zionist tactics which was almost equally applicable to the American Jewish community of the early 1940's:

Almost everywhere the masses are with us. It is they who constitute as well as support the communities. Consequently their wishes must be carried out. . . . That there should be agitations in Jewish communities against Zion has become unbearable. The situation is absurd, impossible. We must end it. *An election campaign must be begun wherever the heads of the communities are not yet with us.* Men with convictions similar to ours, worthy and capable of filling these distinguished positions, must be nominated and elected in the name of the national idea. The prestige of the Jewish community, the means at its disposal, the people whom it supports, must not be used to oppose the will of our people. Therefore I think I voice the sentiments of you all, fellow delegates, in proposing to make the conquest of the Jewish communities one of our immediate aims.
. . . We must not content ourselves with knowing to what extent the Zionist idea has laid hold of Jewry. The facts must be demonstrated. *The ballot is the only suitable, wholly unexceptionable means to this end.*[2]

THE BILTMORE CONFERENCE

During the thirties, predominant Zionist attention was focussed upon the economic upbuilding of Palestine with a view toward providing homes for many thousands of refugees from Europe.[3] Occupied by the concrete tasks of raising funds for Palestine and of drawing non-Zionists into this humanitarian project, American Zionists made few demands regarding the ultimate political status of Palestine. With the outbreak of World War II, however, Zionists evinced marked interest in postwar peace plans and their probable disposition of the Palestine Mandate. Embittered by the tragedy of Jewish massacres in Europe and disillusioned by Great Britain's increasingly narrow construction of the intent of the Balfour Declaration, Zionist writers began to inquire "After the War—Then What?" and to present "Programs for Tomorrow."[4] The terms "Jewish Commonwealth" and "Jewish State" reappeared in common parlance in place of the more politically ambiguous phrase "Jewish Homeland."

Closely related to this renewed interest in the constitutional and international status of Palestine was a rising popular sentiment demanding "Jewish unity for effective Jewish action." Long subjected to the appeals of a host of competing and overlapping national organizations and fund-raising drives, American Jewry indicated a greater desire for communal cooperation in the preparation of a common program for postwar Jewry.[5]

Zionists were quick to exploit this popular demand for unity. Beginning with the dissolution in 1941 of the General Jewish Council—a consultative body composed of representatives of B'nai B'rith, the American Jewish Committee, the American Jewish Congress, and the Jewish Labor Committee—the Zionist Organization of America's *New Palestine* began to carry such editorials as "Toward a United Jewish Front in America," "Reconstituting Jewish Unity," and "On Jewish Unity." [6] The implication was clear: "Jewish unity" and the destiny and welfare of Palestine were compatible, indeed inseparable, concerns of American Zionists. Zionists, one writer advised, should seize this "psychological moment to activate the Jewish masses as well as the intelligentsia and the higher middle class for participation in an ever-expanding program in the interests of the Jewish homeland." And, after erecting a "Jewish Congress for Palestine" representative of all American Jews, Zionists should proceed to "determine the concrete suggestions and demands which the Jewish people must place before the tribunal of the victorious democracies at the end of the present war." [7]

Before Zionists could engineer the creation of an overall body representative of the totality of the American Jewish community, steps had first to be taken to bolster Zionist morale for the arduous undertaking. The various independent Zionist parties had to be coordinated in pursuit of a common objective instead of being left, as previously, to pursue unrelated endeavors. Above all, it had to be determined if some Zionist groups, notably Hadassah, Women's Zionist Organization of America, would support a consciously *political program* for their members in addition to their ordinary philanthropic and humanitarian projects in Palestine.

Formerly, World Zionist Congresses, usually meeting in Switzerland, would bring together Zionist parties from all over the earth in order to mend Zionist cohesion or to formulate needed movement policy. Now, however, the world Zionist movement was fragmented and decimated by war. An international Zionist convocation was out of the question.[8] Accordingly, an "Extraordinary Zionist Conference" was held on May 6–11, 1942, at New York's Biltmore Hotel. Over six hundred delegates representing the four major American parties—ZOA, Hadassah, Mizrachi and Poale Zion—assembled to discuss the future of Palestine, possibilities for cooperation with non-Zionists, and "methods for obtaining a united representation of Jewry at the forthcoming peace conference after victory has been achieved." [9] With Chaim Weizmann, President of the Jewish Agency, David Ben-Gurion, Chairman of the Jewish Agency Executive, and Nahum Goldmann, a member of the Agency Executive, in attendance, the Biltmore gathering took on the character of a World Zionist Congress and lent added importance to this first joint meeting of all major American Zionist parties since World War I.

Exhorted by Ben-Gurion to reaffirm the original political intention of the Balfour Declaration and the Mandate—a "Jewish Commonwealth"—and by Rabbi Abba Hillel Silver to beware of the "unreal, spurious and dangerous" distinctions between "political Zionism" and "philanthropic humanitarianism," the delegates enacted an eight-point program, subsequently known as the "Biltmore Program." [10] Among the demands expressed in this authoritative formulation of Zionist policy, later to be adopted by virtually the entire international Zionist movement, were those calling for the abrogation of the White Paper of May, 1939, and the formation of "a Jewish military force fighting under its own flag and under the high command of the United Nations." Most important, however, was Plank VIII which declared:

> . . . the new world order cannot be established on foundations of peace, justice and equality unless the problem of Jewish homelessness is finally solved. The Conference urges that the gates of Palestine be opened; that the Jewish Agency be vested with control of immigration into Palestine and with the necessary authority for upbuilding the country, including the development of its unoccupied and uncultivated lands; and that *Palestine be established as a Jewish Commonwealth* integrated in the structure of the new democratic world.[11]

Thus it was that American Zionists, who had hitherto "steadfastly refused to formulate the ultimate aim of the movement, preferring instead to concentrate on the practical task of building the Jewish National Home," [12] promulgated the political program which was thenceforth to guide their efforts in the Jewish community. Moreover, the Biltmore Program and the enthusiasm en-

gendered in the process of its formulation seem to have strengthened Zionist cohesion and morale greatly, for after May, 1942, the
Zionist press and leadership assumed an air of new confidence and
determination. Not only was the movement more harmonious
than at any time in the past few years, but Hadassah delegates,
Nahum Goldmann informed his Jerusalem colleagues, had con-
founded their critics by demonstrating "surprising Zionistic education" and great "political maturity" in enthusiastically accepting
the Biltmore Program over the objections of some of their more
timid leaders. Politically speaking, American Zionism had come
of age.[13] In the words of *New Palestine,* the clear task of a coordinated Zionist movement was now to enlist all American Jewry
behind the Biltmore Program: "The day of appeasement is past.
. . . Zionism must now recover the missionary zeal of its early
years. To convert non-Zionists and even anti-Zionists to our cause
must be the task to which every one of us addresses himself." [14]

THE PITTSBURGH CONFERENCE

The Zionist plan to mobilize the entire Jewish community
behind the Biltmore Program was launched in June, 1942. Strikingly enough, on the surface this attempt did not emanate directly
from the ZOA or from the American Emergency Committee for
Zionist Affairs, but rather from Zionist Henry Monsky, President
of B'nai B'rith. Monsky had long resented the continuing bilateral
negotiations between the Zionists and the American Jewish Committee [15] and, after meeting Chaim Weizmann in Chicago in June
and other leading Zionists later, he agreed to sponsor a preliminary conference of national Jewish membership organizations.[16]
In the view of top Zionist leaders, it was tactically useful that such
a conference be called by B'nai B'rith because it was not specifically
a Zionist body and also because B'nai B'rith's public assumption of
the initiative made it more likely that the 150,000 members of the
Order would be effectively committed to the probable Zionist outcome of the conference.[17]

In a letter of January 6, 1943, addressed to thirty-four groups,
Monsky invited delegates to a meeting in Pittsburgh, designed to
consider measures to bring about "some agreement on the part of

the American Jewish community . . . with respect to the postwar status of Jews and the upbuilding of a Jewish Palestine." [18] This action, as Monsky later admitted, was taken "without first consulting the Executive Committee of the B'nai B'rith—an unusual act, a rather bold, and, I think probably, a dangerous one, for which I could have been disciplined." [19]

In answer to this invitation, seventy-eight representatives from every invited organization except the American Jewish Committee and the Jewish Labor Committee assembled in Pittsburgh on January 23-24, 1943. Speaking for approximately one million members, these representatives decided to convene an American Jewish Assembly to arrive at a "common program of action in connection with post-war problems," specifically those relating to the "rights and status of Jews in the post-war world" and "all matters looking to the implementation of the rights of the Jewish people with respect to Palestine." [20]

Although the Pittsburgh meeting took no substantive action on the Palestine question, this controversial issue clearly underlay the discussion which ensued. Monsky, for example, lamented the "state of confusion" in the American Jewish community concerning the political aspirations of Zionism. Noting the conflict then in progress between the anti-Zionist American Council for Judaism and the Zionists, Monsky queried whether, "in the interest of the Jewish people," it would not have been better for the two opposing groups "to compose their quarrels in private, rather than to hold them up for public gaze and criticism." [21]

Representing the Zionist Organization of America, Judge Morris Rothenberg argued that Zionists considered the proposed Assembly necessary in order to obtain "a recording of the opinion of the majority of Jews in this country, as expressed through a democratic forum," so that future delegations to government officials in Washington could rightfully claim to speak for the Jews of America. Zionists wanted an end to the prevailing situation in which, due to the absence of a reliable "testing ground" or "sounding board for Jewish opinion," ninety Reform rabbis could make a statement to the *New York Times* that the "vast majority" of American Jews were opposed to Zionism. Therefore, concluded Rothenberg, Zionists were "willing to come to an open forum. Let everyone have his say, and then let there be a recording of the vote; and that vote . . . is what we want." [22]

For the non-Zionist Union of American Hebrew Congregations (Reform), Robert P. Goldman also injected a word about the necessity for avoiding "fratricidal warfare" and hopefully predicted that all Jews would meet on "a median ground on which we can all unite." With regard to Palestine, Goldman, a Zionist for a quarter of a century, declared:

> We all want Palestine. There is not a person in this country, I think, who does not want Palestine for Jews, and it is just a question of defining terms. . . . If we can sit down together and change a word here and a word there, and compromise on this statement and that statement, as statesmen must do, we will come to a common conclusion.[23]

Hailed by the Zionists and virtually the entire Jewish press as "an historic conference," [24] the Pittsburgh meeting adjourned after creating an executive committee to arrange the terms of participation in the proposed American Jewish Assembly, to fix the date of nationwide elections for delegates, to raise the required funds, and to set the date and place of the forthcoming meeting. It was agreed that five hundred delegates should comprise the Assembly, of whom 375 would be popularly elected through local or regional conferences of the Jewish communities on the basis of their respective populations and 125 named by the cooperating national membership organizations. Regardless of size, national organizations would be represented on the basis of parity, but proportional representation would be observed in all local elections "in order to assure minority representation." [25]

SKIRMISHES IN THE COMMUNITY

Reference has already been made in Chapters 5 and 6 to the ultimately successful efforts of the Zionists to involve the American Jewish Committee and the Jewish Labor Committee in the proposed Assembly. But before this occurred, Zionists had first to win a number of preliminary skirmishes. Objecting to the name "Assembly" on the ground that it implied "a separate political enclave . . . through which sections of America's population would rule themselves, deal with the national government, or negotiate with other governments in the interest of their group," [26] the American Jewish Committee had at first refused to participate in the Pittsburgh deliberations. After considerable discussion and correspondence between the Zionist-led Executive Committee for the Assembly and the American Jewish Committee, however, a compromise agreement was reached. The AJC supposedly accepted the idea that the forthcoming meeting *would* claim to speak for the totality of American Jewry, since "freedom of action" by the constituent organizations would be contrary to the purpose of the Assembly, that is, the forging of a program of *united action.* On the other hand, the proposed name of "American Jewish Assembly" was changed to "American Jewish Conference" and the Assembly Executive Committee conceded "the right of any participating organization to dissent from, and so dissenting, not be bound by, the conclusions of" the Conference.[27] Thereupon, the American Jewish Committee subscribed to the "Call for the American Jewish Conference," released on April 30, 1943. As AJC Executive Secretary Morris D. Waldman later recalled, the Committee was unhappy over being maneuvered into joining the Conference, but had it not joined it "would have suffered much criticism as being oligarchic. The Jewish public would not have shared our fears and reservations. Having participated we have demonstrated our cooperative spirit." [28] Following the lead of the AJC, the Jewish Labor Committee, after being granted sixteen seats in the Conference, agreed to participate, although it did not enter slates in the local elections. A total of sixty-five national Jewish organizations were thus represented in the Conference.[29]

But no sooner was the adherence of these two influential organizations secured than yet another conflict of interests was revealed. And again the conflict was garbed in the ideological robes of democratic organizational life. This new conflict centered upon the role to be played by the prominent philanthropic leaders of the local Jewish federations and welfare funds in the forthcoming elections of delegates to the American Jewish Conference. Non-Zionists argued that federations and funds should be given the status of "national membership organizations," thus enabling them to elect delegates. Zionists, on the other hand, held that federations and welfare funds were not membership groups but primarily fund-raising agencies whose contributors were already overwhelmingly enrolled in local Jewish membership organizations. In order to preserve the sacred democratic principle of "One Man equals One Vote," Zionists held that no "duplicating" representation should be accorded. But, again, a compromise measure conferring token representation upon federations and funds was drafted after the American Jewish Committee vigorously protested that such organizations "constitute the backbone of a substantial part of every Jewish community and to exclude them is to confine membership in the Conference to restricted groups of the community." [30]

Notwithstanding these concessions to his local constituents, Sidney Hollander, president of the Council of Jewish Federations and Welfare Funds and center of the 1941 controversy over a Zionist-opposed national budgeting service for the United Jewish Appeal,[31] protested to Henry Monsky, Chairman of the American Jewish Conference Executive Committee about the "inferior voting status" and "negligible fraction of the representation granted other local membership groups." Pointing out that "active Jewish leaders, though they play an important part in the planning and promotion of Jewish causes through their local federations and welfare funds, are frequently not members of other bodies participating in your Conference," Hollander warned Monsky that the forthcoming Conference was leaving itself open to the charge that it is "not fully responsive to large sections of Jewish life and leadership." [32] But despite this protest, a reconsideration of the issues involved was climaxed by a vote of 22-6 sustaining the original allocation of representation to the local federations and welfare funds.[33]

Although this dispute over representation never took the overt form of a conflict between Zionists and non-Zionists, probably due to a studied attempt by all parties to hold the Conference without additional public controversy, press reports of the period charged that "Jewish Power Politics" were at work behind the scene. *Independent Jewish Press Service,* for example, claimed that once again the Council of Jewish Federations and Welfare Funds was being used "without the knowledge and the approval of the overwhelming majority of Jewish communities which use its services." Noting that the American Jewish Committee's anti-Zionist officers were expecting a difficult time in electing Conference delegates allied with their point of view, *IJPS* saw a plot in the making whereby the Committee, using the mechanism of the Council of Federations which it controlled through interlocking directorates, would gain greater Conference representation. Unable to rely upon "democratic elections," this "handful of men" was merely "preparing an alibi for itself" in anticipation of the Zionist outcome of the American Jewish Conference by creating the diversionary cry of "unfair treatment and discrimination." [34]

Since other philanthropically oriented and predominantly non-Zionist groups—Joint Distribution Committee, Hebrew Immigrant Aid Society (HIAS) and Organization for Rehabilitation and Training (ORT)—had also been excluded from the Conference under a strict interpretation of the term "membership organization," the American Jewish Committee now proposed another maneuver: the co-option of a number of "outstanding personalities" who would "supplement" the locally elected and nationally appointed Conference delegates and thus partially "correct the inequities of the elections." This new proposal, too, was decisively rejected by the Zionist-dominated Conference Executive Committee. Defeated on all counts, the American Jewish Committee henceforth remained aloof from the local elections, characterizing them as dominated by "electioneering, factional log-rolling and personal bitterness." [35]

After the issuance of the "Call for the American Jewish Conference," the scene of conflict shifted to the local communities where spirited election campaigns were waged during the summer of 1943. Unable to secure agreement in the Conference Executive Committee over the feasibility or desirability of direct popular elections,* a "modified form of democratic procedure" was unanimously adopted, namely, the election of delegates through local or regional electoral conferences. In these areas, local membership organizations or branches of national organizations would elect delegates to the electoral conferences on the basis of one delegate for the first fifty members and one for each additional seventy-five members. The rules of election further stipulated that an organization entitled to choose electors must have been established prior to December 7, 1941, and be "engaged in recognized Jewish activi-

---

* Members of the AJC opposed such elections, which they termed Nazi-style "plebiscites." Although the official record of the Conference is silent on the source of opposition to the direct elections, the supposition that it was the AJC (realizing its weakness in terms of mass following) which opposed them, seems tenable.

ties with a membership of more than fifty." Electors were further required to be twenty-one years of age or over and have been a resident of their communities for at least one year.[36]

The 375 locally-elected delegates to the American Jewish Conference were allocated to the local and regional electoral conferences on the basis of one delegate per 10,000 Jewish inhabitants or major fraction thereof. Ostensibly in order to assure minority representation, moreover, a system of proportional representation was applied by means of cumulative or "bullet" voting. In other words, electors were permitted to cast all of their votes for *one* candidate of their choice, rather than be forced to distribute them among the number of candidates allocated to their particular electoral district. With minor exceptions, all voting was by secret ballot. Allowance was also made for individuals unaffiliated with a local organization to express their adherence to the Conference by permitting them to nominate a candidate for it, provided that one hundred such unaffiliated persons signed the nominating petition.[37]

The importance of the community-wide elections for the policy outcome of the Conference was obvious to the Zionist leadership. Immediately after the promulgation of election procedures, *New Palestine* began to carry detailed instructions and exhortations to its membership on how best to win a Zionist victory at the polls. Rabbi James G. Heller, for example, reminding his readers that the forthcoming American Jewish Conference was to be the first "representative expression of the opinion of American Jews" since the American Jewish Congress of 1917, gave this formula for electoral success:

> . . . it is of the utmost importance that all those whose sympathies are with the Zionist ideal should unite so that they may elect a maximum number of delegates from their representative communities and regions.
>
> In order to do this under the election machinery which has been devised, they ought to agree upon a slate of delegates to be nominated and ought also to vote for them "cumulatively,"—that is, by refraining from spreading their votes over the total number of delegates to be elected and concentrating them upon their own candidates.
>
> The Biltmore Platform has become the Magna Charta of Zionist policy. A maximum number of delegates must come to the convention pledged to it.

Zionists unite for action! Organize in your communities! Elect those who will truly represent you! [38]

Issuing a similar "Challenge to Zionists," Rabbi Israel Goldstein warned Zionists against the tendency to elect delegates

. . . whose only qualification is their prominence in the community because of their social standing or philanthropic credentials. The processes of democracy in Jewish life . . . call for a representation of policies rather than of prominent names . . .
Zionists have a tremendous stake in the forthcoming elections. . . .
We Zionists have been constantly asserting that Zionism is the will of the great majority of American Jewry. We are now challenged to prove our claims.[39]

Elections for the Conference took place in 78 communities and 58 regions in every state of the Union and in the District of Columbia. From a total of 968 candidates who stood for election, 379 delegates were chosen by 22,500 electors representing 8,486 local groups with a direct constituency of approximately 1,500,000 persons. In addition, claimed the Conference Executive Committee, at least 750,000 persons, related by family ties to members of participating groups, were indirect or silent partners to the vote. Thus, at least 2,250,000 Jews were represented by the 379 elected delegates. Even allowing for overlapping, the additional 123 organizational delegates represented additional tens of thousands of persons.[40]

As the Zionists confidently expected, the Conference elections resulted in a resounding victory for their cause. Of the 379 elected delegates, fully 240, or 63 percent, were formal members of the Zionist Organization of America or its affiliates. In addition, more than one hundred delegates were elected on slates of the Poale Zion (Labor Zionists) and Mizrachi (Orthodox Zionists).[41] Few Zionist candidates anywhere were defeated in the elections. So complete was the victory that *New Palestine* reported some Zionists were wishing that a few more non-Zionists had been elected, if only "for appearance's sake!" [42]

Following the elections, a Committee of Five—consisting of representatives of the American Jewish Congress, the American Jewish Committee, ZOA, Poale Zion, and B'nai B'rith—was appointed by the Conference Executive Committee to devise procedures permitting "the democratic organization of the Conference, adequate representation on a proportional basis in all committees of all organized opinion, and a balanced discussion on the floor." Such a procedure was ostensibly intended "not just to register a vote," but "to win by persuasion the voluntary cooperation of all concerned in a program of action affecting Jewish life and to secure as large a majority for that action as may be possible." [43]

Among the measures devised by the Committee of Five was a system of nine "blocs" corresponding to "certain points of view that prevail in organized American Jewish life." Once formed, these blocs would serve as a basis for committee appointments and for allocating speaking time at the plenary sessions. A communication addressed to all delegates, accordingly, requested them to adhere to one, and only one, of these blocs, but it was stressed that such adherence would "not abridge the full and complete freedom of action of any delegate with respect to program and ideology." [44] The nine blocs, as ultimately constituted, were as follows:

TABLE 17.   Bloc Voting at the American Jewish Conference [45]

	NUMBER OF DELEGATES
1. AMERICAN JEWISH CONGRESS	111
American Jewish Congress, American Jewish Congress Women's Division, American Federation for Polish Jews, Council of Jewish Fraternal Federations, Free Sons of Israel, Independent Order Brith Abraham, Independent Order Brith Sholom, Progressive Order of the West, United Galician Jews of America, United Roumanian Jews of America	
2. B'NAI B'RITH	63
3. CONSERVATIVE RELIGIOUS GROUP	19
United Synagogue of America, National Women's League of the United Synagogue of America, Rabbinical Assembly of America, National Federation of Jewish Men's Clubs	
4. GENERAL ZIONISTS	116
Zionist Organization of America, Hadassah, Order Sons of Zion	
5. JEWISH LABOR COMMITTEE	16
Forward Association, Jewish Labor Committee, Jewish Socialist Verband, Left Poale Zion, United Hebrew Trades, Workmen's Circle	

TABLE 17.   Bloc Voting at the American Jewish Conference *(cont.)*

	NUMBER OF DELEGATES
6. LABOR ZIONIST BLOC Poale Zion-Zeire Zion, Jewish National Workers' Alliance, Pioneer Women's Organization, League for Labor Palestine	49
7. NON-PARTISAN GROUP American Jewish Committee, National Council of Jewish Women, Jewish War Veterans	42
8. REFORM RELIGIOUS GROUP Union of American Hebrew Congregations, National Federation of Temple Sisterhoods, National Federation of Temple Brotherhoods	21
9. RELIGIOUS NATIONAL ORTHODOX BLOC Mizrachi Organization of America, Mizrachi Women's Organization of America, Hapoel Hamizrachi, National Council of Young Israel, Rabbinical Council of America, Union of Orthodox Jewish Congregations, Union of Orthodox Jewish Congregations —Women's Branch	61
No Designation	3
TOTAL	501

The distribution of registrations among the various blocs thus clearly indicated that formal Zionist parties together with their allies among the Conservative and Orthodox religious groups, B'nai B'rith, and the American Jewish Congress wielded over four-fifths of the voting strength in the American Jewish Conference as it prepared to convene on August 29, 1943. Moreover, many of the organizations not formally affiliated with the Zionist movement, such as the National Council of Young Israel and the American Federation of Polish Jews, were already committed to uphold the Biltmore Program even before the convening of the American Jewish Conference.[46] Whether as the result of accurate representation or due to "rigged" elections and procedures, as the anti-Zionists naturally claimed, Zionist leaders in America could jubilantly report to their Palestinian colleagues that only one important question remained undecided: whether Zionists would (1) have the Conference adopt a militant Zionist program mirroring the Biltmore

Platform, even at the risk of driving non-Zionists out, or (2) accept a compromise resolution designed to achieve a unanimous vote.[47]

THE RESOLUTION ON PALESTINE

Plenary sessions of the American Jewish Conference were devoted to "discussion" of the major questions facing it:—"Rescue of European Jewry, Palestine, and Post-War Rehabilitation and Reconstruction." Because of the size of the assembly (501 delegates), speakers were chosen on the basis of the nine blocs represented and, therefore, "discussion" was limited to prearranged, formal presentations of previously crystallized organizational policy. These statements convincingly illustrate the centrality of the Palestine question to all the work at hand; it was here alone that American Jewry was faced with grossly divergent, probably incompatible, points of view.

Speaking on behalf of the American Jewish Committee, whose "Statement of Views" of January 31 had occasioned widespread criticism from the Zionists,[48] Judge Joseph M. Proskauer, for example, asked the delegates to remember that the "unity of Jewish action" being sought at the Conference must compel no one to sacrifice his principles. Rather than quarrel about *ultimate ideology,* unity should be achieved through *compromise on immediate conduct.* This, cautioned Proskauer, could be done only by emphasizing Jewish agreements instead of Jewish differences.[49]

One such area of agreement, he pointed out, was a unanimous recognition of "the superb achievement made by our people in Palestine." "Jews throughout the world," he continued,

> . . . regardless of their ideologies, have been glad and proud to help in this epic achievement. . . . We are one in our concern for its preservation and upbuilding, and *I do not believe we would ever have a difference in adopting a formula along the lines . . . of keeping the gates of Palestine open.*[50]

The next evening—"Palestine Night"—two leading Zionists, Rabbi Solomon Goldman (a former president of the Zionist Organization of America) and Rabbi James G. Heller (chairman of the ZOA's National Executive Council, but speaking for the "no designation" delegates) took the floor to urge a similar "moderate" stand on Palestine. Neither speaker mentioned the Biltmore Program or its controversial goal of a Jewish commonwealth. As one Zionist aptly observed, a behind-the-scenes "compromise seemed to be in the making whereby the Zionists would give up their demand for a Jewish Commonwealth in return for non-Zionist support of unlimited Jewish immigration into Palestine." [51]

In fact, such a compromise had already been reached more than six weeks earlier. Ignoring Rabbi Abba Hillel Silver, recently elected co-chairman of the re-organized American Zionist Emergency Council and an outspoken advocate of the commonwealth program, Nahum Goldmann, Louis Lipsky, Meyer Weisgal and other Zionist "moderates" agreed that "it would be inadvisable to force the Jewish Commonwealth issue to the breaking point . . . that rather an attempt should be made to obtain from the Conference a set of general principles dealing with all Jewish problems, including Palestine." A standing committee elected in proportion to the strength of the various participants in the Conference would then be elected, a second session of the Conference would be called, and then—later perhaps—a detailed Palestine resolution would be enacted.[52] Under this pacifying plan, "troublemaker" Silver would be allotted no speaking time at the Conference.

Suddenly and dramatically, Silver, who had never in his life been affiliated with the American Jewish Congress, mounted the rostrum to speak on behalf of the militantly-Zionist Congress bloc. Since his unexpected address unquestionably reversed the moderate compromise trend of the previous Conference proceedings and set the tone for the final Resolution on Palestine, it will be quoted at some length.

Silver began his unscheduled speech with a strident reaffirmation of Herzlian political Zionism: "The immemorial problem of our national homelessness which is the principal source of our millenial tragedy remains as stark and as menacing today as it ever was." He then charged that influential Jews were attempting to circumvent the problem by wishful thinking or by appeals to "Jewish unity" in the face of the world crisis. But emergencies and catastrophes are nothing new for the Jew; they have existed in every generation. The only permanent solution is neither ". . .

new immigration opportunities to other countries for fleeing refugees, nor new colonization schemes in other parts of the world. . . . The only solution is to normalize the political status of the Jewish people by giving it a national basis in its national and historic home." [53]

Reviewing the statements of Lloyd George, Woodrow Wilson, Jan Smuts and Winston Churchill on the meaning of the Balfour Declaration, Silver affirmed that this historical document was not intended as "an immigrant aid scheme," but as the basis for a Jewish commonwealth. "Why," he asked,

> . . . has there arisen among us today this mortal fear of the term "Jewish Commonwealth" which both British and American statesmen took in their stride, as it were, and which our own fellow-Jews . . . endorsed a quarter of a century ago? Why are anti-Zionists, or non-Zionists or neutrals—why are they determined to excise that phrase and, I suspect in some instances at least, the hopes?
>
> Why are they asking us, on the plea of unity, to surrender a basic political concept which was so much a part of the whole pattern of the Balfour Declaration? I suspect it is because they . . . have never really reconciled themselves to the fact both of the Declaration and of the Mandate. They would like to forget about them or have the world forget about them or wish them out of existence. Of course, they have no objections to Jews going to Palestine any more than they would have any objections to Jews going to New Zealand, to Australia or any other part of the world.[54]

Denying that the Zionist demand for a Jewish commonwealth was anything new or that it was simply "a matter of ideology," Silver forcefully described the Zionist goal as essential for the "salvation of a people fighting for its very life." Referring to the question of unity raised by Judge Proskauer, he jibed that all such a concept really meant was that when Zionists "agree with certain people, that is unity. If I ask them to agree with me, that, is disunity." The lowest common denominator of this unity would be for Zionists to give up Zionism altogether!

Nor were more rescue and relief schemes adequate to the needs of the hour, as the new head of the American Zionist Emergency Council saw them:

We cannot truly rescue the Jews of Europe unless we have free immigration into Palestine. We cannot have free immigration into Palestine unless our political rights are recognized there. Our political rights cannot be recognized there unless our historic connection with the country is acknowledged and our right to rebuild our national home is reaffirmed. These are inseparable links in the chain. The whole chain breaks if one of the links is missing.[55]

Summing up his case for a forthright demand for a Jewish commonwealth, Silver delineated crucial distinctions between a Zionist and a non-Zionist approach to Jewish problems and he counseled the assembled delegates to ignore the fears and misgivings of supposedly "moderate" Jewish leaders:

A strange thing has occurred here. We are asked not to relinquish our convictions but at the same time not to express them. . . .

Is this Jewish statesmanship? Is this Jewish vision, courage, faith? Or, are we to declare in this great assembly . . . that we stand by those who have given their tears and their blood and their sweat to build for them and for us and for the future generations, at long-last after the weary centuries, a home, a national home, a Jewish Commonwealth, where the spirit of our people can finally be at rest, as well as the body of many of our persecuted people?

Are we going to take counsel here of fear of what this one or that one might say, of how our actions are likely to be misinterpreted; or are we to take counsel of our inner moral convictions, of our faith, of our history, of our achievements, and go forward in faith, to build and to heal? [56]

Silver's appeals touched off an emotional demonstration of unprecedented proportions in the Waldorf-Astoria Ballroom. *Hatikvah* ("The Hope"), the Zionist anthem, was sung over and over again. Shouts and cheering took many minutes to subside. Many delegates wept unashamedly in their seats. Apparently Silver's oratory had acted as a catalytic agent in arousing intense predispositions formed under the press of events occurring in Europe and Palestine. Confronted with daily reports of atrocities committed against the Jews in Nazi-controlled Europe and of official British brutality in Palestine, the delegates were in a state of anxiety as to what could be done about their suffering overseas brethren. Hotel corridors and ante-rooms buzzed with excitement over the scope of Zionist demands in Palestine. "Should the Conference content itself," asked the delegates, "with an appeal for free immigration into Palestine, or go the entire distance to second the so-called 'politically maximum' Biltmore Program with a call for a Jewish commonwealth?"

It was in the Committee on Palestine, consisting of sixty-seven members apportioned on the basis of bloc strength, that this question was forcibly resolved. In five meetings presided over by Abba Hillel Silver, the committee considered three draft resolutions on Palestine. The first, sponsored by the General Zionist, Labor Zionist, Religious National Orthodox and American Jewish Congress blocs (337 of the 501 Conference delegates), spoke unreservedly of the "re-creation of the Jewish Commonwealth." [57] A second, presented by Rabbi Maurice N. Eisendrath on behalf of the Reform Religious Group, was more cautious, merely declaring that "the time has now come for all Jews, irrespective of ideological differences, to unite their efforts toward the establishment of . . . a Jewish homeland in Palestine." Self-government in accordance with the Balfour Declaration and the Mandate was not considered immediately attainable and, therefore, Zionist demands for control of immigration and colonization in the hands of the Jewish Agency for Palestine were not seconded.[58] A third resolution, introduced by three "no designation" delegates also spoke of a Jewish commonwealth, but in a somewhat more guarded and distant sense.[59]

Discussion of the three measures showed that Zionists were far from united on the desirability of proclaiming a Jewish commonwealth as the goal of the united American Jewish community. Rabbi James G. Heller, for example, warned that the American government, in conjunction with Great Britain, was about to issue a statement on Palestine that would "place for the duration of the war, as a matter of patriotic duty, a quietus on discussion of Zionism in this country." Under the circumstances, "extreme demands" by the Zionists or by American Jewry would be "inadvisable"; any statement on Palestine issued by the Conference should be couched in "moderate terms." Besides, declared the influential chairman of the ZOA's National Executive Council, the term "Jewish commonwealth" lent itself to "some misunderstanding" even among Zionists. The best policy to be followed, in short, was to *set up a committee* designed to "formulate further statements to be brought as recommendations to further meetings that may be held before the cessation of hostilities." [60]

Similar statements of caution were made by another prominent Zionist Reform rabbi, Julius Gordon, chairman of the Central Conference of American Rabbis' Palestine Committee, who urged that the Conference transcend differences by emphasizing the "content" of Zionist aims rather than "labels and phraseology," and by Robert P. Goldman, who urged "statesmanlike compromise" instead of "the right of the majority to impose its views on the minority." A representative of the Reform Union of American Hebrew Congregations who also described himself as a formal Zionist for over twenty-five years, Goldman confided that he had it "on very good authority" that the adoption of the Jewish commonwealth program would affect the Jewish cause in Palestine very unfavorably. On the other hand, he repeated, "by adopting a moderate, practical program . . . one that will not excite the Arab world and will strengthen the hands of the opposition to our interests in the British and American Governments, we stand a very good chance of getting what we want immediately, or within a reasonable time." [61]

Similarly, Judge Joseph Proskauer of the American Jewish Committee characterized the Reform resolution as a "moderate platform" and warned that the practice of asking for everything in the hope of getting something was "a very dangerous doctrine": "All the people hostile to Jewry are just waiting for the urging of these maximum demands in order to cement the opposition to the legitimate building up of Palestine itself." Proskauer further stated that he had "spoken to Washington" during the afternoon and he was assured, "from sources which he could not disclose," that "it would be a tragedy to put forth this maximal demand." As far as he was concerned, and he did not wish to imply any threat, "I would be saving Palestine and saving Jewry, if in the event of the adoption of this maximal program I would exercise our right to dissent and withdraw, and I have seriously to consider that possibility." In conclusion, stated Proskauer, unity could be achieved only on the basis of "moderation." Perhaps the Zionists could merely add a preamble on a resolution which would preserve their ultimate claims. After all, he concluded,

Nobody expects a Jewish State now; nobody wants it now. Time is a great healer. . . . This is a particularly fitting situation for the application of caution. . . . There are those who are not identified with Zionists, but who want to help in the building of Palestine, yet they believe that it is a grievous error to ask for statehood now. That is why I say to you, let us have unity.[62]

On the other hand, the position of M. J. Slonim, delegate from St. Louis, may be cited as representative of the more activist element of the Conference which eventually had its way. Noting that every other people in the world was "asking for the maximum" in its postwar peace plans, Slonim queried why the Jews always had to be different by asking for the minimum. Jews should not wait for an overall peace conference which might never take place. Decisions crystallizing the fate of Palestine were being made at meetings of government leaders wherever and whenever they met; "We are not living in a political vacuum today, while the war is going on." Jewish demands, therefore, should be made clear to the world—now! [63]

A third position, represented by Rabbi B. Benedict Glazer of Detroit, while not supporting any particular resolution, protested against "the atmosphere of intimidation which has been generated here in the name of people or officials who are not part of this Conference." Asserting that little could be done to the Jews which would be worse than what they had already suffered in all parts of the world, Glazer declared that he was not frightened by reports of what may be done to Jews if they take or do not take this or that kind of action. If British propaganda agents from the Ministry of Information were active in the United States attempting to influence American public opinion, Glazer asked, why should American citizens as representatives of the largest Jewish community in the world be reluctant to influence their nation? [64]

Other speakers in the Committee on Palestine lined up increasingly on the side of the "maximalists" as represented by the first or Zionist resolution. It soon became apparent that the delegates' Zionist enthusiasm was so great that, even if the leaders had been prepared to compromise, the rank and file would have dissented vigorously.

It is important to note, moreover, that for some of the groups present the Biltmore or Jewish commonwealth program was hardly more than a *minimal* demand. Gedaliah Bublick, for instance, told the assembled delegates that the joint Zionist resolution was, as far as the Religious National Orthodox Bloc was concerned, a compromise between his group and other Zionists "for the sake of unity." Since his group had wanted to demand "a Jewish State on both sides of the Jordan, and a Jewish army led by a Jewish general," the Jewish commonwealth resolution was a minimum from which he could not retreat "even one iota." [65]

At the fifth and final meeting of the Palestine Committee, a new resolution on Palestine was introduced by Chairman Silver. Based mainly on the Zionists' Jewish commonwealth goal, the new version also included recommendations from the Reform and "no designation" proposals. Arrived at as the result of informal negotiations, this synthesis resulted in the withdrawal of all other measures and, consequently, was adopted by a vote "overwhelmingly in the affirmative." Only the two votes of Proskauer and Jacob Blaustein of the American Jewish Committee were specifically recorded in the negative.[66]

According to the memoirs of Morris Waldman, executive secretary of the American Jewish Committee, Proskauer, Blaustein and he now made a desperate eleventh-hour attempt to prevent the approved resolution from coming to a vote before the full Conference. Meeting with Rabbis Wise and Silver and Nahum Goldmann of the Jewish Agency in Wise's hotel room, the three American Jewish Committee spokesmen strenuously urged that the explosive question of Palestine be deferred to a later session of the Conference and, meanwhile, that the former private Zionist-non-Zionist negotiations (Weizmann-Stroock conferences) [67] be re-opened. The Zionist response was stated succinctly by Goldmann: "I am sorry that the Conference sessions were not postponed . . . but in view of the tremendous pro-Zionist emotion generated throughout the country we would be torn limb from limb if we were now to defer action on the Palestine resolution." [68]

The final resolution calling for "the fulfillment of the Balfour Declaration, and of the Mandate for Palestine whose intent and underlying purpose, based on the 'historical connection of the Jewish people with Palestine,' was to reconstitute Palestine as the Jewish Commonwealth," [69] the abrogation of the White Paper of 1939, and the opening of the gates of Palestine to Jewish immigration, was introduced before a tensely expectant plenary session of the American Jewish Conference on September 1. After reading two statements from the Jewish Labor Committee and the National Council of Jewish Women indicating that those organizations would take no official stand on the resolution,[70] Silver read and moved the formal adoption of the resolution on Palestine. Wild applause followed. Seconded enthusiastically by Henry Monsky, President of B'nai B'rith and originator of the Conference, the resolution was put to the vote by Rabbi Stephen S. Wise. Only four votes were recorded as Wise requested the delegates to raise their cards in open dissent; but a veritable sea of cards waved in response to his call for a show of hands in affirmation. A flurry of excitement swept up the gathering and *Hatikvah* was sung again and again.[71]

When order was finally restored, Judge Proskauer stepped forward to register a formal dissent from the resolution. Indicating that he now understood the feelings Daniel must have experienced when he entered the lion's den, the president of the American Jewish Committee declared:

> We are convinced that it is inadvisable to bring to the foreground of public attention at this time political matters that may divide the peoples of the United Nations and create added difficulties. . . .
>
> In entering this Conference, the American Jewish Committee acted on the condition that the . . . right of any participating organization to dissent from and, so dissenting, not to be bound by the conclusions of the Conference was recognized. Pursuant to that provision . . . we regretfully dissent from concurrence with these resolutions.
>
> We express the devout hope that we may still cooperate heartily for the cause of Jewry within the great area in which we have found accord and agreement.[72]

The majority of the Jewish press greeted the Palestine resolution as an "historic," "momentous," "epoch-making" demonstration of the "greater political maturity of the American Jewish community" and the "tremendous acceptance of the Zionist cause by American Jewry." *New Palestine* expressed jubilation that the Conference had

> . . . completely identified itself with the great ideal to which we have been dedicated for almost half a century.
>
> The Zionist position is now the position of American Jewry. The Conference has served to crystallize Jewish opinion in our own country. This marks the end of long discussion and debate. . . . The time has come for action.[73]

Mrs. David de Sola Pool, President of Hadassah, Women's Zionist Organization of America, was even more elated as she described the work of the Conference: "We American Zionists of the past forty years and more are *Halutzim* [pioneers]. We worked in a wilderness of misunderstanding. There have been more misconceptions of Zionism than of any other Jewish cause." Recalling that fifteen and twenty-five years ago Zionists had labored "against all odds" to enlist less that fifty individual Jews of prominence in the Jewish Agency for Palestine, she concluded:

> We have gone infinitely beyond that point. We have now won over not merely individuals; we now have at our side whole national organizations with thousands and hundreds of thousands of members. These are not mere "non-Zionist" bodies. They have pledged their adherence to a full-bodied, positive program of Zionist action. They are now flesh of our flesh, bone of our bone. All that we stand for, all that we struggle for, has become for them, too, an integral ideal.[74]

But different people perceive political reality differently and, at the other end of the political spectrum, Elmer Berger, Executive Director of the anti-Zionist American Council for Judaism, declared that the minor significance of the Conference did not extend beyond the fact that *498 individual Jews* had supported the Biltmore Platform; "No one could say that in the Waldorf-Astoria in New York in 1943, the Jewish 'people' had asked for a Jewish State."[75]

AFTERMATH OF THE PALESTINE RESOLUTION

The actual effect of the Palestine Resolution could not be measured, however, until some months later when the governing bodies of constituent members of the American Jewish Conference had had an opportunity to pass upon its merits. Of those organizations officially adhering to a policy of neutrality on Zionism, B'nai B'rith, the National Council of Jewish Women, the Jewish Labor Committee, the Central Conference of American Rabbis, and the National Federation of Temple Sisterhoods took no action on the demand for a Jewish commonwealth, but several of these groups strongly condemned the White Paper on Palestine and reaffirmed their support for the Balfour Declaration.[76] Jewish War Veterans, on the other hand, adopting its first official stand on Palestine, specifically lauded the Jewish commonwealth demand of the Conference, and approved the entire gamut of Zionist goals relative to immigration and colonization.[77] Most importantly, in the Union of American Hebrew Congregations and the American Jewish Committee, Zionist and non-Zionists clashed openly, with widely different results.

At the October 4, 1943, meeting of the Union of American Hebrew Congregations' Executive Board, resolutions were presented by anti-Zionist rabbis urging the Union to withdraw from the American Jewish Conference on the grounds that the Union's neutrality had been compromised by the Palestine Resolution. Opposing moves advocated by some Zionist rabbis urged the Union to approve the work of the Conference in its entirety. Division of opinion on the matter was too strong for any immediate agreement to be secured, however. Accordingly, the Executive Board contented itself with approval of all aspects of the Conference other than the Palestine Resolution and referred the controversial issue to a special committee of eighteen rabbis charged with devising a compromise solution which could then be ratified by the next meeting of the group's supreme governing body, the Council of the Union.[78]

By the time of the January, 1944, meeting of the Council of the Union it was apparent that most Zionist partisans would be content merely to neutralize the Union as a potential base for anti-Zionist forces in much the same manner that the Central Conference of American Rabbis had been converted from *the* bastion of anti-Zionism to an association sympathetically affiliated with the practical tasks of the Zionist movement. Rabbi Abba Hillel Silver, for example, speaking for the Zionists in the Union, declared:

> I have never . . . come to a Union meeting and urged that we adopt a Zionist platform. I have never come to the C.C.A.R. and urged them to adopt a Zionist platform. I never urged my own congregation to adopt a Zionist platform. I know that there are sharp differences of opinion on this subject and, therefore, a subject that is well to be let alone [*Sic*].

Stating, furthermore, that the recent attempt to unite Zionists and non-Zionists on a common platform was doomed to failure because such a platform could only be reached on a non-Zionist plane, something the Zionists would never agree to do, Silver urged that neither Zionists nor anti-Zionists use the Union for their own purposes: "I would be the last person in the world who would urge the Union to take a Zionist position, but I would be the first person to fight strenuously any resolution that the Union is opposed to the Zionist movement." [79] Neutrality toward Zionism would be the best policy for all concerned, concluded the Zionist leader in the face of persistent demands by anti-Zionists that the UAHC register its disapproval of Zionism and secede from the Zionist-captured American Jewish Conference.

With bitterness over the Zionist question threatening to destroy the effectiveness of the Union's efforts on behalf of Reform Judaism, a compromise resolution, essentially identical to the neutral course urged by Rabbi Silver, was adopted by the Council of the Union:

> Because in the congregations of the Union there are divergent opinions on the question of Zionism, the Union recognizes the right of each individual to determine his own attitude on this controversial question and, therefore, the Union refrains from taking any action on the Palestine Resolution adopted by the American Jewish Conference.[80]

Thus, the courses of action favored by those Zionists and anti-Zionists who wished the Union to second their respective programs were avoided and the voice of moderation prevailed. The Union remained a party to the American Jewish Conference without giving specific sanction to the Zionist's Biltmore Program. At the same time, Zionist fears that the Union might be utilized as a springboard by the anti-Zionists were removed when the Union agreed not to speak on the subject of Palestine.

In the American Jewish Committee, events were to show a different constellation of Zionist-anti-Zionist power relationships. There, leadership was clearly exercised by men who vacillated between the anti-Zionist positions of the American Council for Judaism and the desire to stand completely aloof from the "political implications" of the Zionist program. The adoption of the "Statement of Views" of January 31, 1943, had shown that Zionist members of the Committee were in a decided minority. The forceful conduct of Judge Proskauer at the American Jewish Conference had also demonstrated that the AJC would not be cowed by the fact that pro-Zionist opinion obviously prevailed in the vast majority of national Jewish organizations and local Jewish groups. The question now agitating the Jewish community was whether the AJC would reaffirm its non-Zionist orientation but remain in the Conference "for the sake of Jewish unity," or launch its own program on Palestine in competition with the Zionists and the Zionist-led American Jewish Conference.

It was generally assumed that the answer to this vital question would be given when the annual meeting of the American Jewish Committee convened in January, 1944, four months after the close of the Conference. Unexpectedly, however, the Executive Committee of the AJC, meeting on October 24, 1943, took up the question without consulting the larger membership and, by a vote of 53 to 13 and two abstentions, abruptly decided to secede from the American Jewish Conference. Minutes of this critical meeting are not available but the Committee's Executive Secretary later wrote that the dominant feeling expressed at the time was that the Zionists had overstepped "the bounds of propriety" in forcing the American Jewish Conference to adopt their "maximalist" Biltmore Program. Rabbi Louis Finkelstein, President of Conservative Judaism's Jewish Theological Seminary and virtually the sole non-Reform personality in a position of leadership on the American Jewish Committee, reportedly told the Executive Committee that the Zionists had done "great harm to the Jews of the world" by their actions. Privately, observed Finkelstein, "every responsible Zionist would agree . . . that there isn't one possibility in five hundred that there will be established in the course of the next twenty-five years what is called a Jewish state in Palestine." [81]

Whatever the precise nature of the motives involved, the AJC's leadership announced that it could not remain within the Conference and support the Palestine Resolution now being implemented by the Interim Committee; "remaining in the Conference would give the appearance of unity of action—but only the appearance, not the genuine unity of action that we have always hoped for." [82]

The violent reaction to the American Jewish Committee's secession from the Conference has already been chronicled in Chapter 5 and will not be repeated here. It should suffice to recall that the unprecedented attacks on the Committee—not only by the ZOA, the American Zionist Emergency Council, and the Amer-

ican Jewish Conference, but from practically every organized sector of American Jewry—were of such a magnitude that no other
organization of the sixty-five represented in the Conference chose
to emulate the AJC's "isolationist" and "Jewishly-destructive" act.
Indeed, the only organization which openly complimented the
Committee for its secessionist action was the much-maligned American Council for Judaism. Henceforth, the American Jewish Committee was to discover that regardless of its intellectual merits,
"independence of action" was a very unpopular policy to pursue
in a community craving "Jewish unity" for many of the Zionist
objectives in Palestine.[83]

IMPLEMENTATION OF THE ZIONIST PROGRAM

The enactment of the Palestine Resolution of the American
Jewish Conference marked the practical end of the primary Zion-
ist efforts to convert *American Jewry* to its program. As Rabbi
Israel Goldstein, the new president of the Zionist Organization
of America announced less than two weeks after the Conference
adjourned, the major task of the American Zionist movement would
henceforth be to "win the wholehearted approval of the *American
Government* and people for the Zionist program with respect to
Palestine, which now has become the program of the whole of
American Jewry represented through the democratically elected
American Jewish Conference." [84]

Already the top leaders of the American Jewish Conference
had personally informed Secretary of State Cordell Hull that the
Palestine Resolution represented the unmistakable will of organized American Jewry.[85] At the local level, seminars in numerous
communities were organized so that the policy of the Conference
might trickle down to the entire Jewish population and be trans-
lated into effective, grass roots political action. At the national
level, life memberships were re-instituted by the Zionist Organization and $100 from each of 2,500 individuals was collected for a
"Zionist Emergency Fund" to be used "only for extraordinary purposes in connection with the political struggle which . . . lies
ahead." [86]

In the ensuing Zionist offensive aimed at the American government and non-Jewish population, the Interim Committee of the American Jewish Conference proved to be a consistent ally of the American Zionist Emergency Council. Indeed, no other condition is imaginable since the leadership of the two bodies was virtually indistinguishable. The three co-chairmen of the Interim Committee—Rabbi Israel Goldstein, Rabbi Stephen S. Wise and Henry Monsky—also headed the Zionist Organization of America, the American Zionist Emergency Council, the American Jewish Congress, and B'nai B'rith, while the majority of the other fifty-two Interim Committee members read like a "Who's Who" of the American Zionist movement. For instance, Rabbi Abba Hillel Silver, co-chairman of the American Zionist Emergency Council, simultaneously chaired the Commission on Palestine charged with the implemention of the Conference Resolution on Palestine.[87]

When, therefore, the AZEC proclaimed the opening of a campaign for the abrogation of the Palestine White Paper of 1939, the Interim Committee of the Conference adopted an identical program and urged all Conference delegates to serve on the local Emergency Committees for Palestine then being organized by the AZEC. And, on January 3, 1944, the Palestine Commission of the American Jewish Conference resolved:

> The Palestine Commission shall not do the day-by-day work [which was to be performed by the AZEC], but shall do the political and educational work in order to mobilize American Jewry for the support of the Conference program in relation to Palestine. To that end, the American Jewish Conference shall be fully utilized for the organization of mass activities in support of legislative action deemed necessary to implement the Palestine Resolution.[88]

At the hearings of the U.S. House of Representatives Committee on Foreign Affairs in February, 1944, when the Wright-Compton resolutions approving the ultimate reconstitution of Palestine "as a free and democratic Jewish Commonwealth" were being discussed, Zionists and Conference officials were much in evidence. Earlier, the Conference Interim Committee had dispatched messages to President Roosevelt, Congressional leaders, editors of over six hundred major newspapers, and many influential organizations. Top Zionist spokesmen—Louis Lipsky, Israel Goldstein, Abba Hillel Silver, James G. Heller and Herman Shulman

—took great pains to ensure that the Congress was apprised of the representativeness of the American Jewish Conference. Lipsky, for example, lightly dismissed the anti-Zionist testimony of the American Council for Judaism as the efforts of a mere 2,500 Jews contrasted with the 2,500,000 who had spoken through the Conference in favor of a Jewish Palestine.[89]

Again, in 1945 and 1946, the American Jewish Conference advanced Zionist claims before the United Nations' San Francisco Conference on International Organization and the Anglo-American Committee of Inquiry for Palestine.[90] Seconding every Zionist demand, the American Jewish Conference (which in 1944 reaffirmed its original Resolution on Palestine [91]), declared that it spoke for "ninety-percent" of American Jewry. Only the minuscule anti-Zionist American Council for Judaism was willing to contradict this Zionist contention in public testimony to the contrary.[92]

SUMMARY AND CONCLUSIONS

The foregoing record provides numerous illustrations of the Zionists' and anti-Zionists' profound concern for "democratic procedure" and "democratic ideals" in their jockeying for relative advantage in the Jewish community. Regardless of the substantive issues involved, the democratic mold provided the *sine qua non* of any tactical moves, a convenient appeal for action, and a measuring rod by which to assess the "wrong-doing" of the opposition. Slogans of "unity," "majority rule," "representativeness" and "democracy" provided the ammunition for conflict as well as the cloak for an underlying power struggle between the contending leaderships.[93]

It may also be concluded that the American Jewish Conference marked a considerable victory for the Zionists on their long road to political predominance among American Jewry. After the caucus of Zionist parties at the Biltmore Conference of 1942, a unified and relatively cohesive Zionist leadership emerged, ready to convene the American Jewish Conference. The Conference in turn, speaking for the "overwhelming majority" of American Jewry, proceeded to affirm the Zionist Biltmore Program. For the first time in a quarter of a century, some authoritative measurement of Jewish thinking on the Palestine problem was available for use by the Zionist leadership.

Although the American Jewish Conference was not constituted in a manner to justify the Zionists' oft-repeated claim that at least 90 percent of American Jewry supported a Jewish commonwealth, the magnitude of the community elections and the vote on the Palestine Resolution would seem to confirm Julian Morgenstern's more conservative evaluation of the Conference: "From the consideration of numbers alone it represented, no doubt, the spirit, desire and passions of the majority of American Jewry, though actually of how large a majority we have no way of knowing." [94]

The true merit of the Conference, from the point of view of gauging Jewish public opinion on the Zionist question, was not that it provided an accurate cross-section of the thinking of the *totality* of American Jewry. On behalf of those who were apathetic or those who formed a hard core of "chronic know-nothings" [95] on the subject of Palestine and Zionism, the Conference could not presume to speak. Rather it incontrovertibly measured the thinking of the *organized groups* in American society; it was without question a valid test of Jewish associational support for the Zionist program.*

In this sense, a vote of approximately 480 to 4 on the Palestine Resolution of the American Jewish Conference is a most impressive achievement even when it is remembered that the big American Jewish Congress and B'nai B'rith blocs were largely Zionist all along. It now became possible for Zionist leaders to surmount the tremendous heterogeneity of the American Jewish community in order to pursue their limited objectives in Palestine. It now became possible for Zionist leaders, in their representations before international bodies and statesmen, to claim the virtually unani-

---

* On this point, note Rabbi Joshua Trachtenberg's characterization of the Conference as

> . . . not representative of the American Jewish community. It was not meant to be. The elections were wholly misleading, for they gave the false impression of being based on a real public constituency. Delegates elected on organizational tickets represented and were responsible to no community, local or national; they were bound to "represent" a fractional organizational interest. Since the local communities, as such, played no part in the Conference, delegates selected on a community wide basis were lost sheep, who could find no voice except through the organization blocs, which wiped out their independence and even their identity. Thus the Conference, which was created by the national organizations, never came to represent anything else than these organizations. (*Conference or Assembly?* [Harrisburg, Pa., 1944], pp. 5–6.)

mous approval of organized Jewish opinion for Zionist objectives.

At the same time, the Zionist failure to corral the American Jewish Committee was not without its consequences for Zionist strength and influence. As Rabbi Stephen Wise later conceded, the decision of the Committee to pursue an independent course of action forced the Zionists to spend a great deal of their time and effort in defending themselves against the Committee instead of in more positive pursuits.[96]

Moreover, the Committee's action undoubtedly represented a segment of opinion considerably larger and more influential than was indicated by the four negative votes registered at the Conference. In organizational life, much more than mere numbers must be considered of importance. While the Zionist-led campaign of denouncing the American Jewish Committee apparently kept other non-Zionist groups from leaving the Conference, it could neither force such marginal groups to adopt thoroughgoing Zionists programs nor persuade them to give their wholehearted support to Conference implementation of the Zionist Resolution on Palestine.[97]

It is also necessary to qualify the picture of Zionist victory which emerges from a study of the American Jewish Conference of 1943 because the Resolution on Palestine could probably have been enacted only in the total situation of Jewish suffering unparalleled in history. American Jews, most of whom were only a generation or two removed from Europe and many of whom still maintained contact with relatives there, were naturally moved to "do something" by the almost daily reports of Nazi atrocities. As Chapter 2 demonstrated, the predisposition to alleviate the tragedy of European Jewry and to ameliorate hardships besetting Palestinian Jewry, *when skilfully mobilized and exploited by Zionist leadership,* seems to have produced the public opinion underlying the nearly unanimous Zionist program for Palestine developed in the American Jewish Conference.

This predisposition also apparently induced most non-Zionist organizations to "go along" with the Zionists. While Zionist ideology did not completely "convert" American Jewry, the advocacy by Jewish organizations of a too-zealous policy of "independence" vis-à-vis Palestine was manifestly dangerous. In the final analysis, it was not vague ideological objections to Zionism, such as the fear of "dual loyalty" or the "timeliness and propriety" of the Jewish commonwealth formula, but rather concern for the maintenance of organizational power and prestige in the face of a widely-shared consensus on Palestine, that decided the fate of Zionist claims upon the American Jewish community.

10
zionist propaganda

In the morally neutral terms of the social scientist, propaganda may be defined as "the deliberate use of symbols by representatives of a group in a controversial situation to bring about beliefs, attitudes, and action in accord with the purposes of that group." [1] As such, propaganda is a tool to secure influence, a weapon which may profitably be employed in the political struggle alongside other political weapons, such as organization and personal influence. With specific reference to interest group life, a complicated "propaganda machine" is almost an inevitable concomitant of success. As sociologist C. Wendell King has so aptly observed, "In a mass society, even to bring one's beliefs and proposals into that vague arena called public opinion, simply to get a hearing, calls for elaborate activities. Rousing the apathetic and counteracting the antagonistic are even more difficult matters for the subgroups in such a society." [2]

In their efforts to mobilize the American public behind their program, Zionist leaders employed an extensive variety of public relations techniques, including many types of propaganda organizations, and an abundant number of propaganda themes and media. This chapter is intended as an inquiry into the Zionist use of some of these propaganda weapons vis-à-vis the apathetic and/or uncommitted sectors of the American public, particularly American Jews. The chapter to follow intends to describe the nature and effects of Zionist counterpropaganda against the only organized opposition group in the American Jewish community—the American Council for Judaism.

The hypothesis posed early in this book may profitably be restated at this time: propaganda succeeds in arousing public opinion only where there is an already existent predisposition in the direction urged by the propagandist. This is to say, that propa-

ganda is effective only in certain contexts and "unless it is carefully designed to fit the situation, and related to pre-existing inclinations, it will not succeed." [3] Thus, the "total social situation"
of world Jewry traced in the second chapter should constantly be
recalled when the Zionist "propaganda machine" is studied.

To discuss Zionist propaganda in a more satisfactory manner
than that of a mere cataloging of techniques and media, a great
deal of data would be required which is not presently available.
The reasons for this lack are not difficult to explain. In the first
place, interest groups which pursue controversial objectives take
great pains to protect their archives against the inquiring eyes of
"outsiders." This is particularly true in the case of data concerning interest groups' propaganda activities, for, as David Truman
has generalized, no interest group "admits that it is engaging in
propaganda. Because of the unsavory connotations of the term in
popular usage, only one's opponents use propaganda." [4] To this
general rule, American Zionists offer no marked exception; and,
consequently, available published materials on Zionist propaganda
programs are far from adequate. It is an extremely vexing problem to attempt even a simple reconstruction of what propaganda
measures were utilized by the American Zionist movement in its
long struggle for power and influence, when such measures were
used, and with what frequency. In the second place, and of greater
significance, even when the observer is able to list a particular
technique employed in a past period, no measurements are available which would enable him to gauge the effectiveness, or even
the mere coverage, of that particular device. In other words, the
scant historical material at hand provides no reliable guide to measuring changes in public opinion resulting from Zionist activity
and propaganda.

Nevertheless, it would be useful to survey, even in taxonomic
and chronological fashion, the Zionist propaganda program which
undoubtedly played a significant role in molding public opinion
on the Zionist question. Without such a survey, it would be difficult
to see "Zionists in action"; and, as a result, the erroneous impression might be fostered that changes in public opinion on Zionism
occurred entirely independent of the strivings of organized American Zionists.

The organizational plan for this survey is first to trace Zionist
propaganda techniques which might be termed "constants," that

is, elements which may be found throughout American Zionist history. In this respect, Zionist efforts will be investigated in the spheres of (1) propaganda themes or appeals, (2) press and publications, (3) rallies and public meetings, (4) Jewish education and youth activities, and (5) rabbinical endorsements. Finally, a chronological treatment of Zionist propaganda organizations and programs between 1929 and 1945 will be presented, with the purpose of tracing the use of additional techniques and media and the gradual development of a widely ramified Zionist propaganda machine able to exploit the historical events of the mid-twentieth century.

PROPAGANDA THEMES

The consequences of the lack of reliable content analyses of Zionist propaganda themes or appeals have already been noted.[5] As a partial remedy for this absence of quantitative data, I have chosen to include throughout this study, particularly in the second chapter, a number of quotations from leading addresses and articles by Zionist spokesmen, quotations which an impressionistic survey of Zionist literature seems to confirm as typical expressions of Zionist propaganda. As an introduction to the study of Zionist techniques and media, it may be helpful to generalize about the content or "message" of these appeals. Briefly and popularly summarized, they may be represented by nine statements: [6]

1. Zionism is the Jewish badge of honor—the achievements of Jewish pioneers in Palestine are a shining success and an example for all mankind—Jewish pride and self-respect are enhanced by what happens in Palestine.

2. The Jews everywhere constitute one people—whatever happens to Jews in one land affects their status in another—the unfortunate refugees of Europe must be helped by their more blessed brethren in America—the Jew who cares about his people is a Zionist, for Palestine depends on him.

3. Zionism provides stimulating and pleasant activity of a social nature, as well as work for a worthy cause—Zionism means identifying oneself with the history and destiny of the Jewish people —the Zionist cause is dramatic, for it combats the enemies of the Jewish people while it recreates the Jewish state and nation.

4. Zionism is a constructive way to solve the Jewish problem —auto-emancipation and self-determination are preferable to the endless doles of philanthropy—the Jews must rely upon themselves and not upon the conscience and mercy of the world—no country wants Jewish refugees except Palestine.

5. Zionism perpetuates Judaism and provides for Jewish survival as a distinctive grouping—Palestine will be the cultural center that will enrich American Jewish life by promoting Jewish religion and education—Jewish morale is bolstered by Zionism and the Jew is enabled to express himself in his own unique way, eventually to the benefit of world culture.

6. Zionism will help end anti-Semitism by ending the abnormality of Jewish national homelessness—when anti-Semitism does occur, it can be compensated for by the Jewish sense of belongingness fostered by Zionism.

7. The Jewish state is inevitable—biblical prophecy, a crying world need, and the impressive achievements of Palestinian Jewry all require a statehood solution.

8. Assistance for Palestine is consonant with loyalty to the United States—Palestine is on the front line of the war against Nazism—Palestine is a bulwark of democracy in the midst of feudalism—Zionism brings modernity, progress and democracy to the backward Middle East.

9. The Zionist solution proposes historic justice—a Jewish state is just compensation for innumerable massacres, especially for the 6,000,000 European martyrs of Nazism and Fascism.

PRESS AND PUBLICATIONS

Mention has frequently been made in earlier chapters of the role of the Yiddish and Anglo-Jewish press in fostering Zionist aspirations in Palestine. While measurements of the influence of such periodicals on Jewish thinking are unavailable, a description of their coverage and editorial policy may be attempted.

According to Mordecai Soltes' *The Yiddish Press, An Americanizing Agency* (1923), only one of New York City's daily Yiddish newspapers (*Vorwaerts-Forward*) failed to qualify as "decidedly Zionistic." In fact, no theme transcended Palestine in the frequency and enthusiasm of its reporting.[7] The circulation of the Yiddish press, moreover, was far from insignificant: 535,000 families subscribed to Yiddish dailies in 1927, 425,000 in 1944. Thus, even in the latter days of rapid Americanization, approximately one-third of all American Jewish families subscribed to the Zionist-disposed Yiddish press.[8]

As for the more than two hundred Jewish publications in English, twenty of the twenty-four national periodicals were characterized by one study as very "pro-Palestine, if not actually Zionist," and all of the others were, from the Zionist standpoint, giving Zionist news "adequate" coverage.[9] In addition, Zionist organizations themselves published the following twenty-seven English language publications: *Alliance Voice, Answer, Bnai Zion Voice, Challenge, Furrows, Haboneh, Hadassah Headlines, Hadassah Newsletter, Jewish Frontier, Jewish Horizon, J. N. F. News Bulletin, Jewish Outlook, Junior Hadassah News Bulletin, Junior Mizrachi Women's News, Masada News, Mishmar Bulletin, Mizrachi Women's News, New Palestine, News Bulletin of League for Labor Palestine, Palcor Bulletins, Palestine, Palestine Information, Pioneer Woman, Student Zionist, Unity for Palestine, Young Judaean,* and *Youth and Nation*. Another series of publications—including *Ampal, American Fund News, News Bulletin on the Hebrew University, Pal-Eco News, Technion, United Palestine Appeal Report* —issued by organizations carrying on specific projects in Palestine, supplemented Zionist campaigns for particular objectives. Altogether these numerous publications * had a circulation, overlapping in part, exceeding 300,000 families in 1940 and 600,000 in 1945.[10] To these figures must be added the more than 250,000 subscribers to *Congress Weekly, Reconstructionist, Jewish Spectator, Opinion* and *B'nai B'rith Magazine* (or *National Jewish Monthly*) publications which almost invariably promoted Zionist policies.

---

* Yiddish and Hebrew periodicals included: *Bitzaron, Hadoar, Hamigdal, Harofe Haivri, Mizrachi Weg, Niv, Proletarisher Gedank, Yiddishe Folk,* and *Yiddisher Kempfer*. An additional thirty-nine national Zionist publications operating in 1948 were: *Ahdut Haavodah–Poale Zion Bulletin, Artzenu, Bafraiung Weekly, Bulletin of the United Zionist-Revisionists of America, The Chalutz, Dror, Eretz Yisroel, Hadar, Hadoar Lanoar, Haganah Speaks, Hakol-Hakoreh, Hamelet, Hamenahel, Hamichtav, Hechalutz Halomed, Hechalutz Professional Bulletin, Histadrut Foto News, Histadrut News, Horizon, Iggeret Labogrim, Izfacts, Ivri Tzair, Tzofe Betar, Kolenu, Labor Zionist News, Lamadrich, Land and Life, Leader, Newsletter of Mizrachi National Education Committee, Niv Haboger, Ohalenu, Palestine Affairs, Palestine and Zionism, Sabbath Voice, The Shield, Tel Hai, Undzer Weg, Yiddishe Derzieung, Zionist Issues.*

Zionists also cultivated the general American press by issuing hundreds of press releases and by establishing numerous personal contacts with local newspapers. According to Zionist reports, these efforts yielded over 150 favorable editorials in prominent American newspapers in a single month when the British government threatened to curtail Jewish immigration into Palestine in October, 1938. More than 350 similarly-disposed editorials were also recorded in the spring of 1944 when the White Paper of 1939 became effective.[11] In addition, 10 percent of the 3,300 news columns reprinting Zionist Organization of America press releases in 1944 were to be found in the general American press, as were more than 25 percent of the 4,000 columns printed in 1945.[12] Except for the case of the *New York Times,* no specific Zionist accusations of an "unfair press" are to be noted.*

Zionist organizations also engaged in an ambitious program of pamphlet and book publication and distribution. In 1943–44, a single Zionist group—the ZOA—alone distributed over one million leaflets and pamphlets to selected public libraries, chaplains, community centers, journalists, educators, editors, ministers, writers, and other opinion-molders.[13] Pro-Zionist books and pamphlets by notable non-Jews—for example, Sumner Welles' *Palestine's Rightful Destiny,* Wendell Phillips' *Before the Bar of History,* Eduard Lindeman's *Palestine-Test of Democracy,* Norman MacLean's *His Terrible Swift Sword,* Carl J. Friedrich's *American Policy Toward Palestine,* and Frank Gervasi's *To Whom Palestine?*—were occasionally subsidized by Zionists, sometimes promoted jointly with commercial publishers, and then distributed free to influential persons and groups. Academic studies of Palestine, too, were privately commissioned and commercially released with the aim of producing "help-

---

* An exchange of letters between Arthur Hays Sulzberger, the Jewish publisher of the *New York Times,* and Abba Hillel Silver, dated November 2 and 9, 1943, respectively, reveals Sulzberger's role in the formation of the anti-Zionist American Council for Judaism. Rabbi Silver charged that the *Times* fought Zionism since 1917 and

> . . . has not reported Zionist news impartially and objectively as befits a responsible newspaper. Your anti-Zionist bias has colored its news and determined its editorial policy. . . . Again and again the *Times* has transformed itself into a transmission belt for anti-Zionist propaganda. It never misses an opportunity to focus attention on the anti-Zionist viewpoint.

(Mimeographed copies, 7 pp., in Zionist Archives and Library, New York City.) Earlier, Rabbi Joseph S. Shubow attacked the *Times* at the American Jewish Conference for "its attitude to American Jewish problems . . . for its ignorance and impudence." See *NYT,* September 2, 1943, p. 1; and October 1, 1945, p. 4.

ful" materials devoid of specifically Zionist imprint or sponsorship. American Palestine Institute, Inc. was typical of several non-political and non-profit research organizations initiated by Zionists. At the behest of Chaim Weizmann, the Institute enlisted prominent economists with extensive New Deal experience and useful governmental contacts to study the economic potentialities of Palestine. The result was an imposing scholarly treatise supporting the Zionist argument that Palestine could readily accommodate substantial Jewish immigration.[14]

Perhaps the most successful of these Zionist-inspired and Zionist-disseminated books was Walter Clay Lowdermilk's *Palestine, Land of Promise* (1944), which actually attained a place on the "best seller" lists. This popularized treatment of a Jordan Valley Authority proposal by the Assistant Chief of the United States Soil Conservation Service was specifically commissioned by Emanuel Neumann, director of the public relations program of the American Emergency Committee for Zionist Affairs. The purpose of the work, according to Neumann's superior, Abba Hillel Silver, was manifestly "to dissipate the false propaganda which has been spread concerning Palestine's limited absorptive capacity as an argument for the retention of the White Paper and the curbing of immigration into Palestine." [15]

Moreover, Zionist organizations undertook to supply their own memberships and various libraries with classics of Zionist thought and expositions of Zionist problems and prospects. One of the numerous Zionist book services operating in 1944, that of the ZOA, sold between 3,000 and 4,000 books monthly.[16]

RALLIES AND PUBLIC MEETINGS

In contrast to the "soft-pedaling, quietist" tactics of most non-Zionist organizations, Zionists consistently pursued a policy of arousing public opinion by means of mass meetings, protest rallies, and public petitions. For example, following upon the Arab riots of 1929, Zionists staged a Madison Square Garden rally attracting an overflow audience of more than 25,000 persons. There, Chairman of the U. S. Senate Foreign Relations Committee, William E.

Borah, and Lieutenant Governor Herbert H. Lehman of New York praised Jewish achievements in Palestine and gave encouragement to the crowd which later went on to reaffirm Jewish rights and aspirations in Zion and to "rededicate" itself to the Zionist cause. A similar rally on November 2, 1930, was attended by over 50,000 persons and was coordinated with simultaneous public meetings attracting 750,000 people in more than twenty American cities.[17]

With each new crisis—additional Arab riots, British oppression, Hitlerian atrocities, Allied inaction on the Palestine question— Zionists called new mass meetings or joined other organizations in conducting parades and other public demonstrations. Under the auspices of the Zionist Organization of America or American Emergency Committee for Zionist Affairs, and with the participaion of B'nai B'rith, the American Jewish Congress, the Jewish Labor Committee, Jewish War Veterans, CIO, AFL, and noted non-Jews, rallies at Madison Square Garden, Carnegie Hall, Lewisohn Stadium, Union Square, and Madison Square Park in New York City attracted many hundreds of thousands of Jews and non-Jews. In the last named place alone, over two hundred thousand persons gathered in August, 1945, for a massive open-air protest against British policy in Palestine.[18]

After the establishment in August, 1943, of the American Zionist Emergency Council and local Emergency Committees around the nation, these New York rallies were duplicated in dozens of cities upon instructions from the national AZEC. On the twenty-sixth anniversary of the Balfour Declaration in November, 1943, for example, over fifteen thousand people were turned away from an overflow rally in Carnegie Hall, while tens of thousands of Americans attended more than 119 other rallies around the nation.[19] As all local Emergency Committees were advised, such public demonstrations should not be scattered or sporadic. Rather,

> They must be a united, nationwide effort, carefully planned and organized, utilized at some highly decisive moment in the campaign. It is not difficult to imagine the cumulative effect of a hundred and more mass meetings held simultaneously on one day throughout the United States in all the major communities and extensively reported in the press. It cannot for a moment be doubted that such a demonstration would have a highly significant meaning in Washington.[20]

Two special applications of the mass meeting technique which took place in the thirties are of particular interest. The first was "The Romance of a People," a lavish pageant of Jewish history culminating in the Return to Zion. Sponsored by Zionists and directed by veteran Zionist Meyer Weisgal, this pageant drew 131,000 viewers to Chicago's Soldier's Field on "Jewish Day," a feature of the Century of Progress Exhibition of 1934. Non-Jewish demand for tickets to the spectacle was so great that the *Chicago Tribune* arranged a second performance. In New York City, the *Daily News* sponsored similar performances with the result that 400,000 persons, allegedly something of a record in American theatrical history, came to witness it. Not the least important of the achievements of "The Romance of a People" was a net profit to the Zionist movement of over $300,000 in the five cities in which it played (it was also seen in Philadelphia, Cleveland and Detroit). Such a sum, garnered in the depths of the Great Depression, was nothing short of a windfall for the deficit-ridden ZOA.[21]

Zionists, again led by Weisgal, also constructed a Palestine Pavilion at the New York World's Fair of 1939/40 which depicted Jewish achievements in Palestine and explained the Zionist program. Over one hundred thousand persons attending the opening ceremonies of the Pavilion on May 29, 1939, were addressed by Albert Einstein and other Zionist personalities, including Chaim Weizmann speaking by telephone from Paris. Under the impetus of the speakers' words, the dedicatory ceremony was soon turned into a political demonstration which, by a resounding voice vote, denounced British policy and reaffirmed Jewish rights in Palestine. The Palestine Pavilion was subsequently viewed by more than half a million persons.[22]

JEWISH SCHOOLS AND YOUTH ACTIVITIES

Intimately connected with every synagog and temple in the Jewish community, and with many secular fraternal organizations as well, was the Jewish school. Variously titled the *cheder* or *Talmud Torah* among the Orthodox, or Sunday School among Reform and Conservative Jews, such schools were designed to perpetuate Jewish group survival by offering a diverse curriculum of Hebrew language, Bible tales, religious ritual, and numerous other subjects, depending upon their organizational affiliation. In 1936, over 104,000 children received Jewish instruction on one day a week, while 85,000 studied additional days.[23]

Reference has already been made to a careful study of the Conservative religious schools which indicated that Palestinian and Zionist themes occupied a central position in the teachings of Conservative educators.[24] The same observation seems warranted in the case of other educators, especially those to whom Hebrew language and culture were of prominent concern. As Dr. Noah Nardi concluded from a 1944 survey, Jewish educational bureaus in major American cities were headed by educators, "all of whom, without exception, are Zionists and Hebraists. This with even greater certainty, can be said of the principals and teachers of the Hebrew teaching profession in America." [25] The historian and Jewish educator Rufus Learsi (Israel Goldberg), generalizing from his familiarity with the American Jewish community, similarly observed that "A whole generation of Zionist teachers in the Jewish religious schools approached their work with a sense of dedication, striving to equip their pupils with a knowledge of Hebrew as a living language and inspire them with love of Zion." [26] Obviously, a Palestine reborn, in which Hebrew would reign as a revived and flourishing language, provided powerful appeals for teachers and other professionals in the educational field.

The Zionist tone of many of the Jewish schools was not entirely a natural concomitant of the confluence of Hebraic and Zionist objectives, however. To some extent, too, Zionists affected the curriculum of Jewish schools by consciously infiltrating the boards of directors of pre-existing schools and by establishing pro-Zionist schools wherever local leadership was unsympathetic to Zionism.[27] Through the Histadrut Ivrith, Zionist educators also furthered a broad program of Hebrew-Zionist book and periodical publication, Hebrew-speaking clubs, Hebrew public functions, youth movement and summer camp activity, and a Hebrew theater. Zionist leaders were also instrumental in convening Jewish educational conferences "with a view to more deeply integrating Zionist culture into Jewish education." Finally, hardly a Zionist convention passed without some resolution to the effect that among the most important questions which American Zionism must face was that of Jewish education, whether formally through the schools, or informally through youth groups and related activities. The whole future of Zionism was publicly declared to rest on the willingness of American Zionists to "sponsor the Zionification of the American Jewish youth." [28]

Despite a seemingly natural community of interests between the Zionist movement and Jewish education and the patent official Zionist recognition of the importance of winning Jewish youth for Zionist aspirations, judgments of the effectiveness of Zionist efforts in the area of education vary greatly. On the one hand, a study by Stanley A. Ginsburgh in 1941 claimed that there were twenty-two national Jewish "youth organizations" with a total of 340,000 members, aged 12–25. Of this figure, 173,900 were affiliated with the Jewish Community Center program of the National Jewish Welfare Board, an organization which took no official stand on Zionism. Of the remaining 166,000 youths, 83 percent were reportedly enrolled in groups either directly affiliated with, or sympathetic to, Zionism.[29] Zionist youth commissions operated in at least 147 communities.[30] Moreover, in the National Jewish Welfare Board itself, changes were taking place which would give the Jewish Community Centers and YM-YWHA's a decidedly pro-Zionist atmosphere.*

On the other hand, abundant evidence from those directly concerned with Zionist youth and educational matters supports the impression that Zionist inroads into the younger generation fell short of what might otherwise be expected. Rabbi Israel Goldstein, for example, complained in 1929 that the work of the ZOA's Youth and Education Department consistently remained "un-

---

* Samuel Dinin reports that a 1941–42 survey of the 290 Jewish Centers serving 390,000 affiliated persons revealed that Zionism and Palestine were becoming increasingly paramount in their programs. For example, he notes that many Zionist groups met regularly in such centers, that relations between center personnel and Zionist leadership were growing closer, that many centers developed programs using Palestine as a focus of interest, that their panels, symposia and lectures gave much attention to Palestine and Zionism, that the National Jewish Welfare Board Speakers and Artists Bureau included many prominent Zionists and Palestinian performers, that the NJWB published significant pro-Zionist educational material, and that the National Association of Jewish Center Workers had instituted a Committee on Palestine charged with integrating Palestine into the centers' club programs (*Zionist Education* . . . , p. 62). See also Edidin, *Jewish Community Life* . . . , p. 73 and *Minutes,* ZOA Executive Committee, February 20, 1943, for Zionist negotiations with the Jewish Welfare Board to place literature in the hands of all chaplains and in JWB Army Clubs.

realized due to lack of material resources." [31] Rabbi Edward L. Israel declared in 1935 that Zionists had "failed ignominiously" in attempts to organize Jewish youth.[32] Similar admissions were also made by *Reconstructionist* and *New Palestine* in 1937 and 1940 and by Rabbi Samuel M. Blumenfield, Director of the ZOA's Youth and Education Department, in 1941. And, on the college campus, surveys taken in 1941 and 1946 reveal that Zionist opinions were less prevalent among Jewish students than among adult Jews. Finally, the comprehensive survey conducted by Samuel Dinin and Noah Nardi could be cited at length to indicate that, although the Jewish educational system provided some excellent Zionist instruction and little direct opposition to Zionist objectives, apathy and inertia on the Zionist question were widespread.[33]

RABBINICAL ENDORSEMENTS

Another constant of Zionist propaganda in the United States was the dedicated activity of much of the American rabbinate on behalf of the Zionist program. As noted in earlier chapters, Conservative and Orthodox rabbis were overwhelmingly pro-Zionist in deed as well as in theology, while Reform spiritual leaders provided much of the top leadership of the Zionist groups, of the Zionist funds, and of such related Zionist organizations as the American Jewish Congress. Indeed, it would be a most difficult task to describe the American Zionist movement aside from the work of some of its foremost rabbinical spokesmen—Stephen S. Wise, Abba Hillel Silver, Israel Goldstein, Solomon Goldman, James G. Heller, to mention but a few.

The relevance of rabbinical endorsement of Zionism for the effectiveness of Zionist propaganda is made manifest by the common-sense observation that persons looked to for leadership tend to exert influence far in excess of their mere numbers. Propaganda is thus facilitated by prestigious individuals whose attitudes are valued and respected by others.

Of the prestigious individuals in the Jewish community, the rabbi undeniably exercises very great influence on lay thinking. Although he may not command in America the same measure of authority as he would in much of the Old World, hardly any move of consequence in Jewish life is made in most communities without his participation. Except for a few atypical individuals, the rabbi represents the "only repositor[y] of solid and authentic Jewish knowledge." Moreover, he is the "representative and ambassador" of the Jewish community to the non-Jewish world, the "front man" in Jewish community relations and interfaith activities. As such, many Jews, as well as non-Jews, are heavily dependent upon him for guidance on Jewish issues arising out of the everyday environment as well as for questions of a purely ritualistic or theological nature.[34] In the words of Robert Gordis, "The rabbi in America [is] the dynamo about whom most forms of positive Jewish values cluster and from whom most Jewish activities derive their impetus and direction." [35]

On numerous occasions it was the rabbinical associations and the more than one thousand rabbis enrolled in Zionist groups which lent the authoritative sanction of religion to the activities and goals of the Zionist movement, as, for example, when they urged their congregations to pray and work for the success of the United Palestine Appeal or when they recommended *en masse* membership in the Zionist movement. Many rabbis incorporated Zionist history, ideology and problems into their sermons, services and adult education classes as well as in their religious school programs. They set examples for lay conduct by accepting responsible posts in Zionist groups, by participating in delegations to the American government, by speaking on Zionism before non-Jewish bodies, and by prolific publication of books and articles on the Zionist cause.[36] Rabbis also lent their names to some of the most forceful and widely-circulated Zionist petitions, such as *An Appeal to the Conscience of America,* signed by 1,027 rabbis.[37] Finally, it was the voice of the overwhelming majority of the American rabbinate which so forcefully assailed the anti-Zionist American Council for Judaism and its ninety rabbinical members for their alleged "un-Jewish" attacks on Zionism and for their "misreading" of Jewish history and destiny.*

* See Appendix VII for the assault on the Council by 818 rabbis. Also note the remarks of Rabbi Israel Goldstein (President of ZOA and Synagogue Council of America, Co-Chairman of Interim Committee of American Jewish Conference and Honorary President of Jewish National Fund) before the House of Representatives Committee on Foreign Affairs: "I do not think you will find any instance in American life in which the clergy prodominates [sic] as much as they do in the

In short, like the support of much of the Jewish press and educational system, the help of the organized rabbinate must be evaluated as one of the Zionist movement's most valuable assets. Although we cannot know exactly how much of Zionism's eventual popular acceptance was due to the endorsement of American rabbis, the assumption seems warranted that the respect, prestige and authority of organized religion exerted on behalf of Zionism was a powerful determinant in the attitudes of Jewish laymen and of non-Jews to the Zionist program.

A SURVEY OF ZIONIST PROPAGANDA, 1929–43

Like the organized Zionist movement itself, Zionist propaganda activities were not fully developed before the period of the early forties. To be sure, rallies, petitions, press releases, and numerous other attention-getting techniques had been employed for over forty years before that time, but the general impression obtained from a study of available documents indicates that well-organized propaganda efforts, on a continuing basis and on a large scale, date only to the formation of the American Zionist Emergency Council in August, 1943. To support this generalization, some discussion of earlier Zionist activities is necessary.

It was not until the fall of 1929 that the Zionist Organization of America established a Committee on Public Information charged with the responsibility of explaining the Zionist program to the American public. Even then, the Committee, headed by Emanuel Neumann, was created only in response to Arab riots in Palestine, rather than as part of a long-range public relations program. The Committee functioned vigorously for a time by interviewing governmental officials and foreign ambassadors, by staging mass protest rallies, by securing testimonials from President Hoover and other leading Americans, by promoting meetings of sympathetic non-Jewish spokesmen, and by establishing a Washington office for "follow up" purposes. At this time, the ZOA

Zionist movement, and I submit that that is not accidental. This is in keeping with a place for Zionism in the religious tradition of our people." (*REP-HEAR*, pp. 164–65.)

also consolidated Jewish support by conducting a "Zionist Roll Call" in which Jews could register their approval of the Zionist program upon payment of a token fee of one dollar. Intended "purely for propaganda purposes, and not as a means for raising funds," the Roll Call gathered over 45,000 signatories not formally enrolled in the ZOA in the short space of two months.[38]

With the onset of the Great Depression, however, Zionist propaganda activities were conducted on a hit-or-miss basis. Income from a mere 8,400 memberships failed to cover the ZOA's basic administrative expenses in 1932. Saddled with an oppressive deficit of almost $150,000, the ZOA allowed its Committee on Public Information to lapse. Later attempts to revive mass interest in Palestine through a Palestine Day and another "Zionist Roll Call" in 1935 met with scant success.[39]

Once again, Zionist propaganda activities were stimulated by a crisis situation confronting the Jewish settlement in Palestine. When it seemed likely that an Arab state might be proclaimed in 1938 and the Balfour Declaration scrapped, five Zionist parties and representatives of B'nai B'rith and the American Jewish Congress, formed the National Emergency Committee for Palestine, headed by ZOA President Rabbi Solomon Goldman. Capitalizing upon a widespread indignation with British policy among the American public, Jewish and non-Jewish, this committee called protest assemblies in many Jewish communities and circulated petitions asking President Roosevelt to intervene in the Palestine crisis.[40] In the ensuing months before the issuance of the British White Paper of 1939, more than half a million telegrams urging American action, many from non-Jewish dignitaries and organizations, were reportedly received by the White House and the State Department. Approximately 1,200,000 Jews took the traditional biblical vow from the 137th Psalm ("If I forget thee, O Jerusalem, let my right arm forget its cunning!") at special meetings and regular synagog worship services dedicated to the Palestine crisis. In addition, the Zionist Organization of America alone distributed over half a million pieces of propaganda literature. Finally, the gravity of the situation was demonstrated by a telegraphic summons for key Zionist leaders to meet in Washington. On twenty-four hours' notice, more than two hundred persons, from as far west as California, assembled in the capital for a conference with Secretary of State Cordell Hull.[41]

Despite such *ad hoc* testimony to interest in the Jewish settlement of Palestine, Rabbi Goldman conceded to the 1939 ZOA convention that organized Zionism *on a permanent basis* was woefully weak: "For the simple truth is that our organization has failed to keep pace with our movement. We may even say that the retrogression of the Zionist Organization has been in almost direct proportion to the growth of Zionist sentiment in the country." Illustrating this organizational failure by examples from the propaganda field, the ZOA president went on to remind his listeners that the organization had

> . . . virtually no propaganda department. It has not even a publicity department or a public relations staff. . . . Confronted during the past year with one emergency after another, we were compelled to create a publicity staff on the spot. We have not until this day developed a steady flow of publications on Palestine. . . . We have made only the most occasional and fragmentary use of the radio. We have no Palestine films to speak of. . . .[42]

Obviously, declared Goldman, this was no way to win the support of American Jewry, let alone the American public and government.

On the eve of World War II, the Twenty-first World Zionist Congress, meeting in Geneva late in August, 1939, recognized that its headquarters in Jerusalem might be cut off from the rest of the movement as a result of impending hostilities. Accordingly, the Congress decided to establish an "Emergency Committee for Zionist Affairs" in New York which might be called upon to assume the full authority and functions of Zionist leadership. American Jewry now constituted the "center of gravity" for Zionism outside of Palestine since the impoverished Jewish communities of eastern and central Europe clearly lay in the path of the Nazi juggernaut. It was also acknowledged then that, regardless of the immediate course of the war, the role of the United States government in postwar affairs would be decisive in determining the fate of Palestine; accelerated Zionist propaganda in America was obviously essential.

The Emergency Committee for Zionist Affairs (later to prefix the word "American" to its title) was never asked to direct the political fortunes of the entire Zionist movement as Palestine was spared the direct ravages of war. The Committee did, however, undertake to create an effective public relations instrument which would unite the major American Zionist parties for political action. In its own words, the Committee conceived of its mission as one of bringing home "to the American people and to American political leaders the needs of the Jews as a people and the meaning of Palestine to the Jewish future." [43]

This ambitious program was slow of realization. At the outset, the Committee functioned primarily as "an interparty body for receiving reports and for deciding on matters of common interest" to the four constituent Zionist groups—ZOA, Hadassah, Mizrachi and Poale Zion. Not infrequently it had to resolve an internecine Zionist feud occasioned by the claims of one group at the expense of the others. Not until late 1940 did the Committee acquire a full-time secretary and New York offices of its own; not until January, 1941, did Emanuel Neumann assume the duties of Executive Officer in charge of the Department of Public Relations and Political Action. Thereafter, attempts were made to organize Zionists into local public relations committees and to launch organized propaganda campaigns utilizing the daily press, periodicals, and radio. Organizations for mobilizing non-Jewish support—American Palestine Committee and Christian Council on Palestine—were also established as a result of Neumann's work with the AECZA.[44]

Nevertheless, considerable dissatisfaction was expressed with the "business as usual" manner of the Committee. Neumann himself spoke of the AECZA as a "conference of ambassadors," which committed itself to nothing without "endless consultations" with the constituent organizations. Zionist party factionalism seemed much more important to some Committee participants than the public relations program for which the Committee was ostensibly created. Then, too, the complaint was frequently heard that no Zionist leader existed in that critical period who could command the respect of a Louis D. Brandeis in the critical days of World War I.[45] This state of affairs was made even more acute by Neumann's dramatic resignation from his post in December, 1942. In his explanation to the Jewish press, Neumann declared that Zionist propaganda would never reach its goal as long as the Committee remained unaltered, that is, characterized by "recurrent factional and personal differences . . . vacillation in policy and in action; absence of centralized administrative direction;

failure to adopt a definite program of activities, and budgets wholly inadequate to the immensity of the task." [46]

THE AMERICAN ZIONIST
EMERGENCY COUNCIL

In August, 1943, this course of relatively haphazard Zionist propaganda activities came to an end. At the personal request of World Zionist Organization President Chaim Weizmann, Rabbi Abba Hillel Silver assumed the co-chairmanship (along with Rabbi Stephen S. Wise) of a reorganized American Zionist Emergency Council and the chairmanship of its Executive Committee. The new Council was composed of a total of twenty-six persons: members of the executive committees of the four major Zionist groups together with a number of leading Zionists nominated *ad personem*. In addition, observers from other Zionist groups— Hashomer Hatzair, United Zionist Labor Party (Achdut Avodah– Poale Zion) and Zionist-Revisionists—were in attendance, so that the Council assumed plenary powers, at least in the propaganda field, for the whole of the American Zionist movement. Henceforth, the Council was to act as the activator and coordinator of all Zionist public relations in the United States. The spectacle of various Zionist groups competing for public attention was largely to be ended by an aggressive and centralized political offensive aimed at winning America for the Zionist cause.[47]

Rabbi Silver, who had led an ever more successful United Palestine Appeal for half a decade, was widely known in the community for his outspoken espousal of "Political Zionism"—the campaign for a Jewish commonwealth—in contrast with other Zionists who favored only a campaign against the restrictive White Paper of 1939. Silver's approach to Zionist public relations was also different from that of other Zionist leaders in that it rejected earlier policies of eminent Zionists going to President Roosevelt and Prime Minister Churchill in order to beseech pro-Zionist public statements. The Cleveland rabbi's formula for Zionist success was far more militant:

We must build upon the broad and secure base of public sentiment, the approval of public opinion which in the final analysis determines the attitude and action of governments in democratic society.

With all my supreme admiration for the great personalities who are our friends, and for the significance of great personalities in the world crisis today, with my full admiration and full realization of these two facts, I still say, unto you, what the psalmist said long ago: "Al tivtechu bi-nedivim"—*"Put not your trust in princes . . ."*

Put not the future of our movement in the sole keeping of individuals, however friendly, however great; appeal to the masses of the people of the world; talk to the whole of America; make friends everywhere; carry on an active educational propaganda in your circle, within the sphere of your influence, among your own friends. That will be reflected in the higher political circles. That will guide them. That will sustain them when they come to make important decisions which may involve America's participation in the ultimate solution of the Palestine problem.[48]

In a letter to Chaim Weizmann, March 3, 1944, he stresses the ineffectiveness of unobtrusive methods and recommends direct and forceful political action: *

We are definitely not of the opinion that quiet diplomacy will alone bring about the desired results or that we should pin our hopes entirely upon the good will of one or two people . . . our good friends here, upon whom we have been relying so much [referring to President Roosevelt, primarily] will not move on their own accord, inspired by the moral righteousness of our cause. Nor will the intercession of a few powerful people achieve the desired results. Our friends might be inspired to move and take some definite action as a result of the pressure of five million Jews in a critical election year.[49]

* Publicly, Silver cautioned his followers that they must be "political" yet must assiduously avoid any appearance of favoring one political party against the other; "any other policy would be perilous and in the long run disastrous." Said the Zionist leader, reputedly able to influence high-level Republican policy-makers such as Senator Robert A. Taft: "We have succeeded in getting a friendly hearing from all groups in American public life because of the absolutely non-partisan character of our Movement. The Zionist Movement of the United States is committed to no political party. This . . . is a political asset which we should zealously preserve" (*A Year's Advance* [New York, 1944], pp. 6–7). Rabbi Wise, however, the other co-chairman of the American Zionist Emergency Council, was a long-standing Democrat, staunch defender of the New Deal and of Wilson's New Freedom before it, and a frequent visitor of Franklin D. Roosevelt.

Whatever the cause—the greater forcefulness of Silver's leadership, the greater attractiveness of the policies which he proposed or the greater resources and interest placed at the disposal of the American Zionist Emergency Council—new life seemed to infuse Zionist public relations programs.[50] Under Silver's guidance, the Council greatly expanded its scope of operations from its New York City headquarters. With an annual budget exceeding half a million dollars derived from the Jewish National Fund and the Palestine Foundation Fund (and, thus, indirectly from the non-political United Jewish Appeal),[51] the Council established fourteen professionally staffed committees: Community Contacts, Christian Clergy, American Palestine Committee, Economic Resources, Contact with Allied Post-War Groups, Research, Press, Publications, American Jewish Religious Forces, Post-War Political Planning, Intellectual Mobilization, Special Services and Events, Labor Relations (contact with American Jewish Trade Union Committee for Palestine), and Finance and Personnel.[52] A permanent Washington office, defunct since 1930, was also organized.

At the same time, the AZEC moved to broaden its operations by the formation of over four hundred local Zionist Emergency Committees which would carry Zionist public relations campaigns into every major American community. Such Emergency Committees, though they were purposely kept limited to eight to twelve "select persons," sought to involve not only all locally functioning Zionist parties, but also delegates to the American Jewish Conference, local leaders of the B'nai B'rith, temples and synagogs, congregational brotherhoods and sisterhoods, fraternal lodges, and as many prominent Jews in the community as would accept the program of the American Jewish Conference for the reconstitution of Palestine as a Jewish commonwealth.[53]

In order to develop the political skills of American Zionists preparatory to the ultimate campaign for a Jewish state, the newly-organized AZEC proclaimed a more immediate target early in October, 1943: the mobilization of the American public, Jewish and non-Jewish, for the purpose of abrogating the White Paper of 1939 due to take effect on April 30, 1944. The long-range "educational implications" of a Jewish commonwealth were also stressed during the course of this political offensive. The instructions and letters of guidance sent by the national office of the

AZEC to its local Emergency Committees during the course of this mobilization will serve to illustrate the wide range of propaganda techniques employed by the Zionist movement in its most aggressive activities on the eve of the creation of the State of Israel.[54]

At the outset, local Emergency Committees were directed to establish contacts with their Congressmen, either by dispatching delegations and communications to Washington or, preferably, by arranging "small functions" in honor of such representatives whenever they were at home for holidays or legislative recesses. The purpose of these contacts was "to produce in this country what already exists in the British House of Commons, a group of national legislators who are familiar with the details of the Palestine situation and can discuss it intelligently." [55] Zionists were also instructed to contact the informal holders of power as well as acknowledged officeholders and, above all, to work both sides of the political street:

> . . . it may be deemed wise by your Committee to cultivate the local political leader, who is often a close friend of the Congressman or Senator. That person might be talked to and persuaded to throw the weight of his political influence and power behind our cause. If the officeholder happens to be a member of one party, the other political party should not be neglected. If your present Congressman is a Republican, or vice versa, he may be opposed in the next election by a Democrat. The latter prospective candidate should be cultivated.[56]

Local Emergency Committees, moreover, were encouraged to work for favorable resolutions in local governmental bodies as well as in the national Congress. Expressions of opinion from city councils and state legislatures were deemed important; Washington, advised the AZEC, would be induced to act on Palestinian matters only if it felt there was "a very substantial public opinion on this subject throughout the country. National political leaders follow the lead of their local constituencies." [57]

With specific regard to methods of arousing public opinion on the White Paper issue, Zionist Emergency Committees were instructed in the use of public demonstrations, speakers, seminars, editorials, interviews, and so forth. Like any other segment of the population that desired governmental action, Zionists must be prepared to act:

On certain occasions it will become necessary to produce a dramatic demonstration of . . . American public opinion. That means deluging public officials, Congressmen and Senators, with letters and telegrams. *You must* be prepared at quick notice . . . to go into action to organize *letter-writing and telegram campaigns.* That is why it is so important to keep in close contact with your local Jewish organizations, working through them to produce the results. . . . Those who have the responsibility for formulating American foreign policy must be made to feel that the Jews of America are aroused on the question of the White Paper; that they want it abrogated; and that this is the sentiment of millions of Jews throughout the United States.[58]

With something over two thousand Zionist leaders participating in the work of the Emergency Committees in early 1944, the national AZEC began receiving a series of anti-White Paper resolutions by major Jewish organizations—National Council of Jewish Women, Synagogue Council of America, Jewish Labor Committee, Free Sons of Israel, Rabbinical Council of America, Jewish War Veterans, National Conference of Orthodox Jews for Palestine and Rescue, and many others. In New York City, Herman Hoffman, President of the Council of Jewish Organizations for Palestine, reported that five hundred groups adopted resolutions asking President Roosevelt to help abrogate the White Paper. Similarly, the National Jewish Welfare Board, at the request of the American Zionist Emergency Council, urged its more than three hundred Jewish Community Centers, Young Men's Hebrew Associations and other affiliates to cooperate with all "officially organized local community efforts" against the White Paper. Zionist speakers—Jewish and non-Jewish—were also credited with a growing string of anti-White Paper resolutions from Lions, Rotary, Elks and other fraternal associations, Federations of Business and Professional Women, YMCAs, labor unions, church assemblies, and so on.* More than three thousand groups were quickly listed by the AZEC on its roster of anti-White Paper resolutions.[59]

It is also interesting to note that Jewish support for Zionist

---

* No exact tabulations of the number of speaking engagements arranged by the scores of Zionist and pro-Palestine groups is available. However, the ZOA Speakers' Bureau alone reported that it had supplied 450 speakers for 1,800 public meetings, that an additional thousand meetings had been addressed by the ZOA staff, and that over 300 appearances before non-Jewish groups had been scheduled, all during a *one year period* in 1943–44; ZOA, *Forty-seventh Annual Report,* p. 37.

objectives did not stop at measures designed to abrogate the White Paper. When the Wright-Compton "Jewish commonwealth" resolution was pending before Congress in 1944, numerous Jewish groups sent petitions and resolutions urging enactment. From distant San Francisco alone, certainly not a Zionist stronghold, came communications from such groups as Beth Israel Sisterhood, Temple Sherith Israel Men's Club, San Francisco Chapter of the National Home for Jewish Children, Jewish Educational Society, Pacific Hebrew Orphan Asylum and Home Society, and two B'nai B'rith lodges.[60]

In addition to organizational resolutions, Rabbi Leon I. Feuer, chairman of the Committee on Community Contacts, was able to report to the AZEC's Executive Committee that hundreds of thousands of individual letters, postal cards, petitions, and telegrams had been dispatched to Washington during the course of the anti-White Paper campaign. Examples revealed by Rabbi Feuer included: Leominster, Massachusetts—1,000 telegrams; Portland, Maine—600 telegrams; South Bend, Indiana—60,000 signatures to a petition; Portsmouth, New Hampshire—11,000 letters; Detroit, Michigan—22,000 postal cards and 19,000 letters; and 25 "communities picked at random"—11,500 telegrams. Moreover, according to Feuer, this type of "direct political action," including contacts with Congressmen, seemed to be very popular in the local communities because of its "direct impact" and "promise of tangible results." [61]

A work schedule of AZEC propaganda mailings during the first half of 1945 is revealing for the intensity and breadth of national Zionist activity in support of their local affiliates: [62]

January 8   1) Sympathetic letter from Vice-President Truman to Senators Robert Taft and Robert Wagner.
2) Reprint from *American Mercury*, December, 1945: Gerold Frank, "Fact and Legend About Palestine."
3) "Proceedings of the International Christian Conference on Palestine."

January 17   1) Instructions to all AZEC locals, American Christian Palestine Committee chapters and Christian Council on Palestine groups to write President Roosevelt regarding the opening of Palestine to immigration and the establishment of a Jewish commonwealth.

	2) Declaration, in cooperation with the Synagogue Council of America, of Saturday, January 27, as a "Day of Prayer" for Palestine.
	3) Memorandum explaining reorganization of the AZEC.
	4) Advance notice of Frank Gervasi's *To Whom Palestine?*, four weeks before publication.
January 18	1) Reprint from *New York Times,* December 30, 1944: " 'Arab Menace' Held Fallacy."
	2) Reprint from *New York Times,* January 6, 1945: Anne O'Hare McCormick, "Abroad; American Boys Find Tel-Aviv Like a Home Town."
January 19	1) Model prayer by leading Orthodox, Conservative, Reform rabbis for the forthcoming "Day of Prayer."
	2) Letter sent by Interim Committee of American Jewish Conference to President Roosevelt asking for aid in establishing the Jewish commonwealth.
	3) Pamphlet, *Britain and Palestine,* geared especially to lawyers and others concerned with legality of British actions in Palestine.
February 9	1) Address by Hayim Greenberg on the Zionist situation.
February 14	1) Sympathetic book review by Eduard C. Lindeman of Ernst Frankenstein's *Justice for My People,* from *New York Herald Tribune,* January 28, 1945.
February 16	1) Letter of invitation to regional meeting of AZEC locals in Chicago, March 17–18.
March 1	1) Pamphlet, Albert Einstein and Eric Kahler, *The Arabs of Palestine* (published by American Palestine Committee and Christian Clergy for Palestine).
March 7	1) Political briefing on the international situation.
	2) Advance notices of AZEC activities.
March 9	1) Zionist leaders' letter to editor, *New York Times,* February 24, 1945.
March 16	1) "A Call to Action," notices on approaching San Francisco Conference on International Organization.
	2) Various instructions on preparing public opinion for this international meeting.
March 28	1) Query: What actions have been taken to assure "A Hearing for the Jewish People in San Francisco"?
	2) Pamphlet, Eduard C. Lindeman, *Palestine—Test of Democracy.*

April 3   1) List of publications available from AZEC national office.
             2) Cable from Jerusalem on White Paper struggle.
             3) Suggested resolution for localities on White Paper to be sent to State Department and the President.
April 11   1) Appeal for funds to purchase space in leading New York and Washington newspapers.
April 12   1) Telegram to AZEC locals urging anti-White Paper telegrams to White House and British ambassador.
April 29   1) Alert to possible Arab propaganda at San Francisco Conference.
             2) Resolution adopted at "Rally for Jewish Rights," Lewisohn Stadium, New York.
May 1   1) Reprint from *New York Post,* April 19 by Edgar A. Mowrer.
             2) Appeal to help organize American Christian Palestine Committee locally.
May 15   1) Reprint of newspaper advertisement: "The Ashes of the Dead Speak."
             2) Circular, "Promises, Promises, Promises—When Will They Be Kept?"
May 16   1) Pamphlet, "The Jewish Case"; prepared for delegates and journalists at the San Francisco Conference.
May 21   1) Report and resolution from American Christian Palestine Conference in Boston.
             2) Instructions on conducting a letter from congressman to President Truman campaign: "A Letter to the President of the United States."
May 25   1) Reprint from *PM,* May 15, 1945, on Zionist activities at San Francisco.
June 4   1) May issue of *Survey Graphic,* including article by Ira A. Hirschmann, "Palestine as a Refuge from Fascism."
June 8   1) Follow-up on May 21 mailing, including list of congressmen who had already written to President Truman.
June 14   1) Report on Zionist activities at San Francisco Conference.
June 15   1) Reprint from *New York Post,* June 2, 1945, of article by Catholic leader, Francis E. McMahon.
             2) Pamphlet, Chaim Weizmann, *We Do Not Want to Return to the Past.*

The American Zionist Emergency Council, in conjunction with the ZOA, also purchased radio time on 182 American and 50

Canadian stations. During a thirty-nine week series of fifteen minute programs based on the popular "March of Time" series, Americans in forty-six states heard such stars as Victor Jory, Judith Evelyn, Joseph Schildkraut, Gene Kelly, Joseph Cotten, Eddie Cantor, Walter Abel, Laird Cregar, and Edward G. Robinson in professionally produced dramatizations of "Palestine Speaks!" [63]

There were other aspects of the AZEC's work in the field of public relations: "Vigilance Committees" which would report to its National Office on all anti-Zionist activities in the community, whether by Arabs, British agents, or anti-Zionist Jews; "Veterans' Committees" which sought to influence returning Jewish servicemen; and "high level talks" with pro-Zionist representatives of non-Moslem minorities of the Middle East which had members in the United States.* About these activities, little data is presently available.

With the fate of Palestine nearing a decision at the close of World War II in Europe, Zionist leadership intensified its propaganda efforts still further. In July, 1945, the Washington activities of the Jewish Agency for Palestine were expanded and a division of labor with the American Zionist Emergency Council enacted. According to the terms of this agreement, the New York-based AZEC would be exclusively responsible for all matters concerned with "public relations" and, particularly, for contacts with the Christian Americans and the U.S. Congress. Relations with foreign governments maintaining representation in the United States, on the other hand, were vested in the Washington offices of the Jewish Agency. Negotiations with the executive branch of the American government, finally, were handled by the two groups acting jointly after informal meetings to be held at least every two weeks.[64]

SUMMARY AND CONCLUSIONS

Any Zionist claim that Zionist propaganda was "tremendously successful" in converting Jews to Zionism (or an anti-Zionist claim to the contrary) cannot be proved or disproved by the techniques

* Certain Zionists, for example, were in contact with members of Lebanese Christians sects resident in America, particularly the Maronites, with a view toward establishing a "non-Moslem front" in the Middle East.

and data employed in this study. Perhaps all that can be incontestably stated is that the Zionist propaganda machine made extensive use of a wide variety of themes, techniques and media. As such, American Zionists availed themselves of yet another political weapon in their gradual rise to political influence among American Jews.

As already stated, Zionist propaganda must be evaluated in terms of the total social situation, particularly as it was sketched in our second chapter. This is so because, even at its best, propaganda is only able to aid, not to determine absolutely, the outcome of political struggles. Propaganda, after all, "is not an independent political device that can function effectively apart from other political skills" and apart from the social context in which it operates.[65]

In this light, the hypothesis posed at the beginning of this chapter—propaganda is effective in arousing and mobilizing public opinion only where there is an already existent predisposition in that direction—while not confirmed here, helps to explain the patent increase in pro-Zionist opinion among American Jews which has been traced throughout this study. Assuming that Zionist propagandists knew their public, that is, understood what were the commonly-held opinions of American Jews on world issues (it should be recalled that the principal Zionist spokesmen were rabbis who had intimate knowledge of their congregations), then it is entirely consistent with the data to conclude that Zionist propaganda was effective in arousing and reinforcing pro-Zionist opinions largely because it was aimed at predispositions operative in the Jewish community.

Although the precise nature of these predispositions cannot be assessed, we have described the nature of Zionist propaganda themes aimed at them by a series of nine general statements. The presence of so many distinctive themes in Zionist propaganda suggests that American Zionists found it possible to gather to their banner many organized interests as well as a large variety of variously-motivated individuals. In truth, as Solomon Schechter observed in 1906, Zionism's strength was that it could be all things to all men.[66]

Zionist propaganda was thus able to present multi-faceted and all-inclusive appeals and to unite, with the assistance of external threats to the Jews, a wider sector of the heterogeneous American

Jewish community than had ever been organized before. Like other successful interest groups—the Anti-Saloon League, for example, which was able to mobilize public opinion for prohibition by exploiting popular predispositions in peripheral areas such as sin, vice, and corruption [67]—the American Zionist movement apparently was able to secure popular acceptance by including "platform planks" or appeals to numerous Jewish interests and predispositions.

In short, the eventual success of the American Zionist movement in mobilizing American Jewry for a Jewish state may be explained only by viewing changes in public opinion toward Zionism as a product of interacting and interrelated factors—various types of Zionist activity (including propaganda), historical events and their impact on the status of the Jewish people, and the pre-existing values and goals of American Jews themselves.

11

zionist counterpropaganda: the case of the american council for judaism

We have seen that in its arduous half-century struggle for a Jewish state, the American Zionist movement was able to win effective support from other groups, Jewish and non-Jewish, only in the face of intense opposition from numerous and often powerful interests. Despite this opposition, however, some type of working alliance with the expanding Zionist movement was the end-product of virtually every Zionist encounter with American "non-believers." Thus far I have traced Zionist efforts to mobilize organized support through a variety of traditional forms: winning over existent associations like labor and church groups, forming new ones like the United Jewish Appeal and American Christian Palestine Committee, and utilizing a broad range of propaganda appeals, techniques and media in order to attract unorganized or uncommitted Jewish and non-Jewish support.

This chapter will deal with the manner in which Zionists further built up and solidified group support by exploiting a conflict with the only persistent organized anti-Zionist interest group in the community—the American Council for Judaism. Specifically, we shall observe the nature of a group which rejected the Zionist program, the manner in which Zionists combatted this group, and the probable effects of organized anti-Zionist opposition on the realization of basic American Zionist goals.

ORIGIN, PROGRAM AND ACTIVITIES OF THE COUNCIL

The gradual abandonment of Reform Judaism's traditional antipathy to Zionism under the pressure of world events, changes internal to Reform, and the strivings of organized Zionist partisans have already been traced in Chapter 4. There, too, we sketched the transition of opinion in the Central Conference of American Rabbis which ultimately led ninety Reform rabbis to assemble in Atlantic City in June, 1942, and to formulate a "non-Zionist" program for Reform Judaism.[1] It was the mutually shared opinions expressed at this meeting which, in fact, soon crystallized into the anti-Zionist American Council for Judaism.

Until then, opposition to Zionism between the two world wars had been largely confined to the stray indictments of influential laymen or, more usually, the casual pronouncements of a disapproving rabbi.[2] Consequently, unorganized anti-Zionist opinion, in so far as it existed, was forced to reckon with Zionist victory after victory. In the words of the Council for Judaism's *Information Bulletin* of June 30, 1944 (pp. 2–3):

> If Jewish nationalism has marched from one success to another, it has done so largely because it possessed organization. There has always been opposition to the Zionist-nationalist theory. But it has been sporadic, apologetic, disorganized, and in the end, therefore, usually frustrated. . . .
>
> Evaluate the record! Neutrality, passivity, appeasement, lack of organization have led to an intolerable situation. For a quarter of a century, through default and unorganized opposition, a substantial body of American Jewry has been committed to a program from which it dissented by conviction. At times of crisis this dissent was expressed, but necessarily, for lack of continuing organization, in weak terms. Always, the Zionist-nationalist could say to the dissenter, "Whom but yourself do you represent?"

To correct this obvious weakness of their point of view, anti-Zionists founded the American Council for Judaism with the announced intention of initiating a vast organized movement which would define the Jew as a member of a religious community alone.

In the Council's view, Jews had nothing to do with peoplehood, Palestine or politics; theirs was a religion antipathetically disposed toward Zionism and its "national-chauvinistic" program. The Council's initial sponsors, mostly older rabbis reared in the anti-Zionist tradition of Classical Reform, including Rabbis Julian Morgenstern (president, Hebrew Union College), Louis Wolsey, William Fineshriber, Jonah B. Wise (executive director, Joint Distribution Committee), David Philipson, Samuel H. Goldenson, Morris S. Lazaron, Leo M. Franklin, and laymen Lessing Rosenwald (chairman of the Board, Sears, Roebuck) and Arthur Hays Sulzberger (publisher, *New York Times*), jointly pledged to wake up the "slumbering" American Jewish community and, accordingly, promulgated their doctrine on August 31, 1943, phrased in unmistakable terms:

> We oppose the effort to establish a National Jewish State in Palestine or anywhere else as a philosophy of defeatism, and one which does not offer a practical solution of the Jewish problem. We dissent from all those related doctrines that stress the racialism, the nationalism and the theoretical homelessness of Jews. We oppose such doctrines as inimical to the welfare of Jews in Palestine, in America, or wherever Jews may dwell.[3]

With funds available from wealthy sponsors, the Council embarked upon a multi-faceted campaign to combat Zionism. Among the techniques employed were the sending of pamphlets, letters and telegrams to influential Jews and non-Jews, scheduling of speakers before non-Jewish audiences, purchasing of full-page advertisements in leading newspapers, organization of local chapters and activities, submission of memoranda to government officials, testimony before Congressional committees and visits to prominent statesmen, churchmen and civic leaders.[4]

Recognizing the annoyance of Zionist adherents at the charge of dual loyalty or lack of patriotism to the United States, the Council's propagandists spared no efforts to implant the impression that Zionism endangered the status of American Jewry by encouraging anti-Semitism, that Zionists were "Palestinians first and Americans second," that dollars donated to the United Jewish Appeal would be used for "foreign governmental purposes," and that Zionist ideology meant that all American Jews would eventually have to move to Palestine or, at best, "ghettoize" themselves in

America. The "dual loyalty menace" was, for example, conveyed by Rabbi Louis Wolsey to Congress in his testimony before the House Committee on Foreign Affairs. A Jewish state, he warned, would render the position of American Jews "equivocal," would mean that "I am looked upon as a member of a nation whose headquarters is in Palestine, and that I am subject to suspicion, alienism, and perhaps worse." [5]

Offering what Zionists described as a "cut-rate" membership fee of two dollars (compared with ZOA's annual dues of six dollars), the Council's membership never exceeded, by its own claims, 15,000 persons or 3 percent of peak Zionist enrollments. (Zionist estimates of their opponent's strength ranged from 2,500–8,000.) It is also instructive to note that, according to two unpublished surveys by Mordecai Grossman and the American Jewish Committee, all but one of the national officers and executive board members of the Council were affiliated with Reform Judaism, were of the "upper middle" and "lower upper" classes and were derived from German-Jewish backgrounds. In contrast, the vast majority of American Jews as well as the original bulk of American Zionists were identified with Conservative or Orthodox Judaism, were "middle" to "upper lower" class in economic status, and were East European in national origin. (By the war years, however, Zionist groups also included substantial numbers of upper income bracket Jews as well as Reform Jews of German antecedents.) Thus, Council members were differentiated from the rest of American Jewry on religious, social and economic as well as ideological grounds. These surveys thus confirm some of the "traits" of the "average" anti-Zionist as sketched in Chapters 4 and 5 and revealed by the Roper Poll of 1945.[6]

ZIONIST COUNTERPROPAGANDA

The Zionist reaction to the formation of the American Council for Judaism reveals that the significance of the event was swiftly grasped. In the words of Simon Shetzer, Executive Secretary of the Zionist Organization of America, Zionists found little cause for comfort:

For the first time in decades the Zionist movement faces formal and organized opposition from within Jewish ranks. A group of Reform Rabbis selected this, the most critical hour in Jewish history, to attack the whole Zionist structure and to challenge the validity of our Zionist program. . . . The enemies of Zionism have declared war upon us. They have set out to undermine and discredit the Zionist ideal before the American Public and Government.[7]

Before we turn to the Zionists' counterattack, a brief consideration of anti-Zionism as a social, psychological phenomenon will better enable us to understand the principal propaganda charges of the Zionist counterattack on the Council for Judaism— the charges of "Jewish escapism," "self-hatred," "treason," and "assimilationism." Whether, in fact, such barbs accurately describe the mentality of American Council for Judaism supporters is not the issue here. But, undoubtedly, among countless Zionists, anti-Zionism was perceived *only* as a defect in a person's Jewishness, never as a mere "intellectual difference of opinion." While members of the Council for Judaism viewed themselves as "authentic Jews in the tradition of Classical Reform Judaism," and Judaism as a religious denomination only, Zionists found them not merely "parochial" and "unhistorical," but, worse, actually "traitorously un-Jewish."

The concept of "marginal" or "minimal" Jews was not a unique one improvised by the Zionists as an epithet for their opponents. Jewish history is replete with examples of its members anxious to abandon their underprivileged minority status and "pass" into the more desirable circles of socially higher groupings. Similar phenomena have also been observed in other minorities: Irish, Italians, and, especially, Negroes.[8] Building on the basis of these everyday observations, the eminent social psychologist—and ardent Zionist—Kurt Lewin developed the theory of "Jewish self-hatred." This theory appears to bear directly upon the activities and motivations of the Council for Judaism. Certainly, Lewin's observations provided Zionists with a sophisticated propaganda appeal which they did not hesitate to invoke often and again.

Noting a high degree of assimilation with the majority culture among the upper stratum of the Jewish group, Lewin remarked that the person seeking to enter the higher-status group has to be especially careful to disown any connection with the ideas of the group to which he once belonged. Moreover,

If belonging to a certain group hinders rather than helps the individual in achieving his dominant goals, a conflict between him and the group arises, even an eagerness to leave the group. The well-known anti-Semitism of some Jews is an expression of the individual Jew's dislike of belongingness to the Jewish group. . . . Frequently it is the more privileged people within the underprivileged group, or those people whose open or secret intent it is to pass the line, who are in the position of what sociologists call "marginal men." [9]

On the basis of controlled experiments at the Massachusetts Institute of Technology Research Center for Group Dynamics, Lewin inferred that many prominent Jews were thus frustrated in their attempts to leave the Jewish group. He then went on to hypothesize a "generalized tendency to aggression" on the part of such "marginal men." Since the hostility of the frustrated would-be "passer" cannot be directed against the powerful majority which possesses retaliatory power as well as high status, it is instead diverted toward his own group or against himself. Under such circumstances, that segment of the minority group which is most distinctively "minority culture," or which reminds the "passer" of his inability to leave the minority group, will be the primary target for the hostility of the frustrated.[10]

Such socially and economically prominent individuals, continued Lewin, remain within the minority group but, as likely as not, they assume positions of leadership which enable them, if they so desire, to inflict considerable damage upon their own group. Offered the cloak of communal leadership in recognition of their wealth and eminence, they accept the role "partly as a substitute for gaining status in the majority, partly because such leadership makes it possible for them to have and maintain additional contact with the majority." These "leaders from the periphery," as Lewin terms them, are thus incapable of responding affirmatively to the needs and wishes of the mass of the minority group being led:

Having achieved a relatively satisfactory status among non-Jews, these individuals are chiefly concerned with maintaining the status quo and so try to soft-pedal any action which might arouse the attention of the non-Jew. . . . they are so accustomed to viewing Jewish events with the eyes of the anti-Semite that they are afraid of the accusation of double-loyalty in the case of any outspoken Jewish action. If there is "danger" of a Jew's being appointed to the Supreme Court, they will not hesitate to warn the President against such an action.[11]

As Zionist leadership became aware of activities of the American Council for Judaism, the Zionist press, often utilizing Lewin's insights and terminology, severely attacked it. After the Council released its first membership rolls, Zionist rabbis published articles based on their "intimate and personal knowledge" of "Jewish self-hatred among the Council's sponsors." "Obviously," ran the general tenor of the Zionist reaction, "most of the anti-Zionists are Jewish escapists and assimilationists. Zionists, to the contrary, are aggressively Jewish. Under such circumstances, compromise and persuasion are valueless; anti-Zionism must be vigorously combatted."

Such articles as "They Sharpened the Dagger," "Flying in the Face of Facts," "Those Who Never Learn," "A Stab in the Back," "Anti-Zionist Delusions," "The Die is Cast," "United Front Against Zionism," "The American Council for Judaism: A Current and Timely Study in Frustration and Aggression," "Against Four Million: A Psychoanalytical Examination of the Jewish Anti-Zionist Testimony Offered Before House Foreign Affairs Committee," "Anti-Zionism, a Fear Psychosis," and "They Hate Zionists," [12] are suggestive of the vehement reactions of the Zionist leadership. *New Palestine*'s editorial, "A Stab in the Back," for example, declared:

> The challenge has been hurled, and at a time when we should present a united front against a common enemy [Hitler] we must turn and defend ourselves and the Jewish people from a dastardly stab in the back. The lines have been drawn; there can no longer be neutral Jews, disinterested Jews, apathetic Jews. The Jews of America must either signify their approval of the Zionist movement . . . or they must stand with the anti-Zionists in their negation of the right of the Jew to lift up his head among the peoples of the world. There is no neutral ground between.[13]

Replying to the anti-Zionist manifesto issued by the ninety Reform rabbis assembled at Atlantic City, a forerunner to the establishment of the Council for Judaism, seventeen leading Zionist rabbis, including the presidents of the Synagogue Council of America, Central Conference of American Rabbis, Rabbinical Assembly of America and Rabbinical Council of America, as well as a member of the praesidium of the Union of Orthodox Rabbis of America, prepared a counter-declaration: "Zionism—An Affirmation of Judaism." [14] Signed initially by 733 rabbis, the document was approved by 85 others within a two-month period—"the largest number of rabbis whose signatures are attached to a public pronouncement in all Jewish history." Containing more than 215 Reform rabbis listed as endorsers, this statement condemned the non-Zionists for "misrepresenting and misinterpreting" Zionism and the "historic Jewish religious teaching." "The overwhelming majority of American Rabbis," affirmed the 818 religious leaders, "regard Zionism not only as fully consistent with Judaism but as a logical expression and implementation of it." [15]

Depicting the anti-Zionist challenge as an attack upon Judaism as well as upon Zionism, Zionist leadership urged every synagog to "stand up and be counted." Zionists, who were "whole Jews" and "positive Jews," must see in this "dastardly challenge" of "marginal and minimal Jews"

> . . . the compelling need to marshal all of our available numerical strength—to translate the practically unanimous religious and sentimental attachment to Zionism into active affiliation with our organization.
> The answer to those who would defame our noble ideal and traduce our sacred cause, deeply rooted in Jewish history and tradition, is to continue to build more firmly and widely upon the foundations of our unyielding faith in the incontestable validity of the Zionist aim to restore the land of Israel to the people of Israel. A vastly increased Zionist membership will be our strongest reply to the opposition.[16]

Initial Zionist efforts to counter the activities of the Council included the establishment of District Public Relations Committees to serve as "listening posts" and "combatant units"; the formation of a Chaplain's Committee on Unity for Palestine, composed of 228 rabbis in the United States armed forces, who criticized the Council for its charges of "dual loyalty"; [17] and the launching of a nationwide "Committee to Combat the American Council for Judaism" (later renamed "Committee on Unity for Palestine"), whose purpose was the gathering of "all constructive forces in the fight upon the enemy in our midst." [18]

Zionist leaders sought to arouse greater zeal for their cause by repeatedly warning their membership that the Council, though small in numbers, was equipped with a budget of over $300,000 and was backed by some of America's wealthiest Reform Jews. The Committee on Unity, stated its chairman, Rabbi Felix A. Levy, could marshal only one-sixth of the Council's budget due to the crying demand for funds from other areas of Zionist activity. Nevertheless, the Committee on Unity had to succeed in its role as "missionary to the twenty percent" of American Jewry who had not yet embraced Zionism, for it would be very "unwise to neglect this twenty percent which has plagued us since the organization, through which it is able to express itself, came into being." [19]

Relying primarily upon direct mail and direct contact propaganda, the Committee on Unity assembled a mailing list of all known officers and members of the Council for Judaism. Local Zionist districts then appointed more than 112 Unity for Palestine Committees in order to keep anti-Zionists and local Council activities under surveillance.[20] More than ten thousand circulars, along with hundreds of personal letters, were mailed to persons suspected of being influenced by the Council's propaganda. James G. Heller, Felix A. Levy and Arthur Lelyveld—all distinguished Reform rabbis and officers of the Committee on Unity—toured the nation, including popular Jewish summer resorts in four states. Maurice Samuel, Rev. Richard Evans, Pierre Van Paasen, and numerous other speakers also traveled widely to answer anti-Zionist accusations. Critical statements about the Council by eminent Americans, like Albert Einstein, were given wide circulation. Special editions of pamphlets written by Reform rabbis were distributed in Reform temples that were reputedly Council for Judaism strongholds. Between October, 1944, and April, 1945, over 145,000 items of literature were circulated by the Committee on Unity; in 1946, the figure exceeded 1,000,000 pieces. Numerous "parlor meetings" between persons "affected" by the Council and those espousing Zionism were engineered by Zionist representatives. "Provocative and derogatory" statements issued by the Council were collected by the Committee on Unity and presented to national anti-defamation agencies with the demand that they, in turn, "rise to the defense of the good name of the Jews" by countering the Council's "besmirching attacks" on Zionist Jews. Zionists, moreover, exposed intercepted Council correspondence expressing willingness to confer membership on any anti-Zionist, even one who rejected Judaism as a religion, especially among Reform rabbis and lay leaders who generally maintained that Judaism was a "religion only." [21] In short, the rise of organized anti-Zionism produced intensified Zionist activity adapted to meet the threat to its program.

That the Zionist measures against the Council for Judaism were effective is evident from the fact that over half of the ninety rabbinical sponsors of the Council withdrew from active membership by September, 1943, only one month after its legal incorporation. Moreover, by 1946, less than a dozen rabbis remained on the Council's roster. Even Rabbi Louis Wolsey, one of the founders and provisional chairman of the Council, resigned publicly from the post of vice-president in 1946 in protest against the organization's attempt to block freedom of Jewish immigration into Palestine.[22] Zionists were jubilant over Wolsey's action and widely publicized his denunciation of the Council under the banner of an old rabbinic saying: "Woe to the pastry which its baker admits is no good!"

Wolsey's later address, "Why I Withdrew from the American Council for Judaism," aside from its immediate and widespread use by Zionist leaders, is instructive in that it served to confirm many of the Zionist charges against the Council as well as to illuminate the effect of its activities on Zionist success. Characterizing himself as the Council's "disillusioned founder," Rabbi Wolsey chronicled its history following the "truly religious gathering" of ninety rabbis at Atlantic City in 1942. When the Council for Judaism agreed to accept lay members, there came about an immediate "influx of members who looked upon the Council as a device for assimilation, or for adventuring, or as a balm for those who did not believe in organized religion." What the Council meant by "Americans of the Jewish Faith" was never defined; staff members even allowed membership to those who did not believe in God. The Council's activity, continued Wolsey,

> . . . became completely negative, and instead of majoring religion, it put its full strength into a veto of Zionist ambition—with the result that Jewish nationalism—embittered and angry—moved forward with greater zeal and determination. Zionistic success owes much to the negativism of the Council. . . .
> All in all it developed into an unhappy negative movement of assimilative Jews, of Jews horrified by the possibilities of anti-Semitism, or of Jews who were afraid of losing their fortunes and who planned to hide away to the Smoky Mountains.[23]

We have corroboration of this claim in the report of Rabbi Arthur J. Lelyveld, Vice-Chairman of the Committee on Unity, to the ZOA leadership in September, 1944, after a coast-to-coast tour of areas influenced by the Council for Judaism:

> American Jewry, beyond the shadow of a doubt, is enthusiastically committed to the cause of completing the work of building Palestine as a Jewish Homeland. The movement everywhere is receiving the impetus of new and youthful leadership. *The existence of an organized anti-Zionist group has brought an unprecedented accession of strength to the organizations which are constructively furthering the cause of Jewish Palestine.*[24]

CONCLUSIONS

The American Council for Judaism did not provide effective opposition to the Zionist movement. Founded in the darkest days of World War II, when the tragic fate of European Jewry was rapidly becoming known to American Jewry, it presented no alternative to the Zionist program. That its peak formal membership never amounted to more than 1 or 2 percent of Zionist strength is a significant indication of its failure to stem the tide of Zionist influence in the American Jewish community.

Furthermore, while it cannot be practicably demonstrated that the "psycho-pathological motivations" of Council members were exactly as depicted by Zionist propagandists, the fact remains that the existence of the anti-Zionist group provided Zionists with a potent appeal and a new incentive for intensified activity. Exploiting the alleged danger of Council for Judaism activities to Jewish group survival, and cultivating the picture of wealthy anti-Zionists as "Jewishly escapist" and "self-hating" individuals,* Zionist leadership found a useful device to win over previously apathetic sympathizers to their ranks.[25] The extent to which these attacks upon the American Council for Judaism contributed to Zionism's ultimate success is impossible to measure. The speculation seems warranted that organized anti-Zionist opposition may

---

* An anecdote which made the rounds shortly after the establishment of Israel in 1948 declared that the Council for Judaism would reluctantly recognize the Jewish state—if only Zionist leaders would change the country's name from Israel to Irving (the "Americanized" form).

have produced effects directly contrary to those it desired, for, undoubtedly, the rise of the American Council for Judaism endowed Zionism with the dramatic appeal of a "righteous crusade" and thus helped to bolster Zionist cohesion and the intensity of Zionist efforts.

12

epilogue:
the zionist movement from 1945 to
the establishment of israel

With the Axis humbled by the combined forces of the United Nations, the time was ripe for a full-scale Zionist offensive to win the support of the American government and the United Nations for the creation of a Jewish state in Palestine. Such a campaign could proceed, in the view of the Zionist leadership, upon the firm foundation of an American public opinion in very large measure favorable to its demands. It remained only for organized Zionists to direct this favorable opinion in such a manner that it would eventually be reflected in the highest places. In the firm belief that "the most effective representation in a democracy is through organized public opinion," Zionists set out to channel their popular support into legitimate, but forceful, influence on the American government. "If our cause is just," contended Rabbi Abba Hillel Silver, the acknowledged leader of American Zionism,

> . . . let the American people speak up—its ministers and educators, its writers and journalists, its leaders of capital and labor, its State Legislators, its Congressmen and Senators, of both political parties, Republicans and Democrats alike. . . . Let them make known their will to our Government and to our Chief Executive. . . . Let us rally all men of good will everywhere in the world. . . . Let a mighty chorus of voices rise to the ears of the men whom destiny has chosen for great decisions. Let these men become aware, and be guided and sustained in their own purpose by their awareness, that our cause is overwhelmingly approved by the people of America and of Great Britain, and that it is one of the great and urgent causes of our day in which mankind as a whole is deeply concerned.[1]

Zionists were repeatedly admonished to avoid the illusion that the task of translating their victory in the field of public opinion into effective governmental policy would be a simple matter. At the same time, with characteristic Zionist optimism, Silver assured an audience of devoted followers that Zionist victory was inevitable because of the pressing needs of the Jewish survivors in Europe, because of the determination of the *Yishuv* in Palestine, and because of the new-found strength of the Zionist movement in the United States. "We fully realize that our battle days are far from over," and yet, he emphasized,

> We are not going into the battle empty-handed. We know our strength, our faith, our resolute purposes. We have learned not to yield to wishful thinking and pleasant illusions. We have forged a strong movement. We have a loyal and disciplined army of followers ready to give of themselves, of their substance and of their loyalty and devotion to the cause of a free Israel in a freeland of Israel. This great testing hour of Jewish destiny will not find American Jewry wanting.[2]

On December 17 and 19, 1945, the United States Senate and House of Representatives, by overwhelming voice vote, enacted a Joint Resolution recommending:

> . . . that the United States shall use its good offices with the mandatory power to the end that Palestine shall be opened for free entry of Jews into that country to the maximum of its agricultural and economic potentialities, and that there shall be full opportunity for colonization and development, so that they may freely proceed with the upbuilding of Palestine as the Jewish national home and, in association with all elements of the population, establish Palestine as a democratic commonwealth in which all men, regardless of race or creed, shall have equal rights.[3]

In September, 1947, the American delegation to the United Nations revealed marked sympathy toward the partition plan recommendations of the United Nations' Special Committee on Palestine (UNSCOP) and, in the days preceding a vote in the General Assembly, United States diplomats were active in lining up support for the plan. November 29, 1947, marked the acceptance by the General Assembly (by a vote of 33-13) of the partition proposal calling for the creation of independent Jewish and Arab states in the territory of Palestine. During the next few months, American foreign policy vacillated on Palestine partition.

On May 14, 1948, however, the provisional Jewish government of Palestine proclaimed the independence of the State of Israel. Sixteen minutes later, the United States became the first government to accord *de facto* recognition to the young republic.[4] The central goal of the Zionist movement, "a publicly recognized, legally secured home in Palestine for the Jewish people," had thus been realized.

To what extent the evolving American Zionist power and influence potential chronicled in this study contributed to the creation of the State of Israel is not at all certain. Perhaps little more can ever be claimed than that the Zionist movement was *one* of the necessary prerequisites for the realization of the Zionist program. Thus, while this study does not account fully for the sum total of social phenomena which interacted to create the State of Israel in 1948—not the least of which were the remarkable activity of the Jewish community in Palestine and the prevailing configurations of the East-West struggle of the mid-twentieth century—it does provide explanation of a number of them as they relate to the American scene. As Milton Steinberg incisively summed up the matter almost two decades ago:

> No one knows, when a great decision is made, which factors have been decisive in arriving at that decision; no one can say which of the many influences will precipitate the final result. We don't dare take the chance. American public opinion is crucial—it is necessary; its sympathy must be won.[5]

And American public opinion had been won—after half a century of arduous striving.

13
summary and conclusions:
the building of
american zionism

"Abandonment of generalization . . . means to relinquish understanding altogether."

Albert Einstein

Science has been described as an on-going
process which, building upon the findings of previous investigations, aims at the highest order of generality about a particular set
of phenomena. In this case study of an American interest group
and social movement, I have attempted to utilize the products of
social science as well as other fields of human endeavor. Hypotheses abstracted from the mass of detailed observations about the
American Zionist movement may be of value in future investigations of interest group activity. It is my hope that the findings may
have utility and interest for all students of the political process
and may contribute to the eventual construction of a general
theory of interest group behavior.

In the following pages, all hypotheses, whether my own or
quoted or adapted from the work of other social scientists, are
presented in italics. The interspersed text is intended as illustrative and corroborative material drawn from the history of American Zionism. General readers desiring to avoid this didactic approach may, of course, ignore the hypotheses and proceed directly
to the text itself.

*The behavior of an interest group is limited and largely dictated
by the nature and predispositions of its public. Conquest or neu-
tralization of that immediate public is a prerequisite of effective
demands on government.*[1]

The basic object of this study has been to trace the development of pro-Zionist opinion among American Jews, particularly in the years between 1929 and 1948, on the assumption that predominantly favorable Jewish opinion toward Zionist objectives was *a necessary precondition* of any effective Zionist demand on the American government. Throughout this inquiry we have been concerned with the efforts of Zionist leaders to secure recognition and acceptance, by other Jewish leaders and within the unorganized Jewish public, of demands for establishing a Jewish state or commonwealth in Palestine.

We have not been primarily concerned with the so-called "internal factors contributing to the success of an interest group" —quality of leadership, cohesion of membership, intensity of group feeling, organizational structure, financial resources, group political "know-how," and so forth—although, undoubtedly, these factors had much to do with the success or failure of Zionist demands from government. Rather, our predominant focus was on the *external* relations of an interest group with its public or "political world," in this case, the interaction between organized Zionist groups and the rest of the American Jewish community.

The public of an interest group must be won over or neutralized not only because it is the reservoir from which potential members and support are derived, but also because it contains actual and incipient interests liable to be stimulated for aggressive counteraction if they are ignored or transgressed. Thus, we have been dealing broadly not only with Jewish groups which cooperated and competed with the Zionists regarding the establishment of a Jewish state, but with all American Jews—those persons who, in particular, might be expected to hold an opinion on Zionism. The response of these Jewish groups and unorganized individuals ultimately determined Zionism's influence in the United States.

The special political arena within which group conflict occurs limits and conditions the nature and intensity of the conflict.

Zionist leadership was initially circumscribed in its actions by the "structure of the situation" in which it operated. That is to say, Zionist activities and success were largely conditioned by the particular characteristics of the American Jewish community.

For example, it was hypothesized that due to the disparity of American Jewish socio-economic statuses and multiplicity, heterogeneousness, and competitiveness of various Jewish groups, it would be exceedingly difficult for the American Zionist movement ever to unite all of these interests in behalf of a common endeavor like a Jewish state. In order for Zionist leadership to "represent" American Jewry in political negotiations, numerous Jewish group interests had to be placated or overcome, and a wide variety of competing groups had to be organized for political action. Zionists also had to influence the apathetic, indifferent and unorganized Jewish public. To illustrate the conditioning influences of the arena on Zionist political fortunes: Zionist leaders had to contend with a growing assimilation of Jews to the non-Jewish culture, an assimilation which alienated many American Jews from specifically "Jewish projects" like Zionism. This assimilation also made non-Jewish Americans important reference groups for Jewish thought and action. Therefore, Zionist efforts to influence American Jews had to be relevant to the general American public comprising non-Jewish opinion.

Changes in group influence vary with changes in the conditions prevailing within the public to which the group appeals. Apathy is probably as great an obstacle to the expansion of interest group influence as is organized opposition.

A survey of American Zionism reveals that Zionist strength —measured in terms of formal affiliations, funds raised for Palestine, non-Zionist groups espousing Zionist objectives, and so forth —was not very impressive before World War II. Zionism, in fact, was merely one of a large number of interests competing for the support of American Jewry. Certainly it could not be said that the American Jewish community of 1928 was effectively mobilized to render financial or political aid for the establishment of a Jewish state. While organized anti-Zionism was not a factor in curtailing Zionist influence, American Jews were simply not greatly concerned about the Zionist program. As C. Wendell King has so perceptively stated, "the silent walls of public apathy are probably as great an impediment to the growth of social movements as [is] active vocal opposition." [2]

If Zionist leaders were one day to demand and receive political support from the American people and government, American Jewry itself would have to be transformed into allies or adherents of the Zionist ideal. Increments in Zionist power and influence could only be expected if there were to be changes in the Jewish public from which the Zionist movement was drawn and upon which it depended for support.

"When groups are active over relatively long periods of time, relationships of a fairly stable character will probably develop between them." [3]

Over a period of several decades, Zionist leaders had succeeded in establishing a "hard core" in the Orthodox, Conservative, and Reconstructionist movements and the American Jewish Congress. From these bases, Zionists strove to widen their influence among other groups—Reform Judaism, B'nai B'rith, National Council of Jewish Women, and others. Zionist ranks and funds were gradually enlarged and, more important, in their "conquests" and/or "alliances," Zionists found new platforms or instrumentalities of access to ever wider sectors of the American community. Thereafter, Zionist propaganda was disseminated not only by official Zionist organs, but by the pulpits, press, meetings, convention resolutions, and school curricula, of allies often far larger in number and more influential than the Zionists themselves. Funds for Palestine were obtained from circles many times wider than those of the Zionist parties. Finally, Zionist political demands for a state gradually came to be supported by virtually every organized Jewish group in the United States.

The influence of an interest group varies with the number and quality of alliances it can construct with other groups. Alliances are a means of enlarging a public and of facilitating propaganda. [4]

A major conclusion of this inquiry is that the American Zionist movement cannot realistically be viewed in terms of its formal membership alone. As David Truman has written,

. . . when we speak of the organized dues-paying members of a group, we are not necessarily stating its outer limits. All interest groups have their "fellow travelers" who may or may not be eligible for formal membership, but who act or interact with actual members with a frequency that in certain types of political situations may be of considerable importance.[5]

While the claim of the anti-Zionist American Council for Judaism to the effect that Zionist membership never exceeded 10 percent of the American Jewish community is correct, such a statement fails to take account of Zionism's numerous and influential *effective allies* and *unorganized sympathizers*. Such allies and sympathizers, while often unwilling to identify themselves with "Zionist political ideology," consistently performed the practical tasks demanded by the Zionist movement, whether in fund-raising or in political representations to the American public and to the American and British governments. Zionism's actual base of support, in other words, extended into virtually every organized group in the American Jewish population. Support of Zionist objectives in Palestine did not necessarily entail being a paid member of a Zionist organization. Under the pressure of world events and Zionist proddings, numerous Jewish and non-Jewish groups explicitly made assistance for Palestine a corollary object of their major programs, albeit without the "ideological overtones" of some Zionist party platforms.

Stated in a somewhat different manner, Zionism in the United States was not a *direct movement,* a gathering of organized Zionist groups with large formal memberships. Rather, American Zionism should be viewed as an *indirect movement,* a stream of converging activity gaining strength and substance from various component groups and individual supporters, many of which were not formally Zionist. "Zionists," functionally speaking, were quite often individuals who affirmed the idea of a Jewish state with their financial contributions and political demonstrations, individuals who were not enrolled in Zionist parties, but in various non-Zionist groups. These "non-Zionist" groups, in turn, either subscribed to the Zionist program outright (as for example, the American Jewish Congress, the Rabbinical Assembly of America, the Jewish Reconstructionist Foundation), or else withheld policy statements on the ultimate constitutional status of Palestine, while at the same time consistently supporting the prime Zionist objectives—unrestricted Jewish immigration, land purchase, colonization, self-government, and a Palestinian military force. Together, these two categories of organized Zionist supporters included every important national group in the American Jewish community, and hundreds of thousands of unaffiliated Jews. In truth, aside from its indirect supporters, the American Zionist movement was relatively small in numbers until 1946. The various "non-Zionist" associations in which Zionists were enrolled, the overlapping and multiple roles of Zionists who were also Reform rabbis, B'nai B'rith members or Orthodox laymen gave the Zionist movement its decisive importance in the American Jewish community. To view Zionism only in terms of the Zionist Organization of America, Hadassah, Mizrachi, and Poale Zion, therefore, is to overlook important, indeed decisive, sources of Zionist strength.

It may be argued that groups which supported Zionist objectives in Palestine were not necessarily Zionist-oriented but, rather, were merely *pro-Palestine* in character. In defense of such an argument, it may be recalled that groups like the American Jewish Committee, Jewish Labor Committee, and National Council of Jewish Women never officially approved the idea of a Jewish state until the very eve of the State of Israel's birth, when the Zionist goal was virtually a *fait accompli*. Furthermore, these groups cooperated with Zionists in defense of Palestine only up to the point that the Zionists avowed their "maximum political aims." Thus, for instance, the American Jewish Committee openly opposed the partition of Palestine in 1938, and B'nai B'rith also expressed great uneasiness about the "consequences" for American Jewry of a sovereign Jewish state. Then, too, the Zionists' Biltmore Program of a Jewish commonwealth never received the official approbation of the American Jewish Committee, Jewish Labor Committee, National Council of Jewish Women, Union of American Hebrew Congregations, and B'nai B'rith, although most of these groups felt "morally bound" to support the commonwealth plan by virtue of their membership in the American Jewish Conference.

But again, looked at "effectively" rather than "formally," distinctions between "non-Zionists" and Zionists were largely nominal in character. Certainly, from the Arab and British point of view, the substantive political demands of American Zionists and American non-Zionists were practically identical. The Zionists might openly proclaim a sovereign political entity as their *ultimate* objective while non-Zionists energetically averred that their concern was only with the immediate "humanitarian and non-political upbuilding of Palestine." In fact, however, both were traveling the same road, although, perhaps, from different motivations. It is interesting to note that one of the primary goals of the American Council for Judaism was to "awaken" American non-Zionists, to point out the "inconsistency" and "mistaken notions" of those Jews who did not understand that by helping Palestine philanthropically they were also furthering Zionism politically.

The influence of an interest group varies with the "extent to which its objectives and methods are congruent with the prevailing values" of its public or political world.[6]

That American Zionists, themselves limited in numbers and resources, were able to mobilize a much larger population was due, first, to the fact that the security and well-being of European and Palestinian Jewry were prime values shared by most of the American Jewish community. While some non-Zionist groups assiduously sought to draw a distinction between what they were doing for Palestine and what the Zionists had in mind (even to the point of openly breaking with the Zionists, as the American Jewish Committee did in 1943), no organized Jewish group except the American Council for Judaism was willing to be placed for long in the position of a "wrecker of Jewish unity and welfare." Perhaps this marked unwillingness to harm Jewish interests in Palestine can most succinctly be expressed by a statement of U. S. Supreme Court Associate Justice Benjamin N. Cardozo at the time he joined the Zionist Organization of America in 1918. Confessing to Rabbi Stephen S. Wise that he had signed the Zionist membership application with "some misgiving" since he was not yet an enthusiast for the Zionist cause, Cardozo concluded: ". . . to-day, the line seems to be forming between those who are for the cause and those who are against it, with little room for a third camp. I am not willing to join those who are against, so I go over to the others." [7]

Building upon the common denominator of the value of a Jewish Palestine for the survival of a Jewish people, Zionist leaders were able to evoke varying degrees of sympathetic expression and assistance from very different kinds of organized groups within their public. In Reform Judaism, the Classical anti-Zionist expressions of the Pittsburgh Platform of 1885 were discredited and a new expression of Reform more sympathetic to Zion was substituted for the old. A rising majority of pro-Zionist rabbis and laymen also elected men of their own persuasion to the head of the Reform movement and removed anti-Zionist colleagues from positions of leadership. In B'nai B'rith, an aggressive Zionist leadership gradually led the organization into a working arrangement providing funds, membership, and political support for the Zionist cause. In the Jewish labor movement, pro-Zionist labor leaders erected a number of organizations for the purpose of aiding Palestine—the *Gewerkschaften* campaign, the Jewish National Workers' Alliance, Labor Zionist parties, the American Jewish Trade Union Committee for Palestine—when other organizational forms were not available for their use. Pro-Zionist laborites also gradually forced an originally anti-Zionist labor leadership into a position of neutrality on Zionism while they simultaneously extended generous support for Labor Palestine. In a third major area of conflict, pro-Zionist supporters in the American Jewish Committee were in a decided minority and, therefore, Zionist successes were more limited than in any other sector of the population. Even there, however, the Zionists had the partial support of the Committee from 1919 to 1943. After the American Jewish Committee's secession from the American Jewish Conference, Zionist exploitation of pro-Palestine predispositions in the American Jewish community apparently succeeded in isolating the Committee from its major bases of support in the Reform rabbinate and in several community welfare funds and national organizations. Under the impetus of tragic world events and Zionist attacks, the Committee, in 1947, returned to a stance of active cooperation with the Zionist leadership in behalf of a Jewish state.

Since the strongest anti-Zionist expressions in the Jewish community emanated from the ranks of Reform Judaism (and from Reform Jews' predominant control of the American Jewish Committee and the Joint Distribution Committee), with its economically more privileged and culturally more Americanized membership, the generalization is suggested initially that Zionism's basic appeal was to poor Old World Jews and those only slightly integrated into American society. As a corollary, it might be predicted that the more culturally assimilated American Jews become, the less they will tend to be Zionists.

But anti-Zionist opinion was also originally prevalent at the other end of the socio-economic spectrum, in the Bundist-dominated and proletarian Jewish labor movement composed of recent immigrants. Moreover, simultaneously with the growing Americanization of this laboring class and attendant upon its increasing wealth, there evolved a growing pro-Zionist orientation.[8] As a matter of fact, at the same time that American Jews were becoming more favorably disposed toward Zionism, they were also becoming more "middle class." Increasing wealth and acculturation, in other words, did not lead to the hypothesized anti-Zionist opinions. Furthermore, the generalization posing a direct and inverse relationship between economic class and social acculturation, on the one hand, and acceptance of Zionism, on the other, also fails to account for the large number of avid Zionists, particularly Zionist leaders, drawn from the membership of Reform Judaism and old American Jewish families.

A more valid generalization is that Zionism's appeals were not based on class and acculturation alone, but on an intervening factor as well. This factor may be described as "Jewish perspective," the degree to which an individual felt drawn to identify himself in Jewish ways, to espouse distinctively Jewish beliefs, identifications, and demands concerning issues affecting the Jewish people. Thus, the more affirmative a person was in his Jewish perspective, the more he might be expected to support Zionism, regardless of his socio-economic situation. The individual Jew's approach to Zionism, in other words, was determined primarily by his attitude toward being a member of the Jewish grouping, even though his socio-economic situation may have induced an initial receptivity or hostility to the Zionist program.[9]

The extent to which an interest group will derive support from both effective and formal allies varies with the ability of such allies to derive mutual benefits from the alliance.

The gradually evolved pro-Zionist orientations of much of American Jewry cannot be attributed merely to Zionist victories in relation to Zionist "target groups." Rather, Zionist objectives came to be accepted voluntarily by many Jewish groups because Zionism was able to fulfil certain roles or felt needs. In the religious denominations, for example, Palestine and Zionism provided rabbis and educators with an appealing subject matter and a field of activity which would supplement their theological credos. With

its revival of language and culture, Zionism was the natural concomitant of Jewish education and thus attracted the enthusiastic
assistance of Jewish educators. A progressive Palestine was also
avidly endorsed by rabbis and laymen concerned with "Social Justice" and the ideals of Prophetic Judaism. Projects in Palestine
were widely regarded as worthy causes by numerous local and
national groups seeking a more serious *raison d'être* than that of
social life alone. Finally, Histadrut and Labor Palestine were "made
to order" for Jewish trade unionists eager to lend assistance to
a dynamic laboring society. In other words, groups "used" Zionism
as much as Zionists "used" them; the Zionist program was recognized and accepted partially because it fulfilled certain reciprocal
needs, because support of Zionism rendered something of value
to its allies and supporters.

*The influence of an interest group varies with the relative scope
of its demands. Groups oppose each other on secondary issues
only to the point that resistance to the demands of other groups
threatens the realization of more primary interests.*

The more Zionism came to be accepted by American Jewry, the
more difficult it was for any group to resist its demands. Success in
one sector of the Jewish political world facilitated victory in other
sectors.[10] Groups began to use their Zionist affiliation as a weapon
against their rivals. Conservative Judaism apparently gained numerous adherents at the expense of Reform by virtue of its warm
espousal of Zionism. Eventually, the Reform movement also became pro-Zionist, partially in order to attract families from Orthodox backgrounds who had been alienated by Reform's original
antipathy to Zionism. Similarly, the American Jewish Congress
used its Zionist "democratic-peoplehood" approach as a weapon
against the "oligarchical" American Jewish Committee at a time
when both groups were competing for leadership in the fight against
anti-Semitism. The same might also be said for Hadassah vis-à-vis
non-Zionist women's groups like the National Council of Jewish
Women, and for the Jewish National Workers' Alliance vis-à-vis
Workmen's Circle.

As Zionism became increasingly respectable in the Jewish community, a "bandwagon effect" could be observed. Many journalists

and social historians have pointed out that Zionism became virtually the sole common denominator in an otherwise badly divided community. Zionism was viewed as a "Jewish badge of honor" and a prerequisite for community leadership and eminence. Zionist leadership, in turn, exploited these successes to enhance further its standing among American Jews and to influence recalcitrant groups to adopt a more pro-Palestine posture.[11]

Despite widespread successes in the American Jewish community, Zionist leaders were not able to "Zionize" all of the organized groups in their public. Thorough-going converts to the Zionist cause were not always won. On the other hand, none of these groups were found effectively to oppose Zionism after the mid-forties. Available data indicate that there were strong anti-Zionist inclinations on the part of some leaders of major Jewish groups. Nevertheless, actual anti-Zionist agitation was avoided by such leaders in order that their primary concerns on the American scene would be spared from conflict with an increasingly popular movement. In the case of Reform, the religious unity of the Central Conference of American Rabbis and of the Union of American Hebrew Congregations was considered by Zionists and non-Zionists alike to be more important than a total victory for either side. Among the leaders of the Jewish Labor Committee, Jewish Labor's voice in the general labor movement was universally regarded as too precious to be endangered by conflict concerning the secondary issue of Zionism. Similarly, in the American Jewish Committee and in the National Council of Jewish Women, the program of combatting anti-Semitism and helping American Jews to become integrated into American society was deemed of far greater importance than the Zionist program. In other words, after American Zionism achieved a state of wide acceptance, support of Zionist objectives "cost" American Jewish groups little, while opposition might have "cost" them much in terms of more central concerns. The result was the "effective ally" phenomenon we have already described; groups both refrained from opposing the Zionist movement and, at the same time, from officially affirming Zionist ideology. In practice, however, practically every group eventually rendered actual assistance for the establishment of the Jewish state.

From the Zionist point of view, these "effective allies" were not, of course, all that could be desired, for they had not accepted all of the Zionist program.* Zionist ideology with its "nationalistic overtones" was not universally popular. The Hebraization and communal organization of American Jewry advocated by some Zionists had not been achieved. Some American Jews were worried lest they be charged with dual loyalty by virtue of their support of a Jewish state. Nevertheless, considering that the Zionist movement had begun as a comparatively inconsequential interest group in a community sorely divided by various types of religious, class, and ideological rivalries, even partial success meant a tremendous rise in Zionist influence among American Jews. Zionist leaders not only received the physical support of numerous non-Zionist groups, but they also avoided the risk of being labeled as "a small minority" of American Jewry. Zionist spokesmen, after all, could point to example after example of widespread Jewish support for various objectives in their total program. More importantly, they could proceed to present their demands to the American government in the knowledge that only the American Council for Judaism would actively oppose their claims and activities.

It is axiomatic that the opinions of the total American population regarding the specifically Jewish interest known as Zionism would be of prime importance in determining whether or not Zionist demands on the American government would eventually be realized. Less obvious, however, is the fact that many American Jews looked to non-Jewish groups and individuals as points of reference for determining their own thinking. Many Jews simply would not embrace Zionism unless they could feel that Zionism was thought to be "respectable" by non-Jewish Americans, the models to which "good Jews" were expected to conform in their behavior.

Recognizing the importance of non-Jewish attitudes toward Zionism for the development of more favorable Jewish opinion, as well as for eventual political demands on the American government, Zionist leadership early determined to organize the "Voice

---

* Note C. Wendell King's generalization:

Acceptance, then, is a matter of degree in two respects: a movement and all its goals may not be socially acceptable as a complete package since some items are separable and fare differently in the selective process; furthermore, when it does occur, acceptance rarely involves the entire society but usually means that only certain individuals or subgroups within the society are favorable in their reactions (*Social Movements in the United States* [New York, 1956], p. 54).

of Christian America" in behalf of its program. In this effort, Jewish and Christian Zionists successfully established influential and numerically significant associations of non-Jewish clergymen, educators, labor spokesmen, and local, state and national political leaders, including 80 percent of the American Congress. Pro-Zionist planks were included in both major party platforms during the 1944 presidential campaign, and political promises were made by both presidential aspirants. Finally, much of the American press and numerous key figures in the opinion-molding fields also actively espoused the Zionist position regarding Palestine.

Whether because of a common Judaeo-Christian cultural tradition, "democracy's traditional championship of the under-dog and persecuted minorities," convictions regarding the moral and political "rightness" of the Zionist program,[12] or simply because acceptance of Zionist demands did not require any great expenditure of non-Jewish effort or wealth, the Zionist program came to be ever more acceptable to diverse sectors of the total American population. In contrast, no organized anti-Zionist expression on the part of prominent non-Jews existed anywhere in the United States. The American Council for Judaism's contention that Zionism would impair the status of American Jews with their non-Jewish neighbors was, therefore, without visible substantiation in the years preceding the creation of the State of Israel.

The hypothesis seems confirmed, therefore, that yet another factor responsible for the growth of pro-Zionist opinion among American Jews was that Jewish reference groups—numerous and respected American non-Jews—saw fit to support the movement for the establishment of a Jewish state.*

After tracing the gradual acceptance of Zionist objectives in various sectors of the American Jewish community and noting the generally widespread respectability of the Zionist program in non-Jewish circles, our inquiry next focussed on two particular aspects of Zionist activity: fund-raising for Palestine and the American Jewish Conference of 1943. The purpose of these specialized inquiries was to indicate the manner in which an interest group

* In *The Governmental Process*, Truman suggested that interest groups seek the support of government, partially in order to perform their basic function: "the establishment and maintenance of an equilibrium in the relationships of their members" (p. 105). I have broadened the generalization by including *all* reference groups as factors to be won over as a means of establishing and maintaining group cohesion.

bridges the diversities of its public in order to achieve sufficient cohesion for political objectives.

In the case of fund-raising for Palestine, Zionist leadership enlisted Jewish support through indirect rather than direct channels. Instead of relying entirely upon specifically Zionist funds whose purposes might appeal to only a relatively small segment of the Jewish population, Zionists gradually led American Jewry into various types of joint fund-raising endeavors, enterprises broad enough to encompass the totality of American Jewry. Beginning with the Jewish Agency for Palestine, the Zionist goal was to enroll wealthy Jewish philanthropists in the upbuilding of Palestine. Jointly associated with the "big names" of the American Jewish community, the Zionist cause achieved a degree of prestige it had formerly lacked. Next, through the instrumentalities of the annual National Conferences for Palestine (United Palestine Appeal) and the United Jewish Appeal, the task of reclaiming Palestine was transformed from the sole responsibility of the Zionist movement into a task demanding the loyalties of *all* American Jewry. The utility of furthering the Palestine ideal through such "umbrella organization," rather than solely through Zionist channels, was dramatically illustrated by almost invariant annual increases in funds collected until, in 1948 alone, American Jewry donated over one hundred million dollars to Palestine.

Another Zionist objective in the erection and direction of these "umbrella fund-raising organizations" for Palestine, in addition to the obvious one of seeking larger contributions, was suggested as a direct consequence of the heterogeneity of the American Jewish community. In a public divided by diverse interpretations of Judaism, as well as by rivalries of class, national origin, and political ideology, philanthropy provided the only bridge enabling all Jews to meet on common ground. What could not, perhaps, have been achieved by direct appeals for Palestine and Zionism was realized by incorporating Palestine as a beneficiary of the Jew's religious and moral duty to provide for his less fortunate brethren.

But Zionist fund-raising activity did not cease at the point of obtaining funds for Palestine and bridging chasms in the Jewish community. In addition to these tasks, Zionists used fund-raising mechanisms for the "political education" of American Jewry. Constantly seeking to discredit "mere negative philanthropy," Zionist leadership painted the message of Palestine as a "positive and constructive undertaking." In this way, Zionists eventually came to achieve four important goals. First, Palestine rose from the position of one among many "worthy causes" to be the single largest recipient of American Jewish financial aid. Second, Zionist political instrumentalities in the United States, like the American Zionist Emergency Council, became the indirect financial beneficiaries of such drives by virtue of grants from direct campaign partners, such as the Keren Hayesod and Keren Kayemeth. Third, under the umbrella of fund-raising, Zionist leadership further corralled many American Jewish organizations for limited purposes. This type of union with non-Zionist groups tended to remove the danger that an effective anti-Zionist movement, based on uncommitted sectors of American Jewry, would ever arise; groups that increasingly supported Palestine on a fund-raising basis were unlikely to wage war on the various Zionist political objectives regarding Palestine. Fourth, and perhaps most important for the eventual realization of Zionist objectives, many American Jews were introduced to the political goals of the Zionist movement as a result of propaganda conducted in connection with annual fund-raising drives. The United Palestine and United Jewish Appeals, in short, became vehicles for promoting various Zionist goals not directly related to financial questions—the abrogation of the White Paper, the authorization of a Jewish military force, and even the establishment of a Jewish commonwealth, itself.

After achieving a degree of cohesion in their own ranks judged sufficient to permit of political demands from the American government, Zionist leaders sought to measure and to institutionalize their gains in a manner likely to contribute to further political advances. The numerous and often bitter political struggles in which they engaged in order to win allies, neutralize former opponents, and head off potential antagonists, had to be clothed in the terminology and structures of the American democratic system in order to be successful. With respect to our specific inquiry into the American Jewish Conference of 1943, we saw that American Zionism's gradual rise to an influential position among American Jews was achieved in the democratic mold. The Conference, with its elaborate systems of local elections, delegates, proportional representation, committees and resolutions, lent credibility to the Zionist claim that American Jewry had been "democratically organized" and was now "almost solidly behind" their program. Although Zionist propagandists exaggerated the extent of their victory in the Conference, the fact remains that the Conference gave an indication of a greater unity on a major Jewish question than had ever before been registered in the Jewish community. The Resolution on Palestine, together with the continuing instrumentalities of the American Jewish Conference, were thus added to the Zionist arsenal for later use in the political offensive before the United States government and the United Nations.

"The internal development of an ideology is less important than its use as a means of extending group membership, of increasing the activity of members, or of minimizing the activity of opposition groups." [13]

The record of the American Jewish Conference also indicates the general applicability of David Truman's observation that the democratic mold serves to cloak the struggle for power present in all group life. The fact that "forms of democracy"—types of elections, ballots, representation, and so forth—were the immediate subject of struggle does not mask the fact that great substantive issues were in question at the American Jewish Conference. While the watchwords of the political struggle were phrased in ideological terms, such as "democracy," "majority rule," and "unity," the substantive issues revolved about the explicit proclamation of American Jewry's demands for a state versus the more cautious program of "waiting to see what international developments might bring."

Thus, the American Jewish Conference provides yet another confirmation of several social scientists' observations to the effect that most ideological conflicts in group life are decidedly secondary to the material conflicts of interests of competing groups.[14] While the Zionist question at the Conference—indeed throughout the American Jewish community—was argued in terms of "timeliness," "propriety," and "dual loyalty," more basic interests were actually involved. These may be represented by such questions as whether agreement on the Zionist issue would mean that various groups would have to surrender their "organizational sovereignty" in order to present a united pro-Palestine front, whether opposition to "Jewish unity for Palestine" would harm a group in the furtherance of its primary program, whether a group would be associated in the public mind with the despised anti-Zionist minority if it did not go along entirely with the Zionist's "maximal, political program," and the like.

A public or a potential interest group becomes organized in consequence of disturbances in mutually shared interests or on the basis of "tangent relations." Public opinion remains latent until an issue arises for the group; an issue arises when there is conflict, anxiety, or frustration.[15]

Tracing historical events of the mid-twentieth century, we found that a positive relationship existed between the growth of pro-Zionist opinion in the American Jewish community and a number of these events. With each Arab attack on the Jewish community in Palestine, with each additional British departure from the Balfour Declaration and the Mandate for Palestine, and with each new outbreak of international anti-Semitism, American Jewry increasingly rallied to the Zionist banner. Finally, when the status of world Jewry was revolutionized by the Nazi massacres of European Jewry, support of the Zionist cause was expressed as never before. Zionist political activity, funds for Palestine, formal Zionist memberships, and the number of organized Jewish groups upholding Zionist objectives all soared dramatically. Much engrossed with their own integration into the American economy and society, Jews had always exhibited sympathies for Zionist aspirations. But now, at the close of World War II, American Jewry became better organized and strikingly "politically-minded." External events— "the objective facts of life"—had the last word in determining the reception of the Zionist program. As one leading Zionist conceded with perhaps not too much overstatement: "If Herzl was the Marxist theoretician of Zionism, Hitler was the Leninist prime mover of the Jewish state." Changes in the status of world Jewry, in short, produced changed Jewish predispositions, and to this were added the effects of Zionist propaganda, pointing the way toward a seemingly effective political solution.

Not all of the historical events of the mid-twentieth century worked in favor of the American Zionist movement, however. Two in particular—the Great Depression of the thirties and the early Axis victories in World War II—had a partially demoralizing effect upon the Zionist movement and in addition tended to decrease

Zionist membership. Furthermore, in the absence of a particular threat or crisis affecting world Jewry, Zionist political fortunes waned. Zionist leaders were thus faced with the difficult problem of maintaining the strength of their movement when their goal seemed far from attainment.

Viewing the American Zionist movement as a continuum marked by both mobilizing and demoralizing events, we must recognize the essential correctness of David Truman's generalization: "Perhaps the most significant feature of group politics is that it is a dynamic process, a constantly changing pattern of relationships involving through the years continued shifts in relative influence." [16]

As new issues for the Jewish group arose, public opinion became further activated. Zionist propaganda, which had been focussing for years on a predominantly apathetic audience, now had a fertile field for its operations.[17] Reacting to the emergency conditions facing world Jewry, American Jews sought a program to protect their diverse interests. Some groups, intent on fighting anti-Semitism, wanted the "troublesome" public issue of Palestine settled quickly so that European Displaced Persons would be kept out of the United States and so that Palestinian terrorist activities, which they felt reflected discredit on the Jewish people, would be ended. Other Jews exhibited a marked anxiety about the fate of their relatives and friends abroad and wanted to help in any way possible. For both of these motives, Zionism now presented an attractive program by virtue of its appeals to self-interest; and, as Hadley Cantril has stated, "once self-interest is involved, opinion is not easily changed." [18]

Though far removed from the actual scene of conflict in Palestine, American Jews mobilized to create a Jewish state and, thus, to "solve the Jewish Problem." Though there was no monetary gain from their activity in support of Zionist objectives (and, indeed, pro-Zionist sympathies entailed burdens in the form of dues, financial contributions, and, often, the expenditure of countless hours), millions of American Jews responded to the demands of the Zionist movement with increasing intensity of feeling and activity.

One of the strengths of the Zionist propaganda appeal was its ambiguous and flexible nature. What some Jews could not accept on grounds of religious fiat, they did accept as a result of a belief in the need for "Jewish Unity," because of the "Social Justice of a Jewish Palestine," or because of the "callous indifference of Christendom," all pointed up by the Zionists. Similarly, while the political ideology of "Jewish National Homelessness" was repugnant to some Jews, the claim that Zionism would ensure Jewish survival enjoyed very widespread appeal. Much of Zionist propaganda thus fitted into an "unstructured situation" [19] in which the meaning of the Zionist message was indefinite and subject to widely differing individual interpretation. Since American Zionism was all things to all men, it could enlist a very wide assortment of Jewish and non-Jewish interests under one common banner.

Intense conflict enhanced the mutual identification of those sharing a belief in the need for a Jewish state.[20]

The American Council for Judaism did not provide a serious stumbling block to the rise of Zionist power and influence. Arising at a time of great calamity for world Jewry, the Council posed a dramatic challenge to Zionist leadership which was exploited for all its worth. Representing the anti-Zionist group as a "traitorous," "irreligious" and "anti-Jewish" cause, Zionist counterpropaganda evoked Jewish loyalties and Jewish ardor. While positive documentation is lacking, it seems likely that the net effect of the Council's formation was the intensification of Zionist activity and the enhancement of Jewish cohesion on the Zionist question.

The greater the success achieved by an interest group, the more difficult it becomes to identify it as a discrete unit; success leads to a loss of distinctive identity. Moreover, as an interest group increases in size, the definition of "ideological principles" among its adherents becomes increasingly difficult.[21]

Throughout the history of American Zionism, a number of Zionist writers and leaders persistently pointed out that the growing acceptance of the Zionist program by the Jewish population of the United States was not really a victory for Zionist ideology at all. Rather, they protested, "political Zionism" was surrendering to "Jewish philanthropy." In a similar vein, one contemporary Israeli writer has declared:

The truth is that there never existed in America a Zionist Movement in the accepted (European) sense of the term. Zionist organizations in America *always* have had a purely pro-Israel character and no more. They promoted not personal participation in the upbuilding of the country but political and financial support of a function to be undertaken by other Jews. . . .

The absence of any significant anti-Zionist reaction in the United States is largely conditioned by the absence of a genuine Zionist movement. American Jewry chose a policy of appeasement in foregoing both Zionism and anti-Zionism.[22]

In fact, as the Zionist objective of a Jewish state was accepted by more and more Americans, it became increasingly difficult to identify "the Zionists," as opposed to the non-Zionists, in the Jewish community. In 1929, there were numerous and influential groups which assiduously avoided both Zionist ideology *and* the practical political tasks proposed by the Zionist leadership. The Zionists, by contrast, was easily distinguished by their support of various objectives in Palestine. By 1946, however, it was virtually impossible to distinguish between Zionists and non-Zionists in terms of their actual activities in behalf of a Jewish Palestine. It is possible to argue both that Zionist leadership "succumbed to the lure of philanthropy" and that Jewish philanthropy accepted the "minimal political program" of Zionism. Distinctions between those who had historically been Zionists and those who had played the role of non-Zionists were so blurred that even veteran Palestinian Zionist leader Eliezer Kaplan privately concluded: "I must confess . . . that I found it difficult at times to determine whose bearing was more Zionist and whose appearance made a deeper impression—that of Zionists or non-Zionists . . . those who hoped to find evidence of a split between Jews and Zionists have erred greatly." [23] In any case, the distinction is not very important *in terms of the immediate political consequences* which followed. There now existed a potent coalition of almost every significant group in the American Jewish community, a coalition armed for the struggle to build a Jewish state.

appendix I

SOME NATIONAL AMERICAN JEWISH ORGANIZATIONS

Sources: *American Jewish Year Books,* **XXXI** (1929), **XLVII** (1945–46), and *Palestine Yearbook,* **I** (1944–45), **IV** (1948–49).

Note: Membership figures listed are unverified claims of the organizations themselves.

A. *General Programs* (not primarily pro-Palestine functions)

NAME	FOUNDED	MEMBERSHIP 1930	1945
Agudas Israel	1941	—	29,450
American Birobidjan Committee	1934	—	5,000
American Council for Judaism	1942	—	—
American Jewish Committee	1906	—	450 corporate members
American Jewish Conference	1943	—	120 delegates of 64 national organizations; 378 delegates of local communities
American Jewish Congress	1917, 1922	—	—
American Joint Distribution Committee	1914	—	—
Assembly of Hebrew Orthodox Rabbis of U.S. and Canada	1920	—	125
B'nai B'rith, Order of	1843	85,000	200,000 in world c. 150,000 in US
Central Conference of American Rabbis (Reform)	1899	268	475
Council of Jewish Federations and Welfare funds	1932	—	263 councils in 231 cities
Federation of Orthodox Rabbis of America	1926	102	—
Free Sons of Israel	1849	8,468	10,056
Independent Order B'rith Abraham	1887	110,000	58,000
Independent Order B'rith Shalom	1905	23,676	14,623
Jewish-American Section, International Workers Order (Jewish People's Fraternal Order)	1930	—	47,000
Jewish Labor Committee	1934	—	—
Jewish National Workers' Alliance	1912	5,933	25,000
Jewish Reconstructionist Foundation	1935	—	500
Jewish War Veterans of the United States	1896	8,000	65,000
National Council of Jewish Women	1893	—	65,000

NAME	FOUNDED	MEMBERSHIP	
		1930	*1945*
National Council of Young Israel (Orthodox)	1912	8,000	25,000
Progressive Order of the West	1896	10,347	5,000
Rabbinical Assembly of America (Conservative)	1900	201	354
Rabbinical Council of America (Orthodox)	1923	—	300
Synagogue Council of America	1925	36 delegates	84 delegates
Union of American Hebrew Congregations (Reform)	1873	281 congregations	320 congregations
Union of Orthodox Jewish Congregations of America	1898	—	—
Union of Orthodox Rabbis of U.S. and Canada	1902	350	500
United Synagogue of America (Conservative)	1913	—	350 congregations
Workmen's Circle (Arbeiter Ring)	1900	78,000	75,000
Yeshiva Synagogue Council (Orthodox)	1936	—	500 congregations

B. *Specific Zionist and Pro-Palestine Programs* (Y indicates youth group)

NAME	FOUNDED	MEMBERSHIP		
		1930	*1945*	*1948*
Academic Committee for the Hebrew University	1940	—	300	—
Ahdut Haavodah-Poale Zion; United Labor Zionist Party	1920	—	—	2,000
Ameic-American Eretz Israel Corporation	1944	—	—	—
American Alumni of the Hebrew University	1940	—	70	200
American Beth Jacob Committee	1928	—	—	—
American Committee for the Relief and Resettlement of Yemenite Jews	1938	—	3,000	8,000
American Committee for Weizmann Institute of Science	1945	—	—	—
American Committee of the Universal Yeshivah of Jerusalem	1924	—	—	—
American Economic Committee for Palestine	1932	—	200	—
American Friends of the Hebrew University	1925	—	—	—
American Fund for Palestinian Institutions	1939	—	—	—
American Jewish Dentists' Committee	1936	—	500	—
American Jewish Physicians' Committee	1921	1,000	700	1,250
American Jewish Trade Union Committee for Palestine	1943	—	—	—
American League for a Free Palestine (Revisionist) (non-sectarian)	1944	—	35,000	—

NAME	FOUNDED	MEMBERSHIP		
		1930	*1945*	*1948*
American Palestine Jewish Legion (Hagdud Haivri)	1930	—	5,300	—
American Red Mogen Dovid for Palestine	1941	—	20,000	75,000
American Society for the Advancement of the Hebrew Institute of Technology	1940	—	2,500	5,000
American Zionist Emergency Council	1939	—	—	—
American Zionist Youth Commissions (Y)	1940	—	175 local commissions	—
Americans for Hagana	1947	—	—	—
Ampal-American Palestine Trading Corporation	1942	—	3,000 share holders	8,000 share holders
Avukah, Student Zionist Organization (Y)	1925	1,000	2,000	—
Betar Organization of America (Revisionist) (Y)	1944	—	300	—
B'nai Zion	1908	3,525	5,000	5,000
B'rith Trumpeldor of America (Revisionist) (Y)	1929	—	4,700	4,400
Federated Council of Palestine Institutions	1940	—	—	—
Federation of Palestine Jews of America	1929	—	3,500	3,500
Habonim, Labor Zionist Youth Organization (Y)	1934	—	3,800	4,000
Hadassah, Women's Zionist Organization of America	1912	34,483	142,665	250,000
Haoleh (Y)	1946	—	—	130
Hapoel Hamizrachi of America	1921	—	15,000	16,000
Hashomer Hadati of North America (Y)	1935	—	500	2,300
Hashomer Hatzair (Y)	1923	—	3,000	4,000
Hebrew Committee of National Liberation (Revisionist)	1944	—	8	—
Hebrew Youth Commission (Hanoar Haivri) of Histadruth Ivrith (Y)	1936	—	500	700
Hechalutz Hatzair (Y)	1947	—	—	800
Hechalutz Organization (Y)	1932	—	1,000	2,000
Histadrut Ivrith	1916	3,130	5,800	8,500
Intercollegiate Zionist Federation of American (Y)	1945	—	—	8,000
Jewish Agency for Palestine, American Representatives of	1929	—	115	—
Jewish National Fund (Keren Kayemeth Le-Israel)	1901	—	—	—
Jewish State Zionists of America	1933	—	1,200	—
Junior Hadassah (Y)	1920	—	20,000	20,000
Junior Mizrachi Women's Organization (Y)	1934	—	4,200	9,700
League for Labor Palestine	1934	—	4,000	—
League for Religious Labor in Palestine	1941	—	10 chapters	3,000

NAME	FOUNDED	1930	1945	1948
			MEMBERSHIP	
Masada, Youth Zionist Organization of America (Y)	1933	—	2,500	5,200
Mizrachi Zionist Organization	1911	20,000	35,000	75,000
Mizrachi Women's Organization	1925	—	36,500	50,000
National Council of Organizations for Palestine	1924	—	500 organizations representing 500,000	—
National Labor Committee for Palestine	1923	—	150,000 contributors 3,000 organizations	—
New Zionist Organization of America (Revisionist)	1925	—	10,000	—
Palestine Economic Corporation	1925	—	1,450 stockholders	2,000 stockholders
Palestine Emergency Fund	1945	—	—	5,000
Palestine Foundation Fund (Keren Hayesod)	1922	—	—	—
Palestine Hebrew Culture Fund	1938	—	112 branches	—
Palestine Lighthouse	1927	—	600	—
Palestine Symphonic Choir Project	1939	—	—	—
Palestine Youth Conference (Y)	1947	—	—	—
Pioneer Women's Zionist Organization	1925	3,000	16,000	28,000
Plugat Aliyah (Y)	1946	—	—	200
Poale Zion-Zeire Zion (Labor Zionist Organization of America)	1905–1921	5,000	20,000	65,000
Tel-Hai Fund	1935	—	8 branches	—
United Palestine Appeal	1936	—	—	—
United States Maccabi Association	1934	—	200	—
Women's League for Palestine	1928	—	2,000	3,000
Women's Organization of Hapoel Hamizrachi	1928	—	—	—
Young Judaea (Y)	1908	—	17,000	15,000
Young Zionist Actions Committee (Y)	1944	—	110 affiliated Zionist groups	—
Zeire Hapoel Hamizrachi of America	1945	—	—	2,300
Zionist Organization of America	1897	c. 15,000	136,630	248,566
(With constituent and affiliated organizations —			315,000 in 1945/1946)	

C. Non-Jewish Pro-Zionist Organizations

NAME	FOUNDED	1930	1945	1948
			MEMBERSHIP	
American Palestine Committee	1941	—	7,500	*
Christian Council on Palestine	1942	—	2,500	*

* Merged into American Christian Palestine Committee with 20,000 members in 1948.

appendix II

POLICY ON PALESTINE ADOPTED BY THE GREAT RABBINICAL
COUNCIL OF THE AGUDAS ISRAEL WORLD ORGANIZATION—
1937 (16 ELUL 5697)

Source: Jacob Rosenheim, *Agudist World Problems* (New York, [1941]),
p. 16.

1. The Rabbinical Council declares:

a. Our holy land has been granted to us from the master of the world by a sworn eternal covenant, in order to observe in this land the laws and prescriptions of the Torah and to live there a life in the spirit of the Torah. Thus the Jewish people is forever linked to this land with all the fibres of her soul.

b. Having been expelled on account of our sins from our country G'd has promised us by our holy prophets that He will release us again through the Messiah. The belief in this promise is one of the fundamental principles of the Jewish religion, obligatory for every Jewish person.

c. The right of the Jewish nation to our holy land has therefore its basis in our holy Torah and in the guarantees given by the prophets as the envoys of G'd.

d. The existence of a Jewish state is possible only if the law of the Torah is acknowledged as the constitutional basis of the state, and the sovereignty of the Torah is dominating the administration.

e. A Jewish state that is not based on the foundation of the Torah would mean a denial of Jewish history and of the true essence of Jewish nationality and would destroy the basis of national life.

2. The Rabbinical Council declares in the spirit of Torah that neither negotiations nor decisions concerning the future of Eretz Israel, the inheritance of the whole of Israel, can be considered as legitimate, unless representatives, duly authorized by organized orthodox Jewry, take their part in these negotiations and decisions. Any negotiations without the cooperation of the representatives of orthodox Jewry are a challenge to justice and morality.

appendix III

PALESTINE PROGRAM OF THE RELIGIOUS NATIONAL ORTHODOX BLOC OF THE AMERICAN JEWISH CONFERENCE, 1943

Source: Central Zionist Archives Jerusalem, Z5/758.

PREAMBLE: Abridged

At this time, when the greatest effort in history is being made to right the wrongs committed against small and weak peoples and to guarantee their protection in the future, we the Jews of America, demand the immediate cessation of the wanton slaughter of our fellow Jews throughout Nazi-occupied Europe and elsewhere and that immediate steps be taken to rescue the helpless victims who can and must be saved; we demand that the injustice done the Jewish people centuries ago by devastation of their land and dispersion of their people throughout the world be righted. To this end we submit the following for consideration:

ERETZ ISRAEL:

The demand that Eretz Israel be returned to the Jewish people not only proclaims the historic yearning of our people to return to nationhood, but also is the very foundation of the Jewish religion. God has assured us through the Prophets in clearest terms that Eretz Israel will again belong to the Jews. The daily prayers of the Jew are replete with supplications and hopes for the return to Eretz Israel. The Jews have waited 1874 years that God's promise to suffering Israel be fulfilled, and now, when the opportunity is here for the establishment of freedom and justice on earth, under the inevitable victory of the United Nations, we ask that this be the historic moment when justice to an ancient people, suffering without cause or reason, be accomplished. Eretz Israel is the only hope of millions of persecuted Jews, victims of Nazi barbarism: the only solution to the homelessness of our people. With the establishment of a Jewish Commonwealth on its own ancient soil of Eretz Israel, will the Jewish people have the fullest opportunity for the complete observance of the tenets of the Jewish religion and traditions. Eretz Israel as a Jewish Commonwealth, therefore, is the only solution to the all inclusive centuries-old problem of the Jewish people.

The historic connection between Eretz Israel and the Jewish people was legally recognized by the League of Nations in the Mandate for Palestine. Since then the Jewish people succeeded in reconstructing Eretz Israel as a prosperous land with a Jewish population of nearly 600,000 now already representing the beginnings of a Jewish Commonwealth on its own soil. We, therefore, demand in the name of the Jewish people.

(A) the issuance of a declaration by the United Nations expressing assurance that Eretz Israel be declared a Jewish Commonwealth

(B) the control of immigration into Eretz Israel shall be vested wholly in the hands of the Jewish Agency for Palestine

(C) the immediate abolition of the White Paper which is a contradiction of the Balfour Declaration. It is totally opposed, in word and spirit, to the Mandate of the League of Nations. In fact, the authoritative body of the League of Nations itself declared the White Paper illegal.

appendix

The
of which
search c
(Jerusal
(New Y
mittee
Corpor
Corpor
(Public
1956; I
ish Na
terest
T
to Pal

MEMBERSHIP STATISTICS OF MAJOR AMERICAN ZIONIST GROUPS

Sources: *AJYB; NP* (especially June 27, 1930, 402–406; February 4, 1938, 4); Samuel Dinin, *Zionist Education in the United States* (New York, 1944), 82; ZOA, *Annual Reports;* Letter to author from Hadassah Organization, June 4, 1956; *Reports of the Executives submitted to the Zionist Congresses.*

Note: Membership figures listed are unverified claims of the organizations themselves.

| | ZIONIST ORGANIZATION OF AMERICA | HADASSAH, WOMEN'S ZIONIST ORGANIZATION | LABOR ZIONISTS | | ORTHODOX ZIONISTS | | TOTAL SHEKEL PURCHASES IN THE U.S.[f] |
			POALE ZION	PIONEER WOMEN	MIZRACHI	MIZRACHI WOMEN	
1918	149,235[a]	—	—		18,000		
1919	56,838[b]	—	7,000		18,000		
1920	21,000[c]	—	7,000		18,000		
1921	30,597	—	7,000		20,000		84,310
1922	18,481		7,000		20,000		33,758
1923	24,303		5,000		20,000		32,346
1924	25,934		5,000		20,000		47,251
1925	27,144	27,475	5,000		20,000		131,277
1926	23,784	29,492	5,000		20,000		60,000
1927	21,806	34,466	5,000		20,000		141,221
1928	21,539	37,141	5,000		20,000		55,948
1929	18,031[d]	33,348	5,000		20,000		71,224
1930		34,483	5,000		20,000		34,000
1931	13,008	31,675	5,000	3,000	20,000		79,070
1932	8,484	27,349	5,000	3,000	20,000		44,958
1933	8,927	23,764	5,000	3,500	20,000	4,000	44,955
1934	14,513	28,466	5,000	3,500	20,000	4,500	36,328
1935	16,741[e]	32,496					134,493
1936	18,676	38,497					
1937	26,887	49,250					
1938	27,632	54,200					82,187
1939	43,453	66,000					
1940	43,295	73,837	10,000	7,000	27,000	10,000	171,567
1941	46,022	80,139					148,307
1942	49,952	86,329	12,500	10,000	27,000	32,000	156,308
1943	67,368	95,317	15,000	12,000	27,000	35,000	183,381
1944	111,421	119,934	15,000	15,000	35,000	35,000	257,086
1945	136,630	142,665	20,000	16,000	35,000	36,500	
1946	196,347	176,973					
1947	217,198	198,146					
1948	c. 250,000	242,962	65,000	28,000	75,000	50,000	954,886

Note on the relationship between population concentration and group strength.

A hypothesis suggested in Chapter 3 as a result of the marked urban concentration of American Jews in a few large states might be phrased as follows:

> *The ability of an interest group to influence its public varies directly with the degree to which the public is geographically concentrated; concentration aids group organization and cohesion.*

Although available data on this subject are not fully adequate either to confirm or contradict the hypothesis, there is evidence to suppose that Zionist membership campaigns were relatively more effective in towns and smaller urban areas than in the great metropolises:

1. Harry S. Linfield reported that, in 1927, there were thirteen Zionist organizations per every one hundred congregations in New York City. In contrast, in cities with 100–500,000 Jews, there were thirty-six Zionist groups for every one hundred congregations. Other figures were:

SIZE OF JEWISH POPULATION:	50–100,000	20–50,000	8–20,000	2–8,000	500–2,000
Number of Zionist groups per every 100 congregations	35	63	76	98	76

(See Linfield, *Communal Organization in the United States* [New York, 1930] pp. 115–18.)

2. In 1930, Morris Margulies, Secretary of the New York Zionist Region of the ZOA, complained that due to sheer size of the region (in terms of Jewish population), all communal effort was extremely difficult to organize. Moreover, the problem was compounded by a rapidly shifting population, that is, by the move to different boroughs and suburbs. (See *NP*, January 31, 1930, pp. 69–70.)

---

[a] 87,209 at $2.00; 62,026 at $1.00. Hadassah figures are included under ZOA from 1918–21.

[b] 45,005 at $2.00; 14,833 at $1.00.

[c] Dues fixed at $6.00 until 1938, when they were changed to $5.00.

[d] In addition, 45,200 persons paid $1.00 in the Zionist Roll Call of 1929.

[e] In addition, 20,000 persons paid $1.00 in the Zionist Roll Call of 1935.

[f] A Shekel is a type of poll-tax, fixed at fifty cents, whose purchase is required for elections to the World Zionist Congress. Shekel-purchasers need not be members of a Zionist party.

3. In 1934–35, Margulies noted that the ten leading United States cities contained two-thirds of the nation's Jewish population, but that the same cities accounted for only one-third of the ZOA's membership and one-fifth of the ZOA's total districts. (See ZOA, *Thirty-eighth Annual Report,* p. 9.)

4. On November 6, 1942, *NP* editorialized (p. 5):

It is unfortunately true that the larger the community the smaller is the proportion of Zionist membership. This fact reaches its most obvious demonstration in New York City where, despite the fact that some two million Jews live in a compact and homogeneous community, the proportion of Zionist membership is far, far below the average for the rest of the country.

5. For a suggestive note on the relatively greater political influence of the South's 150,000 Jews than their more than four million Northern brethren, see Harry L. Golden, "The Jews of the South" in Harold Ribalow (ed.), *Mid-Century* (New York, 1955), pp. 216–17.

appendix VI

JEWISH IMMIGRATION INTO PALESTINE

Sources: Jewish Agency for Palestine (Jerusalem), *Statistical Handbook for Jewish Palestine*, 1947, p. 116; *Government of Israel, Statistical Abstract of Israel* 1954–55, No. 6, p. 32.

YEAR	TOTAL JEWISH MIGRATION	TO PALESTINE		TO USA	TO ARGENTINA	TO CANADA	OTHERS
		TOTAL	% OF TOTAL				
1930	42,878	4,944	11.5	11,526	7,805	4,164	14,439
1931	26,066	4,075	15.6	5,692	3,553	3,421	9,325
1932	20,683	9,553	46.2	2,755	1,801	649	5,925
1933	71,095	30,327	42.7	2,372	1,962	772	35,662
1934	61,384	42,359	69.1	4,134	2,215	943	11,733
1935	78,021	61,854	79.3	4,837	3,169	624	7,537
1936	55,300	29,727	53.8	6,252	4,261	880	14,180
1937	35,143	10,536	30.0	11,352	5,178	619	7,458
1938	54,534	12,868	23.6	19,736	1,050	584	20,296
1939	96,000 c.	27,561	28.7	43,450	4,300	890	19,600
1940	59,000 c.	8,398	14.4	36,945	1,850	1,623	9,416
1941	59,000 c.	5,886	15.4	23,737	2,200	626	6,500
1942		3,733		10,608	1,318	388	
1943		8,507		4,705	524	270	
1944		14,464			384	238	
1945		13,121					
1946		17,761					
1947		21,542					
Jan. 1–May 14, 1948		17,165					
May 15–Dec. 31, 1948		101,828					

Note on American Immigration Into Palestine:

According to the Jewish Agency, American immigration into Palestine between 1919 and 1945 numbered 8,057 or 2.3 percent of total Jewish Palestinian immigration. Of this number, only sixteen persons arrived between 1940–45; 1,063 arrived in 1933, 1,028 in 1934 and 1,602 in 1935. The number of Americans resident in Palestine with temporary visas and other non-immigrant statuses was estimated at less than 5,000. References on this subject are: S. Bernstein, "The American Jew and Palestine," *NP*, March 30, 1934, pp. 11–16; *Report of the Executive of the Zionist Organization submitted to the Nineteenth Zionist Con-*

gress at Lucerne, 1935, p. 242; Hechalutz, *Builders and Fighters* (New York, 1948); Chalutziut and Youth Commission of the Labor Zionist Movement, *Chalutz and Youth* (New York, 1952); and Jewish Agency for Palestine, *Statistical Handbook of Jewish Palestine, 1947,* pp. 97, 100, 105.

appendix VII

"ZIONISM AN AFFIRMATION OF JUDAISM"

(A Reply by 818 Rabbis of America to a Statement Issued by Ninety Members of the Reform Rabbinate Charging That Zionism is Incompatible with the Teachings of Judaism.)

Released to the press: November 20, 1942   Abridged

We, the undersigned Rabbis of all elements in American Jewish religious life, have noted with concern a statement by ninety of our colleagues in which they repudiate Zionism on the ground that it is inconsistent with Jewish religious and moral doctrine. This statement misrepresents Zionism and misinterprets historic Jewish religious teaching. . . .

We call attention in the first place to the fact that the signatories to this statement . . . represent no more than a very small fraction of the American rabbinate. They constitute a minority even of the rabbinate of Reform Judaism with which they are associated. The overwhelming majority of American Rabbis regard Zionism not only as fully consistent with Judaism but as a logical expression and implementation of it.

Our colleagues concede the need for Jewish immigration into Palestine as contributing towards a solution of the vast tragedy of Jewish homelessness. They profess themselves ready to encourage such settlement. They are aware of the important achievements, social and spiritual, of the Palestinian Jewish community and they pledge to it their unstinted support. And yet, subscribing to every practical accomplishment of Zionism, they have embarked upon a public criticism of it. In explanation of their opposition they advance the consideration that Zionism is nationalistic and secularistic. On both scores they maintain it is incompatible with the Jewish religion and its universalistic outlook. They protest against the political emphasis which, they say, is now paramount in the Zionist program and which, according to them, tends to confuse both Jews and Christians as to the place and function of the Jewish group in American society. They appeal to the prophets of ancient Israel for substantiation of their views.

Treasuring the doctrines and moral principles of our faith no less than they, devoted equally to America and its democratic processes and spirit, we nonetheless find every one of their contentions totally without foundation.

Zionism is not a secularist movement. It has its origins and roots in the authoritative religious texts of Judaism. Scripture and rabbinical literature alike are replete with the promise of the restoration of Israel to its ancestral home. Anti-Zionism, not Zionism, is a departure from the Jewish religion. Nothing in the entire pronouncement of our colleagues is more painful than their appeal to the prophets of Israel—to those very prophets whose inspired and recorded words of national rebirth and restoration nurtured and sustained the hope of Israel throughout the ages.

Nor is Zionism a denial of the universalistic teachings of Judaism. Universalism is not a contradiction of nationalism. Nationalism as such, whether it be English, French, American or Jewish, is not in itself evil. . . . The prophets of Israel looked forward to the time not when all national entities would be obliterated, but when all nations would walk in the light of the Lord, live by His law and learn war no more.

Our colleagues find themselves unable to subscribe to the political emphasis "now paramount in the Zionist program." We fail to perceive what it is to which they object. . . . There can be little hope of opening the doors of Palestine for mass Jewish immigration after the war without effective political action. . . .

We have not the least fear that our fellow Americans will be led to misconstrue the attitudes of American Jews to America because of their interest in Zionism. Every fair-minded American knows that American Jews have only one political allegiance—and that is to America. There is nothing in Zionism to impair this loyalty. Zionism has been endorsed in our generation by every President from Woodrow Wilson to Franklin Delano Roosevelt, and has been approved by the Congress of the United States. The noblest spirits in American life . . . have lent their sympathy and encouragement to the movement.

Jews, and all non-Jews who are sympathetically interested in the plight of Jewry, should bear in mind that the defeat of Hitler will not of itself normalize Jewish life in Europe. An Allied peace which will not frankly face the problem of the national homelessness of the Jewish people will leave the age-old tragic status of European Jewry unchanged. . . . Following an Allied victory, the Jews of Europe, we are confident, will be restored to their political rights and to equality of citizenship. But they possessed these rights after the last war and yet the past twenty-five years have witnessed a rapid and appalling deterioration in their position. In any case, even after peace is restored Europe will be so ravaged and war-torn that large masses of Jews will elect migration to Palestine as a solution of their personal problems. Indeed, for most of these there may be no other substantial hope of economic, social and spiritual rehabilitation.

The freedom which, we have faith, will come to all men and nations after this war, must come not only to Jews as individuals wherever they live, permitting them to share freedom on a plane of equality with all other men, but also to the Jewish people, as such, restored in its homeland, where at long last it will be a free people within a world federation of free peoples.

notes *

INTRODUCTION

1. To David Easton American Jews are a "social grouping," following his definition of social groupings as ". . . patterns of activity or relations of individuals to one another that are not formally organized, that require no close interaction among the members, and that are not deliberately directed to the pursuit of specified purposes. They are collections of individuals who are classed together as a result of the fact that they have specified characteristics in common." American Jews would seem to be such a category and thus provide the "analytically prior" basis for the formation of specific Jewish groups, such as the various Zionist organizations. But Easton's hypothesis that such a social grouping, based on a common characteristic (in this case, religion), may be expected to yield "similar kinds of activity-responses" in typical circumstances must be modified substantially by the record that follows. See *The Political System* (New York, 1953), pp. 186–87.

2. This plan is suggested in Phillip Monypenny, "Political Science and the Study of Groups: Notes to Guide a Research Project," *Western Political Quarterly*, VII, No. 2 (June, 1954), 183–201.

3. See Harold D. Lasswell and Abraham Kaplan, *Power and Society* (New Haven, 1950), pp. 78–79.

4. Two sources which have vitally influenced the author's conception and use of these terms are Lasswell and Kaplan, *Power and Society*, Chapters IV–V, and Easton, *The Political System*, particularly pp. 116–24.

5. Acknowledgement is made to Irwin Oder, whose unpublished Ph.D. dissertation, "The United States and the Palestine Mandate, 1920–1948: A Study of Public Opinion and Policy-Making" (Columbia University, 1956), provided helpful background for the Zionist question as it affected American governmental authorities.

6. An excellent book on these subjects is Ben Halpern, *The Idea of the Jewish State* (Cambridge, Mass.: Harvard University Press, 1961), published too late to be consulted in this study.

CHAPTER 1

1. For surveys of the Jewish attachment to Palestine see AJC, Abraham G. Duker (ed.), *Palestine in the New World* (New York, 1943), pp. 7–11; Ira Eisenstein, *Palestine in the Life of the Jew* (New York, 1942); Milton Steinberg, *The Making of the Modern Jew* (Indianapolis, 1933), Chapter XVI; *The Bible*, particularly Psalm 137 and the Book of Isaiah.

* See the list of abbreviations on p. xiii. In citations from the Central Zionist Archives (*CZA*), the character "Ƶ" in the file reference appears as "Z."

2. See Berl Locker, *Covenant Everlasting* (New York, 1947); Mildred B. Efros, *The Story of Zionism* (New York, 1952); Nahum Sokolow, *History of Zionism, 1600–1918* (London, 1919); Richard J. H. Gottheil, *Zionism* (Philadelphia, 1914); Arthur Hertzberg (ed.), *The Zionist Idea: A Historical Analysis and Reader* (New York, 1959).

3. For discussion of the social milieu in which Zionism arose, see Salo W. Baron, "The Modern Age," in Leo W. Schwarz (ed.), *Great Ages and Ideas of the Jewish People* (New York, 1956) and Solomon Grayzel, "A Chronicle of Our Generation," in Harry Schneiderman (ed.), *Two Generations in Perspective* (New York, 1957), pp. 3–109.

4. *The Zionist Position, a Statement Submitted to the Delegates to the American Jewish Conference, August 29, 1943*, p. 11. Italics in the original. Concerning the many specific party interpretations of Zionism, the following references may prove helpful to the general reader: AJC, *Palestine in the New World* (New York, 1943), pp. 28–35, 61–70; Basil J. Vlavianos and Feliks Gross (eds.), *Struggle for Tomorrow* (New York, 1954), Part I; Jewish Reconstructionist Foundation, *Zionism Explained* (New York, 1946).

5. Quoted in a widely-circulated ZOA recruiting leaflet and in *REP-HEAR*, p. 225, and *Brandeis on Zionism* (Washington, 1942), pp. 24–25.

6. *Zionism: A Statement*, 3–4; cited in Hertzberg, *The Zionist Idea*, pp. 504–13. In this vein, note also Rabbi Stephen S. Wise's remark that Zionism calls "not so much for definition as for commitment" ("After Twenty-Five Years," in Joseph Shubow [ed.], *Brandeis Avukah Annual of 1932* [New York, 1932], p. 576).

7. A description of these events may be found in the previously cited histories of Zionism as well as in Israel Cohen, *A Short History of Zionism* (New York, 1946), and Rufus Learsi (pseud.), *Fulfillment: The Epic Story of Zionism* (Cleveland, 1951).

8. The meaning of this somewhat cryptic statement has been much debated. For the interpretations of Balfour, David Lloyd George, Winston Churchill and Woodrow Wilson, see AJC, *Palestine in the New World*, pp. 54–55.

9. David de Sola Pool, "Early Relations Between Palestine and American Jewry," in Shubow, *Brandeis Avukah Annual . . .* , pp. 536–48; Milton Plesur, "The Relations Between the United States and Palestine," *Judaism*, III, No. 4 (Fall, 1954), 469–79; M. Eskolsky, "America and Zion, from President Adams to Roosevelt, 150 Years of United States Support," *Palestine and Middle East*, XVI (March, 1944), 44–46; Isidore S. Meyer (ed.), *Early History of Zionism in America* (New York, 1958); ZOA, *Program and Education Bulletin, Tercentenary Issue*, pp. 9 ff.; Abraham Goldberg, "American Zionism up to the Brandeis Era," in Shubow, *Brandeis Avukah Annual . . .* , pp. 549–68; Stephen S. Wise, "The Beginnings of American Zionism," *JF*, XIV, No. 8 (August, 1947), 6–8; and *Theodor Herzl*, special 1929 edition of *NP*.

10. Cited by Judge Louis E. Levinthal in *Credo of an American Zionist* (Washington, 1943), p. 18.

11. Louis Lipsky, *A Gallery of Zionist Profiles* (New York, 1956), p. 156. Also see correspondence between Herzl and Rabbi Stephen Wise in *CZA*, H VIII, 928.

12. Louis Lipsky, *Thirty Years of American Zionism* (New York, 1927), I, 246

13. *AJYB,* XV (1913), 366. A *shekel* is, essentially, a poll tax, the proceeds of which support the World Zionist Organization. Its price, usually fifty cents, enables the purchaser to vote for delegates to World Zionist Congresses. Concerning this period, see also Herbert Parzen, "The Federation of American Zionists" in Meyer, *Early History of Zionism in America;* Julius Haber, *The Odyssey of an American Zionist* (New York, 1956); and Naomi W. Cohen, "*The Maccabaean's* Message: A Study in American Zionism Until World War I," *JSS,* XVIII, No. 3 (July, 1956), 163–78.

14. Dues at this time were only $1.00 or $2.00; and "members," according to the ZOA, were "secured at open-air meetings, in crowds. Most of the names and addresses were either illegible or inaccurate. After paying their dues, they were not reached by any official periodical or any literature They were less members and more registrants." (*NP,* February 4, 1938, p. 4.) See also *AJYB,* XXI (1919), 327; Provisional Executive Committee for General Zionist Affairs' compilation of editorials, endorsements by leading Jews and Christians, *Zionism Conquers Public Opinion* (New York, 1917); Reuben Fink (ed.), *The American War Congress and Zionism* (New York, 1919); Selig Adler, "The Palestine Question in the Wilson Era," *JSS,* X, No. 4 (October, 1948), 303–34; *Brandeis on Zionism* (Washington, 1942); Horace M. Kallen, *Zionism and World Politics* (New York, 1921); Stephen S. Wise, *Challenging Years* (London, 1951), pp. 88–90 and 110 ff.; Chaim Weizmann's autobiography, *Trial and Error* (New York, 1949), pp. 241 ff.; Morton J. Tenzer, "American Zionism and the Palestine Question in the Wilson Era" (incomplete, unpublished Ph.D. dissertation, Yale University).

15. See Irwin Oder, "American Zionism and the Congressional Resolution of 1922 on Palestine," *PAJHS,* XLV, No. 1 (September, 1955), 35–47; and ZOA, *Twentieth Anniversary of the Joint Palestine Resolution of the Congress of the United States (1922–1942)* (Washington, 1942).

16. This group, including such leading Zionists as Robert Szold, Jacob de Haas, Felix Frankfurter, Judge Mack, Justice Brandeis, and Samuel Rosensohn, belabored the Lipsky-led administration for alleged "gross mismanagement," "unsound and unauthorized and furtive financial operations," "undemocratic machine politics," "misdeeds and negligence." See, for example, the Committee for ZOA Reorganization's *The Zionist Awakening* (New York, 1928). Of the numerous accounts of the Brandeis-Weizmann controversy, none are fully adequate, but for brief summaries of the issues involved see Abraham Goldberg, "Zionism in America," in *NP's Theodor Herzl* edition of 1929, especially pp. 221–22; Maurice Samuel, *Level Sunlight* (New York, 1953), Chapter II; Weizmann, *Trial and Error,* Chapter XXIV; Haber, *The Odyssey of an American Zionist,* pp. 176 ff.; *Felix Frankfurter Reminisces* (New York, 1960), p. 178 ff.

17. William Z. Spiegelman's "From Cleveland to Cleveland, American Zionism from 1921 to 1930 in Review," *NP,* June 27, 1930, pp. 402–406 is a valuable source of documentation for the periods. He cites the figure of 18,031 ZOA members in 1929. Sociologist Harry S. Linfield found that the entire Zionist movement in 1927 had a considerably larger popular base— 107,182, of whom 93,677 were adults (*The Communal Organization of the Jews in the United States, 1927* [New York, 1930], p. 113).

18. *A Fratricidal War* (New York, 1928), p. 9. Cf. also Chaim Arlosoroff's incisive pamphlet, *Surveying American Zionism* (New York, 1929).
19. Cited in Frank E. Manuel, *The Realities of American-Palestine Relations* (Washington, 1949), p. 299. Note also Manuel's discussion of the state of the Zionist movement in the early thirities on pp. 299–302; *NP* editorial, April 9, 1926, p. 319; Leo Schwarz, "Zionism in America During the Post-War Era," in Jessie Sampter (ed.), *Modern Palestine* (New York, 1933).
20. "Herzl and Jewish Messianism, Nationalism as a Means to a Greater Goal," in *NP's Theodor Herzl* edition of 1929, pp. 254–56.

CHAPTER 2

1. Leonard W. Doob, *Public Opinion and Propaganda* (New York, 1948), p. 87. Cf. also Hadley Cantril and others, *Gauging Public Opinion* (Princeton, N.J., 1944), pp. 226–27.
2. David Truman, *The Governmental Process* (New York, 1953), pp. 50–55.
3. Stuart A. Queen and others, *The American Social System* (Boston, 1956), p. 148.
4. See *NP*, issue of September 6, 1929 and November 6, 1931, p. 42.
5. Typical of the optimistic expressions in this period are those in *NP*, September 6, 1929, pp. 139, 148, 164; June 20, 1930, pp. 386–87; October 14, 1932, p. 1; December 9, 1932, p. 1; February 14, 1934, p. 4. On the return of the Brandeis-Mack faction and its salutory effects on Zionist cohesion, see issues of May 30, 1930, pp. 338–39; June 13, p. 370; June 27, pp. 399–401; July 25, pp. 13–19, 21–26; August 15, pp. 43–44. Also see ZOA, *Thirty-sixth Annual Report*, in *NP*, July 1, 1933, p. 3 and Morris Rothenberg's *American Interest in Palestine* (New York, [1934]).
6. *NP*, September 9, 1932, pp. 3, 7 and ZOA President Rothenberg's message, p. 1. Cf. also ZOA, *Thirty-fifth* and *Thirty-sixth Annual Reports*, p. 3.
7. *Under Strange Skies* (New York, 1953), p. 315.
8. Morris Rothenberg, "A Grave Peril Threatens," *NP*, January 6, 1931, p. 8. Note similar appeals from non-Zionists Adler and Warburg in the same issue, pp. 6–7, 10, and 15.
9. See Rothenberg's complaint that the very "success" of Zionism militated against ZOA organizational plans, *NP*, July 8, 1932, p. 2; correspondence of World Zionist Organization President Nahum Sokolow on his fifth American visit (1932); and correspondence of Henrietta Szold in *CZA* S49/112.
10. *NP*, June 16, 1933, p. 1.
11. *Agenda for American Jews* (New York, 1950), pp. 57 ff. Also note *NP*, May 12, 1933, p. 1; November 14, 1933, entire issue; December 11, 1933, p. 4; and January 31, 1934, pp. 1–2. See Appendix VI for Palestinian immigration figures. In the period 1933–42, 160,000 Jews entered the United States (thus adding 0.1 percent to the 3.6 percent of the American population which was Jewish), while 214,000 entered Palestine, raising the proportion of that country's Jewish population from 17 to 30 percent. See Cyrus Adler and Aaron M. Margalith, *With Firmness in the Right* (New York, 1946), pp. 441–43, and Mark Wischnitzer, *To Dwell in Safety* (Philadelphia, 1948), p. 247.

12. *Under Strange Skies,* p. 308. The impression is not intended that American Jewry became united in the process of combatting Hitlerism. For interesting accounts of the varied Jewish interpretations of the meaning of Hitlerism for Jewish life, see Henry Cohen, "Crisis and Reaction," *American Jewish Archives,* V (June, 1953), 71–113; Rufus Learsi (pseud.), *The Jews in America* (Cleveland, 1954), pp. 278–80; and Stephen S. Wise, *Challenging Years* (London, 1951), pp. 155 ff.

13. Ginzberg, *Agenda for American Jews,* pp. 57–58. See also David Brody, "American Jewry, The Refugees and Immigration Restriction (1932–1942)," *PAJHS,* XLV (June, 1956), 219–47, for an excellent study of the almost universal Jewish failure to attack American immigration policy despite the critical needs of European Jewry. Thomas A. Bailey cites an unnamed public opinion poll of 1938 to the effect that although 70 percent of American Jews favored further admission of persecuted Jews, 25 percent opposed such measures. See *The Man on the Street: The Impact of American Public Opinion on Foreign Policy* (New York, 1948), p. 25. Note also the American Institute of Public Opinion poll of November 22, 1938: Of 92 percent of the general American sample who had an opinion on the question, "Should we allow a larger number of Jewish exiles from Germany to come to the United States to live?" 77 percent opposed and 23 percent favored such immigration (Hadley Cantril [ed.], *Public Opinion, 1935–1946* [Princeton, N.J., 1951], p. 385).

14. January 17, 1936, p. 1. The paid membership of the ZOA increased from 8,484 in 1932 to 18,676 in 1936; see Appendixes III and IV.

15. "Zionism and the American Jew," *American Scholar,* II (July, 1933), 289–92. Cf. Robert Gordis' observation in *Judaism for the Modern Age* (New York, 1955), p. 32: ". . . in an age when religious loyalties were weak, especially among Jews, [Zionism] supplied a dynamic factor making for Jewish cohesiveness and survival. . . ."; Sol Liptzin, *Generation of Decision: Jewish Rejuvenation in America* (New York, 1958), pp. 292–93: "In working for Israel projects, Jews were being knit together by common anxieties, common fears, common exaltation. They were finding new strength to resist the centrifugal force of the non-Jewish environment . . ."; Eric Hoffer, *The True Believer* (New York, 1958), p. 21: Zionism offered "a new life—a rebirth—or, failing this, a chance to acquire new elements of pride, confidence, hope, a sense of purpose and worth by an identification with a holy cause."

16. Marcus, *American Scholar,* II, 291. Cf. also A. H. Silver's address at a Madison Square Garden rally on March 21, 1944, in *Vision and Victory* (New York, 1949), 42–43; and Rabbi Max Raisin's ecstatic report on the Palestine of 1935 in *The Flight from the Diaspora* (New York, 1935).

17. *NP,* February 7, 1936, p. 10, from an address at the 1936 National Conference for Palestine. Note *NP*'s refutation of the "refugee conception" of Palestine, February 14, 1936, p. 4 and Weizmann's and Wise's similar remarks in the same issue, p. 1, and February 21, 1936, p. 1.

18. *NP,* February 21, 1936, p. 9.

19. The literature on American anti-Semitism of this period is very prolific. Donald S. Strong's *Organized Anti-Semitism in America* (Washington,

1941), for example, studies 121 anti-Semitic groups which operated between 1933 and 1940. Cf. also, Learsi, *Jews in America*, pp. 286–95, 345–46; Cantril, *Public Opinion . . .* , pp. 381 ff.; the sections on "Anti-Jewish Movements" in *AJYB*, XLI–XLIII (1939–1941); and Howard M. Sachar, *The Course of Modern Jewish History* (Cleveland, 1958), pp. 331 ff.

20. See Lawrence H. Fuchs, *The Political Behavior of American Jews* (Glencoe, Ill., 1956), pp. 171 ff.

21. At the first Zionist Congress in 1897, Herzl observed:

> We have been frequently and bitterly attacked because of our feeling of belonging together, but this feeling was on the way to complete disintegration when we were attacked by anti-semitism. It is this attack which has strengthened that feeling once more. We had, as it were, to "go home." Zionism means coming home to Judaism, even before going back to the Jewish land (Federation of American Zionists, *The Congress Addresses of Theodor Herzl* [New York, 1917], p. 5).

A sociological treatment of Lloyd Warner's, Leo Srole's and Charles Marden's commentaries on a very strong Jewish "drive for group survival" which operated as a powerful predisposition in the Jewish community may be found in Marshall Sklare's *Conservative Judaism: An American Religious Movement* (Glencoe, Ill., 1955), pp. 32–34. According to these findings, it seems warranted to assume Zionist "survivalism" met, at least partially, American Jewry's felt need for an activity designed to ensure the perpetuation of the Jewish grouping.

22. Marcus, *American Scholar*, II (July, 1933), 287–88. Note also Johan J. Smertenko's view, "Have Jews a Divided Loyalty?" in Harold U. Ribalow (ed.), *Mid-Century: An Anthology of Jewish Life and Culture in Our Times* (New York, 1955), pp. 519–32; and Benno Weiser's characterization of Zionism as "a sentiment rather than a doctrine," as a *Weltanschauung* or "expression of Jewish pride—a flight into Jewishness, the opposite of many a Jew's flight away from it"; see "Ben Gurion's Dispute with American Zionists," in Ribalow, pp. 537–38.

23. "Anti-Semitism," in Oscar Janowsky (ed.), *The American Jew: A Composite Portrait* (New York, 1942), pp. 202–203.

24. *NP*, April 24, 1936, pp. 1–2; September 25, 1936, p. 4; July 12, 1937, p. 10; December 3 and 17, 1937, p. 1; *Memorandum Submitted to the Palestine Royal Commission on American Interest in the Administration of the Palestine Mandate* by the heads of ZOA, Hadassah, Keren Kayemeth, Keren Hayesod, Palestine Economic Corporation, American Economic Committee for Palestine, and Palestine Endowment Funds, Inc. (New York, 1937).

25. *AJYB*, XLI (1939), 200–205. Cf. also *NP*, issues of October 14, 24, November 4, December 9, 1938 and M. Klavansky-Rabinowitz, "The Struggle for Immigration," *PYB*, III (1947–48), 88–99, for numerous indications of extensive Jewish interest in the Palestine crisis.

26. *Level Sunlight* (New York, 1953), p. 17.

27. In Isacque Graeber and Steuart H. Britt (eds.), *Jews in a Gentile World* (New York, 1942), p. 224. Note also similar observations by Irving Howe, "Sprucetown Jewry Adjusts Itself," in Elliot E. Cohen (ed.), *Commentary on the American Scene* (New York, 1953), pp. 333–35.

28. Fuchs, *Political Behavior* . . . , pp. 100 ff.
29. See Frank E. Manuel, *The Realities of American-Palestine Relations* (Washington, 1949), p. 309; Nahum Goldmann, "Negative and Positive Factors; An Evaluation of the Present Political Status of Zionism; Forces and Influences Working For and Against the Cause," *NP*, October 8, 1943, pp. 46–49; and Emanuel Neumann, "Zionist Policy in the Post-War Period," in *PYB*, III (1947–48), pp. 27–38.
30. Note *REC's* analysis of the Zionist temper, October 13, 1939, pp. 5–7 and the prominent Palestinian leader Eliezer Kaplan's report in *Weekly Press Survey* (London) No. 50, November 22, 1940, 9–10, and his gloomy letter of July 8, 1940 to members of the Jerusalem Jewish Agency Executive, in *CZA*, Z4/10407.
31. A. L. Easterman, "British Jewry Looks West," *NP*, May 16, 1941, pp. 9–10. Cf. also Alfred Werner, "Herzl Looked to America," *NP*, December 20, 1940, p. 9; Benjamin Shwadran, "To Washington," *NP*, May 9, 1941, p. 13; and Silver, *Vision and Victory*, p. 20.
32. *Call to American Zionists* (New York, February 10, 1942), pp. 1–2.
33. Samuel M. Blumenfield, "Pearl Harbor and American Jewry," *NP*, December 4, 1942, pp. 6–10; Silver, *Vision and Victory*, pp. 107–108, 209–20.
34. Manuel, *Realities of American-Palestine Relations*, p. 309; Salo W. Baron, *The Effect of the War on Jewish Community Life* (New York, 1942), p. 11; *Zionist Review*, issue of October, 1942; *IJPS*, September 29, 1942, p. 2.
35. An example of such early reports is Jacob Lestchinsky's "Destruction of European Jewry," *CW*, September 11, 1942, pp. 6–7. Cf. also his *Crisis, Catastrophe and Survival: A Jewish Balance Sheet, 1914–1948* (New York, 1948).
36. *NP*, December 4, 1942, p. 3.
37. See Libby Benedict, "Reaction to Events Overseas," *AJYB*, XLV (1943), 191–98; *CW*, January 8, 1943, pp. 2, 13; March 5, 1943, p. 16; *JTA*, January 28 and February 23, 1943, pp. 2–3; Manuel, *Realities of American-Palestine Relations*, p. 318.
38. *NP*, November 6, 1942, p. 15.
39. Full text in *CW*, April 30, 1943, pp. 11–16.
40. "The Bermuda Conference," *JS*, VIII (June, 1943), 17–18. See also *CW*, May 14, 1943, pp. 11–13; *NP*, May 7, 1943, p. 3; Ben Hecht's "Ballad of the Doomed Jews of Europe," *Answer*, April, 1943, p. 7; The Committee for a Jewish Army of Stateless and Palestinian Jews, *From Evian to Bermuda* (New York, 1943); "Digest to Editorial Opinion," *CJR*, I, No. 1 (September, 1938), 47–56; and Adler and Margalith, *With Firmness in the Right*, pp. 439 ff.
41. Address of March 21, 1945, before the American Zionist Policy Committee (*Vision and Victory*, p. 75).
42. Speech at the World Zionist Congress in Basle, December 10, 1946, quoted in *Vision and Victory*, pp. 108–109. Cf. Judge Louis Levinthal's similar appeal in *NP*, May 7, 1943, pp. 14–15. In concrete terms, American activities in the field of saving refugees were very largely limited to President Roosevelt's authorization, on the eve of the 1944 presidential elections, of a

detention camp at Oswego, New York, for 1,000 refugees. By 1945, according to a National Opinion Research Center poll, 46 percent of the American population favored admission of Jewish refugees (23 percent in 1938), while 46 percent opposed (77 percent in 1938). At the same time, the Jews were considered "less desirable" than Mexicans (48 percent favored), Chinese (56 percent), and Russians (57 percent); poll in *Free World,* January, 1945, p. 23.

43. See Philip S. Bernstein, "Jewish Displaced Persons," *PYB,* III (1947–48), 67–78 and Leo W. Schwarz, *The Redeemers* (New York, 1953).

44. Address of A. H. Silver at American Jewish Conference of 1943, in *Vision and Victory,* p. 18. See similar themes employed on pp. 13–14, 75.

45. See Appendixes I and V for these comparisons.

46. In Cantril, *Public Opinion . . . ,* pp. 385–86; Eric Stern, "Analysis of the Poll," *NP,* April 12, 1946, pp. 165–66; Elmo Roper, *A Survey of American Jewish Opinion on a Jewish State in Palestine,* prepared for the M. Hausman and Son's Foundation, Inc. (New York, October, 1945).

47. Stern, *NP,* April 12, 1946 and *AJYB,* XLVIII (1946), 243–44.

48. *Adventure in Freedom* (New York, 1954), p. 219. See, too, Marshall Sklare and Benjamin Ringer, "A Study of Jewish Attitudes Toward the State of Israel," in Sklare (ed.), *The Jews: Social Patterns of an American Group* (Glencoe, Ill., 1958), pp. 437–50. This study of Baltimore Jewish opinion in May, 1948, found that 90 percent of the respondents favored the establishment of Israel, that 57 percent had favored a Jewish state even before the advent of Hitler, and that 50 percent belonged to Zionist or pro-Zionist organizations.

49. Cantril, *Public Opinion . . . ,* p. 386.

50. See note 31 above.

51. *Jewish Agency Digest of Press and Events* (Jerusalem), February 20, 1946, pp. 10–13.

52. C. Wendell King, *Social Movements in the United States* (New York, 1956), p. 17 (tense changed from present to past). See also King's excellent analysis (pp. 63–64) of the role of crisis in the growth of social movements.

53. *You Never Leave Brooklyn* (New York, 1953), Chapter VII, especially pp. 113–14. Also note his exchange of correspondence with the American Council for Judaism regarding his work in obtaining a pro-Zionist plank in the Democratic campaign platform of 1944; in *Information Bulletin of the American Council for Judaism,* August 1, 1944, p. 2 and October 1, 1944, pp. 2–3.

54. *Nor by Power* (New York, 1953), pp. 265–66, 271.

55. "Problems of Representation in the Government of Private Groups," *The Journal of Politics,* XI, No. 3 (August, 1949), 566–77.

CHAPTER 3

1. The most ambitious efforts in this direction, however, are Marshall Sklare (ed.), *The Jews: Social Patterns of an American Group* (Glencoe, Ill., 1958), and C. Bezalel Sherman, *The Jew Within American Society* (Detroit, 1961). The latter appeared too late to lend its valuable assistance to the preparation of this chapter.

2. There are numerous indications that American Jews regard an unqualified religious definition as inadequate, but since the character of American group life seems to favor the submergence of national distinctions and the promotion of religious affiliation, they accept the familiar stereotype of the Catholic-Protestant-Jewish groupings. On this point see Robert Gordis, *Judaism for the Modern Age* (New York, 1955), pp. 53–55; and Marshall Sklare, *Conservative Judaism: An American Religious Movement* (Glencoe, Ill., 1955), pp. 35–40. Further evidence, on pragmatic grounds, for the inadequacy of a solely religious definition in the period under study may be adduced from the National Opinion Research Center poll (1945) which illustrates the striking differences between Protestant-Catholic and, on the other hand, Jewish "church" attendance:

	Catholic	Protestant	Jewish
Seldom or never attend religious services	6%	19%	32%
Attend once a week or more	69%	36%	9%
Attend once a month or more	81%	62%	24%

(Cited in Sklare, *Conservative Judaism,* pp. 38–39.) A similar inquiry by Ernest Havemann and Patricia Salter West presents results even more definitive in this respect. (*They Went to College* [New York, 1952], pp. 106–107.) Another N.O.R.C. poll (December, 1944) reveals that 49 percent of non-Jewish Americans thought of Jews as a nationality group, while 32 percent conceived of them as a religion, 6 percent "both religion and nationality," 4 percent "neither," 9 percent "don't know." See Hadley Cantril (ed.), *Public Opinion, 1935–1946* (Princeton, 1951), p. 384. Readers are cautioned against a too liberal application of these data to the contemporary American Jewish community. There have been marked changes in the past decades, for example, the "Return to Religion," which were not yet dominant in Jewry during the period covered by this study. On this point, see Will Herberg, *Protestant-Catholic-Jew: An Essay in American Religious Sociology* (Garden City, N.Y., 1956) and Nathan Glazer, *American Judaism* (Chicago, 1957).

3. Abraham G. Duker, *Workshop in Jewish Community Affairs* (New York, 1953), Course 1: "The American Jewish Community: Its History and Development," p. 17. This conception of the Jews is similar to Robin W. Williams'—an "ethno-religious group . . . possessing continuity through biological descent whose members share a distinctive social and cultural tradition," in *The Reduction of Intergroup Tensions* (New York, 1947), p. 42. See also *Forum for the Problems of Zionism, Jewry and the State of Israel,* IV (Jerusalem, 1959), especially pp. 281–303.

4. Gordis is among the many observers who argue that the Hebrew word *am,* "people," is the best single term for the Jewish group as a whole since it connotes strong ties, "religio-cultural in essence," without the political overtones associated with "nationhood," "nation," or "nationality" (*Judaism for the Modern Age,* p. 54).

5. Harry Essrig, "Jewish Americans," in Francis J. Brown and Joseph S. Rouček (eds.), *One America* (New York, 1952), p. 269. See also Liebman Hersch, "Jewish Migrations During the Last Hundred Years," *JP-PP,* I (1946), 407–30.

6. Composite table drawn from Ben M. Edidin, *Jewish Community Life in America* (New York, 1947), p. 17; H. S. Linfield in *AJYB*, XXXII (1930), 219 and XLVI (1944), 419.

7. U.S. Bureau of the Census, *Census of Religious Bodies, 1936: Jewish Congregations* (Washington, 1940).

8. See H. S. Linfield, "The Jewish Population of the United States," *AJYB*, XLVI, 491–98.

9. *Ibid.*, 492, and Essrig, in Brown and Rouček, *One America*, pp. 269–73.

10. Cf. data in Jessie Bernard, *American Community Behavior* (New York, 1949), p. 198; Havemann and West, *They Went to College*, pp. 187–89; Nathan Glazer, "What Sociology Knows About American Jews," *Commentary*, IX (March, 1950), 275–84; Wesley and Beverly Allinsmith, "Religious Affiliation and Politico-Economic Attitude: A Study of Eight Major United States Religious Groups," in Daniel Katz and others, *Public Opinion and Propaganda* (New York, 1954), pp. 151–58; Nathan Reich, "Economic Trends," in Oscar Janowsky (ed.), *The American Jew: A Composite Portrait* (New York, 1942), Chapter VII.

11. Edidin, *Jewish Community Life in America*, pp. 125–26. Bernard cites this Jewish occupational breakdown based on four polls of the American Institute of Public Opinion (1945–1946): business and professional, 36 percent (general average 19 percent); white collar, 37 (20); urban manual workers, 27 (44); farmers 0.6 (17), *American Community Behavior*, p. 198. See also, Sophia M. Robison and Joshua Starr (eds.), *Jewish Population Studies* (New York, 1943); Nathan Glazer, "Social Characteristics of American Jews, 1654–1954," *AJYB*, LVI (1955), 27–28; Bernard D. Weinryb, "Jewish Population Problems," *CW*, March, 1943, pp. 8–10; Nathan Goldberg, "Occupational Patterns of American Jews," *Jewish Review*, III, No. 4 (January, 1946), 262–90; Herberg, *Protestant-Catholic-Jew*, pp. 241–42; and a series of studies in *JP-PP*, I (1946): Jacob Lestchinsky, "The Economic Development of the Jews in the United States," pp. 391–406; II (1948): Nathan Goldberg, "The Jewish Population in the United States," pp. 25–34; IV (1955): Lestchinsky, "Economic and Social Development of American Jewry," pp. 56–96.

12. Bernard, *American Community Behavior*, p. 198. Essrig claims that of 250 periodicals published in English by all ethnic groups, 140 were published by and for Jews (in Brown and Rouček, *One America*, p. 274).

13. This three-wave theory of immigration oversimplifies the facts since, for example, East European Jews were already prominent in America during the colonial period as witness the Polish-born financier of the American Revolution era, Haym Solomon. See especially Jacob R. Marcus, "The Periodization of American Jewish History," *PAJHS*, XLVII, No. 3 (March, 1958), 125–33.

14. This schematic classification, like all generalizations, is admittedly imperfect. Nevertheless, it is a common feature of Jewish sociological writing; Cf. Janowsky, *The American Jew*, Chapter I; Henry Cohen, "Crisis and Reaction," *American Jewish Archives*, V (June, 1953), pp. 71–113; Rufus Learsi (pseud.) *The Jews in America* (Cleveland, 1954), pp. 230–33.

15. Harold D. Lasswell and Abraham Kaplan, *Power and Society* (New Haven,

1950), p. 25. See also Solomon Grayzel, "A Chronicle of Our Generation," in Harry Schneiderman (ed.), *Two Generations in Perspective* (New York, 1957), pp. 12 ff. For a striking example of this, see Mrs. Henry Monsky and Maurice Bisgyer, *Henry Monsky: The Man and His Work* (New York, 1947), pp. 11–12.

16. According to H. S. Linfield, 13,028,234 persons were admitted into the U.S. between 1908 and 1942, of whom 1,248,142 (9.58 percent) were Jews. During the same period, 4,499,597 persons emigrated (34.54 percent of total admissions), including 57,119 Jews (4.58 percent of Jewish admissions). The American Jewish population had a net increase of 1,191,023 persons (13.97 percent of the total American net immigration). Jewish arrivals from 1881–1942 were also estimated at 2,494,537; *AJYB*, XLV (1943), 591. Cf. also Abraham Menes, "The East Side: Matrix of the Jewish Labor Movement," in Theodore Friedman and Robert Gordis, *Jewish Life in America* (New York, 1955), p. 134.

17. Jacob Lestchinsky, "Jews in 1945," *PYB*, I (1945), 28.

18. Abraham G. Duker, *The Impact of Zionism on American Jewry* (New York, 1958); *The Impact of Israel on the American Jewish Community*, Proceedings of a Conference Convened by the Theodor Herzl Institute and the Conference on Jewish Social Studies, December 22–23, 1956 (New York, 1959); and Howard M. Sachar, *The Course of Modern Jewish History* (Cleveland, 1958), pp. 534 ff.

19. Sociologists Arnold and Caroline Rose, for example, believed that American Jewry was rapidly disappearing as a distinct religious and cultural group during the late twenties (*America Divided* [New York, 1949], p. 199) An extended treatment of the influence of Americanization on Jewish group cohesion is Abe L. Weinberger's unpublished Ph.D. dissertation, "Judaism in America: The Influence of America as a New World Frontier upon Judaism of Tradition" (University of Texas, 1953). Cf. also Abba Hillel Silver, *The World Crisis and Jewish Survival* (New York, 1941), p. 56; Jacob B. Agus, *Guideposts in Modern Judaism* (New York, 1954); Max Gottschalk and Abraham G. Duker, *Jews in the Post-War World* (New York, 1945); Ludwig Lewisohn, *The American Jew* (New York, 1950), Chapter V.

20. Duker, *Workshop in Jewish Community Affairs*, Course 1, p. 19.

21. Edidin, *Jewish Community Life . . .* , p. 84.

22. Solomon Sutker, "The Role of Social Clubs in the Atlanta Jewish Community," in Sklare, *The Jews*, p. 264; and Herberg, *Protestant-Catholic-Jew*, pp. 204 ff. For the view that Jews have surpassed their non-Jewish neighbors in "joining" organizations, see William Attwood, "The Position of the Jews in America Today," *Look*, November 29, 1955, p. 31.

23. "Impact of Israel on American Jewish Community Organization and Fund Raising," *JSS*, XXI, No. 1 (January, 1959), 46.

24. Agus, *Guideposts . . .* , p. 11.

25. Concerning the multiplicity of Jewish organizations, see Eli Ginzberg, *Agenda for American Jews* (New York, 1950), pp. 13–14; Bernard G. Richards, "Organizing American Jewry," *Jewish Affairs*, II (May 1, 1947), pp. 1–27; Herberg, *Protestant-Catholic-Jew*, pp. 212 ff.; Isaiah M. Minkoff,

"Development of Jewish Communal Organization in America, 1900–1956," in Schneiderman, *Two Generations* . . . , pp. 110–37; and the following essays in *JP-PP*, II (1948): Charles B. Sherman, "Jewish Communal Organization in the United States," pp. 217–30; Ben-Adir, "Modern Currents in Jewish Social and National Life," pp. 285–329; IV (1955): H. L. Lurie, "Jewish Communal Life in the United States," pp. 187–242; Philip Friedman, "Political and Social Movements and Organizations," pp. 142–86.

CHAPTER 4

1. Truman, *The Governmental Process* (New York, 1951), pp. 251–52.
2. Louis Lipsky, *Thirty Years of American Zionism* (New York, 1927), I, 248. Cf. also the ZOA's official statement in *NP*, July 25, 1930, p. 3; and the list of sympathetically-disposed organizations, particularly fraternal orders, *landsmanschaften* federations, Conservative and Orthodox religious associations which were invited to the 1930 ZOA convention; *NP*, June 13, 1930, p. 373.
3. In this sense, Zionist groups are similar to such an organization as the Chamber of Commerce which attempts to speak for all business interests and, therefore, assiduously avoids taking sides in conflicts between "big" and "little" business interests. See Truman, *The Governmental Process*, p. 183.
4. For summaries of the belief and practices of these groups cf. Frank S. Mead (ed.), *Handbook of Denominations in the United States* (New York and Nashville, 1951), pp. 102–107; Jacob B. Agus, *Guideposts in Modern Judaism* (New York, 1954), Chapters III–IV; Beryl D. Cohon, *Judaism in Theory and Practice* (New York, 1948), Chapter IV–VI; Joseph Zeitlin, *Disciples of the Wise* (New York, 1945), Chapter I; Theodore Friedman and Robert Gordis (eds.), *Jewish Life in America* (New York, 1955), Part I; *UJE*, VI, 237–46; Jacob Agus, "Economic and Social Development of American Jewry," in *JP-PP*, IV (1955), 97–141.
5. *AJYB*, XLVI (1944), 492.
6. Charles B. Sherman, "Jewish Communal Organization in the United States," *JP-PP*, II (1948), 220.
7. Emanuel Rackman, a leading Orthodox rabbi and political scientist at Yeshiva University, describing the multiplicity of Orthodox rabbinical seminaries (at least a dozen, without any joint action or federated union), declared that Orthodoxy's greatest weakness is "its inability to consolidate, or even coordinate, its educational institutions and their alumni." See "American Orthodoxy: Retrospect and Prospect," in Friedman and Gordis, *Jewish Life* . . . , p. 27.
8. Abraham G. Duker, "The Impact of Zionism on American Jewry," in Friedman and Gordis, *Jewish Life* . . . , p. 314. Cf. Hyman B. Grinstein, "Orthodox Judaism and Early Zionism in America," in Isidore S. Meyer (ed.), *Early History of Zionism in America* (New York, 1958), pp. 219–227.
9. See Louis Lipsky, "The Field of Action," in *Thirty Years of American Zionism*, I (New York, 1927).

10. *Ibid.,* I, 192; see also p. 9.

11. Duker, in Friedman and Gordis, *Jewish Life* . . . , p. 314.

12. See Herschel Levine, "Rabbi Kook: Father of Religious Zionism," *Jewish Horizon*, X, No. 10 (October, 1947), 11–13; Jacob B. Agus, "Orthodox Zionism, The Late Rabbi Kuk's Profound Synthesis which Blended Traditional Judaism with Nationalism and National Rebirth," *NP*, June 15, 1945, pp. 225–27; Herbert Weiner, "Rav Kuk's Path to Peace Within Israel," *Commentary*, XVII (March, 1954), 251–63. According to Agus, Rabbi Kuk saw Zionism as

> . . . a noble impulse, akin to religion, implanted by God for the sake of Messianic perfection. Jewish nationalism he regarded as a supremely holy movement, even if its exponents proclaimed from the housetops its total independence of religion. Every one who lends a hand to the upbuilding of the Jewish people in its homeland is working for the revival of the 'sh'chinah' [Divine Presence], for the national genius of Israel is peculiarly suitable for the cultivation of true religion. And the physical health of Israel is a prerequisite for its spiritual growth.

See Agus, *Guideposts* . . . , p. 35, and *Banner of Jerusalem: Life, Times and Thought of Abraham Isaac Kuk* (New York, 1946).

13. The National Council of Young Israel, with approximately 40,000 members in 1944, also aided the Zionist program of fund-raising, political rallies, Palestine education, and so forth. Samuel Dinin, *Zionist Education in the United States* (New York, 1944), pp. 63–64.

14. See Appendix III for the "Palestine Program of the Religious National Orthodox Bloc of the American Jewish Conference" (1943). The "Bloc" consisted of seven Orthodox associations: Mizrachi, Women's Mizrachi, Hapoel Hamizrachi, Rabbinical Council (Histadrut Harabbonim), National Council of Young Israel, Union of Orthodox Jewish Congregations of America, and Women's Branch of Union of Orthodox Jewish Congregations of America. The numerous other Orthodox Zionist resolutions adopted by Orthodox bodies are not discussed here for they were essentially identical with the formal acts of Conservative Jews to be treated later in this chapter. However, for an indication of one of these wherein 600 rabbis and 1200 laymen at the January, 1944, "National Conference of Orthodox Jewry for Palestine and Rescue" assailed the British White Paper, attacked the anti-Zionist American Council for Judaism, demanded the establishment of a Jewish state, endorsed the Palestine resolution of the American Jewish Conference and lauded the work of the AZEC, see Joshua Trachtenberg, "Religious Activities," in *AJYB*, XLVI (1944), 91–92 and *IJPS*, January 31, 1944, pp. 6–7. Referring to the American Jewish Conference, Rabbi Wolf Gold, Honorary President of Mizrachi, told the House Committee on Foreign Affairs that 1,500,000 American Orthodox Jews "enthusiastically endorsed the entirety of the program for a Jewish Commonwealth." See *REP-HEAR*, p. 231.

15. See Isaac Lewin's sympathetic sketch on Agudas Israel in Basil J. Vlavianos and Feliks Gross (eds.), *Struggle for Tomorrow* (New York, 1954), Chapter IX.

16. *The Zionist*, February 27, 1931, p. 2.

17. Rackman, in Friedman and Gordis, *Jewish Life* . . . , p. 29.
18. *CJR*, III, No. 5 (September–October, 1940), 532.
19. *Agudist World Problems* (New York, 1941), p. 5. By 1942, Agudas Israel made good its offer to negotiate with other groups in the community and was participating in the preliminary talks for the American Jewish Conference. Subsequently, however, the Agudah reverted to a separatist role. See Chapter 9, below.
20. *IJPS*, June 26, 1944, pp. 2–3.
21. *Ibid.*
22. *Palcor News Agency Cable*, March 13, 1946, p. 2. Agudah testimony before the Anglo-American Committee of Inquiry in 1946 revealed few significant differences from the Zionist demands.
23. *UJE*, VIII, 128.
24. *Jewish Agency Digest of Press and Events* (Jerusalem edition), December 27, 1943, pp. 10–11; *Jewish Horizon*, VII (April, 1945), pp. 12–13. Breuer is also quoted as saying: "If the State which is coming will accept the sovereignty of God, we shall recognize it *de jure;* otherwise we can only recognize *de facto* a Jewish State which is not based on Torah." See H. A. Goodman, "Three Voices," *Jewish Life*, XXVI (February, 1959), 46–49.
25. *JTA*, October 29, 1944, p. 4; Isaac Lewin (ed.), *Material for the Preparation of a Constitution for the Jewish State* (New York, 1948); and *CZA*, Z5/1069, especially documents dated July 25, 1944.
26. Milton Steinberg, *The Making of the Modern Jew* (Indianapolis, 1933), p. 283.
27. Quoted reverently over one hundred years later by Classical Reformists in Congregation Beth Israel, *A Handbook of True Facts Concerning the "Basic Principles" of Congregation Beth Israel* (Houston, 1944), p. 9.
28. *CCARY*, VII (1897), xli. The Conference, a continuing assembly meeting annually, acts as a "clearing house" for Reform thought and practice. Its pronouncements on Jewish problems are generally regarded as authoritative by Reform Jews. See Samuel S. Cohon, "Reform Judaism in America," in Friedman and Gordis, *Jewish Life* . . . , p. 98.
29. Cited by Moshe Davis in Louis Finkelstein (ed.), *The Jews: Their History, Culture, and Religion* (New York, 1949), p. 393. Davis quotes Hirsch as proclaiming himself a Zionist, however, after America was shocked by news of the brutal Kishinev pogroms of 1903 (p. 409).
30. Quoted by James W. Wise in "Liberal Judaism and Zionism," *Avukah Annual, Fifth Anniversary Edition 1925–1930* (New York, 1930), p. 30. Cf. also Melvin Weinman, "The Attitude of Isaac Mayer Wise Toward Zionism and Palestine," *American Jewish Archives*, III, No. 2 (January, 1951), 3–23; Israel Knox, *Rabbi in America* (Boston, 1957), pp. 110 ff.; Joseph P. Sternstein, "Attitude of Reform Judaism Toward Zionism as Evinced in the 'American Israelite,' 1895–1904"; and Joseph Tabachnik, "Report on American Jewish Reaction to the First Zionist Congress," papers read at the "Second Conference on the History of Zionism in America," New York, Herzl Institute, 1957. For scattered evidence of pro-Zionist sympathies among Reform rabbis, see Herschel Levin, "The Other Side of the Coin," paper read at this conference.

31. Steinberg, *Making of the Modern Jew*, p. 297.
32. Max Gottschalk and Abraham G. Duker, *Jews in the Post-War World* (New York, 1945), p. 123.
33. Nathan Glazer, *American Judaism* (Chicago, 1957), pp. 46 ff.
34. See Abram Sachar, *A History of the Jews* (New York, 1953), pp. 354–55.
35. Leon Fram, "Reform Judaism and Zionism: A Zionist Interpretation," in Hebrew Union College Alumni, *Reform Judaism* (Cincinnati, 1949), p. 192.
36. Cited in Rufus Learsi (pseud.), *Jews in America* (Cleveland, 1954), pp. 234–35.
37. Caspar Levias, *The Justification of Zionism;* reprint from the *CCARY* of 1899; Max Schloessinger, *Reform Judaism and Zionism: An Examination of Dr. David Philipson's Thesis That They Are Irreconcilable;* reprint from the *Jewish Comment* (Baltimore), January 4–11, 1907, p. 14. Cf. also Bernard G. Richards, *Reform Judaism and Zionism*, reprint from *NP*, September 11, 1942.
38. Learsi, *Jews in America*, p. 233; and Louis Lipsky, *A Gallery of Zionist Portraits* (New York, 1957). On the founding of a "Zionist Association of Liberal Rabbis," see Justine W. Polier and James W. Wise, *The Personal Letters of Stephen Wise* (New York, 1956), p. 180.
39. Learsi, *Jews in America*, p. 30.
40. For a different view of the "purge," see Samuel S. Cohon, "The History of the Hebrew Union College," *PAJHS*, XL, No. 1 (September, 1950), 40–41.
41. The period of anti-Zionist orientation is best treated in Naomi Wiener Cohen, "The Reaction of Reform Judaism in America to Political Zionism (1897–1922)," *PAJHS*, XL, No. 4 (June, 1951), 361–94; and David Philipson, "The Central Conference of American Rabbis: 1899–1939," in *AJYB*, XLII (1940), especially 197–203.
42. Non-Zionist skepticism of a Jewish state is mirrored in the correspondence of Louis Marshall; see Charles Reznikoff (ed.), *Louis Marshall, Champion of Liberty* (Philadelphia, 1957), II, Chapter VII.
43. Justifying his cooperation with the Zionists, Marshall declared:

> I have belonged to a Reform Congregation for nearly sixty years. I have never understood that there is anything basically inconsistent between belief in Palestine and Reform Judaism. If there is then so much the worse for Reform Judaism . . . *indifference to Palestine on the part of any Jew to me spells inconsistency with the spirit of Judaism.*

Quoted in United Jewish Appeal, *The Rebuilding of Palestine* (New York [1927]), p. 6.

44. *NP* editorialized on January 24, 1930, that the truce arranged in 1929 to facilitate "practical cooperation between equal partners" was endangered by some Reform rabbis who "have taken up their discarded tomahawks and emit resonant ear-splitting shouts, as if to confound an enemy. . . ." (pp. 43–44). See also Wise's view in *Challenging Years* (London, 1951), p. 218.
45. *NP*, July 25, 1930, p. 4.
46. *CCARY*, XLII (1942), 108, 132.

47. *CCARY*, XLIV (1944), 131. Reform laymen expressed similar sentiments in a resolution on the "Development of Palestine as a Land of Refuge for the Oppressed":

> Whatever may be our diversities of opinion as to the place of Palestine in Jewish life, we all rejoice that such of our coreligionists as are fleeing from lands of oppression are finding a haven and a new home in the land which has played so large a part in Jewish historical experience.

Quoted in *Proceedings* of the UAHC, *Sixty-first Annual Report*, p. 123. The remarkable progress being made in the Yishuv (Palestine) evidently impressed visiting Reform rabbis deeply, for Felix A. Levy, who had argued against President Wilson's espousal of the Zionist cause, and G. George Fox became ardent Zionist supporters upon their return from Palestine. See Philip P. Bregstone, *Chicago and Its Jews* (Chicago, 1933), pp. 272–73.

48. *CCARY*, XLIV (1934), 66. Debate on the Zionist-sponsored motion is recorded on pp. 72–80.

49. *Ibid.*, 132.

50. According to Rabbi Bernard J. Bamberger, the "Platform" was the product of only nineteen rabbis' thinking. Even Kaufmann Kohler, who wrote most of it, never regarded the "Platform" as sacrosanct. Yet, in the absence of supplanting or supplementing formulations, it came to be a rallying point for anti-Zionist rabbinical authorities. See Hebrew Union College Alumni, *Reform Judaism*, p. 16.

51. *The Pittsburgh Platform* (1885), cited in *CCARY*, I (1890), 120–23 and XLV (1935), 198–200.

52. *The Rabbis of America to Labor Palestine* (New York, 1935), pp. 7–8. Note also, the 1937 survey of 30 percent of the Reform rabbinate which revealed that over half of those surveyed agreed with, and only 20 percent disagreed with the statement: "The cultivation of the Hebrew language and literature and loyalty to the cause of rebuilding Palestine as a Jewish homeland are essential to the Jewish pattern of life." See Zeitlin, *Disciples of the Wise*, p. 92.

53. *CCARY*, XLV (1935), 148–50.

54. *Ibid.*, 342–54.

55. *Ibid.*, 103. Rabbi Edward L. Israel, a leader of the Zionist bloc in the Conference, claimed that the Zionists had sufficient votes to force through a positive Zionist plank. That they were content with this "neutrality" clause was due largely to a desire to avoid splitting the Conference, especially at a time when it seemed that the drift to Zionism was irresistible. Zionists hoped to capture the entire Conference in time by a "process of education" and without forcing non-Zionists to the defensive ("A Critique of 'Reformism,'" *REC*, January 8, 1937, p. 9). As evidence of the continuing rabbinical ferment on Zionism, see Israel's "Reform Judaism and Zionism" and the "Symposium" of the same title in *Hebrew Union College Monthly*, XXIV, No. 3 (January 15, 1937), 3–4; and XXIII, No. 6 (May 23, 1936), 12–30, respectively.

56. *CCARY*, XLVII (1937), 419–20.

57. *Ibid.*, 98–99. Cf. also Glazer, *American Judaism*, pp. 102 ff. Of the 1937 statement Glazer writes (p. 104): "This is, in effect and in detail, a Zionist statement: both a bitter minority and a triumphant majority considered it as such. . . ."

58. *Proceedings* of the UAHC, *Fifty-third Annual Report*, pp. 158. Compare also Agus, *Guideposts* . . . , pp. 70–74.

59. *CCARY*, LI (1941), 43.

60. Rabbi Israel was simultanously President of the Synagogue Council of America (the deliberative and consultative body of most of the American rabbinate) and a member of the executives of both B'nai B'rith and World Jewish Congress; see *NP*, July 18, 1941, p. 16.

61. *The Zionist* (New York), September, 1941, p. 1.

62. *NP*, July 18, 1941, p. 16.

63. *NP*, February 20, 1942, pp. 4, 24.

64. *CCARY*, LII (1942), 169–70.

65. *Ibid.*, 172–81. Cf. also Rabbi Goldenson's press release of March 16, 1942, in which he denied the veracity of London dispatches employed by the Zionists attesting to the "unanimous support of American Jewry" for a Jewish Army, *IJPS*, pp. 6–7

66. *CCARY*, LII, 182. Including absent members, fifty-seven Reform rabbis dissented from the Jewish Army resolution. To offset this significant group, the AECZA gathered the endorsements of over five hundred other rabbis, publishing their names and approval in leading American newspapers; see *NP*, March 27, 1942, pp. 4–5, 16.

67. Except where otherwise indicated, documentation on the founding of the American Council for Judaism is drawn from records in *LAJC* and in *CZA*, Z5/733 and 1399, particularly "Minutes of Lay-Rabbinical Chapter Committee Meeting, November 2, 1942" and "Confidential Minutes of the Meeting of the Eastern Contingent of Non-Zionist Rabbis, November 23, 1943," both held in Temple Rodeph Shalon, Philadelphia.

68. *IJPS*, June 2, 1942, pp. 1–3. That such a pledge was ever made was categorically denied by Rabbis Heller and Freehof, the latter known as a "neutralist" on the Zionist question.

69. This was Elmer Berger's "Flint Plan," a program of "anti-nationalism and integration," later to provide a tactical approach for the American Council for Judaism.

70. *IJPS*, June 2, 1942, pp. 1–3. See also *JTA*, June 14, 1942, p. 4. A favorite theme of the anti-Zionists at this period, overlooking their own activities, was to condemn the Zionists for pursuing a "politics as usual" policy despite raging World War II.

71. *JTA*, June 3, 1942, p. 4.

72. This committeee was headed by Rabbi Morris S. Lazaron of Baltimore, among the most ardent of anti-Zionists. Eleven years earlier Lazaron had taken sharp issue with Wolsey and other anti-Zionists in a brilliant essay avowing his own personal Zionist affiliation and contesting the conceptions of his opponents; see his *Reform Judaism and Jewish Nationalism* (reprint from *The Jewish Times*, January 2, 1931).

73. The "Statement" is obviously a compromise document; not all the rabbis

felt equally alarmed about the dangers of Zionism. Some favored a much more forceful denunciation of the "secular nationalists." Wolsey, the conference chairman, however, assured the press that there was perfect agreement on the measures to be taken (*NYT*, June 3, p. 9). The "Statement" is extant in various mimeographed copies of 2–4 pages and was also printed in *NYT*, August 30, 1942.

74. *IJPS* succeeded in obtaining minutes of two closed anti-Zionist meetings; see *CW*, December 18, 1942, pp. 2, 11–12; *IJPS*, December 14, 1942, pp. 1–8; and note 67, above.

75. *CW*, December 18, 1942, pp. 2, 11–12.

76. *Ibid*. Rabbi Lazaron agreed to inform Secretary of the Interior Harold Ickes, scheduled speaker at a United Palestine Appeal conference on December 6, of the anti-Zionist cause. Formerly an outspoken friend of the Zionist movement, Ickes addressed the conference but said nothing whatsoever concerning Palestine. Zionists thereafter began to speak of "A Conspiracy of Silence," that is, a definite deterioration in relations with the Roosevelt administration.

77. According to the first issue of the Council's *Information Bulletin*, October 15, 1943, twenty Reform rabbis served on its Board of Directors. A total of 97 rabbis, all Reform, were identified with the Council at its inception. After the Zionist victory in the American Jewish Conference of 1943, however, and with the expression of increasingly a-religious attitudes of the Council, this rabbinical support swiftly waned; numerous public withdrawals from the Council for Judaism were announced. Those withdrawals continue, as witness the report in *NYT*, July 22, 1956, p. 43.

78. Jewish entrance into Palestine was scheduled to terminate on March 31, 1944, according to the 1939 White Paper issued by the Palestinian Mandatory.

79. An account of these negotiations and excerpts of Heller's report to CCAR members are contained in *NP*, February 19, 1943, pp. 8–9 and Minutes of ZOA Executive Committee, November 16, 1943. Heller alleged that anti-Zionist literature was mailed to 10,000 persons on a mailing list and with a free postal permit number supplied by the Joint Distribution Committee, a non-Zionist organization dominated by Reform laymen and rabbis.

80. *CCARY*, LIII (1943), 29–30.

81. *Ibid.*, 183–84.

82. *Ibid.*, 184–87.

83. *Ibid.*, 187–94. Heller later told the House Committee on Foreign Affairs that the vote on this resolution was 137–45 (*REP-HEAR*, p. 211).

84. *CCARY*, LIII (1943), 92–93. This resolution was described by Rabbi Elmer Berger, Executive Director of the American Council for Judaism, as the "end of a cycle":

> The last, great source of opposition to Jewish nationalism—an opposition deriving from liberal religion—had succumbed to the relentless pressure of the Zionists. The last chance of a formidable opponent meeting Jewish nationalism with a policy of integration was apparently lost. (*The Jewish Dilemma* [New York, 1951], pp. 241–42.)

85. *CCARY,* LIII (1943), 93–94.
86. *Ibid.,* 94–96.
87. *Ibid.,* 96–98.
88. The actual roll-call voting is published in *CCARY,* LIII, 20–24.
89. *CCARY,* LIV (1944), 28–29.
90. *Ibid.,* 27–34.
91. Congregation Beth Israel, *Annual Report,* May 30, 1944, p. 28.
92. See *Get Thee A Teacher* (Houston, 1945), Congregation Beth Israel's collection of theological writings purporting to prove the centrality of anti-Zionism in Reform thought.
93. Congregation Beth Israel, *Annual Report,* May 30, 1944, pp. 30–31. Avowedly anti-Zionist temples were also reported in Pontiac, Michigan; Baton Rouge, Louisiana; and Lincoln, Nebraska, and, to some extent, wherever an American Council for Judaism rabbi held a pulpit. See Joshua Trachtenberg, "Religious Activities," in *AJYB,* XLVII (1945), 215–28 and *JTA,* February 21, 1945, p. 1.
94. Beth Israel adopted the "Principles" by a vote of 632–168, but 142 of the dissenters opposed the new credo so vigorously that they resigned their temple membership. Assistant Rabbi Robert Kahn, who also resigned in protest, later headed a rival Reform temple formed by the secessionists. See Anne Nathan Cohen, *The Centenary History: Congregation Beth Israel of Houston, Texas, 1854–1954* (Houston, 1954), pp. 57–58.
95. Congregation Beth Israel, *Annual Report,* May 30, 1944, p. 60.
96. *CCARY,* LIV, 31–41.
97. *JTA,* March 21, 1944, p. 4. Compare with Rabbi Louis I. Newman's "Houston 'Reform Judaism': Folly in Masquerade," *IJPS,* January 28, 1944, pp. 1–30, and reply by Beth Israel's rabbi in the same issue: Hyman J. Schachtel, "Explaining the Basic Principles," pp. 1–4D. The Zionists' effort to counteract Beth Israel's actions, including the dispatch of leading rabbis Maurice Eisendrath and Joshua Liebman to Houston, is detailed in Minutes of the ZOA Executive Committee, New York, November 16, 1943.
98. Congregation Beth Israel, *The President of Congregation Beth Israel Replies to Dr. Solomon B. Freehof, President, Central Conference of American Rabbis* (Houston), May 1, 1944, pp. 4–5. Additional protests were addressed to the Union of American Hebrew Congregations and the Hebrew Union College, the latter being charged with neglecting traditional reform principles of anti-Zionism in the training of the rabbinate. The UAHC publicly rejected Beth Israel's charges in a press release dated April 11, 1944.

    A letter from Rabbi Elmer Berger to Maury Travis, Houston Chapter of the American Council for Judaism, September 12, 1947, in the files of the Council's New York office, criticizes the policies of Rabbi Julian Morgenstern, former President of Hebrew Union College, as pro-Zionist, attributing to him primary responsibility for the degeneration of Reform Judaism by the filling of leading Reform pulpits with Zionists. This charge seems unwarranted, however, for Morgenstern was a constant critic of the Zionists; see two examples of his statements: "Reform Leader Warns Rabbinical Students Against Zionism," *IJPS*, September 29, 1942, pp. 1–2; and "Palestine is Only a Secondary Issue with American Jews," *JTA*, October 11, 1944, pp. 3–4.

99. Congregation Beth Israel, Policy Formulation Committee, *A Handbook of True Facts Concerning the "Basic Principles of Congregation Beth Israel,"* (Houston, 1944), pp. 14–15.

100. See Baruch Braunstein, "The Reform Rabbis' Unity Conference," *IJPS*, July 9, 1943, pp. 1–4E.

101. Berger, *Jewish Dilemma*, pp. 248–52.

102. *CCARY*, LVI (1946), 212–13. One member of this committee of three was arch anti-Zionist David Philipson.

103. *Ibid.*

104. On this point, see Israel, *REC*, January 8, 1937, p. 9; Bregstone, *Chicago and Its Jews,* p. 143; Norman Miller, "The Jewish Leadership in Lakeport," in Alvin Gouldner (ed.), *Studies in Leadership* (New York, 1950), pp. 198–99; Sklare, *Conservative Judaism,* pp. 73–74; and Abraham G. Duker, *Workshop in Jewish Community Affairs* (New York, 1953), Course I: "The American Jewish Community: Its History and Development," Syllabus for Session 5: "Social and Organizational Trends Within the American Jewish Community Today," p. 15.

105. UAHC, *Reform Judaism in the Larger Cities—A Survey,* p. 10; cited in Sklare, *Conservative Judaism,* p. 267. According to the official historian of Congregation Beth Israel, one reason for the bitter controversy in the Houston temple was this rapid East European influx into Reform. Beth Israel, the only Reform temple in Houston, a city whose population doubled between 1930 and 1942, was faced overnight with a flood of traditionalist newcomers eager for admittance. Under these circumstances, the Classical Reform "Old Guard" felt compelled to make a stand against the infiltrations of Zionist feeling; Cohen, *Centenary History,* pp. 53–54.

106. Israel, *REC,* January 8, 1937, p. 8; Duker, *Workshop in Jewish Community Affairs,* p. 15; Glazer, *American Judaism,* p. 102.

107. Tables 5–8 drawn from David Polish, "Zionism in Reform Rabbinate," *CW,* March 19, 1943, p. 13. Due largely to the continuing hostility to Zionism of the Reform seminary, Hebrew Union College, in Cincinnati, Stephen S. Wise founded a second seminary, the Jewish Institute of Religion, in New York City. Influenced by a hand-picked Zionist faculty, J.I.R. graduates became noted for their avid espousal of Zionism. Of J.I.R. students, wrote Armond E. Cohen: ". . . theirs is an insatiable love for Zion: this means that they not only think of Zion, but are actively engaged in bringing about the restoration; this means that they are unsurpassed in Zionist activity by any other group of theological students. . . ." Cohen also claimed that over one-third of the rabbinical students at the Hebrew Union College were Zionists, while only 10 percent were anti-Zionists: in "Palestine and Our Rabbinical Schools," in Joseph S. Shubow (ed.), *The Brandeis Avukah Annual of 1932* (New York, 1932), pp. 593–98.

108. Sylvan D. Schwartzman, *Reform Judaism in the Making* (New York, 1955), p. 161.
109. Conservatism's United Synagogue of America was founded by 22 congregations in 1913 and then grew to 190 in 1940, 350 in 1950, and 668 in 1959. Source: Letter to author from Marjorie Wyler, Jewish Theological Seminary of America, December 11, 1959. By 1953, Reform's Union of American Hebrew Congregations had remarkably accelerated its growth —to 150,000 families and 450 congregations.
110. Leon Fram, "Reform Judaism and Zionism: A Zionist Interpretation," in Hebrew Union College Alumni, *Reform Judaism* (Cincinnati, 1949), 176.
111. *Reform Judaism*, Introduction, p. 17.
112. See David H. Wice, "Reform Judaism and Zionism: A Non-Zionist Interpretation," in *Reform Judaism*, pp. 197–98 and Samuel S. Cohon, "Reform Judaism in America," in Friedman and Gordis, *Jewish Life . . .* , p. 98.
113. Sklare, *Conservative Judaism*, pp. 23–24.
114. The Board of Directors of the Seminary retained its Reform character well into the forties. The 1941 *AJYB*, for example, reveals that such stellar figures in Reform and the American Jewish Committee as Sol M. Stroock, Cyrus Adler, Irving Lehman, Mrs. Felix M. Warburg, and Arthur Oppenheimer dominated the J.T.S.' lay leadership; XLII (1941), 531. This may account, in part, for the fact that Louis Finkelstein, President of the Seminary after the death of Solomon Schechter, was virtually the only Conservative rabbi to resist Zionist demands in the mid-forties; see Chapter 5 below, and Glazer, *American Judaism*, pp. 74 ff.
115. On Schechter's decisive influence in shaping a Conservative alliance with Zionism, see Louis Finkelstein, "Solomon Schechter as a Zionist," *NP*, December 13, 1950, p. 10; Louis Lipsky, *A Gallery of Zionist Profiles* (New York, 1956), pp. 184–91; and Norman Bentwich, *Solomon Schechter, A Biography* (Philadelphia, 1948), pp. 309–31.
116. In his 1906 *Statement on Zionism*, portions of which were cited on p. 8, above.
117. Wives of Seminary faculty were among the founders and directors, in 1912, of Hadassah, Women's Zionist Organization of America, most successful of all American Zionist groups; see Rose G. Jacobs, "Beginnings of Hadassah," in Meyer, *Early History of Zionism . . .* , p. 242.
118. A sociological study of Stamford, Connecticut by Samuel Koenig in 1938, for example, revealed that the local Conservative synagog looked upon Zionism as "the most important Jewish movement" and, accordingly, made Zionist philosophy the basis of many of its teachings and educational activities; in Isacque Graeber and Steuart H. Britt (eds.), *Jews in a Gentile World* (New York, 1942), p. 229. Cf. also Robert Gordis, *Conservative Judaism, An American Philosophy* (New York, 1945), pp. 33–35 and his *The Jew Faces A New World* (New York, 1941), p. 207. Sklare (*Conservative Judaism*, pp. 219–20) stresses that Zionism helped to fill Conservatism's "ideological void" by "indicating an appealing program of activity," thus adding practical to theoretical reasons for Conservative en-

thusiasm about Zionism. Cf. also Herbert Parzen's comprehensive paper, "Conservative Judaism and Zionism (1903–1922)," read at the "Second Conference on Zionist History in America," New York, Herzl Institute, 1957; and Beryl D. Cohon, "Conservative and Reconstructionist Judaism," in Hebrew Union College Alumni, *Reform Judaism*, pp. 107–34.

119. *PRAA*, II (1927), 32, 51.

120. *PRAA*, V (1933–38), 188–89. The following year (1934), the Palestine Committee reported that the ZOA had amended its constitution to permit greater participation by organized Jewish groups. Resolutions of this Assembly included a plea for active affiliation of all rabbis in the ZOA and an expression of appreciation for the work of the Histadrut in Palestine (*PRAA*, V, 55, 59). See also, Conservative rabbis' endorsement of Labor Palestine in *The Rabbis of America to Labor Palestine*, compiled by the League for Labor Palestine (New York, 1935).

121. *PRAA*, V, 362–63, 388–400.

122. *Pronouncement on Zionism* (New York, 1938), p. 8.

123. *Ibid.*, p. 10. This document is not a complete endorsement of every facet of Zionist policy. On the contrary, pp. 3–8 contain sharp criticisms of various practices of the Palestinian Zionist movement.

124. *PRAA*, V, 406, 419, 428.

125. *Disciples of the Wise* (New York, 1945), pp. 96–98. For an interesting comparison, in part, see Eliezer Whartman, "Attitudes of American Rabbis on Zionism and Israel," *JSS*, XVII, No. 2 (April, 1955), 121–32.

126. *PRAA*, VI (1940), 168.

127. *PRAA*, VIII (1947), 127, 166, 277.

128. See *REC*, April 2, 1943, p. 7 and *NP*, March 5, 1943, p. 13. Sklare (*Conservative Judaism*, p. 220) claims the joint membership plan did not work too well, most Zionists preferring to support the movement outside the synagog. Some laymen feared that Zionism would conflict with other values, such as "institutional maintenance." Nevertheless, by early 1944 there were eighty congregations entirely enrolled in the ZOA, the majority of them affiliated with Conservatism. The United Synagogue of America, Conservative Judaism's equivalent of Reform's Union of American Hebrew Congregations, apparently shared the Zionist sentiments of its rabbinical mentors, for the more than three hundred synagogs affiliated with the United Synagogue approved this resolution in 1944:

> In the firm belief that the survival of the Jewish people and their religion is linked with the future of Palestine, and believing that in Palestine the Jewish people can best fulfill their historic destiny, we demand that the Jews be permitted to establish an autonomous Jewish State in Palestine. (Dinin, *Zionist Education in the United States*, p. 63.)

On the local level, too, Conservative and Orthodox rabbis in St. Louis, representing twenty-two congregations, issued a rabbinical edict imposing upon every congregation in the city "The sacred duty" to join a Zionist organization (*NP*, April 2, 1943, p. 19).

129. Louis Katzoff, *Issues in Jewish Education: A Study of the Philosophy of the Conservative Congregational School* (New York, 1949), p. 92.

130. *REC*, January 11, 1935, p. 4. An editorial in the same issue warned American Jewry against the visit of the Revisionist leader, Vladimir Jabotinsky, labeling him a "tool of economic reaction," "a betrayer of the Zionist vision," and a "destroyer" of the Jewish labor movement in Palestine (pp. 8–9). Cf. also Mordecai M. Kaplan's authoritative statement of Reconstructionism, *Judaism As A Civilization* (New York, 1935), especially pp. 273–74.

131. *REC*, February 23, 1945, p. 15.

132. See, for example, these *REC* articles: "Zionism Is Not Enough," January 11, 1935, pp. 5–6; Ira Eisenstein, "The Place of Palestine in Jewish Life," November 1, 1935, pp. 6–11; Eugene Kohn, "The Role of Reconstructionism in the Zionist Movement," October 13, 1939, pp. 7–13; Jack J. Cohen, "Zionism for Jews or for Judaism?" May 12, 1944, pp. 9–15; "Preparing for the Jewish Commonwealth," November 3, 1944, pp. 14–20; the numerous books of Mordecai M. Kaplan; Ira Eisenstein, *Creative Judaism* (New York, 1941), pp. 66–67, 88–90, 103, 199; Milton Steinberg, "Current Philosophies of Jewish Life," in Janowsky, *The American Jew*, Chapter IX; the official statement of the Reconstructionist Foundation Policy Committee, and Arthur Hertzberg (ed.), *The Zionist Idea* (New York, 1959), pp. 534–44.

133. See "Mordecai M. Kaplan and Reform Judaism: A Study in Reciprocity," in Ira Eisenstein and Eugene Kohn (eds.), *Mordecai M. Kaplan: An Evaluation* (New York, 1952), pp. 235–39.

134. In addition to those mentioned in preceding notes, Morton Berman, Louis M. Levitsky, Jacob J. Weinstein, Harold Weisberg, Samuel M. Blumenfield, Philip S. Bernstein, Joshua Trachtenberg, Solomon Goldman, and Joshua L. Leibman were some of the other rabbis who played leading roles in American Zionism. Outstanding lay educators and professionals like Abraham G. Duker, Israel S. Chipkin, and Judah Pilch were also notably influenced by Reconstructionist thought.

CHAPTER 5

1. See Harry Schneiderman (ed.), *Two Generations in Perspective* (New York, 1957), especially pp. 59–65, 110–37. On the American Jewish Committee's program and achievements, see *UJE*, I, 242–47; Oscar Handlin, "The American Jewish Committee; A Half-Century View," *Commentary*, XXIII (January, 1957), 1–10; and Nathan Schachner, *The Price of Liberty: A History of the American Jewish Committee* (New York, 1948).

2. Ben Halpern's "The American Jewish Committee" is one of the more reasoned expositions of these charges; see *JF*, X, No. 12 (December, 1943), 13–16. Cf. also his "The Impact of Israel on American Jewish Ideologies," especially pp. 68–70 in *The Impact of Israel on the American Jewish Community* (New York, 1959). Other writers often employed terms expressing the greatest contempt and derision. In 1939, the AJC raised its million dollar budget from a mere 400 subscribers, a major achievement for that period. See *Proceedings of the Fiftieth Anniversary Observance of the American Jewish Committee* (New York, 1958), p. 247.

3. *UJE*, I, 242; and AJC, *Proceedings . . . ,* p. 176.

4. Halpern, *JF*, X, No. 12, 15–16.

5. *Ibid.*, p. 16. The Committee's abundant financial resources were derived not only from its wealthy constituency but also from the Joint Defense Appeal conducted in conjunction with B'nai B'rith's Anti-Defamation League. In this way, the Committee obtained funds from local federations and welfare funds for the purpose of combatting anti-Semitism, but other facets of the Committee's activities could be supported through the same undifferentiated collection.

6. *Thirty Years of American Zionism* (New York, 1927), I, 30. See also Howard M. Sachar, *The Course of Modern Jewish History* (Cleveland, 1958), pp. 520 ff.; and Moses Rischin, "The Early Attitude of the American Jewish Committee to Zionism (1906–1922)," *PAJHS*, XLIX, No. 3 (March, 1960), 188–201.

7. AJC, *To the Counsellors of Peace* (New York, 1945), p. 5; *Twelfth Annual Report, 1918–1919*, pp. 43–45.

8. See Schachner, *Price of Liberty . . .* , p. 136, and Charles Reznikoff (ed.), *Louis Marshall, Champion of Liberty* (Philadelphia, 1957), II, Chap. VII.

9. AJC, *To the Counsellors of Peace*, p. 6. See also AJC, *Twenty-third Annual Report*, in *AJYB*, XXXII (1930–31), 309–10, 321–24 and *Twenty-fourth Annual Report*, *ibid.*, XXXIII (1931–32), 368–69.

10. AJC, *Twenty-ninth Annual Report*, *AJYB*, XXXVIII (1936–37), 617 and *UJE*, I, 246.

11. *Thirtieth Annual Report*, *AJYB*, XXXIX (1937–38), 819–20.

12. On the running organizational feud between the American Jewish Committee and the American Jewish Congress, see any issue of the *Congress Bulletin* in 1935, and Henry Cohen, "Crisis and Reaction," *American Jewish Archives*, V, No. 2 (June, 1953), 71–113.

13. Maurice J. Karpf, *Partition of Palestine and Its Consequences* and *American Non-Zionists and Palestine Partition* (both New York, 1938). Although the non-Zionists' interest in Palestine was supposedly limited to "philanthropic" pursuits only, Karpf later challenged a declaration to the League of Nations Permanent Mandates Commission by Colonial Secretary Malcolm MacDonald to the effect that the phrase *Jewish National Homeland* "should mean something less than a Jewish State." Karpf insisted upon the legitimacy of an earlier statement by Colonial Secretary William Ormsby-Gore which affirmed that the Balfour Declaration "was still a binding obligation and would remain so until replaced by an independent State." (Morris Fine, "Review of the Year 5699, Part I, The United States," *AJYB*, XLI [1939–40], p. 204.)

14. *New Judaea* (London), August–September, 1937, p. 233, carries reports of meetings of the Zionist Congress and Council of the Jewish Agency at which partition was discussed. Warburg warned against empowering the Agency to ascertain conditions for *any* Jewish state and declared that Americans had agreed to help relieve Jewish suffering and to aid in making Palestine self-supporting, but never to assist the establishment of a Jewish state. Warburg hoped that the Mandate could be revived with Jews and Arabs induced to live together in peace without the necessity of independent statehood.

15. Karpf, *Partition* . . . , pp. 15–16. The non-Zionists' threat to withdraw from the Agency was further motivated by the fact that it had come to be dominated by the Zionists; some of the European "non-Zionists" represented therein consistently voted with the Zionist bloc. Correspondence in *CZA*, S25/237, S29/76, S53/311 and S53/322d illuminates other facets of the non-Zionists' opposition to a Jewish state. Particularly revealing is Karpf's letter to Ben-Gurion, dated June 7, 1937, threatening that the non-Zionist Joint Distribution Committee may undertake programs in Palestine in competition with the World Zionist Organization (S53/322d).

16. AJC, *Thirty-first Annual Report*, in *AJYB*, XLI (1939–40), 634, and *To the Counsellors of Peace*, pp. 6–7. The Committee gave wide distribution to three pamphlets opposing partition. These, claimed the *Annual Report*, "undoubtedly contributed to a wider knowledge of the dangers inherent in the partition proposal." Zionist reactions to these attacks may be found in *NP* editorials, April 15, 1938, p. 6, and April 29, 1938, p. 4, which counter the "obsessed fears" of Rabbi Morris Lazaron and Maurice Karpf, respectively. See also, "After the Zionist Congress," *JS*, III (September 1937), 3–4, and Bernard G. Richards, "In Reply to a Pamphlet—An Open Letter to Dr. Maurice J. Karpf," *NP*, April 15, 1938, p. 7.

17. Adler, President of the Committee, dispelled Zionist fears of a rupture of relations with the non-Zionists by a letter to Stephen S. Wise, President of the ZOA, pledging continued financial assistance to Palestine regardless of the outcome of the partition question. Karpf, too, in an address before the National Conference for Palestine, attempted to placate Zionist attackers of the Committee by assuring the assembled delegates that everyone involved was devoted to Palestine. But, "at the present time," he added, a Jewish state "can only confuse and divide where there should be clarity and unity." See *NP*, February 28, 1938, p. 10, and January 28, p. 2, respectively.

18. AJC, *To the Counsellors of Peace*, p. 7.

19. *Ibid.*

20. The statement of this delegation, claiming to be "representative of every section of organized Jewish life in the United States and reflecting the sentiment of four and a half million citizens," is reprinted in *CJR*, I, No. 2 (November, 1938), 7–10.

21. Various unpublished documents in *LAJC* and Schachner, *Price of Liberty* . . . , p. 138. This period was marked by a virtual consensus among American Jewry concerning the necessity of maintaining Palestine as a haven for Jewish refugees from Europe. One product of the Hitlerian threat was a *rapprochement* between the erstwhile rivals of the Committee: American Jewish Congress, B'nai B'rith and Jewish Labor Committee. The four groups, all dedicated to the "safeguarding of Jewish rights" and the fight against anti-Semitism, formed the General Council for Jewish Rights, later renamed the General Jewish Council, on June 13, 1938. This consultatory body specifically excluded "the consideration of questions involving racial, national or religious philosophies," for example, Zionism. See *CJR*, I, No. 2 (November, 1938), 20, 68.

22. See Schachner, *Price of Liberty* . . . , pp. 139 ff., and Morris D. Waldman, *Nor by Power* (New York, 1953), Chapters XIX and XX, for a record of these negotiations. Earlier, leading non-Zionists, like Maurice Karpf and Maurice Hexter, declined to participate in the work of the newly-constituted American Emergency Committee for Zionist Affairs (letters from Nahum Goldmann to Eliezer Kaplan, October 25, 1940, and September 18, 1941, in *CZA*, S53/210b).

23. The *Struma* was one of the ships carrying "illegal" or uncertified immigrants to Palestine. Turned away from Palestine by the Mandatory Government, it sank in a Black Sea minefield with a loss of over seven hundred Jews fleeing from the Balkans. See Jon and David Kimche, *The Secret Roads* (New York, 1955), pp. 56–57.

24. AJC, *Thirty-fifth Annual Report,* p. 46.

25. Waldman, *Nor by Power,* p. 207.

26. *Ibid.,* pp. 207–209.

27. Cited in *ibid.,* p. 240. Waldman adds that Proskauer wrote Judge Samuel Rosenman, a leading member of the Committee and Special Counsel to President Roosevelt, that cooperation with the Zionists was a "tragic error." Apparently, Proskauer and other members of the Committee were also much incensed at the vow given by another Committee member, Judge Louis Levinthal, as he accepted the presidency of the ZOA: "In assuming the Presidency with which this convention has honored me, I renew my pledge to dedicate my efforts to make Zionism the major concern of the Jews in America" (*ibid.,* p. 243).

28. AJC, *Thirty-fifth Annual Report,* pp. 46–47.

29. "Our Brother's Keeper," *CW,* May 29, 1942, pp. 11–12; and Louis Lipsky, "The Equal of Others," *ibid.,* pp. 13–14.

30. Letter dated April 16, 1942, in *CZA,* S25/41.

31. *Ibid.;* and Waldman, *Nor by Power,* p. 238.

32. The Committee had not taken a stand on the Zionist demand for a Jewish military force, the immediate provocation for the rift in the CCAR. However, J. C. Hurewitz cites a letter of Morris Waldman, dated April 3, 1942, asserting that while Palestine remains in the process of development it "should not go beyond the idea of Jewish units as part of the British forces." Current Zionist pressures for an army were "a legitimate democratic process," Waldman believed, but they also constituted "an embarrassment to the United Nations" (Hurewitz, *The Struggle for Palestine* [New York, 1950], pp. 129–30).

33. "The Conspiracy Against Zionism," *CW,* December 18, 1942, pp. 2, 11–12, presents an outspoken expression of the anti-Zionists' hopes for capturing the AJC. According to Waldman, Judge Proskauer was approached by anti-Zionist rabbis to accept the presidency of the American Council for Judaism. Already a candidate for the presidency of the infinitely more influential Committee, Proskauer expressed himself in full sympathy with the anti-Zionist group, but declined to accept the post (*Nor by Power,* p. 239).

34. The furious Zionist reaction to this breach of negotiations is mirrored in

letters from Nahum Goldmann to Eliezer Kaplan, October 26 and December 21, 1942; in *CZA*, S25/237 and S53/210a, respectively.

35. Joseph M. Proskauer, *A Segment of My Times* (New York, 1950), p. 237; and Schachner, *Price of Liberty* . . . , p. 140. Proskauer's construction of the Biltmore Platform seems entirely too formal and legalistic. It was widely recognized at the time that the establishment of a Jewish commonwealth required a transition period in order to transfer the European remnants to Palestine. What was *immediately* demanded was international sanction to effect such a transfer. In any case, most Zionists never advocated a "purely Jewish state" but only a Jewish majority in Palestine.

36. AJC, *Thirty-sixth Annual Report*, pp. 39–41; and letter from Nahum Goldmann to Eliezer Kaplan, December 21, 1942, in *CZA*, S53/210a.

37. AJC, *Thirty-sixth Annual Report*, pp. 14–15; also published in *NYT*, February 1, 1943, p. 13. Emphasis added. Obviously, the document did not represent the thinking of all its sponsors, for Medalie was known as a Zionist and Lehman told the press that the "Statement" did not go far enough in its advocacy of Jewish rights and intimated that, if the Committee did not make an additional statement on Palestine, he would have to "dissociate himself from that view." See *IJPS*, February 1, 1943, p. 7.

38. Though the "Statement" did not, theoretically, preclude a Jewish state "within a reasonable period of years," it did deny the Zionists' demand for the *immediate right* to a commonwealth. It was, therefore, regarded in Zionist circles as a maneuver to frustrate statehood indefinitely. Waldman's memoirs relate that rumors of the "Statement's" contents caused the Zionists to conclude that all Zionist-Committee negotiations were at an end. Weizmann reportedly telephoned Waldman, the Zionists' best contact in the Committee, that the proposed document was regarded as unfriendly to Zionism since it carried no mention even of the Balfour Declaration or of the Mandate. Waldman's assurances that the "Statement" was merely an attempt to preserve the cohesion of the AJC by providing a compromise between Zionists and anti-Zionists in the Committee were unavailing. *Nor by Power*, pp. 251–52.

39. AJC, *Thirty-sixth Annual Report*, pp. 43–49. Objections to the "Statement" made by Zionist members of the Committee at the Annual Meeting are deleted from the *Report;* only Proskauer's arguments are printed. Proskauer's election was a disappointment to the Zionists. Nahum Goldmann, for example, had written: "There are rumors that Proskauer will be elected, but I do not believe it because they will be afraid to provoke us by choosing a rabid anti-Zionist, so will probably choose a more neutral man." (Letter to Eliezer Kaplan, December 21, 1942, in *CZA*, S53/210a.)

40. *Ibid.*, pp. 46–50.

41. The *Annual Report* does not indicate the vote on these matters. A check of the attendance at the meeting reveals that many of the delegates of pro-Zionist organizations represented in the Committee were absent at the time (for example, Free Sons of Israel, Independent Order Brith Abraham, Rabbinical Assembly of America, and others). It is doubtful that Proskauer's election could have been averted regardless of the attendance,

however, since the Committee was dominated by known non- or anti-Zionists. See membership lists, *ibid.*, pp. 103–105. In view of Judge Proskauer's vigorous objections to the Zionist program all during 1942, the following passage from his autobiography casts doubts on the "rationality" of his earlier opposition to Zionism:

> Prior to 1943, I had no contact with the Zionist movement and no special interest in it. My knowledge of its principles and program was scant. Instinctively I was opposed to the creation of a state identified, however remotely, with a religion. But in 1943, *when I assumed the presidency of the American Jewish Committee,* a detailed study of the entire problem became a necessary duty (*A Segment of My Times,* p. 229 [my italics]).

42. Waldman, *Nor by Power,* pp. 252–53, and his memorandum of September 13, 1943, in *CZA,* Z4/15072.
43. "The End of a Long Discussion," *NP,* February 19, 1943, pp. 4–5; and see letter from Nahum Goldmann to Eliezer Kaplan, January 11, 1943, in *CZA,* S53/210a.
44. See editorials in *REC,* March 5 and 19, pp. 3–5 in both issues.
45. Schachner, *Price of Liberty* . . . , p. 146. AZEC minutes of January 7, 1943, record the Zionists' understanding that any organization could secede from the proposed Assembly and, indeed, "must do so if unwilling to accept a decision of the majority. That is to say that decisions are binding on the constituent organizations unless they withdraw." At the same time, a majority of the AZEC agreed to press the Assembly for acceptance of the Biltmore Program unless the opposition proved to be too strong. In that event, "changes might be made in phraseology in order to insure unity." See *CZA,* Z4/15365.
46. Schachner, *Price of Liberty* . . . , p. 145.
47. Proskauer, *A Segment of My Times,* p. 199.
48. On March 11, 1943, the ZOA Executive Committee debated Proskauer's demands long and hard and finally rejected them. Rabbi Israel Goldstein summed up the majority view:

> . . . the American Jewish Committee is not accustomed to taking positions merely on a whim or on a technicality. They know what they are doing and when they want a change of name, they want it for a very special purpose. Their purpose is to make this Assembly in the eyes of public opinion as noncommittal and unimportant and as impersonal as possible, and they believe that the name of Conference conveys that tentativeness much better than the name of Assembly, and therefore it is not ridiculous for them to insist on a change. It is therefore important and very fundamental for us to oppose that change.

(In *CZA,* Z4/15365. See also the spirited exchange of correspondence on the name change issue between Proskauer, on the one hand, Wise and Monsky on the other in *CZA,* Z5/759.)
49. *Nor by Power,* pp. 253–54.
50. "From Assembly to Conference," p. 3. See also *NP,* May 7, 1943, pp. 3–4, which averred that since the Conference's objectives and election pro-

cedures remained unaltered, a change of name was a small price to pay for the adherence of the AJC.

51. *The Conference Record,* January 15, 1944, pp. 6–7. Elliott E. Cohen, editor of the Committee-sponsored *Commentary* magazine also complained to Meyer Weisgal of "pushing around" by the Zionist press and its allies, particularly *Congress Weekly.* Said Cohen, "I still don't like being called an anti-Semite and I don't like the magazine being smeared" (*CZA,* Z5/1136).

52. *Nor by Power,* p. 265. Waldman was a prime mover in the Committee's secession; see his confidential memorandum, dated September 13, 1943, in *CZA,* Z4/15072. Minutes of the AJC's Palestine Committee meeting of December 31, 1944, also reveal how deeply concerned its leadership was with the untenable position of a neutralist stand on Palestine. Said David Sher: "The failure of the American Jewish Committee to speak either for or against the Jewish Commonwealth resulted in a virtual declaration of war upon the Committee by the Zionists." Therefore, a more "affirmative" policy, similar to the one followed by the B'nai B'rith, was held to be unavoidable.

53. See *NP,* November 12 and December 24, 1943, and January 21, 1944, pp. 105, 171, and 210, respectively; ESCO Foundation for Palestine, *Palestine: A Study of Jewish, Arab, and British Policies* (New Haven, 1947), pp. 1092–94; *CJR,* VI, No. 6 (December 1943), 635; VII, No. 1 (February, 1944), 67; Press Releases of I. L. Kenen (American Jewish Conference), October 24 and November 18, 1943; *The Conference Record,* January 15, 1944, pp. 6–7. The Progressive Order of the West further rebuked the Committee and affiliated with the Zionist Organization of America. For Zionist efforts to secure these withdrawals, see Minutes of ZOA Executive Committee, November 16, 1943.

54. Waldman, *Nor by Power,* pp. 271–72.

55. AJC, *Thirty-seventh Annual Report,* pp. 22–23, 40, 42. Compare the revised by-laws on pp. 147 ff. with the more restrictive membership provisions in *Thirty-sixth Annual Report,* pp. 121 ff. Despite this move, however, the Committee was still weak in numbers by 1945 when the ZOA alone totalled over 135,000 members. At that time, the Committee had 450 corporate members and 21 local chapters with 2,080 members, but it also received financial support from the Joint Defense Appeal to which 20,104 individuals and 600 local Jewish community agencies contributed in 1944–1945; see *AJYB,* XLVII (1945–46), 566 and note 5, above. The AJC's membership growth came later: from 33 chapters and 9,000 members in 1947 to 38 chapters and 26,000 members in 1957. See AJC, *Proceedings . . . ,* p. 166.

56. AJC, *To the Counsellors of Peace,* pp. 7–8.

57. *REP-HEAR,* pp. 276–77.

58. Cf. Proskauer's statements in *Committee Reporter,* March, 1944, pp. 1, 7–8, and *A Segment of My Times,* p. 211.

59. *Committee Reporter,* March, 1944, p. 2.

60. Waldman, *Nor by Power,* p. 273.

61. F. D. R.'s October 15 message to the ZOA's national convention read in part: "I know how long and ardently the Jewish people have worked and prayed for the establishment of Palestine as a free and democratic Jewish commonwealth. I am convinced that the American people give their support to this aim; and if reelected I shall help to bring about its realization." Dewey made an equally forthright promise three days earlier. Texts in *NP*, October 27, 1944.

62. Waldman, *Nor by Power*, p. 275.

63. Letter in *CZA*, Z4/14773.

64. "An Exchange of Letters," *The Conference Record*, April, 1945, pp. 2, 4; and *IJPS*, March 2, 1945, pp. 5–6.

65. *Committee Reporter*, March, 1945, p. 2 (my italics). The AJC's Committee on Peace Problems, after analyzing various plans for Palestine, similarly stressed that a Jewish commonwealth was not foreseeable in the near future and, therefore, a "common denominator" for Zionist and non-Zionist action might be found, *if* only the Zionists would drop their demand for the immediate establishment of a Jewish commonwealth; AJC, *Proposed Plans on the Future of Palestine* (New York, 1944), p. 36; and *To the Counsellors of Peace*, p. 87.

66. For examples of the Zionists' continuous attack on the Committee, see "A Statement on Recent Activities of Certain Minority Groups," *The Conference Record*, December 1945, pp. 11–12; Ludwig Lewisohn, "An Emigré Zionist Speaks Out," *NP*, March 3, 1944, pp. 292–93; Daniel Frisch, "The Layman on Minority Rule: The Story of the Long Misrepresentation and Betrayal of Our Interests by the American Jewish Committee," *NP*, May 18, 1945, pp. 201–203; "Whither the American Jewish Committee," *REC*, February 7, 1941, pp. 4–5; Milton Steinberg, "Commentary Magazine," in his *A Believing Jew* (New York, 1951), pp. 136–65; and others in *CZA*, Z5/1136.

67. *LAJC* and *CZA*, Z5/400. At about the same time, the AZEC's Washington office attempted to induce influential non-Zionists, like Judge Samuel Rosenman and Rabbi Louis Gerstenfeld, to have the AJC and even the American Council for Judaism, cooperate in a large-scale program of Palestinian immigration; see file Z5/400 in *CZA*, particularly report of Dr. Benjamin Akzin, November 14, 1945.

68. See AJC, *In Peace and Dignity* and *Toward Peace and Equity: Recommendation of the American Jewish Committee* (both New York, 1946), especially pp. 8, 109–37. Note also the Committee's large advertisements in *NP*, offering free copies of Proskauer's appeal for "The Opening of Palestine." The ad clearly implies that the Committee is a reliable friend of the Zionist movement (issue of April 12, 1946, p. 6).

69. On Proskauer's political activities in this period, see *LAJC* and *CZA*, Z5/421 as well as *A Segment of My Times*, pp. 238–60; *JTA*, August 20, 1946, p. 4; and *Palcor*, August 20, 1946, pp. 2–3.

70. Minutes, American Section of the Executive of the Jewish Agency, January 22, 1948, in *CZA*, Z5/421.

71. Proskauer, *A Segment of My Times*, p. 260. For recent official views of the Committee's pro-Israel activities, see *Of Freedom and Faith: Viewpoint*

and *Program of the American Jewish Committee* (New York, 1956), and *The American Jewish Committee—What It Believes and What It Does* (New York, 1954).

72. *LAJC* and *CZA*, Z4/15072.

73. Eli Ginzberg sees this motive as a more basic determinant of Jewish organizational rivalries than the much-debated "ideological principles" usually tendered as explanations of conflicts; see his *Agenda for American Jews* (New York, 1950), p. 81.

74. Staff paper in *LAJC*.

75. Samuel Dinin, *Zionist Education in the United States* (New York, 1944), p. 64.

76. *Jewish Life in Our Times* (New York, 1943), p. 132. See also, Rufus Learsi (pseud.), *The Jews in America* (Cleveland, 1954), p. 347; Abram L. Sachar, "B'nai B'rith," *Current History*, LI (April, 1940), 24–27, 60; and Howard M. Sachar, *The Course of Modern Jewish History* (Cleveland, 1958), pp. 529–30. Although B'nai B'rith was never officially critical of Zionism, see the negative, unsigned report of the First Zionist Congress, in *The Menorah*, XXIII, No. 3 (September, 1897), 129–37.

77. Bernard Postal, *This is B'nai B'rith, A Book of Facts* (Washington, 1943), pp. 24–27, 60, 123–25; and Mrs. Henry Monsky and Maurice Bisgyer, *Henry Monsky: The Man and His Work* (New York, 1947), pp. 139 ff. World Zionist Organization President Chaim Weizmann, a founder of B'nai B'rith in Manchester, England, listed additional pro-Palestine acts of the organization—"the things which Zionists remember with gratitude when they think of B'nai B'rith"—in an address before the 1941 triennial convention (*ibid.*, p. 127). Note also that succeeding presidents of the ZOA —Rabbis Wise, Goldman, Levinthal, Goldstein, and Silver—were all leading members of the B'nai B'rith.

78. See *B'nai B'rith Magazine*, XLVII, No. 3 (December, 1932), 66–67 and Maurice Samuel's "Prosperity in Palestine," *ibid.*, pp. 68–70, 95.

79. *Ibid.*, XLVIII, No. 2 (November, 1933), 58, and XLVIII, No. 5 (February, 1934), 156.

80. See *Proceedings* of the Fourteenth General Convention of the Constitution Grand Lodge (Supreme Lodge) (Washington, 1935), pp. 73–75; *B'nai B'rith Magazine*, XLIX, No. 5 (February, 1935), 168–69.

81. *B'nai B'rith Magazine:* XLIX, No. 10 (July, 1935), 354 and L, No. 1 (October, 1935), 3; Meyer F. Steinglass, "Palestine Unites American Jewry," L, No. 6 (March, 1936), 186, 195, 213–14; LI, No. 2 (November, 1936), 44; LI, No. 3 (December, 1936), 74 and 92–93 ("The Whole Country is Talking About B'nai B'rith's $100,000 Gift to Palestine"); LI, No. 4 (January, 1937), 115; LI, No. 5 (February, 1937), 146–47 and LI, No. 6 (March, 1937), 179. See also the ZOA's grateful reaction to B'nai B'rith's support in *NP*, February 14, 1936, p. 3; October 23, 1936, pp. 1, 6; November 6, 1936, p. 6.

82. *B'nai B'rith Magazine*, LII, No. 1 (August–September), 1937, 18. The organization's Anti-Defamation League was also conspicuously concerned about the effects of a Jewish state upon the status of American Jewry. See Fireside Discussion Group of the Anti-Defamation League, *Previewing the Jewish State* (Chicago, 1937).

83. *B'nai B'rith Magazine,* LIII, No. 3 (November, 1938), 99.
84. See Edward E. Grusd, "Welcome, Dr. Chaim Weizmann," *ibid.,* LIV, No. 6 (February, 1940), pp. 164–65; Postal, *This is B'nai B'rith,* p. 125; and *CJR,* II, No. 2 (March–April, 1939), 181.
85. *Proceedings* of the Sixteenth General Convention of the Constitution Grand Lodge (Supreme Lodge) (Washington, 1941), pp. 40–43. Consult also, *NP's* glowing testimonial to Monsky's leadership on B'nai B'rith's one-hundredth birthday, November 6, 1942, p. 5.
86. *B'nai B'rith Magazine,* LVII, No. 7 (March, 1943), 217–18, 231–32; and Monsky and Bisgyer, *Henry Monsky* . . . , pp. 34–38, 86 ff.
87. *B'nai B'rith Magazine,* LVIII, No. 2 (October, 1943), 80.
88. *Ibid.,* p. 43. Monsky's personal views on a Jewish commonwealth were never in doubt, for the *B'nai B'rith Magazine* had earlier published his telegram to the Emergency Committee for Zionist Affairs on the occasion of the 25th anniversary of the Balfour Declaration: ". . . let us reconsecrate ourselves to the winning of the war, followed by a full realization of the intent of the Balfour Declaration, namely, a Jewish commonwealth in Palestine," LVII, No. 4 (December, 1942), 114.
89. *The Conference Record,* June, 1944, pp. 2–3; *Summary of the Seventeenth Convention, Supreme Lodge* (Washington, 1944), pp. 30–35. An editorial in B'nai B'rith's *National Jewish Monthly* of the same month gives further justification for remaining in the Conference and participating in a common program of action while not officially endorsing a commonwealth, "an ideological concept." Cf. *IJPS,* June 16, 1944, p. 5.
90. *Thirty Years of American Zionism,* I, 51. Lipsky continues to relate the stages in the Congress' formation—"the most interesting struggle American Zionism went through in all its history" (I, 51–58). Cf. also Lipsky's "Early Days of American Zionism (1897–1929)," in *PYB,* II (1946), 447–88.
91. *UJE,* I, 247–50. See also, Rabbi Stephen Wise's autobiography, *Challenging Years* (London, 1951), Chapter X; Learsi, *Jews in America,* p. 278; Pilch, *Jewish Life in Our Times,* pp. 124–25; Bernard G. Richards. "Is United Jewish Action Possible?", *REC,* December 30, 1938, pp. 13–16; and Justine Wise Polier, "The American Jewish Congress," in Schneiderman, *Two Generations* . . . , pp. 259–74.
92. The Executive Committee of the Congress in the late twenties included such nationally-known Zionist leaders as Louis Lipsky, Gedalia Bublick, Abraham J. Feldman, Abraham Goldberg, Solomon Goldman, Max Heller, Isaac Hamlin, Mordecai M. Kaplan, B. L. Israel, and Louis Levinthal, William B. Lewis, Hugo Pam, Bernard A. Rosenblatt, Emanuel Neumann, Morris Margulies and Elihu D. Stone, to mention but a few. This pattern of Zionist-Congress overlapping has continued until the present day. Concerning this point, see the letter of Chicago Rabbi S. Felix Mendelsohn who complained that the ZOA was constantly being drained of its best workers by the programs undertaken by Congress. Rabbi Mendelsohn proposed a merger of the two organizations since virtually every Congress member was a loyal Zionist; *REC,* April 2, 1943, p. 20.
93. Congress membership figures are not readily available, although in the

nationwide elections of June 25–27, 1938, held in connection with the meeting of the World Jewish Congress Executive, 698, 993 Americans paid a registration fee and 351,674 actually voted. On the basis of these elections, 550 delegates representing Jews in thirty states convened in New York on the following October 29–31; *UJE*, I, 252, and *CJR*, I, No. 1 (September, 1938), 59.

94. See American Jewish Conference, *A Survey of Facts and Opinions* (New York, 1943), pp. 114 ff. and *AJCOP*, p. 361 and *AJCOP* (Second Session), p. 361

95. See, for example, issues of December 12, 1935, p. 2; December 18, 1942, p 13; May 29, 1942, pp. 13–14, 19–21; December 6, 1946, pp. 4–5. Cf. also *The Conference Record*, July, 1944, p. 3; and *Resolutions on Palestine* of the "War Emergency Conference of the World Jewish Congress" (Atlantic City, November 26–30, 1944): "The War Emergency Conference of the World Jewish Congress associates itself with the program of the Jewish Agency for Palestine and its claims that . . . there must be a definitive and permanent termination of the national homelessness of the Jewish people by the establishment of Palestine as a Jewish Commonwealth.

"This Conference urges the British Government to abrogate the policy set out in the White Paper of 1929 and to open Palestine to unrestricted Jewish immigration and resettlement.

"This Conference appeals to the United Nations to ensure that the general scheme of post-war reconstruction shall include the establishment of Palestine as a free and democratic Jewish Commonwealth and that appropriate public financial aid and other resources be provided for that purpose, including the speedy transfer to Palestine of all Jewish survivors of Nazi persecution who desire or need to have part in the rebuilding of the Jewish National Home."

96. See Mildred G. Welt, "The National Council of Jewish Women," in *AJYB*, XLVI (1944–45), 59. The delegates' action was popularly endorsed by the next convention of the Council; report in *CJR*, VII, No. 1 (February, 1944), 67.

97. Hook, *The National Council of Jewish Women on the Present-Day Jewish Scene* (New York, 1946), pp. 14–18.

98. See *JS*, XX, No. 1 (January, 1955), 6–7.

CHAPTER 6

1. C. Bezalel Sherman, *Three Centuries of Growth: The American Jewish Community Today* (New York, 1954), p. 25.

2. *JP-PP*, II (1948); J. C. Rich, "The Jewish Labor Movement in the United States," 399–430; Raphael R. Abramovitch, "The Jewish Socialist Movement in Russia and Poland (1897–1919)," 369–98; IV (1955): Abraham Menes, "The Jewish Labor Movement," 334–90; Max D. Danish, "The Jewish Labor Movement: Facts and Prospects," 391–410; Will Herberg, "Jewish Labor Movement in the United States," *AJYB*, LIII (1952), 3–74; Henry Cohen, "Crisis and Reaction," *American Jewish Archives*, V, No. 2 (June, 1953), 73. The ideological and political conflict between Bundists

and Zionists is treated in Melech Epstein, *Jewish Labor in U.S.A., 1882–1952* (New York, 1950), II, 305–306; Basil J. Vlavianos and Feliks Gross (eds.), *Struggle for Tomorrow: Modern Ideologies of the Jewish People* (New York, 1954), Chapter VIII; David Wertheim, "Poale Zion Organization," *PYB*, II, (1945–46), 392; Harry Rogoff, *An East Side Epic* (New York, 1930), Chapter XVII; and A. L. Patkin, *The Origins of the Russian-Jewish Labour Movement* (Melbourne, 1947).

3. Cited in C. Bezalel Sherman, "Secularism and Religion in the Jewish Labor Movement," in Theodore Friedman and Robert Gordis (eds.), *Jewish Life in America* (New York, 1955), p. 110. See also Sherman's "Nationalism, Secularism and Religion in the Jewish Labor Movement," *Judaism*, III, No. 4 (Fall, 1954), 355.

4. "Foreword" to Samuel Kurland, *Cooperative Palestine, The Story of the Histadrut* (New York, 1947), p. xiv.

5. Sherman, in Friedman and Gordis, *Jewish Life . . .* , p. 114. Sherman's explanation of early Jewish union instability corroborates Martin Kriesberg's study of Catholic reactions in Communist-dominated unions: "Cross Pressures and Attitudes: A Study of the Influence of Conflicting Propaganda on Opinions Regarding American-Soviet Relations," *Public Opinion Quarterly*, XIII, No. 1 (Spring, 1949), 5–16. See David Truman's explication of the disruptive effects of "overlapping membership" in *The Governmental Process* (New York, 1953), pp. 156 ff.; J. B. S. Hardman, "Jewish Workers in the American Labor Movement," *YIVO Annual of Jewish Social Science*, VII (1952), 229–54; Selig Perlman, "Jewish-American Unionism, Its Birth Pangs and Contribution to the General American Labor Movement," *PAJHS*, XL, No. 4 (June, 1952), 297–337.

6. Dates of these events are variously stated in available sources. Melech Epstein, for example, gives June, 1910, as the founding date of the Farband while *AJYB*s cite the year 1912. The best short treatment of this anti-Zionist and Jewish socialist milieu is C. Bezalel Sherman, "The Beginnings of Labor Zionism in the United States," in Isidore S. Meyer (ed.), *Early History of Zionism in America* (New York, 1958). See also Harry J. Kahn, *Fifty Years of Poale Zionism in America* (New York, 1953) and Yiddisher Kempfer, *History of the Labor Zionist Movement in North America* (2 vols.; New York, 1955) (Yiddish).

7. A Jewish Workers' Congress, held in New York in February, 1917, representing all wings of Jewish labor, reportedly "almost" adopted a resolution approving Zionist aspirations in Palestine. Upon the resolution's defeat, the Labor Zionists withdrew and staged their own Congress for Palestine (Epstein, *Jewish Labor in U.S.A.*, p. 66).

8. Sherman, *Three Centuries of Growth . . .* , p. 26.

9. Louis Lipsky, *Thirty Years of American Zionism* (New York, 1927), I, 211.

10. Epstein, *Jewish Labor in U.S.A.*, pp. 253–58 and Melech Epstein, *The Jew and Communism, 1919–1941* (New York, 1959), Chapter XXXVII.

11. See *Report of the Executive of the Zionist Organization Submitted to the Nineteenth Zionist Congress at Lucerne, 1935*, p. 249: ". . . [through the *Gewerkschaften* campaign] the party succeeded in penetrating to the organized Jewish bodies and enlisting the co-operation of their leaders for

the movement. The great Labour Order "Arbeiter-Ring," which was formerly dominated by elements inimical to Zionist and Palestine, is now actively participating in the campaign for a working Palestine."

12. Kurland, *Cooperative Palestine*, p. 50; Samuel Dinin, "Zionist and Pro-Palestine Activities," *AJYB*, XLVI (1944), 185; Isaac Hamlin, "National Labor Committee for Palestine," *PYB*, I (1944–45), 440–43.

13. Poale Zion–Zeire Zion claimed 5,000 members in 1930 and 20,000 in 1945. Its auxiliary, Pioneer Women's Organization, enlisted 3,000 and 16,000 members in comparable periods. Farband grew from 5,036 members in 1917 to 26,570 in 1946. See Epstein, *Jewish Labor in U.S.A.*, pp. 269–71; *CW*, December 10, 1943, pp. 4–5; and my Appendix V.

14. Louis Brandeis, Albert Einstein and a host of eminent American business-men were captured by the idealistic appeal of Labor Palestine, while the Reform and Conservative rabbinate was deeply impressed by the "Social Justice" ideals of Labor Palestine. See Epstein, *Jewish Labor in U.S.A.*, pp. 409–11; Kurland, *Cooperative Palestine*, pp. xv–xvi; and *The Rabbis of America to Labor Palestine* (New York, 1935).

15. *UJE* (New York, 1939), VI, 133. One estimate of Jewish Labor strength, attributed to Will Herberg, listed 125,000 Jews in the ILGWU; 100,000 in the Amalgamated; 75,000 in fraternal societies, and over 100,000 in other unions during 1945 (document in *LAJC*).

16. "This Is Our Home" Series, No. 2. See also, Samuel Koenig's sociological study of Stamford, Connecticut; the 65 members of the local Workmen's Circle branch were mostly small businessmen and practically all were aged, first generation immigrants. Many of these persons simultaneously belonged to the local Poale Zion group. In Isacque Graeber and Steuart H. Britt (eds.), *Jews in a Gentile World* (New York, 1942), p. 225.

17. See the article on the JLC in *UJE*, VI, 133, and Epstein, *Jewish Labor in U.S.A.*, pp. 258 ff. and 402 ff.

18. Cf. Abraham G. Duker, *Jewish Survival in the World Today* (New York, 1941), Part III-B, p. 13; Samuel Dinin, "Reflections on Jewish Community Organization in the United States," *REC*, June 3, 1938, p. 9; Koenig, in Graeber and Britt, *Jews in a Gentile World*, p. 225; Samuel Dinin, *Zionist Education in the United States* (New York, 1944), p. 66. Also note a typical Zionist allusion to the Bundist nature of the Workmen's Circle and the Labor Committee in "The Die-Hard Bundists," *CW*, June 6, 1941, pp. 4–5. Commenting on a noncommittal resolution adopted by the 1941 Workmen's Circle convention, *CW* blamed the group's hesitancy vis-à-vis Zionism to the recent arrival of Bundist refugees from Poland, who, like their Agudist brethren, were setting the American clock backwards since they "had not receded one step from their Marxian orthodoxy of forty years ago and refuse to reckon with the new world realities."

19. *JTA*, December 15, 1943, p. 2.

20. *AJCOP*, pp. 41–42; and "Harbinger of Unity," *CW*, May 28, 1943, pp. 3–4 The Committee qualified its support for the Conference, however, by failing to participate in the community-wide elections and by limiting its role to the sending of sixteen organizational delegates.

21. *AJCOP*, pp. 94–95.

22. *Ibid.*

23. *Ibid.*, p. 279. At about the same time, Nochum Chanin, General Secretary of the Workmen's Circle, was quoted as saying: "Some members of the Socialist Bund have been opposed to Zionism as an absolutely harmful ideal. I never held that view. I was among those who considered it absolutely impossible of realization. Today I am ready to strike out the word 'absolutely.'" ("A Non-Zionist Looks at Israel," *American Israel Review*, I, No. 1 [December–January, 1957–58].)

24. See "Collective Jewish Responsibility," *CW*, November 19, 1943, pp. 5–6; "The Labor Committee's Decision," *CW*, December 10, 1943, pp. 3–4; and *Conference Record*, January 15, 1944, p. 5. *Conference Record* states that the vote was 45 to 38 in favor of full participation in the Conference.

25. *A Declaration by The American Jewish Trade Union Committee*. Note also Zaritsky's testimony before the House Committee on Foreign Affairs, *REP-HEAR*, pp. 236–38. Citing AFL and CIO resolutions, Zaritsky concluded: "In short, American organized labor—12,000,000 strong—unreservedly and unequivocally supports the aspirations of the Jewish people for the establishment of their homeland in Palestine."

26. The record of the JPFO's admission may be found in *AJCOP* (Second Session), pp. 281–304.

27. *Ibid.*, pp. 287–88.

28. *Ibid.*, p. 302. See the Conference Interim Committee's "Statement on the Withdrawal of the Jewish Labor Committee," January 12, 1945, in *Conference Record*, January, 1945, pp. 4–5.

29. See, for example, "Misrepresenting Jewish Labor," *CW*, April 27, 1945, pp. 4–5; and Zev Baumgold, "Jewish Neutrality on Palestine," *Furrows*, III (June, 1945), 13–15. The "holdout" of the ILGWU was reportedly due to the Bundist ideology of its president, David Dubinsky. But Dubinsky's biographer, Max D. Danish, paints a picture of rapid pro-Palestine personal development in *The World of David Dubinsky* (Cleveland, 1957), pp. 273 ff.

30. Long aloof from Zionism, Hillman was shocked by the loss of half his family in Nazi extermination centers and horrified by a visit to German crematoria and D.P. camps. Thereafter, he devoted much of his last two years of life to the establishment of the Jewish state; his entreaties to President Truman were very favorably received by the White House, according to Hillman's biographer. See Matthew Josephson, *Sidney Hillman, Statesman of American Labor* (Garden City, N.Y., 1952), pp. 642, 657

31. "Misrepresenting Jewish Labor," *CW*, April 27, 1945, pp. 4–5.

32. Letter from Perlow to Louis Lipsky, Chairman of the Conference Interim Committee, March 22, 1945, in *CZA*, Z5/1022.

33. *CZA*, Z5/1022.

34. Learsi, *Jews in America*, p. 319.

35. See *Acts and Pronouncements of the American Federation of Labor on Palestine and the Jewish Race* (New York, 1938); *JTA*, October 15, 1942, p. 4; *NP*, November 6, 1942, p. 5; National Labor Committee for Palestine, *Report to American Labor* (New York, 1944); and C. Bezalel Sherman's

unpublished study of Zionism and American Labor read at the Herzl Institute's "Second Conference on the History of Zionism in America," New York, December, 1957.

36. See, for example, Philip Murray's statement before the House Committee on Foreign Affairs, in *REP-HEAR*, pp. 234–35. Lewis G. Hines, National Legislative Representative of the AFL, similarly supported the demands for a Jewish commonwealth, claimed that 6,500,000 AFL members approved the pro-Zionist Wright-Compton resolutions; *REP-HEAR*, pp. 149–50.

37. Epstein, *Jewish Labor in America*, p. 411. Epstein observes correctly that labor "used" Zionism just as Zionism "used" it. Labor leaders obtained broad audiences between national conventions by frequent appearances before Zionist groups, the JLC, *Gewerkschaften* campaign, and so forth, and simultaneously enhanced their prestige in much of the Yiddish press.

38. Reuben Fink (ed.), *America and Palestine* (New York, 1944), p. 67; and *AJCRIC*, p. 77. Louis Segal, General Secretary of the Jewish National Workers Alliance, solicited and received widespread political support for the Zionist movement from prominent non-Jewish labor leaders. A portion of his correspondence is in *CZA*, Z5/1034.

39. According to Earl Browder's unsubstantiated testimony before the Dies Committee on September 6, 1939, Jewish Communist party members numbered 2,500, or $2\frac{1}{2}$ percent of the total Communist party membership. Thus, the Jews were under-represented in the CPUSA relative to their proportion of the total American population, e.g., $3-3\frac{1}{2}$ percent. See *CJR*, II, No. 6 (November–December, 1939), 59; and Alexander S. Kohanski "Communist Propaganda for Jews: The New Line," *CJR*, II, No. 5 (September–October, 1939), 470–83.

40. P. 11. Reprint in Duker, *Jewish Survival in the World Today*, Source Book on Part III-B, pp. 13–15. Duker also reprints a speech on Zionism by Earl Browder delivered on June 8, 1936, along with reports of the anti-Jewish agitation fomented by the Jewish Section of the Palestine Communist party (pp. 15–18).

41. See C. Bezalel Sherman, *The Communists in Palestine: The Mufti's Moscow Allies* (New York, 1934), a documented record of CP participation in the Palestine riots; and Epstein, *The Jew and Communism*, Chapter XXVIII. Typical of the Zionist attacks on the Communists are the articles in *NP*, May 1, 1936, p. 4; May 15, 1936, p. 4; July 17, 1936, p. 7; *REC*, March 6, 1936, pp. 3–5, and June 26, 1936, pp. 7–13. The last mentioned article by Rabbi Ira Eisenstein ("Zionism and The Communists") is a Zionist refutation of the official line of The Jewish Buro's Paul Novick, whose pamphlets may be consulted as the authoritative position of American Communists. Cf. the fiery indictment of Communists by Albert Findley in the Trotskyite *Labor Action*, February 3, 1947, pp. 5–6: "Stalinism's Dirty Record on the Jewish Question."

42. Alex Bittelman, *Should Jews Unite?* (New York, [1943]), p. 14 (separately published English translation of Introduction to the Yiddish edition of Earl Browder's *Victory—After*). Bittelman was General Secretary of the *Morning Freiheit* Association, official Yiddish newspaper of the Jewish

Communists. Contrast this work with his *Palestine: What is the Solution?*
(New York, 1947), and *To Secure Jewish Rights: The Communist Position*
(New York, 1948), and see *NYT,* November 24, 1960, p. 15, on Bittelman,
"The Lenin of American Communism," and his expulsion from the Communist party.

43. *Should Jews Unite?* pp. 9, 13–14.

44. *The Jewish People Will Live On!* (New York, 1944), pp. 35–37, 47.

45. *IJPS,* July 30, 1945, pp. 6–7. Earlier, observers had detected a gradual
improvement in Communist attitudes toward Zionism; see Norman Bentwich, "Soviet Russia and Zionism, Mutual Sympathy Replaces Suspicion—
Each Marks Rebirth of a People," *NP,* April 16, 1943, pp. 11–12; Hertzel
Fishman, "Moscow and Jerusalem, Recent Events Reveal Striking Manifestations of a Reversal in Russia's Negative Policy Toward a Jewish
Palestine," *ibid.,* May 5, 1944, pp. 374–76, 386; Martin Ebon, "Communist
Tactics in Palestine," *Middle East Journal,* II, No. 3 (July, 1948), 255–69;
Irving Howe and Lewis Coser, *The American Communist Party: A Critical
History (1919–1957)* (Boston, 1957), pp. 342–43, 401 ff.; William Z. Foster,
History of the Communist Party of the United States (New York, 1952),
pp. 480–81.

46. For views of recent labor thinking about Israel and Zionism, see the
statements by Jacob Pat (executive secretary of the Jewish Labor Committee), "We Are One Camp," in *Forum for the Problems of Zionism,
Jewry and the State of Israel,* IV (Jerusalem, 1959), 195–98; and George M.
Harrison and Jacob S. Potofsky (of the AFL-CIO), *Ten Years of Progress
. . . A Report on Israel* (Washington, 1959).

CHAPTER 7

1. See Kurt Lewin, *Resolving Social Conflicts* (New York, 1948); Alvin W.
Gouldner (ed.), *Studies in Leadership* (New York, 1950), pp. 195–271; Sol
Liptzin, *Generation of Decision* (New York, 1958); and Eric Hoffer, *The
True Believer* (New York, 1958), p. 95.

2. On Herzl's view of negotiation with non-Jewish notables, see *Theodor
Herzl,* 1929 special edition of *NP,* especially 140. A vivid example of
Zionist exhortation to convert non-Jews to Zionism can be found in *NP,*
January 24, 1930, p. 52. An overt usage of Lewin's "reference group"
teachings is found in Arthur Lelyveld's "The Anti-Zionists Seize an Opportunity," *Student Zionist,* IV, No. 12 (December, 1946), 25.

3. For indications of Christian interest in Zionism before 1930, see Reuben
Fink (ed.), *The American War Congress and Zionism* (New York, 1919);
Isidore S. Meyer (ed.), *Early History of Zionism In America* (New York,
1958); Frank E. Manuel, *The Realities of American-Palestine Relations*
(Washington, 1949); Carl H. Voss, *The Palestine Problem Today* (New
York, 1946); Irwin Oder, "American Zionism and the Congressional Resolution of 1922 on Palestine," *PAJHS,* XLV, No. 1 (September, 1955), 35–47;
Selig Adler, "Whither U.S. Policy?" *CW,* October 22, 1956, pp. 7–9; Milton
Plesur, "The Relations Between the United States and Palestine," *Judaism,*
III, No. 4 (Fall, 1954), 469–79; M. Eskolsky, "America and Zion," *Palestine
and Middle East,* XVI (March, 1944), 44–46.

4. On the Federation's program and leadership, see *Pro-Palestine Herald,* January, 1932, and succeeding issues, and *Principles and Program of the Pro-Palestine Federation of America* (Chicago, [1931–32]). On Zionist contacts with leading Christians in this period, see *CZA,* Z4/3215 III.

5. Reuben Fink (ed.), *America and Palestine* (New York, 1944), pp. 58–59.

6. Letter to Israel Cohen in *CZA,* S25/237, dated January 29, 1934.

7. Text in *NP,* June 4, 1936, p. 9. Signatories included James F. Freeman, Episcopal bishop of Washington; Samuel Harden Church, president of Carnegie Institute; S. Parkes Cadman, president of the Union of Congregational Churches in America; Ivan Lee Holt, president of the Federal Council of Churches in America; Frederick B. Robinson, president of City College of New York; and others.

8. *NP,* September 11, 1936, p. 2.

9. *NP,* December 18, 1936, p. 1.

10. *CJR,* I, No. 2 (November, 1938), 71–72.

11. *Ibid.,* 73–75.

12. *CJR,* II, No. 2 (March–April, 1939), 84; U.S. *Congressional Record,* March 7, 1939, p. 2915 and May 25, 1939, p. 6167; *AJCOP* (Second Session), p. 298.

13. *NP,* May 15, 1942, pp. 13–14. The same issue (p. 9) carries an article by Samuel I. Feigin, "Zionism and American Intellectuals," appealing for more adequate public relations with the academic world. One indication of anti-Zionism on the part of American intellectuals is the unpublished memorandum of the Council on Foreign Relations, "The New Zionism and a Policy for the United States," October 19, 1943. This document, classified "Confidential," circulated to a number of distinguished foreign-relations experts; in *CZA,* Z5/669. Other indications of Zionist work among intellectuals can be found in *CZA,* Z5/1175 and Z5/1213.

14. See *CZA,* S53/469a and S53/210b; "Zionist Public Relations Committees in Communities Throughout America," p. 3; *AJCRIC,* p. 75; Neumann's "Shall America Speak? The Importance of the American Palestine Committee and the Political Tasks of American Zionists," *NP,* March 28, 1941, pp. 10–11; *NP,* April 4, p. 25; *NP,* May 9, 8–10, p. 16.

15. AZEC, *A Report of Activities, 1940–1946,* pp. 7–8. A similar declaration was again submitted by Senator Wagner to the President on December 18, 1942.

16. Numerous relevant documents can be found in Fink's *America and Palestine.* See also congressional petition of 54 senators and 251 representatives to President Truman, July 2, 1945, in *AJYB,* XLVIII (1946), 228.

17. See the American Zionist Emergency Council's press books: *American Public Opinion on British Policy in Palestine; America Speaks on Palestine; The Balfour Declaration and American Interest in Palestine; Palestine in the Press; Press Book on the 1939 British White Papers on Palestine;* and *Press Book on Palestine Jewry's Contribution in the War Against the Axis* (New York, 1943–46).

18. Emergency Committee to Save the Jewish People of Europe, *Memorandum on the Findings of the Emergency Conference to Save the Jewish People of Europe* (New York, 1943), p. 2.

19. Note, for example, New Zionist Organization of America, *The American-British Convention on Palestine* (New York, 1944).
20. The Executive Committee of this clerical body included Carl H. Voss, Howard D. Warren, John W. Bradbury, Reinhold Niebuhr, James Luther Adams, Richard E. Evans, Daniel A. Poling, Paul Tillich, William F. Albright, Karl M. Chworowsky, S. Ralph Harlow, John Haynes Holmes, Leslie T. Pennington, Howell Paul Sloan, and Pierre van Paassen, in addition to its president, Henry A. Atkinson. See their testimony in *REP-HEAR*, pp. 192–94, 238–39. In 1946, the CCP merged with the APC to form the American Christian Palestine Committee. Howard M. LeSourd, on leave as Dean of the Graduate School at Boston University, was ACPC director, while officers included seven congressmen: Owen Brewster, James Mead, Arthur Vandenberg, Warren Magnuson, John McCormack, Joseph Martin, and Helen Douglas. Other committee members were Fiorello La-Guardia, William Green, Phillip Murray, Edgar A. Mowrer, Reinhold Niebuhr, Robert E. Smith, Ralph W. Sockman, Eduard C. Lindeman, Francis J. McConnell, Eric Johnston, Daniel Poling, Daniel L. Marsh, Sumner Welles, John H. Holmes, George B. Ford, Carl H. Voss, Dean Alfange, Ruth B. O. Rohde. Carl J. Friedrich and Walter Clay Lowdermilk were also among the prominent non-Jews who added their voice to the Zionist demand for a Jewish commonwealth; *REP-HEAR*, pp. 97–106 and 175–92, respectively. For an example of the Council's pro-Zionist literature see *Truth About Palestine* (New York, 1946). Note, also, the memorandum of the Emergency Committee for Zionist Affairs, "Palestine and the Arab World," June 17, 1941, which stressed to its Christian audience the "community of interest" between the Jews of Palestine and the Maronites and other Christians of Lebanon; the delegation of Christian religious leaders, led by Archbishop Athenagoras, which presented petitions of 500,000 Americans to the White House and Congress, *NYT*, August 30, 1944, p. 15; and the appeal of 5,000 Protestant ministers to Roosevelt, Churchill and Stalin; *NYT*, March 15, 1945, p. 11.
21. See "The Voice of Christian America," *Proceedings* of the National Conference on Palestine; and *AJCRIC*, pp. 75–77. The National Conference further voted to engage in continuing cooperation with the APC with a view toward adopting a common "program of action." Named to a committee for this purpose were Daniel Marsh, president of Boston University; Carl J. Friedrich, of Harvard; Norman Littell, assistant attorney-general of the United States; David Henry, executive vice-president of Wayne University; Daniel A. Poling, editor of the *Christian Herald;* Henry A. Atkinson, general secretary of the Church Peace Union and of the World Alliance for International Friendship; and two newspapermen. A larger conference, the "International Christian Conference for Palestine," was convened by similar sponsors on November 1–2, 1945. Delegates from 29 countries there established a "World Committee for Palestine" to cooperate with the APC and the Zionist movement. See *Proceedings* of the International Christian Conference for Palestine (Washington, 1945); *CZA*, Z5/399; and Carl H. Voss, "Christians and Zionism in the

United States," *PYB*, II (1946), 493–500; III (1947), 431–37, IV (1948), 413–23.

22. The Club Program Service of the APC and Christian Council, which supplied lecturers for thousands of colleges, churches, women's clubs, and others, invariably was able to obtain prominent Christian speakers for such local conferences; AZEC, *A Report of Activities, 1940–1946*, pp. 8–9, and "Report on Community Contacts Submitted to the Executive Committee of the American Zionist Emergency Council," May 15, 1944, pp. 1–2. Another technique employed by the APC was a collective agreement whereby ministers would simultaneously offer either sermons about Palestine (see the *Program* of the Greater New York Conference of the American Christian Palestine Committee, October 14–16, 1945) or a specially-written prayer for an end to Jewish suffering (see *A Suggestion for Memorial Sunday*, May 27, 1945).

23. A press release of AZEC, January 25, 1945, states these figures. A printed version of the *Petition*, issued earlier, contains about 1,600 signatures; see *JTA*, March 31, 1944, p. 1, May 17, 1944, p. 2.

24. The American Palestine Committee's *A Christian Point of View on Palestine* (New York, 1946), a portfolio of "exhibits testifying to Christian America's overwhelming support for a Jewish Commonwealth," was presented to the Anglo-American Committee of Inquiry in January, 1946. This document reprints many of the petitions and testimonials cited above.

25. See the Council's *Christian Opinion on Jewish Nationalism and a Jewish State* (Philadelphia, [1944]) and the Institute's *Papers on Palestine*, I and II (New York, 1945, 1947).

26. On anti-Zionism and the political struggle for Palestine, see Manuel, *The Realities of American-Palestine Relations*, pp. 214–15, 322–24, 341–42; and ESCO Foundation for Palestine, *Palestine: A Study of Jewish, Arab and British Policies* (New Haven, 1947), p. 1119.

27. On this point, see "Bases of Our Concern," *A Christian Point of View on Palestine*, p. 4; and Eric Goldman, *Rendezvous with Destiny* (New York, 1958), p. 171.

28. Memorandum from Waldman to leaders of the Committee, September 13, 1943, *CZA*, Z4/15072.

29. See previous note.

CHAPTER 8

1. Maurice Samuel, *Level Sunlight* (New York, 1953), p. 217, and cf. see Harry Golden, *For 2¢ Plain* (Cleveland, 1959), pp. 58–67.

2. Chaim Weizmann, *Trial and Error* (New York, 1949), p. 311.

3. Cited in Morris D. Waldman, *Nor by Power* (New York, 1953), p. 203. Concerning similar views and treatment of Zionist-non-Zionist relations in this period, see Charles Reznikoff (ed.), *Louis Marshall, Champion of Liberty* (Philadelphia, 1957), II, Chapter VII.

4. "Palestine—The Task of All Jewry," in Allied Jewish Campaign, *The Rebuilding of Palestine* (New York, 1930), p. 4.

5. Jacob de Haas, *Thirty Years After Herzl* (reprint from *Menorah Journal*, June, 1927), p. 15.
6. *Challenging Years* (London, 1951), p. 218.
7. January 10, 1941, pp. 3–4.
8. ZOA, *Thirty-second Annual Report*, in *NP*, June 21, 1929, pp. 542–43. The Agency alliance with non-Zionists also helped bolster Zionist confidence and repair long-aggravated internal relations. *NP*, July 19, 1929, for example, gives many indications of a greater acceptance of Zionist goals in American life. A speech of Rabbi Julius Morgenstern, President of the formerly anti-Zionist Hebrew Union College (Reform), was regarded as a significant symptom of growing Zionist "respectability." See also *NP*, May 2, 1930, pp. 267–68; and Ludwig Lewisohn, *This People* (New York, 1933), pp. 154–55.
9. See *NP*, December 14, 1934, p. 4 and January 4, 1935, p. 4; Stephen S. Wise, *As I See It* (New York, 1944), pp. 31–32.
10. The subject is treated in my Ph.D. dissertation, "American Zionism: The Building of a Political Interest Group" (St. Louis, Washington University, 1956), pp. 254 ff.
11. Zionist Organization and The Jewish Agency for Palestine, *Reports of the Executives Submitted to the Twenty-third Zionist Congress at Jerusalem, 1951* (hereafter *ZC 23*), p. 31, and Jewish Agency for Palestine, *Statistical Handbook of Jewish Palestine, 1947* (Jerusalem).
12. ZOA, *Thirty-eighth Annual Report*, pp. 5–6.
13. See *Proceedings* of National Conference for Palestine, especially pp. 6–7, 79; Zionist evaluation in *NP*, January 25, 1935, pp. 1–4; and ZOA, *Thirty-eighth Annual Report*, p. 6.
14. *NP*, November 1, 1935, pp. 1–2.
15. See "Jewish Press Deplores Passing of the U.J.A.," *ibid.*, pp. 1–2. For substantiation of these rumors, see the Philadelphia *Jewish World* editorial (reprinted in *NP*, November 15, 1935, p. 5) reporting that JDC Executive Director Rabbi Jonah B. Wise was disparaging the role of Zionism and Palestine and promoting his own anti-Zionist "pet projects" for Jewish resettlement in Ecuador and Birodidjan (U.S.S.R.). Cf. *NP*, November 15, 1935, p. 4 and "The New J.D.C.," *Congress Bulletin*, December 20, 1935, p. 2, which criticizes the JDC for its "strange absence of discussion," "undemocratic nature," and habit of treating Jewish affairs as if they were "the private projects of their leaders," all typical of Zionist attacks on the non-Zionist "social service barons" or *shtadlanim*.
16. *NP*, November 1, 1935, p. 1 and February 7, 1936, p. 4.
17. "Palestine and the Jewish Masses," January 25, 1935, p. 5. Cf. "Agreeing to Disagree," *Congress Bulletin*, November 1, 1935, p. 2 and Rabbi Paul Reich, *NP*, December 11, 1936, p. 6.
18. *NP*, February 7, pp. 1–4; February 14, p. 1; March 13, p. 8; April 3, p. 6; April 17, p. 4; April 24, p. 4; and May 1, pp. 1–2, all 1936.
19. *ZC 23*, p. 31.
20. Note the remarks of political Zionism's founder, Theodor Herzl, in his diaries:

Those who are all too well fed, whose imagination has been weakened by their comfortable lives, certainly do not yet wish to understand us. All the better are we understood by the poor and the needy; they have the imagination which grows out of suffering. . . . I wanted to get the poor together, in order to exercise pressure on the lukewarm and hesitant rich. . . . The Jews who are comfortable are, all of them, my enemies.

In *Theodor Herzl* issue of *NP* (1929), pp. 146–47, 166, and Federation of American Zionists, *The Congress Addresses of Theodor Herzl* (New York, 1917), p. 21.

21. Abraham G. Duker, "Structure of the Jewish Community," in Oscar Janowsky (ed.), *The American Jew: A Composite Portrait* (New York, 1942), p. 153 note.

22. See "Our Un-Jewish 'Leaders' " by "One Who Knows," in *REC*, June 7, 1940, pp. 12–15. The anonymous author, a professional communal employee, charged that in many communities "Every positive, constructive, traditional, specifically Jewish movment is handicapped or discouraged or throttled, and Zionism is the first victim for the very reason that it is too 'Jewish' " (p. 15). Cf. Joseph S. Shubow, "The New Totalitarianism," *NP*, April 25, 1941, pp. 7–8, 16. Similar conclusions are reached in Norman Miller's sociological study of an unidentified Jewish community: "The Lakeport Jewish community is not so much led as controlled by a moneyed oligarchy which is only vaguely responsive to the 'needs' and 'interests' of the individuals supposedly being 'served' " ("The Jewish Leadership of Lakeport," in Alvin Gouldner [ed.], *Studies in Leadership* [New York, 1950], pp. 195–227). More difficult to document is the role of professional Jewish social workers and non-Zionist organizational staff members in mapping non-Zionist policy. It would seem that many communal workers were culturally assimilationist in their Jewish values, while there were others who were consciously Communist-oriented negators of "Jewish peoplehood." Both of these groups were correspondingly anti-Zionist. Their role in guiding the policies of the local welfare funds, although it was of less importance than the role of the philanthropists, is nonetheless worthy of study.

23. Trachtenberg's examination of leadership in eight *major* national Jewish organizations revealed that 28 individuals occupied a total of 108 directorships, and four families held 31. One family occupied eleven directorships, another eight, and another seven. One man held seven posts (his wife held an eighth), another six, and four persons five positions each. All of these interlocking directorates were held by persons "conspicuously identified" with local federations and welfare funds. The implication drawn is obvious but instructive: the millions of dollars collected in the community for various causes were dispensed by the "arbitrary wishes" of a few wealthy individuals. See "Time to Talk Out," *REC*, June 12, 1942, pp. 8–15, and the suggestive analysis of non-Zionist social composition and power structure in Ben Halpern, "The American Jewish Committee," *JF*, X, No. 12 (December, 1943), 13–16; and Harry Schneiderman (ed.), *Two Generations in Perspective* (New York, 1957), pp. 114–17.

24. *NP*, March 20, 1936, pp. 1–4; April 3, 1936, p. 4; May 8, 1936, p. 4; June 25, 1937, p. 29.

25. *NP*, January 14, 1938, p. 4; entire issue of January 28, 1938; February 28, 1938, p. 6; and *ZC 23*, p. 31.

26. *NP*, January 14, 1938, p. 4.

27. *NP*, February 11, 1938, p. 4; April 8, p. 4; January 6, 1939, pp. 1, 4; January 20, pp. 1–6; February 24, p. 4; December 29, pp. 1–4; January 12, 1940, p. 4; and December 27, p. 13, contrasted with November 1, 1935, p. 1.

28. *Ibid.*, December 27, 1940, pp. 5–10; and *CZA*, S53/411. The successor of the National Refugee Service since 1947 has been the United Service for New Americans.

29. *NP*, December 27, 1940, p. 5. On popular pressure for Jewish unity, see *CZA*, S53/314, letter of Israel Goldstein to Henry Montor, May 14, 1945.

30. *NP*, December 27, 1940, p. 5.

31. January 10, 1941, p. 6. See also *CW*, January 10, 1941, pp. 3–4.

32. "Prelude to a Real Union," *CW*, January 17, 1941, p. 7.

33. *Ibid.*

34. *Ibid.*, p. 8; *NP*, December 27, 1940, p. 10; *CZA*, S53/314.

35. Abba Hillel Silver, "A Call to American Jewry," *NP*, January 3, 1941, p. 5.

36. Silver, "The Cause of Zion Must Not Be Minimized," *NP*, January 3, 1941, p. 5.

37. *NP*, January 3, 1941, p. 25. Silver's charges were substantiated by B'nai B'rith President Monsky, who simultaneously pledged that the 150,000 men and women of his nominally non-Zionist organization would give the UPA their "complete and unqualified support." See "Jewish Leadership in a Crisis," *NP*, January 3, 1941, pp. 15–18.

38. *NP*, January 3, 1941, p. 26. Silver also described other "undemocratic" efforts to "steam-roller" this plan into effect.

39. *NP*, January 3, 1941, p. 22. Other indications of the Zionist struggle to defeat the budgeting service may be found in *NP*, February 7, pp. 3–6; February 14, pp. 3–4; March 14, p. 4; March 28, p. 5; April 25, p. 3 and June 6, pp. 4–5, 13, all 1941.

40. "No Centralized Budgeting," *CW*, February 14, 1941, pp. 4–5. Cf. M. Z. Frank, "We, Democrats?" *ibid.*, pp. 6–7; Louis Lipsky, "Behind Budget Control," *ibid.*, February 21, 1941, pp. 7–9; Henry Montor, *A Minority Report on the Proposal to Establish a National Advisory Budget Service; PRAA*, VIII (1947), 18–19; Morton Berman, "Is American Jewry Losing Its Democracy?" *REC*, April 4, 1941, pp. 7–9. Not all Zionists opposed the budgeting service, however; see Elisha Friedman's position as reported in *JTA*, March 28, 1941, p. 4.

41. "Is J.D.C. Non-Political?" *CW*, February 28, 1941, p. 3.

42. According to Lipsky, Silver suggested this local referendum in order to avoid the "inevitable acceptance" of the budgeting service plan if it were submitted to the Board of Directors of the Council of Jewish Federations. "A Referendum of Big-Givers," *CW*, February 28, 1941, pp. 10–11.

43. Note the view of Rabbi Israel Goldstein in *ibid.*

44. *Ibid.*, p. 11.
45. See Henry Montor, "Democracy Takes the Count," *CW*, May 23, 1941, pp. 5–7; and Trachtenberg, *REC*, June 12, 1942, p. 12.
46. The exact relationship between "big givers" and non-Zionist organizations is difficult to assess, but Zionists generally believed the JDC capable of influencing the biggest donors, and vice versa. Cf. correspondence in *CZA*: Kurt Blumenfeld to Arthur Hantke, April 19, 1940: "the most important contributors are making promises to the Joint on a large scale provided that the money is not used for Palestine. . . . The Joint is supported by 200 well-to-do Jews. In New York half of the total income is contributed by 41 people"; and similar letters from George Landauer to Leo Lauterbach, January 3, 1940, S25/237; Nahum Goldmann to Eliezer Kaplan, October 25, 1940, S53/210. See also Philip Houtz, "Current Theories and Techniques in Fund-Raising," *JSSQ*, XVIII, No. 4 (June, 1942), 339–56; and Lawrence L. Blaine, "Failure of the Wealthy," *CW*, August 8, 1941, pp. 5–7. Houtz reported that in the New York Federation drive of 1940, 903 persons—less than 2 percent of all donors—gave 51.4 percent of the funds collected. Blaine's analysis revealed that numerous wealthy persons, including *New York Times* publisher Arthur Hays Sulzberger, publicly reduced their gifts to the New York City campaign because of unwillingness to support Palestinian projects. (Of the $638,020,496 collected by the UJA between 1941 and 1950, 65.6 percent was derived from local welfare funds, 27.3 percent from the UJA of greater New York, and 7.1 percent from other funds; *ZC 23*, p. 27.) A more contemporary view of this question is Maurice Taylor's "Jewish Community Organization and Jewish Community Life," *YIVO Annual of Jewish Social Science*, IX (1954), 179–204. In 1952, Taylor reports, 20.2 percent of the givers of $100 or more to 94 welfare funds contributed 90.3 percent of all monies collected.
47. *NP*, March 14, 1941, p. 16 and Louis Lipsky, "The Way to Communal Unity," *CW*, March 21, 1941, pp. 5–6.
48. See *The Zionist* (New York), March, 1941, p. 4; *REC*, March 21, 1941, pp 3–4. Only *CW* publicly regretted the "Happy Ending"; this "peace at any price" agreement was held to be harmful to the Zionist cause in the long run; March 14, 1941, pp. 4–5; and March 21, 1941, p. 4.
49. March 14, 1941, p. 4.
50. "Foreword" to Abba Hillel Silver, *Vision and Victory* (New York, 1949), pp. 1–2.
51. See David Ben-Gurion, "Zionist Policy Today," *NP*, January 17, 1941, pp. 7–8.
52. *NP*, January 31, 1941, p. 27.
53. *Ibid.*, p. 22. The Conference also endorsed other Zionist political goals, including the fight against the White Paper and the drive for a distinctively Jewish military force for service against the Nazis.
54. Drawn from ZOA, *Annual Reports;* letter to the author from Hadassah, June 4, 1956; and *Reports* of Executives of Jewish Agency to World Zionist Congresses. Of all funds allotted by federations for local purposes, 5.9 percent was earmarked for Jewish education in 1941, but ten years later more than 9 percent was devoted to the same purpose. See William

Avrunin, "Jewish Communal Developments: Perspective and Assessment," *JSSQ*, XXX, No. 1 (Fall, 1953), 1–8.

55. See *ZC 23*, p. 27; Arnold Gurin, "The Outlook for Financing Jewish Communal Services," *JSSQ*, XXIX, No. 1 (Fall, 1952), 15–23; *NP*, November 6, 1942, p. 34; and Arnold Gurin, "Impact of Israel on American Jewish Community Organization and Fund Raising," in *The Impact of Israel on the American Jewish Community* (New York, 1959). On philanthropy as "the dominant new form of communal allegiance," see Salo W. Baron, in Leo Schwarz (ed.), *Great Ages and Ideas of the Jewish People* (New York, 1956), p. 461.

56. *AJYB*, XLIX (1947), 137; L (1948), 141–42; 775–76; LI (1949), 176–81. Collections of the American Red Cross were $231,710,000 in 1945; $117,-641,000 in 1946; $57,530,000 in 1947; and $39,619,000 in 1948, while the American Cancer Society in the same period raised $4,292,000; $10,106,000; $12,126,000; and $13,221,000 (from *Annual Reports* and data supplied by the Comptrollers of these associations). Prominent non-Jews, too, gave generously to the UJA. John D. Rockefeller, Jr., for example, donated $100,000 in 1946. See *A Report to Members of the National Campaign Council of the U.J.A.*, March 12, 1946, p. 1.

57. These figures are composites of research reported in my Ph.D. dissertation, pp. 491–93, and charts. Note also that (1) over 100 separate fundraising campaigns for Israel were conducted between August and November, 1948, according to the Council of Jewish Federations and Welfare Funds; and (2) private American investments in Palestine in 1946 were also reported in excess of $45,000,000. See *AJYB*, LI (1949), 181; and AZEC, *Economic Aspects of American Interest in Palestine* (New York, 1946).

58. The source of Tables 15 and 16 is *Reports of the Executive Submitted to the Twenty-third Zionist Congress at Jerusalem, 1951*, pp. 28–29. Currently, United Israel Appeal, successor to the UPA, receives 67 percent of net UJA income up to the first $55,000,000 collected, and seven-eighths of all additional collections. Approximately 50 percent of the JDC's current spending is centered in Israel.

59. In the eyes of veteran Zionist leader Kurt Blumenfeld, Schwartz "makes the impression of a Zionist in disguise." Speaking fluent Hebrew and Arabic and well-versed in Palestinian affairs, Schwartz was regarded as unlike his "plutocratic employers" (letter by Blumenfeld cited in note 46).

60. See *U.S. Department of State Bulletin*, September 30, 1945, pp. 456–63; and related comments in President Harry S. Truman's *Memoirs* (Garden City, N.Y., 1955), II, Chapter X.

61. Staff documents advising AJC leaders on these themes may be seen in *LAJC* and *CZA, Z4/15072*.

62. David Brody, "American Jewry, The Refugees and Immigration Restriction (1932–1942)," *PAJHS*, XLV, No. 4 (June, 1956), 247. Brody documents the almost universal Jewish failure to attack the U.S.'s restrictive quota system in a period when European Jewry badly needed a refuge, but he

fails to distinguish Zionist from non-Zionist motivations for this silence. For it seems probable that many Zionists accepted, perhaps even "welcomed," the quota system as "proof" of their contention that only in a sovereign Jewish state could Jews be free of discrimination and, thus, control their own destinies.

CHAPTER 9

1. *The Governmental Process* (New York, 1953), pp. 129–39.
2. Federation of American Zionists, *The Congress Addresses of Theodor Herzl* (New York, 1917), pp. 11–12 (my italics).
3. For conspicuous examples of this policy, see Robert Szold, "An Economic Program; Toward an Accelerated Rebuilding of the National Home," *NP*, September 19, 1930, pp. 70–71; and similar articles in issue of October 3, 1930.
4. See the articles by A. Revusky and Benjamin Akzin in *ibid.*, March 27 and April 24, 1942, respectively, and ESCO Foundation for Palestine, *Palestine: A Study of Jewish, Arab and British Policies* (New Haven, 1947), pp. 1079–80.
5. Cf. Oscar Handlin, *Adventure in Freedom* (New York, 1954), p. 225; and Abraham G. Duker, "Efforts to Build an Over-All Jewish Body in the U.S.," *Conference Record*, July, 1947, pp. 5–7, 15. Duker argues (p. 5):

> The generalization is therefore in order that proposals for a central representative body of American Jews have been motivated by emergencies facing the Jewish people, rather than by the desire for a more efficient and democratic organization of American Jewry. . . . The establishment of central organizations as the authoritative representatives of the diaspora communities has been predominantly the result of outside pressure rather than voluntary action.

6. *NP*, issues of April 11, April 25, May 9, and May 16, 1941, pp. 3, 4–5, 5 and 5, respectively.
7. Abraham Goldberg, "Needed: A United Congress of American Zionists," *JS*, VI, No. 6 (June, 1941), 6–7. A similar appeal was made earlier by Louis Lipsky in "Why Not a Zionist United Front?" *CW*, May 23, 1941, pp. 10–12. Cf. also *The Zionist* (New York), December, 1941, pp. 14, 23, 55, 76.
8. Preliminary planning for a Zionist conference is reflected in the correspondence of Nahum Goldmann of the Jewish Agency in New York with his colleagues in Jerusalem (letter of September 18, 1941, to Eliezer Kaplan, in *CZA*, S53/210b). See also "Report of a meeting with Mr. [David] Ben-Gurion . . . Winthrop Hotel, New York City, December 5, 1940" (11 pp., typewritten), in files of AZEC. Present at this critical meeting were top leaders of American Zionism: Israel Goldstein, Nahum Goldmann, Louis Lipsky, Robert Szold, Mrs. David de Sola Pool, Stephen S. Wise, Abba Hillel Silver and Arthur Lourie.
9. *NP*, April 24, 1942, p. 4, stresses the independence of the various Zionist participants and notes that the Biltmore gathering was an "extra-legal body" whose resolutions would be effective only insofar as they proved

acceptable to the constituent organizations and the World Zionist Executive. Nevertheless, predicted *NP*, "the policy that the Conference adopts will have powerful moral force behind it."

10. *IJPS*, May 12, 1942, p. 5. Other speeches made by key Zionist leaders may be found in *NP*, issue of May 15, 1942, and "Minutes of the Extraordinary Conference of American Emergency Committee for Zionist Affairs, May 8–11, 1942," in *PYB*, III (1948), 424–26.

11. *IJPS*, May 12, 1942, p. 4 (my italics). See also ESCO, *Palestine: A Study . . .*, pp. 1079–87 and J. C. Hurewitz, *The Struggle for Palestine* (New York, 1950), Chapter XII, which place the Biltmore Platform in its international and Palestinian context.

12. Isaac Levitats, "Pro-Palestine and Zionist Activities," *AJYB*, XLV (1943–44), 207. Other evaluations of the Biltmore Conference are: "The Zionist Conference," *JF*, IX, No. 6 (June, 1942), 4–6; "The Zionist Quasi-Congress," *REC*, May 29, 1942, pp. 4–5.

13. Undated memorandum to Jewish Agency Executive in *CZA*, S25/237

14. May 15, 1942, p. 4. The titles of *NP* editorials are expressive of the "new look" in the ZOA following the Biltmore Conference: "The Need for Militancy," "The Need for Unity," "The Need for Disciplined Loyalty," pp. 4–5. Cf. also *ibid.*, issue of November 6, 1942, which argues that Zionism had "returned to Maximal, Herzlian, Statehood Zionism"; and comments in *JS*, VIII (November, 1942), 4–5; *REC*, November 13, 1942, pp. 3–4; *CW*, October 23, 1942, pp. 12–13.

15. See letter, Nahum Goldmann to Eliezer Kaplan, December 21, 1942, in *CZA*, S53/210a.

16. Zionist initiative in convening this meeting is demonstrated by letters of Nahum Goldmann to Eliezer Kaplan, December 21, 1942, January 11 and 28, 1943, in *ibid.* Cf. Mrs. Henry Monsky and Maurice Bisgyer, *Henry Monsky: The Man and His Work* (New York, 1947), pp. 34–38, 86 ff.

17. Letter, Arthur Lourie to L. Lauterbach, January 14, 1943, in *CZA*, Z4/10207 IV.

18. Text of this invitation may be found in *AJCOP*, p. 319.

19. *AJCOP* (Second Session) (New York, 1945), p. 179. At the same time, he characterized himself as "Henry Monsky, the Zionist" (p. 28).

20. *AJCOP*, pp. 323–26: Organizations participating in the Pittsburgh meeting are listed on pp. 320–21.

21. *Ibid.*, p. 18 and Monsky, *Toward a Common Program of Action* (Washington, 1943), p. 9.

22. *AJCOP*, pp. 20–21.

23. *Ibid.*, pp. 22–23.

24. *NP* declared that a "turning point had been reached in the long history of a divided American Jewish community." Lavish praise was also heaped on Monsky for his "historic leadership" (February 3, 1943, pp. 3–5). Records and correspondence related to the Conference may be found in *CZA*, Z5/764.

25. *AJCOP*, pp. 32–34, 324–26 and *Rules of Election for the American Jewish Conference* (April, 1943). The proposal to use proportional representation originated from a representative of the UAHC, not from the Zionists.

26. *AJCOP*, p. 40. Dr. Nahum Goldmann described the Pittsburgh Conference as "a complete success . . . more successful even than we had expected." Explaining that the Zionists had convened the meeting a week before the annual meeting (January 31) of the AJC, in the correct expectation that this would keep the dissension-torn Committee from being represented, Goldmann wrote: "It was the mistake of their life not to have participated, because with them absent, we took over the real leadership. Had they been there, they would have organized a non-Zionist bloc and even the B'nai B'rith would not have gone along with us 100%, as they did." (Letter to Eliezer Kaplan, January 28, 1943, in *CZA*, S53/210a.)

27. *AJCOP*, p. 41. See also, *Minutes, ZOA* Executive Committee, March 11, 1943, and April 1, 1943, in *CZA*, Z5/1220.

28. *AJCOP*, pp. 332–33. Waldman's remarks were circulated in a confidential memo. of September 13, 1943, in *CZA*, Z4/15072.

29. *AJCOP*, pp. 41–42, 328. Correspondence between Monsky and Jacob Pat, Executive Secretary of the JLC, may be found in *CZA*, Z5/750.

30. Nathan Schachner, *The Price of Liberty: A History of the American Jewish Committee* (New York, 1948), p. 147 and *AJCOP*, pp. 42–43.

31. See p. 201, above.

32. Document, dated May 7, 1943, in *LAJC*. See also *CZA*, Z5/752.

33. *AJCOP*, p. 44.

34. June 4, 1943, pp. 1A–2A.

35. Documents in *LAJC* and Schachner, *Price of Liberty* . . . , p. 148.

36. *AJCOP*, p. 46.

37. *Ibid.*, pp. 46–47. Critics of Zionism later ascribed numerous "devious effects" to this electoral procedure. Schachner, for example, states that the "bullet" system gave undue weight to candidates of organized supporters, most of whom were disposed favorably to Zionism. In this way, many acknowledged local leaders, such as those affiliated with the AJC or federations and welfare funds, were bereft of support and either refused to stand for election or were badly defeated (*Price of Liberty* . . . , p. 148).

38. *NP*, May 21, 1943, p. 8 (my italics).

39. *Ibid.*, p. 12. Cf. also the "Joint Zionist Statement on American Jewish Conference" by the three General Zionist groups, in *ibid.*, p. 20; *REC*, May 14, 1943, pp. 3–4; and "There Are No Neutrals," *NP*, June 11, 1943, pp. 3–4. In the *NP* editorial, Zionists were cautioned against electing delegates whose support of the Biltmore Program was of too recent origin. Rather, what was desired was the election of those "whose adherence to the Zionist cause is based on life-long conviction, not on sudden expediency." *CZA*, Z5/760 also mirrors Zionist preparations for the coming elections.

40. *AJCOP*, pp. 47–48, 62–63, 345–48.

41. ZOA, *Forty-sixth Annual Report*, p. 7. ZOA delegates included 24 members of their national Executive Committee. The General Zionist slate (ZOA, Hadassah, Order Sons of Zion) was promoted by an extensive use of leaflets, pamphlets, and full-page advertisements in both the Yiddish and Anglo-Jewish press.

42. July 16, 1943, p. 3. See also, *JS*, VIII (July, 1943), 4; *NP*, August 20, 1943, pp. 2, 5; and *CW*, June 18, 1943, entire issue.
43. *AJCOP*, pp. 48–49.
44. *Ibid.*, p. 50.
45. *Ibid.*, pp. 361–62.
46. See American Jewish Conference, *Survey of Facts and Opinions on Problems of Post-War Jewry in Europe and Palestine; Call of the Labor Zionist Movement to the Delegates to the American Jewish Conference;* and American Emergency Committee for Zionist Affairs, *The Zionist Position* (all New York, 1943), which contain numerous organizational policy declarations and expositions of Zionist aims presented to all Conference delegates. The President of the American Jewish Committee later characterized the Conference thus:

> The members of the conference were chosen by a most complicated system of local elections, which in my opinion clearly loaded the voting with a preponderant Zionist majority . . . long before the opening date it was obvious that the cards had been stacked, and that the Zionist majority intended to push through its program and endeavor to make it, if not legally binding perhaps, at least morally binding on *all* Jews in this country (Joseph M. Proskauer, *A Segment of My Times* [New York, 1950], p. 22).

47. Letter, Nahum Goldmann to Moshe Shertok, July 14, 1943, in *CZA*, S25/237.
48. See pp. 127 ff., above.
49. *AJCOP*, p. 74.
50. *Ibid.*, p. 75 (my italics). In an earlier address, Rabbi Stephen S. Wise had not urged the Conference to adopt the Biltmore Program of a Jewish commonwealth, but merely to denounce the discriminatory White Paper of 1939 (*ibid.*, p. 72).
51. Harold P. Manson, in notes for Silver, *Vision and Victory* (New York, 1949), p. 14.
52. Minutes, New York Jewish Agency Executive, July 12, 1943, in *CZA*, Z5/641 and see note 47 above; Goldmann's letter predicts that no controversial resolutions will be adopted, but merely that deliberative machinery will be established.
53. *AJCOP*, pp. 98–99.
54. *Vision and Victory*, p. 14.
55. *AJCOP*, pp. 100–101.
56. *Ibid.*, pp. 101–103. This speech was widely considered "responsible" for the subsequent passage of the Palestine Resolution. *B'nai B'rith Magazine*, LVIII, No. 2 (October, 1943), for example, reports that Silver's words shook the audience, causing one known anti-Zionist to turn to his fellow delegates and exclaim: "Boys, I'm a Zionist!" (p. 42).
57. *AJCOP*, pp. 131–33. Drafts of various negotiations and resolutions on Palestine may be found in *CZA*, Z5/775 and 771.
58. *AJCOP*, pp. 133–34.
59. *Ibid.*, pp. 134–35. An analytical treatment of the three resolutions may be found on pp. 136–39.

60. *Ibid.*, pp. 139–41

61. *Ibid.*, pp. 144–45.

62. *Ibid.*, pp. 167–69.

63. *Ibid.*, pp. 143–44.

64. *Ibid.*, pp. 145–46.

65. *Ibid.*, p. 158.

66. *Ibid.*, pp. 176–77. Earlier, a procedural resolution offered by Blaustein, which would have deferred any action on Palestine until a future session of the Conference, was decisively defeated (p. 176).

67. See pp. 121 ff., above.

68. *Nor by Power* (New York, 1953), p. 258.

69. Entire text of the resolution may be found in *AJCOP*, pp. 178–81.

70. *Ibid.*, pp. 279–80.

71. See Carl Alpert's report of the proceedings in *NP*, September 10, 1943, pp. 18–19; *B'nai B'rith Magazine*, XLVIII, No. 2 (October, 1943), 42–43, 80; and letters from Arthur Lourie, Emergency Committee for Zionist Affairs to L. Lauterbach, Jerusalem, September 2, 1943, in *CZA*, Z4/10207 IV; and Nahum Goldmann to Moshe Shertok, September 16, 1943, in *CZA*, S25/237.

72. *AJCOP*, pp. 280–81. A more forthright indictment of Zionist activities may be found in Proskauer's *A Segment of My Times*, pp. 200–204; and Schachner, *Price of Liberty* . . . , pp. 149–52.

73. September 24, 1943, p. 29. See also a leaflet issued by the ZOA in the same tone, entitled: *"Onward to Victory!" Jewish Commonwealth in Palestine Endorsed by United American Jewry; Forty-five Years of American Zionist Effort Culminate in Adoption of Resolution by Conference Representing 5,000,000 American Jews;* in *Palestine*, December, 1943, pp. 11–12; *CW*, September 24, 1943, pp. 5–11; October 8, 1943, pp. 5–6; December 10, 1943, p. 4; *JS*, IX (October, 1943), 5; Meier Steinbrink, "American Jewish Conference," *Liberal Judaism*, XI (December, 1943), 6–9, 57–60.

74. *NP*, October 8, 1943, pp. 49–50.

75. *The Jewish Dilemma* (New York, 1951), pp. 164–65. Other critical comment may be found in *NP*, September 10, 1943, pp. 15–17; and Rubin Saltzman, *The American Jewish Conference* (New York, 1943).

76. See *AJCRIC*, pp. 65, 86–88; *The Conference Record*, June, 1944, pp. 2–3, July, 1944, p. 3; and discussions in Chapter V, above.

77. *NP*, September 24, 1943, p. 20. Two years earlier, Benjamin Kaufman, National Commander of the JWV, had assured the forty-sixth annual convention of the ZOA that "there are no more ardent Zionists to be found than in our ranks" (*ibid.*)

78. See Joshua Trachtenberg, "Religious Activities," *AJYB*, XLVI (1944), 94. For earlier "neutrality" statements of the Union, see *Proceedings* of the Union, *Sixty-eighth–Seventieth Annual Reports*, pp. 108, 268; and *Liberal Judaism*, XI (June, 1943), 3–4.

79. *Proceedings* of the Union, *Seventy-first–Seventy-third Annual Reports*, p. 29.

80. *Ibid.*, pp. 20–30. For the debate among Zionists over this proposed compromise, see Minutes, Office Committee, AECZA, June 14, 1944, pp. 1–2.

81. Waldman's *Nor by Power*, p. 259; see pp. 245, 355 (note 114), above,

indicating why many Jews considered Finkelstein a captive of the rich Reform Jews who dominated the Board of Directors of the J.T.S.

82. In *Statement of the American Jewish Committee on withdrawal from the American Jewish Conference,* November 7, 1943, p. 6. This document also contains a long list of charges directed at the Zionists for their alleged perversion of the Conference. Cf. also Schachner, *Price of Liberty* . . . , p. 152; Waldman, *Nor by Power,* pp. 258–62; and Waldman's memo. of September 13, 1943, in *CZA,* Z4/15072.

83. See Interim Committee, *Statement of the American Jewish Conference on the Withdrawal of the American Jewish Committee;* press releases of ZOA, October 26, 1943; American Jewish Conference, October 24, November 18, 1943; and AZEC, October 28, 1943; in *CZA,* Z5/766.

84. *NP,* September 24, 1943, p. 4 (my italics).

85. Minutes of the delegation to the State Department, September 18, 1943, may be found in *CZA,* Z4/15391.

86. *NP,* p. 3; and November 12, 1943, p. 89.

87. See *AJCRIC,* pp. 4, 62.

88. *Ibid.,* pp. 66–68. Conference political plans for aiding the Zionist cause are revealed in I. L. Kenen's memoranda to the Palestine Commission, in *CZA,* Z5/1076.

89. *Ibid.,* pp. 68–77; and *REP-HEAR,* pp. 113, 274.

90. See the American Jewish Conference, *The Jewish Position at the United Nations Conference on International Organization* (New York, 1945) and *Statement Submitted to the Anglo-American Committee of Inquiry* (New York, 1946); and Mrs. Henry Monsky and Maurice Bisgyer, *Henry Monsky: The Man and His Work* (New York, 1947), pp. 38 ff. and 103 ff. In preparation for the San Francisco Conference, the American Jewish Conference and AZEC jointly sponsored 88 mass public rallies calling for a Jewish commonwealth. The largest of these attracted over 60,000 persons on April 29, 1945, in New York City. The more than two dozen Jewish organizational delegates who participated in UNCIO included eleven representatives of the American Jewish Conference and nine members of AZEC. They issued more than forty different statements in approximately 50,000 stencilled sheets in three languages to UNCIO delegates and the press corps. See Arthur Lourie, "Report on the San Francisco Conference," 1945 (mimeographed).

91. See *AJCOP* (Second Session), pp. 310–11. The resolution was approved with only one dissenting vote while the Union of American Hebrew Congregations abstained (*ibid.,* p. 143). On the Zionists' evaluation of the second session, see notes in *CZA,* Z5/1058.

92. The three major organizations unrepresented in the Conference in 1945— American Jewish Committee, Jewish Labor Committee, and Agudas Israel —supported all substantive claims of the Zionists and the Conference while refraining from the use of the phrase "Jewish commonwealth" as the preferred ultimate constitutional status of Palestine. See, for example, AJC, *To the Counsellors of Peace* (New York, 1945) and *The Problem of Palestine, A Review of Developments in 1945* (New York, 1946). See also,

the Conference's earlier attack on the American Council for Judaism in *AJCOP*, pp. 105, 276–78, 286–90.

93. See Truman, *The Governmental Process*, pp. 139–55, for a discussion of this point.

94. *Unity in American Judaism* (Cincinnati, 1945), p. 5.

95. See Herbert H. Hyman and Paul B. Sheatsley, "Some Reasons Why Information Campaigns Fail," in Daniel Katz and others, *Public Opinion and Propaganda* (New York, 1954), especially pp. 523–24.

96. *AJCOP* (Second Session), p. 194.

97. *REC* viewed the non-Zionist groups as "too frightened by popular resentment to leave the Conference, and so, although they remain within it, their collaboration with the work of the Conference is not one hundred percent active and genuine" (January 7, 1944, p. 3). Cf. also *CW*, January 14, 1944, pp. 3–4; and Israel Goldstein, "The American Jewish Conference," *NP*, November 17, 1944, p. 29.

CHAPTER 10

1. Stuart A. Queen, William N. Chambers, Charles M. Winston, *The American Social System: Social Control, Personal Choice, and Public Decision* (Boston, 1956), p. 147.

2. *Social Movements in the United States* (New York, 1956), p. 16. Also note Truman's similar point, cited on pp. 2–3, above.

3. See p. 16, above.

4. *The Governmental Process* (New York, 1953), p. 223.

5. See pp. 16–17, above.

6. See Inis L. Claude, Jr.'s excellent survey of Zionism in *National Minorities: An International Problem* (Cambridge, 1955), especially pp. 106–109.

7. Soltes believes that similar attitudes characterized the out-of-New York press, too. The 1950 reissue of this work again stressed the devotion of the Yiddish press to Zionist objectives by revealing that a content analysis of 1,500 editorials showed that Israeli questions were the most frequently treated theme (pp. xi, 18, 107).

8. Ben Edidin, *Jewish Community Life in America* (New York, 1947), p. 84. Julius Haber reports that the leading Yiddish newspaper, *The Day (Der Tag)*, was founded by Zionists in 1914 (*The Odyssey of an American Zionist* [New York, 1956], p. 149).

9. Isaac Imber in *NP*, March 21, 1941, pp. 11–12.

10. *PYB*, I (1945), 477–80 and Emanuel Neumann, "Memorandum on Coordination of Zionist War-Time Propaganda," November 19, 1940 (mimeographed). See *PYB*, IV (1949), 455–66.

11. *Report of the Executives of the Zionist Organization and of the Jewish Agency for Palestine Submitted to the Twelfth Zionist Congress . . . 1939*, p. 95; and Leon I. Feuer, "Report on Community Contacts Submitted to the Executive Committee of the American Zionist Emergency Council," May 15, 1944, p. 3.

12. ZOA, *Forty-seventh* and *Forty-eighth Annual Report*, pp. 25 and 33, re-

spectively. These figures compare with 5 percent of 2,000 newspaper columns printed in 1940–1941 (*NP*, September 5, 1941, p. 14).

13. ZOA, *Forty-seventh Annual Report*, pp. 32–33.

14. AZEC, *A Report of Activities, 1940–1946* (New York, 1946), pp. 10–11. Publications sold or distributed by AZEC in April, 1945, in addition to those already mentioned, included: Ephraim Broido, *Jews, Arabs and the Middle East;* Albert Einstein and Eric Kahler, *The Arabs and Palestine;* Arthur Lourie, *Britain and Palestine* and *The Facts About Palestine;* Dorothy Thompson, *I Speak Again as a Christian;* Louis D. Brandeis, *Brandeis on Zionism;* Ernst Frankenstein, *Justice for My People;* Pierre Van Paassen, *The Forgotten Ally;* Maurice Samuel, *Harvest in the Desert.* The API study is: Robert R. Nathan, Oscar Gass, and Daniel Creamer, *Palestine: Problem and Promise, An Economic Study* (Washington, 1946). In a similar vein, note ESCO Foundation for Palestine, *Palestine: A Study of Jewish, Arab, and British Policies* (New Haven, 1947). Particularly illuminating records of Zionist publicity efforts may be found in Minutes, AZEC Public Relations Committee, March 8, 1943 and April 5, 1944, in GZA, Z5/641, 867, 1207 and Z4/10207V. Zionist participation in promoting a "helpful" series of Nation Associates Inc. studies is documented in the latter archive file; see Nation Associates' 1) *Arab Higher Committee, Its Origins, Personnel and Purposes: The Documentary Record Submitted to the United Nations, May 1947;* 2) *British Record on Partition, As Revealed by British Military Intelligence and Other Official Sources: A Memorandum Submitted to the Special Session of the General Assembly of the United Nations, April, 1948;* 3) *Could the Arabs Stage an Armed Revolt Against the United Nations? Memorandum Submitted to the General Assembly of the United Nations, October, 1947;* 4) *Oil and the State Department Policy on Palestine: The Documentary Evidence of How ARAMCO Attempts to Destroy the Partition Resolution of the United Nations: Memorandum Submitted to the President of the United States, June, 1948;* 5) *Palestine: A Pattern of Betrayal; The Role of the United States, Great Britain, and the United Nations Since November 29, 1947;* 6) *Palestine Problem and Proposals for Its Solution: Memorandum Submitted to the General Assembly of the United Nations by Freda Kirchwey, President, The Nation Associates; Henry A. Atkinson, Secretary, The Church Peace Union; Raymond G. Swing; James G. Patton, President, Farmers Educational and Cooperative Union; Philip Murray, President, Congress of Industrial Organizations; Frank P. Graham, Chairman, Advisory Council, The Nation Associates; Frank Kingdom, Co-Chairman, The Progressive Citizens of America* (New York, 1947).

15. *A Year's Advance* (New York, 1944), p. 4. This report by Silver alludes to other Zionist public relations programs which, "because of their confidential nature," were not fully discussed. Cf. also Samuel Dinin's description of the work of the Zionist "Commission on Palestine Surveys," which enlisted Robert R. Nathan of the War Production Board, Oscar Gass of the Treasury Department, Louis Bean of the Bureau of the Budget, and Colonel Theodore B. Parker of the Tennessee Valley Authority in various economic surveys of Palestine's economic capacity; in *AJYB*,

XLVI (1944–45), 179–80; and *CZA*, Z5/313. On the political significance of this work, see also Ben Halpern, "Forecasting Palestine's Population: Statistical Anti-Zionism," *JF*, XIII, No. 3 (March, 1946), 38–41.

16. ZOA, *Forty-eighth Annual Report*, p. 15. A contrast to this record is provided by *NP*'s lament of February 7, 1930, that even Zionists were ignoring Jewish and Zionist books (p. 76).

17. See entire issue of *NP*, September 6, 1929; and ZOA, *Thirty-fourth Annual Report*, in *ibid.*, November 6, 1931, p. 42.

18. Records of some of these rallies, including lists of the principal speakers and resolutions enacted, may be found in *Mass Demonstration Against Hitler Atrocities*, July 21, 1942; *JTA*, January 25 and February 5, 1942, p. 4 and p. 2, respectively; *PYB*, I (1945), 370; April 30, 1945, p. 22; March 15, 1945, p. 11; July 15 and 16, 1946, pp. 5 and 9, respectively; April 5, 1948, pp. 1, 3; AZEC, *A Report of Activities, 1940–1946* (New York, 1946).

19. Minutes, ZOA Executive Committee, November 16, 1943.

20. AZEC, "An Outline of Activities for Local Zionist Emergency Committees," November 3, 1943, p. 6, issued in connection with a campaign to abrogate the White Paper. Cf. also "Memorandum of Instructions with Respect to Mass Demonstrations," March 22, 1943, in *CZA*, Z5/912.

21. ZOA, *Thirty-seventh Annual Report*, in *NP*, June 29, 1934, pp. 13–15 In 1936, too, the Zionist-produced motion picture, "The Land of Promise," was viewed by many thousands of people in a five-week run at New York's Astor Theater on Broadway and in gala theater parties in numerous other cities as well.

22. *Ibid.*, May 30, 1939, and subsequent issues of *NP* in 1939–40 which re ported the apparent success of the project.

23. United States Bureau of Census, *Census of Religious Bodies* (Washington, 1940), p. 16.

24. See pp. 106–107, above.

25. Samuel Dinin, *Zionist Education in the United States* (New York, 1944), p. 67. Similar claims were made by Jacob S. Golub in *Some Principles of Jewish Education* (New York, 1937), p. 1; Samuel Blumenfield, *Annual Report of the Department of Education of the Z.O.A., 1941*, p. 16; and Abraham Duker, "The Impact of Zionism on American Jewry," in Theodore Friedman and Robert Gordis (eds.), *Jewish Life in America* (New York, 1955), p. 312.

26. *Fulfillment: The Epic Story of Zionism* (Cleveland, 1951), pp. 296–97. Cf. also Nathan Glazer, *American Judaism* (Chicago, 1957), p. 93.

27. See Max Shulman, "The First American Disciples," in *Theodor Herzl*, special 1929 edition of *NP*, pp. 222–24.

28. Edidin, *Jewish Community Life . . .* , p. 89 (The Histadruth Ivrith reported directly to the ZOA annually on its year's activities; see any ZOA annual report); *Report of the Executive of the Zionist Organization to the Eighteenth Zionist Congress (1933)*, p. 170; Israel Goldstein, Chairman of ZOA's Committee on Youth and Education, in ZOA, *Thirty-second Annual Report*, in *NP*, June 21, 1929, p. 555. Cf. also Chaim Arlosoroff, *To the Jewish Youth* (New York, 1938), p. 17.

29. "Facts and Figures Concerning American Jewish Youth," in ZOA, *Jewish Youth—Challenge and Promise* (New York, 1941), pp. 7–8. Appendix I lists many of these Zionist youth groups.

30. Minutes, Special Meeting, ZOA Executive Committee, May 25, 1944.

31. *NP*, June 21, 1929, pp. 554–55.

32. "Labor Zionism," *JF*, II, No. 11 (November, 1935), 22.

33. *REC*, February 5, 1937, p. 4; and *NP*, November 1, 1940, p. 6, respectively; Blumenfield, *NP*, March 7, 1941, p. 12; and his *Problems Facing Zionist Education in America* (New York, 1941). Dr. Jesse Orlansky was quoted in *NP*, April 25, 1941, as saying that polls at Harvard and the University of Denver found less than half of the Jewish student bodies favored a Jewish national home in Palestine and 25 percent of them opposed such a home anywhere (p. 9). Arthur Lelyveld observed some five years later that a poll in which 30 percent of the interviewees were in the youth segment found 40 percent of the total anti-Zionist sentiment in this age grouping; *Student Zionist*, IV (December, 1946), p. 23; and Dinin, *Zionist Education . . .* , especially pp. 72–73, 81.

34. See Samuel Blumenfield, "Pearl Harbor and American Jewry," *NP*, December 4, 1942, pp. 6–10; Bernard J. Bamberger, "The American Rabbi: His Changing Role," in Friedman and Gordis, *Jewish Life . . .* , pp. 322–37; Abraham G. Duker, *Workshop in Jewish Community Affairs* (New York, 1953), Course I, Syllabus for Session 4: "Americanization and Its Specific Effects on the Jews," p. 15; and Eli Ginzberg, *Agenda for American Jews* (New York, 1950), pp. 14–15.

35. *Jewish Life . . .* , p. 17.

36. Cf. *NP*, March 7, 1941, p. 5; June 23, 1939, p. 13; November 6, 1942, p. 3; Dinin, *Zionist Education . . .* , p. 35; Blumenfield, *NP*, December 4, 1942, p. 9. Note also that fully 20 percent of the delegates to the American Jewish Conference of 1943 (98 persons) were rabbis (*Conference Record*, August 30, 1943, p. 8; and *NP*, September 10, 1943, p. 7).

37. See *NP*, May 31, 1945, pp. 1, 11–12. This document, addressed to the American people and world statesmen on the eve of the San Francisco Conference on International Organization, appealed for unfettered Jewish immigration into Palestine and the establishment there of a Jewish commonwealth.

38. The work of the Committee on Public Information is described in ZOA, *Thirty-third Annual Report*, in *NP*, June 27, 1930, pp. iii ff. Previous to this committee's formation, a Committee on Political Relations organized public meetings and receptions in order to attract "attention to Zionist ideals and Jewish accomplishments in Palestine." See *Thirty-second Annual Report*, in *ibid.*, June 21, 1929, p. 553; and *CZA*, Z4/3215 III.

39. See *NP*, June 29, 1934, p. 6; ZOA, *Thirty-eighth Annual Report*, in *NP*, April 24, 1936, p. 5.

40. *Ibid.*, October 21, 1938, p. 1. Note also Hilda Gruen's impressionistic account of feverish Zionist activity: "Zionist Workers Spring Into Action; Tension Marks Activity of Zionist Headquarters; Workers Burn Midnight Oil," *ibid.*, October 14, 1938, p. 6.

41. ZOA, *Forty-second Annual Report*, in *ibid.*, June 23, 1939, p. 13.

42. *Ibid.*, p. 9. One achievement registered in the previous year, however, was a Zionist theater group which utilized the avenue of the arts for the popularization of the Palestinian enterprise (*ibid.*, p. 15).

43. AZEC, *A Report of Activities, 1940–1946*, p. 3.

44. Note the Committee's exhortations to local Zionists: "The policy in Washington will be determined by public opinion, by the attitude of the thousands of American communities across the continent. . . . The purpose of your Public Relations Committee is to make and keep public opinion in your community favorable to our Cause" ("Zionist Public Relations Committees in Communities Throughout America, Manual for Their Organization and Function," 1941 [mimeographed], pp. 1–2); ZOA, *Forty-sixth Annual Report*, pp. 37–40; and Harold P. Manson, "A President Leaves Office," *NP*, May 27, 1949, p. 5. In *CZA*, Z5/1176 contains data on the Committee's work. Cf. also *CZA*, Z5/274 for elaborate plans for the 1942 Balfour Day celebrations: a declaration by Congressmen, a rabbinical delegation to the Secretary of State, publicity in at least nine large-circulation national magazines, a radio forum at Northwestern University, a rally at Carnegie Hall with Free World Association and League of Nations Association, etc. (Minutes, Office Committee of AECZA, October 20, 1942.)

45. See *NP*, May 15, 1942, p. 4; Louis Lipsky, "Why Not a Zionist United Front?" *CW*, May 23, 1941, pp. 10–12; and Meyer W. Weisgal, "Events and Trends in American Jewry," *ibid.*, September 11, 1942, p. 20.

46. *IJPS*, February 12, 1943, pp. 1–3.

47. AZEC, *A Report of Activities, 1940–1946*, pp. 4–5.

48. From his *A Year's Advance*, p. 13. On the poor state of Zionist political effectiveness before the advent of Silver to Zionist leadership, see Carl J Friedrich, *American Policy towards the Jewish National Home in Palestine* (Washington, 1944), pp. 29–30; and Emanuel Neumann's Foreword to Silver's *Vision and Victory* (New York, 1949), a collection of Silver's most important addresses (pp. 2–5). For Silver's repeated emphasis on the greater value of public opinion than of political promises, see particularly pp. 81–83 in that collection.

49. On the same theme, see Marvin Lowenthal, "Memorandum on Zionist Strategy," March 3, 1944, in *CZA*, Z5/669.

50. Three later references attributing the transformation of the AZEC to Silver's leadership may be found in *REC*, November 17, 1944, pp. 5–6; *Jewish Outlook*, IX (January, 1945), 8–10; ZOA, *Forty-seventh Annual Report*, pp. 59–63.

51. Data is scant concerning the financing of the Council, but for incomplete references see Samuel Dinin, *Zionist Education* . . . , p. 41, and documents in *CZA*, S53/469a and Z5/653. In the period from October 15, 1943, to May 21, 1945, the AZEC received $779,940 and spent $762,759. Some items of expenditure were: Administration, $312,992; Press, $53,768; Publicity, $83,105; Research, $51,463 ("Statement of Receipts and Expenditures," in *CZA*, S53/469a). Much fund-raising occurred locally, too, as when Philadelphia Zionists raised over $50,000 for combatting the White Paper by $100-a-plate dinners.

52. AZEC Press Release, October 28, 1943; *CZA*, Z5/1176 and memorandum

on "Intellectual Mobilization Committee," November 23, 1943, *CZA*, Z5/1213.

53. AZEC, "An Outline of Activities for Local Zionist Emergency Committees," p. 1; and Minutes, Special Meeting of ZOA Executive Committee, May 25, 1944.

54. See *NP*, October 8, 1943, p. 2. The author is indebted to a prominent American Zionist leader who provided unpublished documentary materials from the period of 1943–45, materials now in the author's possession.

55. AZEC, "An Outline of Activities for Local Zionist Emergency Committees," p. 3. A similar confidential memorandum was sent by ZOA Executive Secretary Simon Shetzer to local ZOA leaders on April 14, 1943.

56. AZEC, "Outline . . . ," p. 3.

57. *Ibid.*, p. 4. *CZA*, Z5/402 is a remarkable collection of correspondence from local Zionists to national AZEC showing contacts made and promises elicited from leading political figures at the local level.

58. AZEC, "Outline . . . ," pp. 4–5.

59. AZEC Press Releases, December 13, 16, 20, 1943; *JTA*, January 7, 20, February 1, 1944; AZEC, *Confidential Bulletins* and *Emergency Council Bulletins,* January–July, 1944. In Colorado alone, more than 200 non-Jewish groups, including the state legislature and Denver city council, passed anti-White Paper resolutions. In Brooklyn, the Jewish Community Council, claiming to represent one million Jews and over 600 groups, cabled Truman, asking him to help abrogate the Paper; see *Palestine: A Statement of the Position of the Brooklyn Jewish Community, 1946.* For suggestive materials on the "Zionist hold" over Brooklyn Jewry, see Ralph Foster Weld, *Brooklyn is America* (New York, 1950), p. 187; and Samuel P. Abelow, *History of Brooklyn Jewry* (Brooklyn, 1937), pp. 145–57. Note Abelow's conclusion: "Many years have passed since the first Zionist society was organized. While the Zionists were tabooed by many Jews in the early history of the movement, today [1937] it is not only fashionable to be a Zionist but it is considered an honor."

60. *REP-HEAR*, p. 8. Note also the American Jewish Conference's "Suggestions for Part of Public Relations Program—Wright-Compton Resolution," January 31, 1944; and I. L. Kenen's memorandum on public opinion, both in *CZA*, Z5/1076.

61. "Report on Community Contacts Submitted to the Executive Committee of the American Zionist Emergency Council," May 15, 1944, pp. 1–2. Several Congressmen, according to Feuer, remarked that they were "amazed" at the number of communications on the subject they had received, including a substantial number from non-Jews.

62. *CZA*, Z5/1204.

63. ZOA, *Forty-seventh* and *Forty-eighth Annual Reports,* pp. 50–51 and 18, respectively.

64. See "Palestine and the Arab World," issued by the Emergency Committee for Zionist Affairs, June 17, 1941; "Maronites and their Attitude Toward Zionism," *Zion Yugent* (Jerusalem), March, 1946, pp. 8–9; Archbishop Ignatius Moubarak, "Shall History be Denied?" *Palestine,* December, 1947,

pp. 163–64; Isaac ben Tzvi, "Christian Lebanon and Jewish Palestine," *JF*, XIII, No. 7 (July, 1946), 11–12. On the division of Zionist labor, see Minutes, Executive of Jewish Agency for Palestine, New York, July 2, 1945; and Minutes, AZEC, July 12, 1945, in *CZA*, Z5/641; I. B. Berkson, "Proposals submitted to the Executive Committee of the American Zionist Emergency Council for expansion and intensification of Zionist political education in the United States," September 10, 1945 (8 pp.); and Benjamin Akzin, "Memorandum to the Executive Committee of the American Zionist Emergency Council," June 9, 1945 (6 pp.), in *CZA*, Z5/1207.

65. Truman, *The Governmental Process*, p. 224.

66. See p. 8, above.

67. See Peter H. Odegard, *Pressure Politics: The Story of the Anti-Saloon League* (New York, 1928), especially pp. 36 ff.; and Truman, *The Governmental Process*, pp. 228 ff.

CHAPTER 11

1. See pp. 79 ff., above.

2. See for example, Morris S. Lazaron, *Common Ground* (New York, 1938), and other works listed in the bibliography; Samuel H. Goldenson, *Zionism, Jews and Judaism* (New York, 1942). Consult also *REC*, January 5, 1940, pp. 4–5; January 19, 1940, pp. 15–16; March 29, 1940, pp. 5–7; October 17, 1941, pp. 3–4; and Morris Jastrow, Jr., *Zionism and the Future of Palestine* (New York, 1919), especially pp. 151–59.

3. American Council for Judaism, *Statement of Views* (Philadelphia, 1943). The issuance of this statement was widely publicized, especially in *NYT*, August 31, 1943, and coincided with the Zionist-dominated American Jewish Conference.

4. For examples of these techniques, see Sidney Wallach, *The Struggle for Integration* (Philadelphia, 1945); the Council's *Information Bulletin; Zionism vs. Judaism* (Philadelphia, 1944); *The American of Jewish Faith* (Philadelphia, 1945); *A Post-War Program for Jews* (Submitted to Cordell Hull, September 25, 1944); testimony before the U.S. House of Representatives' Committee on Foreign Affairs, *REP-HEAR*, 120–45, 159–71, 197–209, 327–43 and 346–55; and Frank C. Sakran, *Palestine Dilemma: Arab Rights versus Zionist Aspirations* (Washington, 1948), pp. 168 ff.

5. *REP-HEAR*, p. 204; and Lazaron's "Foreword" to *Christian Opinion on Jewish Nationalism and a Jewish State* (Philadelphia, [1944]); and Sidney Wallach, *Jews Must Choose* (Philadelphia, n.d.). Unpublished content analyses of more recent documents issued by the Council have been made by the staff of the American Jewish Committee and bear out the author's contention that the "dual loyalty" issue is the mainspring of the Council's propaganda.

6. See pp. 37–9, above. According to Grossman's study, "Opinions of Leaders of American Council for Judaism on Jewish Integration and Group Survival," the great majority of the respondents to his questionnaire held that "Jew" always has a religious connotation and no other, but that, "in an unguarded moment," many admit a person may lose his

religious affiliations and still remain a Jew. Richard A. Schermerhorn, in whose *These Our People* (Boston, 1949) Grossman's work is cited, concludes that the leadership of the Council was composed of "minimal" Jews as opposed to the Zionist "maximal" Jews (p. 441). This distinction is further highlighted by Robert Gordis who relates the story of the Council's attempt to enlist a prominent Orthodox rabbi known for his anti-Zionist leanings. The rabbi approached by the Council allegedly replied: "For you, Zionism is too much; for me, it is not enough. We have no basis for agreement" (*Judaism for the Modern Age* [New York, 1955], p. 54). Cf. also Solomon Sutker, "The Role of Social Clubs in the Atlanta Jewish Community," in Marshall Sklare (ed.), *The Jews: Social Patterns of an American Group* (Glencoe, Ill., 1958), especially p. 268.

7. "Memo to All Z.O.A. District and Regional Chairmen and Secretaries and Members of the National Administrative Council," December 29, 1942 (mimeographed). Cf. letter, Nahum Goldmann to Eliezer Kaplan, September 17, 1942, in *CZA*, S53/210b.

8. See Oliver C. Cox, "Leadership Among Negroes in the United States," in Alvin W. Gouldner (ed.), *Studies in Leadership* (New York, 1950), pp. 228–71.

9. *Resolving Social Conflicts* (New York, 1948), pp. 157, 176–79.

10. *Ibid.*, pp. 190–93. Cf. Marshall Sklare, *Conservative Judaism* (Glencoe, Ill., 1955), pp. 39–40; Abraham G. Duker, *Jewish Survival in the World Today* (New York, 1941), Part II-B, pp. 1–4; and Mordecai M. Kaplan, *The Future of the American Jew* (New York, 1948), pp. 5–6.

11. *Resolving Social Conflicts*, p. 196. Lewin's study was first published in 1941, several years before the establishment of the Council for Judaism. His conclusions appear to be applicable to Grossman's survey of the Council, cited above, which revealed that Council leaders favored the "melting pot" over the "cultural pluralism" theories of Americanism, opposed the extension of Jewish communal life in America, and rejected Hebrew studies.

12. See *NP*, issues of December, 1942; January–March, 1943; January, July–September, 1944; March, 1945; *REC*, January 22, 1943, p. 19; May 15, 1942, pp. 5, 20.

13. December 18, 1942, p. 5. Also see the ZOA's *Why Zionist Manpower Today!* (Washington, [1943]).

14. Press Release of the American Emergency Committee for Zionist Affairs, November 20, 1942. This statement was later approved by the student bodies of five leading rabbinical seminaries (including Reform's Hebrew Union College by a vote of 42–9); in *NP*, February 19, 1943, p. 14. For a detailed and recent example, see Chaim Lieberman, *Strangers to Glory: An Appraisal of the American Council for Judaism* (New York, 1955).

15. Portions of this statement are contained in Appendix VII. Other denunciatory statements by Zionists and their allies may be consulted: Rabbinical Assembly of America (Conservative), *REC*, February 5, 1943, pp. 17–18; Executive Committee of the American Jewish Conference, *Conference Record*, December, 1945, pp. 11–12; and Judge Louis E. Levinthal, President of ZOA, Press Release of December 16, 1942.

16. "Memo to All Z.O.A. Districts . . . ," December 29, 1942.

17. A letter from this Chaplain's Committee was printed in *NYT*, January 21, 1946:

> . . . In view of the defamatory statements and innuendos made repeatedly by responsible representatives of the American Council for Judaism, impugning the patriotism of American Zionists, we the undersigned rabbis, serving as Chaplains in the armed forces of our nation, register our deep resentment and disapproval of such reckless and un-American allegations.
>
> Of the 305 surviving Chaplains of the Jewish faith who responded unhesitatingly to the call of our country in its hour of need, 228 have already identified themselves with Zionism, with replies expected from many still overseas. For anyone to insinuate that Zionism tends to diminish the full measure of devotion of these 228 rabbis to America is the height of impudence.
>
> Such an accusation comes with particularly bad grace from an organization which numbers amongst its leadership men who did not respond to the call of the responsible Jewish Commission to serve in the Chaplaincy.

Cited in American Zionist Council, *False Witness: The Record of the American Council for Judaism* (New York, 1955), pp. 12–13.

18. *NP*, January 7, 1944, p. 192; and Memo from Simon Shetzer to All ZOA Districts . . . , January 17, 1944.

19. ZOA, *Forty-ninth Annual Report*, p. 29.

20. Minutes of ZOA Administrative Council, July 9, 1944. The findings of Zionist counterpropagandists provide an interesting commentary on the rationality of both Zionist and Council for Judaism members. The ZOA's *Forty-seventh Annual Report* (1944), for example, reveals several instances of its members also belonging to the Council. One individual paid the Council $2 in dues and the ZOA $100 in order to fight the Council (p. 47).

21. A cross-section of printed Zionist propaganda material in this period includes a reprint from *Survey Graphic* on Palestinian development, *Briefing It* ("Tips to Chart the Course of the Campaign to Widen the Area of Zionist Influence—a Newsletter for Unity for Palestine Chairmen"), flyers entitled "You are in Good Company" and "The Seal of Congressional Approval"; a pro-Zionist letter from architect Marion S. Dimmock to Council for Judaism President Elmer Berger; "Palestine and the Peace"— a fortnightly commentary by the investment survey *The Value Line;* and reprints of letters, articles and pamphlets by Arieh Tartakower, Edgar Ansel Mowrer, Edward M. Warburg, Senators Robert Taft and Robert Wagner; Carl Alpert, M. Z. Frank and Dr. Louis Finkelstein. See also ZOA, *Forty-ninth Annual Report*, pp. 28–29; *"Should Jews Defame Jews?"* (Houston Committee on Unity); *Unity Committee on Palestine,* Special Section of the Secretary's Report on the Activities and Achievements of the ZOA, October 1, 1944, to March 31, 1945, p. 1; *CZA*, Z5/1145; and Minutes of the Executive Committee of the ZOA, November 19, 1944. Einstein was quoted as saying:

> The American Council for Judaism is a fairly exact copy of the *Zentralverein Deutscher Staatsburg Juedischen Glaubens* (Central As-

sociation of German Citizens of Jewish Faith) of unhappy memory, which in the days of our crucial need showed itself utterly impotent, and corroded the Jewish group by undermining that inner certitude by which our people could have overcome the trials of this difficult age.

In American Zionist Council, *False Witness*, p. 1.

22. *False Witness*, pp. 3–4.

23. In Wolsey, *Sermons and Addresses* (Philadelphia, 1950), pp. 14–15. Recalling the remark of Israel Friedlander, that "what Zionism needed to arouse it from its indolence of 40 years ago was some strong opposition," Wolsey conceded that the Council had provided it. He also went on to charge that Council leadership was "intolerant" of rabbinical suggestions, "snubbed" rabinical cooperation, was "dictatorial," and "generally irreligious." As a result, its rabbinical supporters after 1948 numbered only five active members, "one of whom flirts with Zionism." Cf. also *NYT*, July 22, 1956, p. 43, for yet another resignation. The author's interviews with responsible persons have also revealed that Wolsey was particularly incensed by the failure of Council Executive Secretary Elmer Berger to accept a chaplaincy in the war and by Berger's "personal morality."

24. *Unity for Palestine,* September, 1944, p. 4.

25. Note Harold D. Lasswell's and Abraham Kaplan's proposition in *Power and Society* (New Haven, 1950), pp. 38–39; similar observations in Truman, *The Governmental Process* (New York, 1951), p. 209; and Eric Hoffer, *The True Believer* (New York, 1958), p. 336; and C. Wendell King's generalization about techniques employed by social movements in fostering group morale and loyalty, all of which seem well illustrated by this study:

> . . . in-group loyalties are cultivated by an emphasis on ethnocentrism in the movement's ideology and tactics . . . [by playing] up a real or fancied enemy, contrasting the movement's values with contrary values in the society, linking the movement's goals and their superiority with the aspects of the status quo which are to be changed. . . . (*Social Movements in the United States* [New York, 1956], p. 78.)

CHAPTER 12

1. Address of Abba Hillel Silver before American Zionist Policy Committee, March, 21, 1945; in his *Vision and Victory* (New York, 1949), p. 83.

2. Address at World Zionist Congress in Basle, Switzerland, December 10, 1946; in *ibid.*, p. 114.

3. See AZEC, *A Report of Activities, 1940–1946* (New York, 1946), pp. 11–15, for a detailed legislative history of this resolution which had been pending before Congress since January 1944. Also see *NYT*, December 18, 1945, p. 1, and December 20, p. 12, for an account of the passage of the resolution and *NP*, January 18, 1946, pp. 79, 87–89, for typical Zionist reactions to this victory.

4. The political record here summarized is of necessity over-simplified. For detailed studies, see J. C. Hurewitz, *The Struggle for Palestine* (New York, 1950), pp. 212 ff.; ESCO Foundation for Palestine, *Palestine: A Study of*

Jewish, Arab, and British Policies (New Haven, 1947), pp. 1187 ff.; Joseph J. Zasloff, *Great Britain and Palestine* (Geneva, 1952).

5. *NP*, November 6, 1942, p. 32.

CHAPTER 13:
SUMMARY AND CONCLUSIONS

1. See David Truman, *The Governmental Process* (New York, 1951), p. 114.

2. *Social Movements in the United States* (New York, 1956), p. 103.

3. Howard E. Freeman and Morris Showel, "Differential Political Influence of Voluntary Associations," *Public Opinion Quarterly*, XV, No. 4 (Winter 1951–52), p. 705; and Truman, *The Governmental Process*, p. 114.

4. Phillip Monypenny, "Political Science and the Study of Groups: Notes to Guide a Research Project," *Western Political Quarterly*, VII, No. 2 (June, 1954), 198.

5. Truman, *The Governmental Process*, p. 114.

6. *Ibid.*, p. 248.

7. In Stephen S. Wise's autobiography, *Challenging Years* (London, 1951), p. 88.

8. See Mordecai M. Kaplan, *A New Zionism* (New York, 1955), p. 89; and Abraham Menes, "The East Side: Matrix of the Jewish Labor Movement," in Theodore Friedman and Robert Gordis (eds.), *Jewish Life in America* (New York, 1955), pp. 153–54.

9. Note Eli Ginzberg's similar generalization in his *Agenda for American Jews* (New York, 1950), p. 78; and Marshall Sklare and Benjamin B. Ringer:

> . . . merely being Jewish was enough to evoke pro-Israel sympathies; however, it is equally apparent that something more was generally needed to transform the sympathies into active involvement with and support for Israel. A firm attachment to Jewish life and the sharing of strong sentiments and feelings about Jewishness played an important part in producing this involvement and support.

("A Study of Jewish Attitudes Toward the State of Israel," in Sklare [ed.], *The Jews: Social Patterns of an American Group* [Glencoe, Ill., 1958], p. 442.)

10. Compare Hadley Cantril's "law of public opinion": ". . . an accomplished fact tends to shift opinion in the direction of acceptance." (*Gauging Public Opinion* [Princeton, N.J., 1944], p. 228.)

11. See King, *Social Movements* . . . , p. 58.

12. An example of speculation about what motivated non-Jewish supporters of the Zionist program may be found in Kaplan, *A New Zionism*, p. 89:

> . . . the role of the Bible in forming the American mind exercises a subconscious influence and rises clearly to consciousness from time to time among those who mold opinion. There is something about the American spirit of democracy and justice which is definitely conducive to a sympathetic interest in the upbuilding of Israel.

13. Monypenny, *Western Political Quarterly*, VII, No. 2, 199.

14. Cf. Ginzberg's discussion in *Agenda* . . . , p. 81.

15. Truman, *The Governmental Process*, pp. 50–55; Ginzberg, Agenda . . . , p. 3; Eric Hoffer, *The True Believer* (New York, 1958), p. 13; and see p. 16, above.

16. *The Governmental Process*, p. 65. See Emanuel Neumann's "Foreword" to Abba Hillel Silver, *Vision and Victory* (New York, 1949), p. 1.

17. Freeman and Showel, *Public Opinion Quarterly*, XV, No. 4, 705. In this connection, note Truman's generalization: "When it has become organized, moreover, a major function of the organization is to speed up and sharpen its members' perceptions of the consequences of actions (events) occurring or impending in the environment and related to the group's interests" (*The Governmental Process*, p. 218).

18. *Gauging Public Opinion*, p. 228. Cf. also Monypenny, *Western Political Quarterly*, VII, No. 2, 197: "The greater the degree to which a given object of activity is indispensable for the maintenance of an optimum state by a given group, the more intense will be the activity of that group. . . . It is probable that there are equally intense reactions to non-economic objects, of which we as yet know little."

19. Truman, *The Governmental Process*, p. 245. Cf. also Hoffer, *The True Believer*, p. 45:

> . . . in order to succeed, a mass movement must develop . . . a capacity to absorb and integrate all comers. It is futile to judge the viability of a new movement by the truth of its doctrine and the feasibility of its promises. What has to be judged is its corporate organization for quick and total absorption of the frustrated.

20. Harold D. Lasswell and Abraham Kaplan, *Power and Society* (New Haven, 1950), p. 39. Cf. also Truman, *The Governmental Process*, p. 209.

21. *Power and Society*, p. 43.

22. Eliezer Livneh, *State and Diaspora* (Jerusalem, 1953), pp. 15, 19. Perceptive Zionist observations of a similar nature may be found in: Samuel M. Blumenfield, "Problems Facing American Zionism," *NP*, October 7, 1938, pp. 3, 6; ZOA, *Reorienting Zionist Education Today* (New York, 1948), particularly the address of Professor Simon Halkin; Simon Greenberg, "Auto-Emancipation and Zionism," in Joseph Shubow (ed.), *Brandeis Avukah Annual of 1932* (New York, 1932), pp. 110–14; Salo W. Baron, "Prospects for the Diaspora," *NP*, June 20, 1947, pp. 143–46; Walter Turnowsky, *Zionist Propaganda, A Critical Survey of its Methods* (Jerusalem, 1938); Judd L. Teller, "America's Two Zionist Traditions: Brandeis and Weizmann," *Commentary*, XX (October, 1955), 343–52. These may also be studied for their commentary on the "ideological content" of American Zionism.

23. See p. 40, above.

bibliography

A. *Unpublished Documents*

Press releases, mimeographed leaflets, letters and other documents from the archives or libraries of American Council for Judaism, American Emergency Council for Zionist Affairs, American Jewish Committee, American Jewish Conference, American Jewish Congress, American Zionist Emergency Council, Central Zionist Archives (Jerusalem), Jewish Agency for Palestine, Zionist Archives and Library, Zionist Organization of America.

Akin, Benjamin. "Memorandum to the Executive Committee of the American Zionist Emergency Council." New York, June 9, 1945.

American Emergency Committee for Zionist Affairs. "Zionist Public Relations Committees in Communities Throughout America: Manual for Their Organization and Function." New York, n.d. [c. 1941].

American Jewish Committee (Louis Shub). "The Jewish Agency and the Non-Zionists." New York, June 14, 1944.

American Zionist Emergency Council. "Confidential Bulletins." New York, 1943–44.

———. "An Outline of Activities for Local Zionist Emergency Committees." New York, November 3, 1943.

Ben Gurion, David. "The ABC of Zionist Policy." Habonim Labor Zionist Youth, New York, 1944.

Berkson, I. B. "Proposals submitted to the Executive Committee of the American Zionist Emergency Council for expansion and intensification of Zionist political education in the United States." New York, September 10, 1945.

Council on Foreign Relations. "The New Zionism and a Policy for the United States." New York, October 19, 1943.

Emergency Committee for Zionist Affairs. "A Jewish Military Force to Serve Under British Command in the Defense of Palestine and the Middle East." New York, December, 1941.

Extraordinary Zionist Conference (Biltmore Hotel, New York). "Excerpts of Addresses, May 9 and 10, 1942."

Feuer, Leon I. "A Memorandum on the Zionist Political Front." New York, 1946.

———. "Report on Community Contacts Submitted to the Executive Committee of the American Zionist Emergency Council." New York, May 15, 1944.

Friedrich, Carl J. "American Policy Towards the Jewish National Home in Palestine." n.d. [c. 1942].

Hook, Sidney. "The National Council of Jewish Women on the Present-Day Jewish Scene; A Program Survey of the Organization." National Council of Jewish Women, New York, 1946.

Lowenthal, Marvin. "Memorandum on Zionist Strategy." New York, March 3, 1944.

Montor, Henry. "A Minority Report on the Proposal to Establish a National Advisory Budget Service." New York, February 24, 1941.

Neumann, Emanuel. "Memorandum on Coordination of Zionist War-Time Propaganda." New York, November 19, 1940. (Mimeographed.)

Oder, Irwin. "The United States and the Palestine Mandate, 1920–1948: A Study of Public Opinion and Policy Making." Unpublished Ph.D. dissertation, Columbia University, 1956.

Rubinow, I. M. "Economic and Industrial Status of American Jewry," Paper presented to the National Conference of Jewish Social Service, Philadelphia, 1934.

Tenzer, Morton J. "American Zionism and the Palestine Question in the Wilson Era." Unpublished, incomplete Ph.D. dissertation, Yale University, n.d.

Weinberger, Abe L. "Judaism in America: The Influence of America as a New World Frontier Upon Judaism of Tradition." Unpublished Ph.D. dissertation, University of Texas, 1953.

Zionist Organization of America. Committee on Unity for Palestine. "Briefing It: Tips to Chart the Course of the Campaign to Widen the Area of Zionist Influence: A Newsletter for Unity for Palestine Chairmen." New York, 1944.

B. *Yearbooks, Convention Reports, Proceedings and Hearings*

American Christian Palestine Committee. *Proceedings* of the International Christian Conference for Palestine, November 1–2, 1945. Washington and New York, 1945.

American Jewish Committee. *The American Jewish Year Book*. Vols. XXIX–LVIII,. Philadelphia: Jewish Publication Society of America, 1927–50.

——. *Proceedings of the Fiftieth Anniversary Observance of the . . .* New York, 1958.

——. *Twenty-third–Fortieth Annual Reports*. New York, 1929–49.

American Jewish Conference (Alexander S. Kohanski, editor). *Organization and Proceedings of the First and Second Sessions, 1943, 1944.* New York: American Jewish Conference, 1944, 1945.

Avukah, Student Zionist Organization. *Avukah Annual, Fifth Anniversary Edition, 1925–1930.* New York, 1930.

B'nai B'rith. *President's Message to the Supreme Lodge, Seventeenth Convention.* New York, 1944.

——. *Proceedings of the General Convention of the Constitution Grand Lodge (Supreme Lodge), Fourteenth General Convention–Seventeenth General Convention.* Washington, 1935–44.

Central Conference of American Rabbis. *Yearbook*, Vols. XL–LVIII, 1930–48.

Congregation Beth Israel. *Annual Report*. Houston, May 30, 1944.

Executives of Zionist Organization and The Jewish Agency for Palestine. *Reports of the Executives Submitted to the Twenty-third Zionist Congress at Jerusalem 1951.* New York, 1951.

Forum for the Problems of Zionism, Jewry and the State of Israel. Vol. IV:

Proceedings of the Jerusalem Ideological Conference. Jerusalem: World Zionist Organization, 1959.

Hechalutz Organization of America. *Hechalutz Yearbook: Builders and Fighters.* New York, 1948.

The Impact of Israel on the American Jewish Community. Proceedings of a Conference Convened by the Theodor Herzl Institute and the Conference on Jewish Social Studies, December 22–23, 1956. New York, 1959.

National Conference for Palestine. *Proceedings of the . . . , January 20 and 21, 1935.* New York: American Palestine Campaign, 1935.

Rabbinical Assembly of America. *Proceedings of the . . .* Vols. II–XIV, 1928–50.

Shubow, Joseph S., editor. *The Brandeis Avukah Annual of 1932: A Collection of Essays on Contemporary Zionist Thought.* New York: Avukah, 1932.

Udin, Sophie A., editor. *The Palestine Year Book 5706–9.* Vols. I–IV, Washington and New York: Zionist Organization of America, 1945–49.

Union of American Hebrew Congregations. *Proceedings of the . . . , Fifty-sixth– Seventy-third Annual Reports.* Cincinnati and New York, 1930–47.

United Jewish Appeal. *A Report to Members of the National Campaign Council of the U.J.A.* New York, March 12, 1946.

U.S. Bureau of the Census. *Census of Religious Bodies 1936; Jewish Congregations: Statistics, History, Doctrine and Organization.* Washington: U.S. Government Printing Office, 1940.

U.S. House of Representatives, Committee on Foreign Affairs. *Hearings before the . . . , The Jewish National Home in Palestine.* Seventy-eighth Congress, Second Session on H. Res. 418 and H. Res. 419; February 8, 9, 15, 16, 1944. Washington: U.S. Government Printing Office, 1944.

Weizmann Archives. *Report of Activities for the Period of October 1951– January 1958 presented to the First Meeting of the Editorial Board Held on March 31, 1958, at Rehovot.* Rehovot, Israel: Weizmann House, 1958.

World Zionist Organization. *Central Zionist Archives, Report for Period 1951– 1955.* Submitted to the Twenty-fourth Zionist Congress, Jerusalem, 1956.

———. *Central Zionist Archives, Report for Period April 1954–May 1955.* Submitted to the Zionist General Council, Jerusalem, 1955.

———. *Report of the Executive of the . . . , submitted to the Sixteenth, Seventeenth, Eighteenth, Nineteenth Zionist Congresses at Zurich, Basel, Prague, Lucerne.* London: Central Office of the Zionist Organization, 1929, 1931, 1933, 1935.

——— and Jewish Agency for Palestine. *Report of the Executives of the . . . , submitted to the Twentieth, Twenty-first, Twenty-second Zionist Congress and the Fifth, Sixth Session of the Council of the Jewish Agency at Zurich, Geneva, Basle.* Jerusalem: Executives of the Zionist Organization, 1937, 1939, 1946.

Zionist Organization of America. *Report to the Annual Convention, Thirtieth– Fifty-third Conventions.* New York and Washington, 1927–50.

C. *Periodicals* (*1928–60*)

American Israel Review
American Jewish Archives
American Jewish Chronicle
American Zionist (Zionist Organization of America)
Answer
B'nai B'rith Magazine
Bulletin of the Rabbinical Assembly of America
Commentary (American Jewish Committee)
Committee Reporter (American Jewish Committee)
Conference Record (American Jewish Conference)
Congress Bulletin (American Jewish Congress)
Congress Weekly (American Jewish Congress)
Congressional Record, United States
Conservative Judaism (Rabbinical Assembly of America)
Contemporary Jewish Record (American Jewish Committee)
Farband Newsletter (Jewish National Workers Alliance)
Furrows (Habonim, Labor Zionist Youth Organization)
Hadassah Newsletter (Hadassah, Women's Zionist Organization of America)
Hebrew Union College Monthly
Independent Jewish Press Service
Information Bulletin of the American Council for Judaism
Jewish Affairs (American Jewish Congress)
Jewish Agency Digest of Press and Events (Jerusalem, London and New York)
Jewish Frontier (Labor Zionist Organization of America)
Jewish Horizon (Hapoel Hamizrachi of America)
Jewish Outlook (Mizrachi Organization of America)
Jewish Social Service Quarterly
Jewish Social Studies (Conference on Jewish Social Studies)
Jewish Spectator
JTA [Jewish Telegraphic Agency] *Daily News Bulletin*
Judaism (American Jewish Congress)
Liberal Judaism (Union of American Hebrew Congregations)
Menorah Journal
National Jewish Monthly (B'nai B'rith)
New Judaea (London)
New Palestine (Zionist Organization of America)
New York Times
Opinion, A Journal of Jewish Life and Letters
Palcor News Agency Cables
Palestine (American Zionist Emergency Council)
Palestine and Middle East (Tel Aviv)
Palestine and Zionism (Zionist Archives and Library of the Palestine Foundation
    Fund)
Pioneer Woman (Women's Labor Zionist Organization of America)
Pro-Palestine Herald (Pro-Palestine Federation of America)

Publications of the American Jewish Historical Society
Reconstructionst (Jewish Reconstructionist Foundation)
Seven Arts Feature Syndicate
Statistical Abstract of Israel (Jerusalem)
Student Zionist (Intercollegiate Zionist Federation of America)
Unity for Palestine (Committee on Unity for Palestine)
Voice of the Unconquered (Jewish Labor Committee)
Workmen's Circle Call
Young Israel Viewpoint (National Council of Young Israel)
Young Judaean (National Young Judaea)
Youth and Nation (Hashomer Hatzair)
Zionews (New Zionist Organization of America)
Zionist (New York Region of the Zionist Organization of America)
Zionist, Voice of Jewish Opinion (Zionist Organization of Chicago)
ZOA Program and Education Bulletin (Zionist Organization of America)

D. *Pamphlets and Leaflets*

Allied Jewish Campaign. *The Pact of Glory: The Jewish Agency for Palestine discussed by Louis Marshall, Chaim Weizmann,* and others. New York, n.d. [c. 1929].

American Christian Palestine Committee. *Program of Greater New York Conference of* . . . New York, October 14–16, 1945.

———. *A Suggestion for Memorial Sunday,* New York, May 27, 1945.

American Council for Judaism. *The Anglo-American Committee of Inquiry.* New York, 1946.

———. *The American of Jewish Faith.* Philadelphia, 1945.

———. *Christian Opinion on Jewish Nationalism and a Jewish State.* Philadelphia, n.d. [c. 1944].

———. *Zionism and Judaism.* Philadelphia, 1944.

American Emergency Committee for Zionist Affairs. *The Balfour Declaration and American Interest in Palestine: Issued in Connection with the Twenty-fifth Anniversary of the Balfour Declaration.* New York, 1942.

———. *Call to American Zionists.* New York. February 10, 1942.

———. *Zionism an Affirmation of Judaism: A Reply by 757 Orthodox, Conservative, and Reform Rabbis of America to a Statement Issued by Ninety Members of the Reform Rabbinate Charging That Zionism is Incompatible with the Teachings of Judaism.* New York, 1942.

———. *The Zionist Position: A Statement Submitted to the Delegates to the American Jewish Conference, August 29, 1943.* New York, 1943.

American Federation of Labor. *Acts and Pronouncements of the A.F.L. on Palestine and the Jewish Race (1917–1938).* New York: National Committee for a Leon Blum Colony, 1938.

American Jewish Committee. *In Peace and Dignity: Testimony before the Anglo-American Committee of Inquiry on Palestine.* New York, 1946.

———. *Jewish Post-War Problems: A Study Course, Unit VI "Palestine in the New World," Research Institute on Peace and Post-War Problems.* New York, 1943.

American Jewish Committee. *Palestine, Your Questions Answered.* New York, 1946.
———. *Statement on Withdrawal from the American Jewish Conference.* New York, 1943.
———. *Survey of Developments Re Palestine: 1945–1946.* New York, 1946.
———. *This Is Our Home, II: Jewish Labor in the United States.* New York, 1954.
———. *To the Counsellors of Peace: Recommendations of the American Jewish Committee.* New York, 1945.
———. *Toward Peace and Equity, Recommendations of the American Jewish Committee.* New York, 1946.
———, Committee on Peace Problems. *The Problem of Palestine: A Review of Developments in 1945.* New York, 1946.
———. *Proposed Plans on the Future of Palestine.* New York, 1944.
American Jewish Conference. *The Jewish Position at the United Nations Conference on International Organization, A Report to the Delegates.* New York, 1945.
———. *Report of the Interim Committee and the Commissions on Rescue, Palestine, Post-War, To the Delegates.* New York, November, 1944.
———. *Rules of Election for the American Jewish Conference, National Board of Elections.* New York, April, 1943.
———. *A Statement of the Organization of the Conference and a Summary of Resolutions Adopted at the First Session.* New York, 1943.
———. *Statement on the Withdrawal of the American Jewish Committee, Adopted by the Interim Committee.* New York, November 7, 1943.
———. *Statement Submitted to the Anglo-American Committee of Inquiry.* New York, January 2, 1946.
———, Committee on Preliminary Studies. *A Survey of Facts and Opinions on Problems of Post-War Jewry in Europe and Palestine.* New York, 1943.
American Jewish Congress. *Statement to the Anglo-American Committee of Inquiry.* New York, January, 1946.
American Jewish Trade Union Committee for Palestine. *A Declaration.* New York, n.d. [c. 1944].
American Palestine Committee. *The American Palestine Committee—What It Is.* New York, n.d. [c. 1941].
———. *A Christian Point of View on Palestine.* New York, 1946.
———. *"The Common Purpose of Civilized Mankind," A Declaration by Sixty-eight Members of the Senate and 194 Members of the House of Representatives of the Seventy-seventh Congress on the Occasion of the Twenty-fifth Anniversary of the Balfour Declaration.* New York, November 2, 1942.
———. *The Voice of Christian America: Proceedings of the National Conference on Palestine, Washington, March 9, 1944.* New York, 1944.
American Zionist Bureau. *American Public Opinion on British Policy in Palestine.* Washington, n.d. [c. 1939].
American Zionist Council. *False Witness: Record of the American Council for Judaism.* New York, 1955.
American Zionist Emergency Council. *After the Victory: A Blueprint for the Rehabilitation of European Jewry.* New York, n.d. [c. 1944].
———. *America Speaks on Palestine.* New York, n.d. [c. 1944].

———. *Economic Aspects of American Interest in Palestine: Statement Submitted to the Anglo-American Committee of Inquiry.* New York, January, 1946.

———. *The Jewish Case, The Place of Palestine in the Solution of the Jewish Question.* New York, 1945.

———. *Palestine in the Press.* New York, 1946.

———. *A Petition to the President of the United States, Respectfully Submitted by Members of the Faculties of American Schools of Higher Learning.* New York, n.d. [c. 1945].

———. *Press Book on the 1939 British White Paper on Palestine.* New York, n.d. [c. 1943].

———. *Press Book on Palestine Jewry's Contribution to the War Against the Axis.* New York, n.d. [c. 1944].

———. *Rally for Palestine.* New York, 1944.

———. *A Report of Activities, 1940–1946.* New York, 1946.

———. *The American Zionist Case: Statement Submitted to the Anglo-American Committee of Inquiry.* New York, January, 1946.

American Zionist Policy Committee. *Public Opinion on the Zionist Controversy.* New York, 1945.

American Zionist Youth Commission. *Palestine Royal Commission Report: Palestine and the Jews: A Brief Historical Survey.* New York, 1946.

Anti-Defamation League of B'nai B'rith. *Previewing the Jewish State.* Chicago: Fireside Discussion Group, 1937.

Arlosoroff, Chaim. *Surveying American Zionism.* New York: The Zionist Labor Party "Hitachduth" of America, 1929.

———. *To the Jewish Youth.* New York: Zionist Labor Party "Hitachduth" of America and Canada, 1938.

Baron, Salo W. *The Effect of the War on Jewish Community Life.* New York: Harry L. Glucksman Memorial Committee, 1942.

Ben-Jacob, Jeremiah. *Guide to Zionism.* New York: American Zionist Youth Commission, n.d. [c. 1949].

Berger, Elmer. *Why I Am a Non-Zionist.* Flint, Michigan: Myron Winegarden, n.d., [c. 1942].

Bernstein, Philip S. *A Jew Looks at the Christian Problem.* See Voss, Carl H.

———. *The World Jewish Crisis and Palestine Today.* Rochester, New York: Privately printed, 1940.

Bick, Abraham, editor. *Exponents and Philosophy of Religious Zionism.* Brooklyn: Hashomer Hadati of North America, 1942.

Bittelman, Alex. *The Jewish People Will Live On!* New York: Morning Freiheit Association, 1944.

———. *Palestine: What is the Solution?* New York: Morning Freiheit Association, 1947.

———. *Should Jews Unite? Jewish People's Unity As a Force for American National Unity.* New York: Morning Freiheit Publishers, n.d. [c. 1943].

Blumenfield, Samuel M. *Annual Report of the Department of Youth and Education of the Z.O.A. and Problems Facing Zionist Education in America.* New York: Zionist Organization of America, 1941.

———. *The Zionist Situation in Chicago: An Evaluation.* Chicago: Zionist Organization of Chicago, 1938.

Blau, Joseph L. *The Spiritual Life of American Jewry 1654–1954*. New York: American Jewish Committee, 1955.

Brickner, Barnett R. *The Jewish Army Controversy*. Reprint from *The Jewish Review and Observer* (London), April 3, 1942.

Brooklyn Jewish Community Council. *Palestine: A Statement of the Position of the Brooklyn Jewish Community*. Brooklyn, 1946.

Browder, Earl. *Zionism*. New York: Jewish Bureau of the Central Committee of the Communist Party, U.S.A., 1936.

Chalutziut and Youth Commission of the Labor Zionist Movement. *Chalutz and Youth, A Yearbook Devoted to the Cause of Chalutziut in America*. New York, 1952.

Christian Council on Palestine. *Truth About Palestine*. New York, 1946.

The Committee for a Jewish Army of Stateless and Palestinian Jews. *From Evian to Bermuda*. New York, 1943.

Committee for ZOA Reorganization. *The Zionist Awakening: A Summary Report of the Washington Conference Held April 29th, 1928*.

The Committee of Christian Leaders, Clergymen and Laymen. *Memorandum in Behalf of Jewish Immigration into Palestine*. New York, n.d. [c. 1942].

Committee on Unity for Palestine of the ZOA. *Should Jews Defame Jews? A Factual Account of Certain Happenings at Houston, Texas, During April, May and June 1945*. Houston, 1945.

Congregation Beth Israel. *The President of Congregation Beth Israel Replies to Dr. Solomon B. Freehof, President, Central Conference of American Rabbis*. Houston, May 1, 1944.

———, Policy Formulation Committee. *A Handbook of True Facts Concerning the "Basic Principles" of Congregation Beth Israel*. Houston, 1944.

Dinin, Samuel. *Zionist Education in the United States, A Survey*. New York: Zionist Organization of America, 1944.

Douglas, Helen G. *To Christian Youth*. New York: American Christian Palestine Committee, 1945.

Efros, Mildred B. *The Story of Zionism*. New York: Education Department of Hadassah, 1952.

Eisenstein, Ira. *Palestine in the Life of the Jew*. New York: The National Academy for Adult Jewish Studies, 1942.

Emergency Committee for Zionist Affairs. *Revisionism: A Destructive Force*. New York, 1940.

Emergency Committee to Save the Jewish People of Europe. *Memorandum on the Findings of the Emergency Conference To Save the Jewish People of Europe, July 20th to 25th, 1943*. New York, 1943.

Epstein, Elias. *Zionism and the Jewish Youth of America*. New York: Privately printed, n.d.

Executive of the Zionist Organization. *The Jubilee of the First Zionist Congress, 1897–1947*. Jerusalem, 1947.

Feldman, Abraham J. *Why I Am A Zionist: A Reform Rabbi's Viewpoint*. New York: ZOA Committee on Unity for Palestine, 1945.

Fertig, M. Maldwin. *The Pittsburgh Conference*. New York: American Emergency Committee for Zionist Affairs, 1943.

Fox, G. George. *American Jewish Nationalism—Unity—and the Conference!* Reprint from *The Sentinel* (Chicago), n.d. [c. 1944].

Frisch, Daniel. *Thoughts of a Layman: What Happened to the American Jewish Conference?* Indianapolis: Privately printed, n.d. [c. 1944].

Fuss, Samuel. *A Comparative Analysis of the American Jewish Conference Resolution on Palestine and Consideration of the Dissent Therefrom.* Pittsburgh: Privately printed, 1943.

Glazer, Nathan. *Social Characteristics of American Jews, 1654-1954.* New York: American Jewish Committee, 1955.

Goldenson, Samuel H. *Zionism, Jews and Judaism.* New York: Temple Emanu-El, 1942.

Goldstein, Israel. *The Road Ahead: A Program for American Zionism.* Washington: Zionist Organization of America, 1944.

Golub, Jacob S. *Some Principles of Jewish Education.* New York: Zionist Or ganization of America, n.d. [c. 1937].

Greenberg, Simon. *Israel and Zionism: A Conservative Approach.* New York: The National Academy for Adult Jewish Studies, The United Synagogue of America, 1956.

Haber, Julius. *The Unpaid Debt of American Jewry to its Brethren.* New York: Privately printed, 1945.

Hadassah. *Statement to the Anglo-American Committee of Inquiry.* Washington, 1946.

Harrison, George M. and Potofsky, Jacob S. *Ten Years of Progress: A Report On Israel.* Washington: American Federation of Labor—Congress of Industrial Organization, 1959.

Hearst, William R. *A Homeland for Dispossessed or Persecuted Jews.* Reprint from *New York Journal-American,* New York, n.d. [c. 1938].

Heller, James G. *An Answer to the American Council for Judaism and to Published Criticisms of the American Jewish Conference.* San Francisco, 1943.

Herzl, Theodor. *The Congress Addresses of Theodor Herzl.* New York: Federation of American Zionists, 1917.

Hirsch, David E. *A Record of American Zionism* (ZOA Pamphlet Series No. 13). New York: Zionist Organization of America, 1955.

Holmes, John Haynes. *Jews and the Christian Conscience: A Plea for Palestine.* New York: The Community Church, 1945.

Ickes, Harold L. *Cycles of Darkness.* New York: United Palestine Appeal, 1938.
———. *Palestine and the Destiny of the Jewish People.* New York: United Palestine Appeal, 1936.

Institute of Arab American Affairs, Inc. *Papers on Palestine II: A Collection of Articles by Leading Authorities Dealing with the Palestine Problem.* New York, 1947.

Israel, Edward L. *On Marshy Ground.* New York: Zionist Organization of America, n.d. [c. 1938].

Jackson, Robert H. *The Challenge to the Christian Conscience.* New York: United Palestine Appeal, 1939.

Jewish National Fund. *Pocket Diary, 1954-1955.* New York, 1954.

Jewish Reconstructionist Foundation. *Zionism Explained.* New York, n.d. [c. 1946].

Karpf, Maurice J. *Partition of Palestine and Its Consequences.* Reprint from *Jewish Social Service Quarterly,* March, 1938.

Labor Zionist Council for the American Jewish Conference. *Call of the Labor*

Zionist Movement to the Delegates to the American Jewish Conference.
New York, 1943.

Lazaron, Morris S. *Homeland or State: The Real Issue.* Baltimore: Privately
printed, 1941.

———. *Is This The Way?* Baltimore: Privately printed, 1942.

———. *Judaism A Universal Religion.* Reprint from *The Christian Century*,
August 30, 1939.

———. *Palestine: The Dream and the Reality: A Survey of Jewish Nationalism.*
Reprint from *Atlantic Monthly*, November, 1944.

———. *Reform Judaism and Jewish Nationalism.* Reprint from *The Jewish
Times* (Baltimore), January 2, 1931.

Lesourd, Howard M. *Christian Looks at Palestine.* New York: American Christian Palestine Committee, 1947.

Lestchinsky, Jacob. *Crisis, Catastrophe and Survival: A Jewish Balance Sheet,
1914–1948.* New York: Institute of Jewish Affairs, World Jewish Congress,
1948.

Levias, Caspar. *The Justification of Zionism.* Reprint from Central Conference
of American Rabbis *Yearbook*, 1899.

Levinthal, Louis E. *The Credo of an American Zionist.* Washington: Zionist
Organization of America, 1943.

MacDonald, James G., and others. *Palestine—A Jewish Commonwealth in Our
Time.* Washington: Zionist Organization of America, 1943.

Mack, Julian W. *Americanism and Zionism.* New York: Zionist Organization of
America Committee on Unity for Palestine, n.d. [c. 1944].

McNutt, Paul V. *Palestine, A Symbol of Democracy.* New York: United Palestine
Appeal, 1941.

Marshall, Louis and Weizmann, Chaim. *The Rebuilding of Palestine.* New York:
United Palestine Appeal, n.d. [c. 1927].

Mizrachi, Orthodox Religious Zionist Organization of America. *Religious and
Spiritual Aspects of Zionism: Statement Submitted to the Anglo-American
Committee of Inquiry.* Washington, January, 1946.

Monsky, Henry. *Toward a Common Program of Action:* Address at Conference
of National Jewish Membership Organizations, January 23, 1943, Washington: B'nai B'rith, 1943.

Morgenstern, Julian. *Nation, People, Religion—What Are We?* Cincinnati:
Hebrew Union College, 1943.

———. *Unity in American Judaism, How and When?* Cincinnati: Hebrew Union
College, 1945.

National Conference on Palestine. *Resolution Adopted on March 9, 1944.* New
York: Christian Council on Palestine, 1944.

National Labor Committee for Palestine, Trade Union Division. *Report to
American Labor.* New York, 1944.

New York State Jewish Buro, Communist Party. *The Meaning of the Palestine
Partition.* New York, 1937.

Niebuhr, Reinhold. *Jews After the War.* Reprint from *The Nation*, February 21
and 28, 1942.

Novick, Paul. *Palestine: The Communist Position: The Colonial Question.* New
York: The Jewish Buro of the Central Committee of the Communist Party,
U.S.A., 1936.

————. *Solution for Palestine: The Chamberlain White Paper.* New York: National Council of Jewish Communists, 1939.

————. *Zionism Today.* New York: The Jewish Buro of the Central Committee of the Communist Party, U.S.A., 1936.

Patai, Rafael, editor. *Current Jewish Social Research.* New York: Theodor Herzl Foundation, 1958.

Postal, Bernard, editor. *This is B'nai B'rith, A Book of Facts.* Washington: Supreme Lodge of B'nai B'rith, 1943.

Pro-Palestine Federation of America. *Principles and Program of . . . ,* Chicago, n.d. [c. 1930].

Proskauer, Joseph M. *The Call of the Hour.* New York: American Jewish Committee, 1945.

————. *Our Duty as Americans—Our Responsibility as Jews.* New York: American Jewish Committee, 1948.

Provisional Executive Committee for General Zionist Affairs. *Zionism Conquers Public Opinion.* New York, 1917.

Rabbinical Assembly of America. *Pronouncement on Zionism.* New York, 1938.

The Rabbis of America to Labor Palestine. New York: The League for Labor Palestine, 1935.

Raisin, Max. *The Flight From the Diaspora.* New York: Association of Reform Rabbis of New York City and Vicinity, 1935.

Roper, Elmo. *A Survey of American Jewish Opinion on a Jewish State in Palestine.* New York: M. Hausman and Son's Foundation, Inc., October, 1945.

Rosenheim, Jacob. *Agudist World-Problems.* New York: Agudath Israel World Organization, n.d. [c. 1941].

Rothenberg, Morris. *American Interest in Palestine.* New York: Zionist Organization of America, n.d. [c. 1934].

Saltzman, Rubin. *The American Jewish Conference, Facts and Documents Which Should Be Known to the Jewish Public.* New York: Jewish-American Section, International Workers Order, 1943.

Schachner, Nathan. *Statesmanship in American Jewish Life.* New York: American Jewish Committee, 1949.

Schechter, Solomon. *Zionism: A Statement.* Reprint from *The American Hebrew,* December 28, 1906.

Sherman, C. Bezalel. *Bund, Galuth Nationalism, Yiddishism.* (Herzl Institute Pamphlet No. 6.) New York: Theodor Herzl Foundation, 1958.

————. *The Communists in Palestine: The Mufti's Moscow Allies.* New York: The League for Labor Palestine, 1939.

————. *Three Centuries of Growth: The American Jewish Community Today.* New York: Labor Zionist Organization of America—Poale Zion, 1954.

Schloessinger, Max. *Reform Judaism and Zionism: An Examination of Dr. David Philipson's Thesis That They Are Irreconcilable.* Reprint from *Jewish Comment* (Baltimore), January 4–11, 1907.

Silver, Abba. *"Advance on All Fronts!"* New York: United Palestine Appeal, 1943.

————. *A Year's Advance: A Political Report Submitted to the Convention of the Zionist Organization of America, October 15, 1944.* New York: American Zionist Emergency Council, 1944.

————. *Zionism—What It Is . . . What It Is Not.* Cleveland: The Temple, n.d.

To Secure Jewish Rights: The Communist Position. New York: New Century Publishers, 1948.

Trachtenberg, Joshua. *Conference or Assembly? An Analysis and a Challenge.* Harrisburg, Pennsylvania: Privately printed, 1944.

Turnowsky, Walter. *Zionist Propaganda: A Critical Survey of its Methods.* Jerusalem, author, 1938.

Ulitzur, A. *Foundations: A Survey of Twenty-five Years of Activity of the Palestine Foundation Fund—Keren Hayesod.* Jerusalem: Keren Hayesod, 1946.

United Palestine Appeal. *Palestine Unites, A Stirring Chapter in American-Jewish History Recording the Union of Forces for the Upbuilding of Palestine.* New York, n.d. [c. 1929].

Voss, Carl H. *A Christian Looks at the Jewish Problem.* Together with Bernstein, Philip S., *A Jew Looks at the Christian Problem.* New York: American Christian Palestine Committee, 1946.

Wallach, Sidney. *Jews Must Choose.* Philadelphia: American Council for Judaism, n.d.

———. *The Struggle for Integration.* Philadelphia: American Council for Judaism, 1945.

Weizmann, Chaim. *The Jewish People and Palestine.* Jerusalem: Head Office of the Zionist Organization, n.d. [c. 1936].

———. *Palestine's Role in the Solution of the Jewish Problem.* New York: United Palestine Appeal, 1942.

Zaar, Isaac. *Hebrew Independence: The Contribution of the Hebrew Committee of National Liberation.* New York: American League for a Free Palestine, 1945.

Zionist Organization of America. *A Brief Statement of the Basis and Scope of the Right of the United States to Participate in Any Disposition of Palestine.* New York, 1937.

———. *A Jewish Commonwealth in Palestine, Our Contribution to a Better World.* Washington, n.d. [c. 1944].

———. *Program and Education Bulletin, Tercentenary Issue.* New York, 1955.

———. *Twentieth Anniversary of the Joint Resolution of the Congress of the United States (1922–1942).* Washington, 1942.

———. *Two Generations of Zionism.* Washington, 1944.

———. *Why Zionist Manpower Today! A Symposium.* Washington, n.d. [c. 1943].

———. *Zionism and Judaism: A Symposium.* Washington, 1943.

Zionist Organization of America, Committee on Public Information. *The Program of the Zionist Organization of America: Resolutions Adopted by the National Executive Committee.* New York, 1931.

———. Committee on Unity. *An Appeal to the Conscience of America by One Thousand Twenty-seven Rabbis.* New York, 1945.

———, Committee on Unity for Palestine. *The Facts: Zionism and Our Non-Jewish Neighbors.* New York, n.d.

———, Department of Youth and Education. *Jewish Youth—Challenge and Promise.* New York, 1941.

———. *Zionism Today—Restatement and Evaluation.* New York, 1941.

———, Education Department. *Reorienting Zionist Education Today, Proceedings of Conference on.* New York, 1948.

————. *What We Mean By A Jewish Commonwealth.* New York, 1945.

————, Hadassah, Keren Hayesod, Keren Kayemeth, Palestine Economic Corporation, American Economic Committee for Palestine and Palestine Endowment Funds. *Memorandum submitted to the Palestine Royal Commission on American Interest in the Administration of the Palestine Mandate.* New York, 1937.

E. *General and Special Studies*

Abelow, Samuel P. *History of Brooklyn Jewry.* Brooklyn: Scheba Publishing Company, 1937.

Adler, Cyrus and Margalith, Aaron M. *With Firmness in the Right: American Diplomatic Action Affecting Jews, 1840–1945.* New York: American Jewish Committee, 1946.

Adler, Selig. *The Palestine Question in the Wilson Era.* New York: Conference on Jewish Relations, 1948.

Agus, Jacob B. *Banner of Jerusalem: Life, Times and Thought of Abraham Isaac Kuk.* New York: Bloch Publishing Co., 1946.

————. *Guideposts in Modern Judaism: An Analysis of Current Trends in Jewish Thought.* New York: Bloch Publishing Co., 1954.

————. *Modern Philosophies of Judaism: A Study of Recent Jewish Philosophies of Religion.* New York: Behrman's Jewish Book House, 1941.

Apenszlak, Jacob, editor. *The Black Book of Polish Jewry: an Account of the Martyrdom of Polish Jewry Under the Nazi Occupation.* New York: American Federation for Polish Jews, 1943.

Attwood, William. "The Position of the Jews in America Today." *Look,* November 29, 1955, pp. 27–35.

Bailey, Thomas A. *The Man in the Street: The Impact of American Public Opinion on Foreign Policy.* New York: Macmillan Co., 1948.

Baron, Salo W., editor. *Bibliography of Jewish Social Studies, 1938–39.* New York: Conference on Jewish Relations, 1941.

Bentwich, Norman. *Solomon Shechter, A Biography.* Philadelphia: Jewish Publication Society of America, 1948.

Berger, Elmer. *The Jewish Dilemma.* New York: Devin-Adair Co., 1951.

————. *Judaism or Jewish Nationalism: The Alternative to Zionism.* New York: Bookman Associates, 1957.

————. *A Partisan History of Judaism.* New York: Devin-Adair Co., 1945.

Bernard, Jessie. *American Community Behavior.* New York: Dryden Press, 1949.

Brandeis, Louis Dembitz. *Brandeis on Zionism, A Collection of Addresses and Statements.* Washington: Zionist Organization of America, 1942.

Bregstone, Philip P. *Chicago and Its Jews.* Chicago: Privately printed, 1933.

Brown, Francis J., and Rouček, Joseph S., editors. *One America: The History, Contributions, and Present Problems of Our Racial and National Minorities.* New York: Prentice-Hall, Inc., 1952.

Cantril, Hadley and others. *Gauging Public Opinion.* Princeton: Princeton University Press, 1944.

————, editor. *Public Opinion, 1935–1946.* Princeton: Princeton University Press, 1951.

Celler, Emanuel. *You Never Leave Brooklyn.* New York: John Day Co., 1953.

Claude, Inis L., Jr. *National Minorities, An International Problem.* Cambridge: Harvard University Press, 1955.

Cohen, Anne N. *The Centenary History: Congregation Beth Israel of Houston, Texas, 1854–1954.* Houston: Congregation Beth Israel, 1954.

Cohen, Elliot E. *Commentary on the American Scene: Portraits of Jewish Life in America.* New York: Alfred A. Knopf, 1953.

Cohen, Israel. *Contemporary Jewry.* London: Methuen & Co., Ltd., 1950.

———. *A Short History of Zionism.* London: Frederick Muller, Ltd., 1951.

———. *The Zionist Movement.* New York: Zionist Organization of America, 1946.

Cohon, Beryl D. *Judaism in Theory and Practice.* New York: Bloch Publishing Co., 1948.

Cohon, Samuel S. *Judaism, A Way of Life.* Cincinnati: The Union of American Hebrew Congregations, 1948.

Danish, Max D. *The World of David Dubinsky.* Cleveland: The World Publishing Co., 1957.

Davis, Moshe, editor. *Israel: Its Role in Civilization.* New York: Harper & Bros., 1956.

Doob, Leonard. *Public Opinion and Propaganda.* New York: Henry Holt, 1948.

Duker, Abraham G. *Jewish Survival in the World Today.* New York: Hadassah, 1941.

———. "Workshop in Jewish Community Affairs, Course I: The American Jewish Community: Its History and Development." New York: American Jewish Congress, n.d. [c. 1953]. (Mimeographed)

———. "Workshop in Jewish Community Affairs, Course II: The Status and Security of the American Jew: Background for Jewish Community Relations." New York: American Jewish Congress, 1953. (Mimeographed)

Easton, David. *The Political System: An Inquiry Into the State of Political Science.* New York: Alfred A. Knopf, 1953.

Ebersole, Luke E. *Church Lobbying in the Nation's Capital.* New York: Macmillan Co., 1951.

Edidin, Ben M. *Jewish Community Life in America.* New York: Hebrew Publishing Co., 1947.

Editors of Fortune. *Jews in America.* New York: Random House, 1936.

Eisenstein, Ira. *Creative Judaism.* New York: Behrman's Jewish Book House, 1941.

——— and Kohn, Eugene. *Mordecai M. Kaplan: An Evaluation.* New York: Jewish Reconstructionist Foundation, Inc., 1952.

Epstein, Melech. *Jewish Labor in U.S.A., 1882–1952.* 2 vols. New York: Trade Union Sponsoring Committee, 1950.

———. *The Jew and Communism, 1919–1941.* New York: Trade Union Sponsoring Committee, 1959.

ESCO Foundation for Palestine, Inc. *Palestine: A Study of Jewish, Arab, and British Policies.* New Haven: Yale University Press, 1947.

Feuer, Leon I. *Why A Jewish State.* New York: Richard R. Smith, 1942.

Findley, Albert. "Stalinism's Dirty Record on the Jewish Question." *Labor Action,* February 3, 1947, pp. 5–6.

Fink, Reuben, editor. *America and Palestine: The Attitude of Official America and of the American People Toward the Rebuilding of Palestine as a Free and Democratic Jewish Commonwealth.* New York: American Zionist Emergency Council, 1944.

———. *The American War Congress and Zionism: Statements by Members of the American War Congress on the Jewish National Movement.* New York: Zionist Organization of America, 1919.

Finkelstein, Louis, editor. *The Jews: Their History, Culture, and Religion.* 2 vols., New York: Harper & Bros., 1949.

Foster, William Z. *History of the Communist Party of the United States.* New York: International Publishers, 1952.

Fox, G. George. *An American Jew Speaks.* Chicago: Falcon Press, 1946.

Frankfurter, Felix. *Felix Frankfurter Reminisces.* Recorded in talks with Dr. Harlan B. Phillips. New York: Reynal & Co., 1960.

Freeman, Howard E., and Showel, Morris. "Differential Political Influence of Voluntary Associations." *Public Opinion Quarterly,* XV, No. 4 (Winter 1951–52), 703–14.

Friedman, Elisha M. *Inquiry of the United Jewish Appeal, Report to the Allotment Committee of the United Jewish Appeal 1940 for Refugees and Overseas Needs.* New York: United Jewish Appeal, 1941.

Friedman, Theodore and Gordis, Robert, editors. *Jewish Life in America.* New York: Horizon Press, 1955.

Friedrich, Carl J. *American Policy Toward Palestine.* Washington: Public Affairs Press, 1944.

Fuchs, Lawrence H. *The Political Behavior of American Jews.* Glencoe, Illinois: Free Press, 1956.

Get Thee a Teacher. Houston: Congregation Beth Israel, 1945.

Ginzberg, Eli. *Agenda for American Jews.* New York: King's Crown Press, 1950.

———. *Report to American Jews, on Overseas Relief, Palestine and Refugees in the United States.* New York: Harper & Bros., 1942.

Gittelsohn, Roland B. *Modern Jewish Problems.* Cincinnati: Union of American Hebrew Congregations, 1943.

Glazer, Nathan. *American Judaism.* Chicago: University of Chicago Press, 1957.

Goldberg, Abraham. *Pioneers and Builders: Biographical Studies and Essays.* New York: Abraham Goldberg Publications Committee, 1943.

Goldberg, Israel (Rufus Learsi, pseudonym). *Fulfillment: The Epic Story of Zionism.* Cleveland: World Publishing Co., 1951.

———. *The Jews in America: A History.* Cleveland: World Publishing Co., 1954.

Golden, Harry. *For 2¢ Plain.* Cleveland: World Publishing Co., 1959.

Goldman, Eric F. *Rendezvous with Destiny: A History of Modern American Reform.* New York: Vintage Books, 1958.

Goldman, Solomon. *Undefeated.* Washington: Zionist Organization of America, 1940.

Goldstein, Israel. *Toward a Solution.* New York: G. P. Putnam's Sons, 1940.

Gordis, Robert. *Conservative Judaism, An American Philosophy.* New York: Behrman's Jewish Book House, 1945.

———. *The Jew Faces A New World.* New York: Behrman's Jewish Book House, 1941.

414   *Bibliography*

Gordis, Robert. *Judaism for the Modern Age*. New York: Farrar, Straus, & Cudahy, 1955.

Gordon, Albert I. *Jews in Transition*. Minneapolis: University of Minnesota Press, 1949.

Gottheil, Richard J. H. *Zionism*. Philadelphia: Jewish Publication Society of America, 1914.

Gottschalk, Max, and Duker, Abraham G. *Jews in the Post-War World*. New York: Dryden Press, 1945.

Gouldner, Alvin W., editor. *Studies in Leadership: Leadership and Democratic Action*. New York: Harper & Bros., 1950.

Graeber, Isacque, and Britt, Steuart H., editors. *Jews in a Gentile World*. New York: Macmillan Co., 1942.

Gross, Feliks. *European Ideologies, A Survey of 20th Century Political Ideas*. New York: Philosophical Library, 1948.

Gurevich, D., compiler. *Statistical Handbook of Jewish Palestine, 1947*. Jerusalem: Jewish Agency for Palestine, 1947.

Haber, Julius. *The Odyssey of an American Zionist: Fifty Years of Zionist History*. New York: Twayne Publishers, 1956.

Halpern, Ben. *The American Jew—A Zionist Analysis*. New York: Theodor Herzl Foundation, 1956.

Handlin, Oscar. *Adventure in Freedom: Three Hundred Years of Jewish Life in America*. New York: McGraw-Hill Book Co., Inc., 1954.

Havemann, Ernest, and West, Patricia S. *They Went to College: The College Graduate in America Today*. New York: Harcourt, Brace & Co., 1952.

Hebrew Union College Alumni. *Reform Judaism*. Cincinnati: Hebrew Union College Press, 1949.

Heller, Joseph. *The Zionist Idea*. London: The Joint Zionist Publications Committee, 1947.

Herberg, Will. *Protestant—Catholic—Jew: An Essay in American Religious Sociology*. Garden City, New York: Doubleday & Co., Inc., 1956.

Hertzberg, Arthur, editor. *The Zionist Idea: A Historical Analysis and Reader*. Garden City, New York: Doubleday & Co., and Herzl Press, 1959.

Herzl, Theodor. *Excerpts From His Diaries*. New York: Scopus Publishing Co., 1941.

———. *The Jewish State: An Attempt at a Modern Solution of the Jewish Question*. New York: Scopus Publishing Co., 1943.

History of the Labor Zionist Movement in North America. 2 vols. New York: Yiddisher Kempfer, 1955 (Yiddish).

Hitler's Black Record: The Documented Story of Nazi Atrocities Against the Jews. New York: American Jewish Congress, 1943.

Hoffer, Eric. *The True Believer: Thoughts on the Nature of Mass Movements*. New York: Mentor Books—New America Library of World Literature, 1958.

Howe, Irving, and Coser, Lewis. *The American Communist Party: A Critical History (1919–1957)*. Boston: Beacon Press, 1957.

Hull, Cordell. *The Memoirs of . . .* , Vol. II. New York: Macmillan Co., 1948.

Hull, William L. *The Fall and Rise of Israel, The Story of the Jewish People During the Time of Their Dispersal and Regathering*. Grand Rapids, Mich.: Zondervan Publishing Co., 1954.

Hurewitz, J. C. *The Struggle for Palestine.* New York: W. W. Norton & Co., Inc., 1950.

Janowsky, Oscar I., editor. *The American Jew: A Composite Portrait.* New York: Harper & Bros., 1942.

———. *The Jews and Minority Rights (1898–1919).* New York: Columbia University Press, 1933.

Jastrow, Morris, Jr. *Zionism and the Future of Palestine: The Fallacies and Dangers of Political Zionism.* New York: Macmillan Co., 1919.

The Jewish People–Past and Present. 4 vols. ("Jewish Encyclopedic Handbooks.") Central Yiddish Culture Organization (CYCO), 1946–55.

Johnsen, Julia E., compiler. *Palestine: Jewish Homeland?* ("The Reference Shelf," Vol. XVIII, No. 6.) New York: The H. W. Wilson Co., 1946.

Johnson, Gerald. *An Honorable Titan: A Biographical Study of Adolph S. Ochs.* New York: Harper & Bros., 1946.

Josephson, Matthew. *Sidney Hillman, Statesman of American Labor.* Garden City, N.Y.: Doubleday & Co., 1952.

Jung, Leo, editor. *Israel of Tomorrow.* New York: Herald Square Press, Inc., 1946.

Kahn, Harry J. *Fifty Years of Poale Zionism in America.* New York: Farlag Biderman, 1953 (Yiddish).

Kallen, Horace M. *"Of Them Which Say They Are Jews" And Other Essays on the Jewish Struggle for Survival.* New York: Bloch Publishing Co., 1954.

———. *Zionism and World Politics: A Study in History and Social Psychology.* Garden City, N.Y.: Doubleday, Page & Co., 1921.

Kaplan, Mordecai M. *The Future of the American Jew.* New York: Macmillan Co., 1948.

———. *Judaism as a Civilization.* New York: Macmillan Co., 1935.

———. *A New Zionism.* New York: Theodor Herzl Foundation, 1955.

Karpf, Maurice J. *Jewish Community Organization in the United States.* New York: Bloch Publishing Co., 1938.

Katz, Daniel and others. *Public Opinion and Propaganda: A Book of Readings.* New York: Dryden Press, 1954.

Katzoff, Louis. *Issues in Jewish Education: A Study of the Philosophy of the Conservative Congregational School.* New York: Bloch Publishing Co., 1949.

King, C. Wendell. *Social Movements in the United States.* New York: Random House, 1956.

Kimche, Jon and David. *The Secret Roads.* New York: Farrar, Straus & Cudahy, 1955.

Kohn, Eugene. *The Future of Judaism in America.* New Rochelle, New York: Liberal Press, 1934.

Knox, Israel. *Rabbi in America: The Story of Issac M. Wise.* Boston: Little Brown & Co., 1957.

Kriesberg, Martin. "Cross Pressures and Attitudes: A Study of the Influence of Conflicting Propaganda on Opinions Regarding American-Soviet Relations." *Public Opinion Quarterly,* XIII, No. 1 (Spring, 1949), 5–16.

Kurland, Samuel. *Cooperative Palestine: The Story of Histadrut.* New York: Sharon Books, 1947.

Labor Zionist Handbook: The Aims, Activities and History of the Labor Zionist Movement in America. New York: Paole Zion Zeire Zion of America, 1939.

Lasswell, Harold D., and Kaplan, Abraham. *Power and Society: A Framework for Political Inquiry.* New Haven: Yale University Press, 1950.

Lazaron, Morris S. *Common Ground, A Plea for Intelligent Americanism.* New York: Liveright Publishing Corp., 1938.

Learsi, Rufus (pseudonym). See Goldberg, Israel.

Lee, Alfred M., editor. *New Outline of the Principles of Sociology.* 2nd ed. New York: Barnes & Noble, 1951.

Leiserson, Avery. "Problems of Representation in the Government of Private Groups." *The Journal of Politics,* XI, No. 3 (August, 1949), 566–77.

Levinthal, Israel H. *Judaism: An Analysis and an Interpretation.* New York: Funk & Wagnalls Co., 1935.

Lewin, Kurt. *Resolving Social Conflicts.* New York: Harper & Bros., 1948.

Lewisohn, Ludwig. *The American Jew: Character and Destiny.* New York: Farrar, Straus & Co., 1950.

———. *This People.* New York: Harper & Bros., 1933.

Lieberman, Chaim. *Strangers to Glory: An Appraisal of the American Council for Judaism.* New York: Rainbow Press, 1955.

Linfield, Harry S. *The Communal Organization of the Jews in the United States.* New York: American Jewish Committee, 1930.

Livneh, Eliezer. *State and Diaspora.* Jerusalem: Youth and Hechalutz Department of World Zionist Organization, 1953.

Lipsky, Louis. *A Gallery of Zionist Profiles.* New York: Farrar, Straus & Cudahy, 1956.

———. *Thirty Years of American Zionism.* 2 vols. New York: Nesher Publishing Co., 1927.

Liptzin, Sol. *Generation of Decision: Jewish Rejuvenation in America.* New York: Bloch Publishing Co., 1958.

Locker, Berl. *Covenant Everlasting: Palestine in Jewish History.* New York: Sharon Books, 1947.

McDonagh, Edward C., and Richards, Eugene S. *Ethnic Relations in the United States.* New York: Appleton-Century-Crofts, Inc., 1953.

Manuel, Frank E. *The Realities of American-Palestine Relations.* Washington: Public Affairs Press, 1949.

Marcus, Jacob Rader. "Zionism and the American Jew." *The American Scholar,* II (July, 1933), 279–92.

Marden, Charles F. *Minorities in American Society.* New York: American Book Co., 1952.

Mead, Frank S. *Handbook of Denominations in the United States.* New York and Nashville: Abingdon-Cokesbury Press, 1951.

Meyer, Isidore S., editor. *Early History of Zionism in America.* New York: American Jewish Historical Society and Theodor Herzl Foundation, 1958.

Miller, Irving. *Israel, the Eternal Ideal.* New York: Farrar, Straus & Cudahy, 1955.

Mizrachi Jubilee Publication, 1911–1936. New York: Mizrachi Organization of America, 1936.

Monsky, [Daisy] Mrs. Henry, and Bisgyer, Maurice. *Henry Monsky: the Man and His Work*. New York: Crown Publishers, 1947.

Monypenny, Phillip. "Political Science and the Study of Groups: Notes to Guide a Research Project." *Western Political Quarterly*, VII, No. 2 (June, 1954), 183–201.

Nathan, Robert R., Gass, Oscar, and Creamer, Daniel. *Palestine: Problem and Promise, An Economic Study*. Washington: Public Affairs Press, 1946.

Parkes, James. *The Emergence of the Jewish Problem, 1878–1939*. London: Oxford University Press, 1946.

Patkin, A. L. *The Origins of the Russian-Jewish Labour Movement*. Melbourne: F. W. Cheshire Pty. Ltd., 1947.

Philipson, David. *The Reform Movement in Judaism*. New York: Macmillan Co., 1931.

Pilch, Judah. *Jewish Life in Our Times*. New York: Behrman's Jewish Book House, 1943.

Polier, Justine W. and Wise, James. *The Personal Letters of Stephen Wise*. Boston: Beacon Press, 1956.

Proskauer, Joseph. *A Segment of My Times*. New York: Farrar, Straus & Co., 1950.

Queen, Stuart A., Chambers, William N., and Winston, Charles M. *The American Social System: Social Control, Personal Choice, and Public Decision*. Boston: Houghton Mifflin Co., 1956.

Raisin, Max. *A History of the Jews in Modern Times*. New York: Hebrew Publishing Co., 1949.

Reznikoff, Charles, editor. *Louis Marshall, Champion of Liberty: Selected Papers and Addresses*. 2 vols. Philadelphia: Jewish Publication Society of America, 1957.

Ribalow, Harold U., editor. *Mid-Century: An Anthology of Jewish Life and Culture in Our Times*. New York: The Beechhurst Press, 1955.

Rischin, Moses. *An Inventory of American Jewish History*. Cambridge: Harvard University Press, 1954.

Robinson, Jacob. *Palestine and the United Nations: Prelude to Solution*. Washington: Public Affairs Press, 1947.

Robison, Sophia M., and Starr, Joshua, editors. *Jewish Population Studies*. New York: Conference on Jewish Relations, 1943.

Rogoff, Harry. *An East Side Epic: The Life and Work of Meyer London*. New York: The Vanguard Press, 1930.

Rose, Arnold and Caroline. *America Divided: Minority Group Relations in the United States*. New York: Alfred A. Knopf, 1949.

Rosenberg, J. Mitchell. *The Story of Zionism: A Bird's-Eye View*. New York: Bloch Publishing Co., 1946.

Rosenberg, Stuart E. *The Jewish Community in Rochester, 1843–1925*. New York: Columbia University Press, 1954.

Sachar, Abram Leon. "B'nai B'rith." *Current History*, LI (April, 1940), 24–27, 60.

———. *A History of the Jews*. New York: Alfred A. Knopf, 1953.

Sachar, Howard M. *The Course of Modern Jewish History*. Cleveland: World Publishing Co., 1958.

Sakran, Frank C. *Palestine Dilemma: Arab Rights versus Zionist Aspirations.* Washington: Public Affairs Press, 1948.

Samuel, Maurice. *Level Sunlight.* New York: Alfred A. Knopf, 1953.

Schachner, Nathan. *The Price of Liberty: A History of the American Jewish Committee.* New York: The American Jewish Committee, 1948.

Schappes, Morris U. *The Jews in the United States: A Pictorial History, 1654 to the Present.* New York: Citadel Press, 1958.

Schermerhorn, Richard A. *These Our People: Minorities in American Culture.* Boston: D. C. Heath & Co., 1949.

Schneiderman, Harry, editor. *Two Generations in Perspective: Notable Events and Trends, 1896–1956.* New York: Monde Publishers, 1957.

Schwartzman, Sylvan D. *Reform Judaism in the Making.* New York: Union of American Hebrew Congregations, 1955.

Schwartz, Leo W., editor. *Great Ages and Ideas of the Jewish People.* New York: Random House, 1956.

———. *The Redeemers: A Saga of the Years 1945–1952.* New York: Farrar, Straus & Young, 1953.

Sherman, C. Bezalel. *The Jew within American Society: A Study in Ethnic Individuality.* Detroit: Wayne State University Press, 1961.

Silver, Abba H. *Vision and Victory: A Collection of Addresses, 1942–1948.* New York: Zionist Organization of America, 1949.

———. *The World Crisis and Jewish Survival: A Group of Essays.* New York: Richard R. Smith, 1941.

Simonhoff, Henry. *Under Strange Skies.* New York: Philosophical Library, 1953.

Sklare, Marshall. *Conservative Judaism: An American Religious Movement.* Glencoe, Ill.: Free Press, 1955.

———. *The Jews: Social Patterns of an American Group.* Glencoe, Ill.: Free Press, 1958.

Sokolow, Nahum. *History of Zionism, 1600–1918.* London: Longmans, Green & Co., 1919.

Soltes, Mordecai. *The Yiddish Press: An Americanizing Agency.* New York: Teachers College, Columbia University, 1950.

Steinberg, Milton. *A Believing Jew.* New York: Harcourt, Brace & Co., 1951.

———. *The Making of the Modern Jew.* Indianapolis: The Bobbs-Merrill Co., 1933.

———. *A Partisan Guide to the Jewish Problem.* Indianapolis: The Bobbs-Merrill Co., 1945.

Strong, Donald S. *Organized Anti-Semitism in America: The Rise of Group Prejudice During the Decade 1930–1940.* Washington: American Council on Public Affairs, 1941.

Taylor, Alan R. *Prelude to Israel: An Analysis of Zionist Diplomacy, 1897–1947,* New York: Philosophical Library, 1959.

Thirty Years: The Story of the Joint Distribution Committee. New York: Joint Distribution Committee, 1945.

Truman, David. *The Governmental Process: Political Interests and Public Opinion.* New York: Alfred A. Knopf, 1951.

Truman, Harry S. *Memoirs.* 2 vols. Garden City, N.Y.: Doubleday & Co., 1955.

Universal Jewish Encyclopedia. 10 vols. New York, 1939.

Vlavianos, Basil J., and Gross, Feliks, editors. *Struggle for Tomorrow: Modern Political Ideologies of the Jewish People.* New York: Arts, Inc., 1954.

Voss, Carl H. *The Palestine Problem Today.* Boston: Beacon Press, 1953.

Waldman, Morris D. *Nor by Power.* New York: International Universities Press, 1953.

Weisgal, Meyer W., editor. *Chaim Weizmann: Statesman, Scientist, and Builder of the Jewish Commonwealth.* New York: Dial Press, 1944.

Weiss-Rosmarin, Trude. *Jewish Survival, Essays and Studies.* New York: Philosophical Library, 1949.

———, editor. *On the Road to Zion: Selected Writings of Daniel Frisch.* New York: Zionist Organization of America, 1950.

Weizmann, Chaim. *Trial and Error: The Autobiography of* . . . New York: Harper & Bros., 1949.

Weld, Ralph F. *Brooklyn is America.* New York: Columbia University Press, 1950.

Werner, M. R. *Julius Rosenwald, The Life of a Practical Humanitarian.* New York: Harper & Bros., 1939.

Williams, Robin W. *The Reduction of Intergroup Tensions.* New York: Social Science Research Council, 1947.

Wischnitzer, Mark. *To Dwell in Safety: The Story of Jewish Migration Since 1800.* Philadelphia: Jewish Publication Society of America, 1948.

Wise, Stephen S. *As I See It.* New York: Jewish Opinion Publishing Corp., 1944.

———. *Challenging Years.* London: East and West Library, 1951.

Wolsey, Louis. *Sermons and Addresses.* Philadelphia: Congregation Rodeph Shalom, 1950.

Zaar, Isaac. *Rescue and Liberation, America's Part in the Birth of Israel.* New York: Bloch Publishing Co., 1954.

Zasloff, Joseph J. *Great Britain and Palestine: A Study of the Problem before the United Nations.* Geneva: Librairie E. Droz, 1952.

Zeitlin, Joseph. *Disciples of the Wise: The Religious and Social Opinions of American Rabbis.* New York: Teachers College, Columbia University, 1945.

index

World War II, influence on Zionism, 16, 29-31 *passim,* 42, 69, 80, 181, 220-21, 313
World Zionist Congresses, 4, 6, 71, 221, 268, 328, 358, 369
World's Fair (New York) of 1939–40, Palestine Pavilion at, 261

Yiddish language and publications, 52, 56, 57, 256-57, 371, 387
Young Men's–Women's Hebrew Associations, 56, 263, 274
Youth activities, 261-64, 390. *See also* Education; Propaganda

Zaritsky, Max, 163, 166, 370
Zeitlin, Joseph, 105
Zionism, defined, 1, 5-7
Zionist Organization of America, 12, 17, 52, 75, 79, 95-96, 104, 106, 118, 121, 128, 155, 162, 179, 183, 193-95, 210, 258, 263-69, 284, 291, 302, 337, 352, 356, 360, 363-66, 385; and American Council for Judaism, 284-91 *passim;* and American Jewish Conference, 221-47 *passim,* 382-86
Zionist parties, 1, 7, 111. *See also* Hadassah; Mizrachi; Poale Zion; Revisionist Zionists; Zionist Organization of America

Manuscript edited by Barbara Woodward
Designed by S. R. Tenenbaum
Set in Linotype Baskerville with
Beton Medium Condensed
Printed on Warren's Olde Style Antique White Wove
and bound in Holliston Zeppelin
Manufactured in the United States of America